Comp 3

odd

even

Comp

$1 \le n \le 4$, 2

$5 \le n \le 8$, 4

Assembler
for COBOL
Programmers

Ranade IBM Series

K. BOSLER • *CLIST Programming* 0-07-006551-9

H. MURPHY • *Assembler for COBOL Programmers: MVS, VM* 0-07-044129-4

H. BOOKMAN • *COBOL II* 0-07-006533-0

P. MCGREW, W. MCDANIEL • *In-House Publishing in a Mainframe Environment, Second Edition* 0-07-046271-2

J. RANADE • *DB2: Concepts, Programming, and Design* 0-07-051265-5

J. SANCHEZ • *IBM Microcomputers Handbook* 0-07-054594-4

M. ARONSON • *SAS: A Programmer's Guide* 0-07-002467-7

J. AZEVEDO • *ISPF: The Strategic Dialog Manager* 0-07-002673-4

K. BRATHWAITE • *System Design in a Database Environment* 0-07-007250-7

M. CARATHANASSIS • *Expert MVS/XA JCL: A Complete Guide to Advanced Techniques* 0-07-009816-6

M. D'ALLEYRAND • *Image Storage and Retrieval Systems* 0-07-015231-4

R. DAYTON • *Integrating Digital Services* 0-07-016188-7

P. DONOFRIO • *CICS: Debugging, Dump Reading, and Problem Determination* 0-07-017606-X

T. EDDOLLS • *VM Performance Management* 0-07-018966-8

P. KAVANAGH • *VS COBOL II for COBOL Programmers* 0-07-033571-0

T. MARTYN • *DB2/SQL: A Professional Programmer's Guide* 0-07-040666-9

S. PIGGOTT • *CICS: A Practical Guide to System Fine Tuning* 0-07-050054-1

N. PRASAD • *IBM Mainframes: Architecture and Design* 0-07-050686-8

J. RANADE • *Introduction to SNA Networking: A Guide to VTAM/NCP* 0-07-051144-6

J. RANADE • *Advanced SNA Networking: A Professional's Guide for Using VTAM/NCP* 0-07-051143-8

J. TOWNER • *CASE* 0-07-065086-1

S. SAMSON • *MVS: Performance Management* 0-07-054528-6

B. JOHNSON • *MVS: Concepts and Facilities* 0-07-032673-8

P. MCGREW • *On-Line Text Management: Hypertext* 0-07-046263-1

L. TOWNER • *IDMS/R* 0-07-065087-X

A. WIPFLER • *Distributed Processing in the CICS Environment* 0-07-071136-4

A. WIPFLER • *CICS Application Development Programming* 0-07-071139-9

J. RANADE • *VSAM: Concepts, Programming, and Design, Second Edition* 0-07-051244-2

J. RANADE • *VSAM: Performance, Design, and Fine Tuning, Second Edition* 0-07-051245-0

Assembler for COBOL Programmers

MVS, VM

Hank Murphy

University of California, Los Angeles
Business, Management, and Engineering Extension

McGraw-Hill, Inc.

New York   St. Louis   San Francisco   Auckland   Bogotá
Caracas   Hamburg   Lisbon   London   Madrid
Mexico   Milan   Montreal   New Delhi   Paris
San Juan   São Paulo   Singapore
Sydney   Tokyo   Toronto

Library of Congress Cataloging-in-Publication Data

Murphy, Hank
    Assembler for COBOL programmers : MVS, VM /Hank Murphy.
        p. cm.

    1. Assembler language (Computer program language) 2. MVS
(Computer system) 3. VM/CMS (Computer operating system) 4. COBOL
(Computer program language)   I. Title.
    QA76.73.A8M85   1990
    005.13'6—dc20   90-5852
                                                                        CIP

*ESA/370, MVS/ESA, MVS/XA, and MVS/SP are trademarks of the
International Business Machines Corporation; Librarian is a
trademark of Computer Associates; PanValet is a trademark of
Pansophic Software; Post-It is a trademark of 3M; Bartles & Jaymes
is a trademark of E & J Gallo. All other trademarks used are the
property of their respective holders.*

ISBN 0-07-044129-4

*The sponsoring editor for this book was Theron Shreve, the editing
supervisor was Jim Halston, and the production supervisor was
Suzanne W. Babeuf.*

Printed and bound by R. R. Donnelley and Sons.

*Subscription information to BYTE Magazine: Call
1-800-257-9402 or write Circulation Dept., One Phoenix
Mill Lane, Peterborough NH 03458.*

For information about our audio products, write us at:
Newbridge Book Clubs, 3000 Cindel Drive, Delran, NJ 08370

Contents

Preface

Who Are You?

If you picked up this book because of its title, you can probably benefit from it. Who are you?

This book's approach represents a method of learning IBM mainframe assembler language that capitalizes on the strengths and knowledge of you, the knowledgeable COBOL programmer. This book is oriented towards experienced professional programmers — or fairly advanced students — rather than towards the computer science college student taking an introductory assembler language class.

As such, this book expects that you have a good foundation in data processing. You will probably benefit most if currently employed as a COBOL programmer in an MVS shop. You may also find this book a valuable reference if you are taking an assembler class and know the COBOL language fairly well.

As such, this book also avoids most of the elementary descriptions which make other assembler language books less desirable for experienced programmers. If you feel that you need a picture of a tape drive to comprehend the concept of sequential file access, this book is not for you. If you aren't sure where you fall, read this introduction and you should get a fair idea of what this book expects from you — and what it purports to deliver to you in exchange for your investment in time and money.

The approach of this book uses the "compare and contrast" method. Almost everything covered is explained in terms of how a COBOL feature or technique works in assembler. Basic definitions are avoided, unless there is no corresponding COBOL feature. This book avoids complex examples — assembler is complicated enough. Wherever possible, a direct conversion from COBOL to assembler is used to explain things. Additionally, this book explains some common assembler coding techniques. This sometimes includes the history behind their use. The assembler language covered is the IBM 370 assembler language. This covers the majority of mainframe CPUs in use today. The specific computers described by the term "IBM 370" include the IBM 3090, 4381, and 9370 CPUs, the older IBM 308x and 43xx CPUs, 303x CPUs, the even older IBM 370 CPU family, and (to a large degree) even the original IBM 360 computers. This also covers a large number of plug-compatible CPUs from Amdahl and HDS (formerly National Advanced Systems, as well as older plug-compatible CPUs from Magnuson, IPL, and other manufacturers.

This book is oriented towards the MVS operating system. It also explains most operating system functions in terms of how they differ under VM. In addition, many of the coding examples will also work under other, similar environments. These include the older versions of MVS, the VS1 operating system, and perhaps even the MVT operating system. We will also cover a few things which are unique to VM. Most of these will be discussed in Appendix 4, which will describe some VM-unique macro instructions. In addition, we will provide separate examples for VM where appropriate. Most of the book's examples will run unchanged under VM's OS simulation. However, Chapters 19 (sort exits) and 21 (VSAM) have not been tested under VM, but these are the only exceptions.

The assembler program used is IBM's Assembler H program product, IBM order number 5668-962. Almost all of the examples will also run under the older OS/VS Assembler. Some will also run with the OS/360 Assembler F. Assembler H was used to run most of the examples.

To most effectively use this book, you'll need access to a computer. You should have a good knowledge of COBOL and experience in coding JCL or CMS commands. If you don't know what JCL is, you should probably buy another book — for example, "Expert MVS/XA JCL" by M. Carathanassis, McGraw-Hill. You will also need access to a number of IBM manuals, which are listed in Chapter 1.

You should know how to do hexadecimal arithmetic. (If you don't, Appendix 1 shows the basics of hexadecimal and binary arithmetic.) Use of a calculator is OK, but you should eventually learn how to do hex arithmetic by yourself. You should know how to convert from decimal to hex and back. You should know how to convert from hex to binary, using references if needed.

You should also know how to go about looking up things you don't know about COBOL, JCL, or CMS. This means that you should know where the manuals are, if you don't have your own, and how to use these manuals.

How To Use This Book

If you desire, you could just read the book. The chapters are organized into up to four separate types of information. First, and always present, is a discussion of fundamental assembler features. This is material which you should read in every chapter. Second, where needed, a separate section called "esoterica" discusses additional facets of the instructions covered in the chapter. You don't necesarily need to read the esoterica section. It presents less-used or specialized information which you may never need to know to use assembler language. However, it's there if you ever need it.

Most chapters have a summary section which reiterates the points covered in the chapter. This allows you to have an informal checklist of the concepts in what you just read.

Finally, to learn the most from the book, you should use the sections called "Things to Do" at the end of most chapters. You can think of these as assignments, although they tend to teach you as much about how your data processing installation works as about assembler language per se.

Other activities which may make this book more valuable include:

- Get listings of assembler programs in use at your company and try to understand them as you go through the chapters

- Assemble a COBOL program with the COBOL compiler PMAP and DMAP options to see how COBOL uses the 370 instruction set

Learning assembler won't be complete after reading one book. This book is designed to help both at the beginning of and later during that extended process. To that end, Appendix 3 includes a complete cross-reference from COBOL verbs and features to the corresponding assembler implementation.

What This Book Will Teach You

As a working computer programmer, your time is valuable. Everybody wants it. Your boss wants schedules met. Your time is money.

Even when you want to do something yourself — go to a ball game, visit your relatives, talk to your stockbroker, watch TV, or anything else — you have to give up doing something else to do it.

Even outside of work, your time isn't limitless — or free.

So what will you get from your investment of money (to buy it) and time (to read and learn from it)?

To start with, you'll have a better understanding of the concepts behind assembler in general. You'll learn the mechanics of an assembler program and its interfaces to MVS, VM, and to other programs.

You will learn 40 to 50 assembler instructions. These include the most commonly used assembler instructions. Additionally, you will be exposed to most of the others and get some idea of how and when to use them.

You won't learn the floating point instructions. This writer has taught assembler language to over five hundred students at Pierce College and through UCLA extension. No single student has ever demonstrated a need to know it for their work. For those of you who may need this, there are other books out there — but how many people code floating point in COBOL?

Depending on your own ability and the opportunities where you work, you'll learn enough to start maintaining assembler programs, making modifications of increasing difficulty. Also, you'll learn enough to write assembler subroutines for COBOL programs, allowing you to use your new-found expertise in your present job.

Finally, you'll gain a better understanding of the IBM mainframe architecture, which will enhance your debugging skills and help you understand how the COBOL compiler does things.

You won't be able to leap tall buildings with a single bound. But you have to start someplace.

A few other notes on the book are appropriate at this point. The COBOL programs in this book were compiled with the APOST option, which specifies that the single quote mark (apostrophe) is used to delimit character constants in VALUE clauses and in literals. The alternative is use of double quote marks, which few if any COBOL programmers use.

Assembler uses the single quote mark for all character constant values. As a result, we will reserve the double quote marks (",") to set off examples included in a text paragraph, like "PERFORM 0900-END-ROUTINE." If code is specified outside of a text paragraph, no double quote marks will be used, like:

PERFORM 0900-END-ROUTINE.

Thus, if you see something like "DC   C' RECORD:'" in the text, it should be read as:

DC   C' RECORD:'

and the double quote marks at each end should be ignored.

— Hank Murphy

Acknowledgements

The creation of a book involves a lot of work beyond the writing. This effort would not be possible without the help and advice of many people.

Jay Ranade, series editor, deserves credit for his insight into what typical programmers need. With Jay's advice, I went from a general dissatisfaction with existing assembler books to a clear focus on a unique approach.

Theron Shreve, senior editor for McGraw-Hill, was most helpful in the contract matters involved in bringing out the book. I also thank Nancy Sileo for her assistance in getting things resolved quickly.

The majority of the preproduction work fell to Jim Halston, senior editing supervisor at McGraw-Hill. Jim's patience and thoroughness are sincerely appreciated. Naomi Auerbach, book designer, provided timely and specific guidance on the details of type and print. I also thank the proofreaders and copy editors — Gretlyn Cline, James Madru, and Meg Tobin — for their efforts, which saved me from egregious (and embarassing) errors more than once.

The knowledge, approaches, and techniques which went into this book were developed through experience with many students and peers, as well as in work situations. I thank all my former students for their interaction over the last ten years. Also, my courses were critiqued and shaped by my colleagues: Anne Delaney, Art Sherman, Pete Schleppenbach, Jim Reidy, Pat Davis, and Dr. Ernest Sobel, among many others. All played a part in developing the foundation for this book. I am also indebted to many former employers and co-workers, who are truly too numerous to mention.

I also thank my other reviewers — Greg Hamer and Lana Karlsen. Their insight during the formulation of this book helped greatly.

Every aspiring writer will understand when I thank my wife, Barbara, and children, Joe, Jennifer, Jessica, and Matthew, for their patience while the inmate ran the asylum. Barbara has a career of her own to work through, and put up with...well...a great deal. Honest, honey, you can use the dining room table now. Really.

I also have to thank my parents and stepmother, both for making Hank Murphy possible, but also for their appreciation for reading and learning. In retrospect, this made writing a book unavoidable. I also have to thank my journalism teacher at Taft High School, Ernie Pearl, who taught me the organization needed for writing and, as it turned out, for programming.

Needless to say, any errors remaining in the book are my own. I hope you enjoy the book in spite of them.

Learning Assembler Language

1.1 WHY?

Why would anyone in their right mind want to learn assembler language? It has a wide range of perceived drawbacks. It's complex. It's difficult to code and debug. It provides very few services to the programmer. It's hard to maintain. And most managers don't like it.

So why would anyone in their right mind want to learn assembler? That's easy. By and large, programmers aren't in their right minds.

In fact, the detractors of assembler language have some grounds for some of their complaints. Assembler language is complex — on almost any machine. This reflects the complexity of computers themselves, since assembler is traditionally the only way to have complete control over the computer. In the IBM world, with the MVS or VM operating systems, the complexity of the operating system rivals or surpasses that of the 370 hardware, making it even more difficult.

A result of this complexity is that assembler language is more difficult to code than most other languages — certainly more so than COBOL. Whether assembler is more difficult to debug is more debatable, particularly when using a dump. Better debugging skills, based on more thorough understanding of how the IBM 370 architecture works, represents a common side benefit of learning assembler.

Assembler language can also be very hard to maintain. However, incomprehensible programs are no monopoly of assembler. Bad programmers — let's just say unenlightened programmers — can write incomprehensible programs in any language. APL, BASIC, C, FORTRAN, PASCAL, PL/I, and RPG come to mind as languages also used for incomprehensible programming.

The skill of writing maintainable programs probably transcends the language used. Just point out to your boss how much easier his or her programs are to maintain than anyone else's. (If necesary, try to keep a straight face while you do this.)

So why — or perhaps when — should you use assembler? Generally three situations clearly merit its use. The first is for direct interface to the operating system to use some MVS service which isn't available in COBOL. In this case, there is simply no alternative. The second situation covers those cases where data is presented, or required, in some special format which isn't directly usable in COBOL. This usually arises when sending or receiving data to or from another type of computer, or from programs written in a language other than COBOL.

The third case is the one most commonly used to justify use of assembler — speed. This justification for using assembler is not as good as the other two, although more common. The speed of a program's execution depends on many things — design, the speed of the computer running it, the speed of the I/O devices used, and competition from other work in the system running at the same time. The programming language used may have an insignificant effect on the total time needed to do the processing required.

However, there are still many cases where well-designed assembler language programs run markedly faster than well-designed programs in other languages. But a poorly planned assembler program can be slower than a well-designed COBOL program. Like incomprehensible programs, slow programs can be written in any language. But speed and size are still valid justifications for using assembler language.

In summary, assembler language is often less desirable than COBOL for many reasons. However, there are several cases where assembler language is still preferable or even required.

1.2   SOME DIFFERENCES BETWEEN COBOL AND ASSEMBLER

Assembler language differs from all of the other languages mentioned above in that assembler closely follows the actual instruction facilities available on the 370. This means that we have to understand the 370 architecture in order to program in it. By contrast, COBOL and other high-level languages run on several different central processing unit (CPU) types with (usually) minimal changes.

Assembler also has a markedly different syntax from COBOL. COBOL tries to look like the English language. As such, a line of input may contain more than one COBOL statement (although that's normally avoided). A COBOL statement requires a special delimiter (the period) to mark the end of a statement.

By contrast, assembler language statements have only one statement per line. To continue a statement in assembler, each line of the statement except the last must contain a special continuation indicator. And assembler language statements terminate with a blank, not a period. In addition, assembler language commands bear no resemblance to COBOL's English-like structure.

Another difference between COBOL and assembler is that COBOL statements may create many 370 machine instructions to process one COBOL command. By contrast, assembler language statements normally generate only one machine instruction per assembler language statement. (Macro instructions represent an exception to this, which will be covered later.) As a result, you normally need to code several lines of assembler to get the same effect as one line in COBOL. Many examples of this will be shown later in the text.

Another difference, which requires a real shift in one's thinking, lies in the order of operands. In COBOL, one normally does something with some variable to something else. For example,

MOVE A TO B.

or

ADD 1 TO ITEM-CT.

The first operand (A or 1) in these statements is used to do something (move or add) to the second operand.

Unfortunately, in the 370 architecture, the second operand is normally used to do something to the first operand. The statements above might appear in assembler language as

MVC   B,A

or

AP   ITEMCT, = P'1'

When thinking as a COBOL programmer, it's a natural trap to interpret "MVC B,A" as "move B to A". In fact, the statement means the opposite.

Another big difference between the two languages lies in assembler's lack of an orderly organization of the program. In COBOL, you separate a program into divisions, sections, and paragraphs which contain one or more statements. By contrast, in assembler language you just start coding. (Well, actually not, but you have to decide on your own organization and enforce it yourself throughout the program.) This means that you have to plan the program's layout, which COBOL does for you.

Another difference this entails is that there is less of a fixed order of statements in assembler. With a couple of exceptions, assembler language statement types (data, linkage, and instructions) may appear in almost any order. Thus, in COBOL, programs always contain four divisions, each of which may contain one or more sections. In assembler, each executable program contains a header statement (CSECT or START) and an END statement, but no other rules need be followed regarding the order of statements.

There are many other differences which will be brought out as we go through the two languages. In many ways, though, assembler has fewer outright rules than COBOL, forcing more discipline on the programmer. Additionally, assembler requires different thought patterns.

1.3   ASSEMBLING A PROGRAM

This book will generally show the differences between assembler language and COBOL by indicating how the same thing is done in the two languages. We'll do this by showing how to convert a COBOL verb or statement to a corresponding assembler statement or series of statements. This is not to recommend that you convert COBOL programs to assembler — the idea is to allow you to understand assembler based on your knowledge of COBOL. Later on in the book, we will also discuss some of the many things you can do in assembler which you can't do in COBOL, but first things first.

To start on this, let's investigate something we have to use to learn assembler — how to assemble a program. To do this at your shop, you'll need to determine some things about how your shop runs. This will be described for MVS first, then the changes you would make to do this under VM/SP will be discussed.

The first consideration is your shop standards on how to store source programs. There are several ways to do this under MVS — as individual data sets under TSO or ISPF, as members of a partitioned data set (PDS) or library, or in a source maintenance package, such as Librarian (marketed by Computer Automation) or Pan Valet (marketed by Pansophic). In VM, we'll assume that you will put the programs on your A-disk.

A second point is whether it's customary to include the MVS assembly (compile) JCL with the source program or to keep it separate.

The safest way to handle these two questions is to find an existing assembler language program in your shop and copy the JCL (and possibly the program as well). Make sure that you don't accidentally modify *production* copies of source programs when you run the JCL you obtain this way.

Alternatively, you can use standard IBM-supplied MVS assembler procedures. These are available at most shops. These may be found as ASMHC to assemble a program, ASMHCL to assemble and link edit a program, and ASMHCLG to assemble, link edit, and execute a program. (These are for the 'H' version of the IBM assembler, which is in use at most MVS shops. If these aren't found at your shop, the corresponding procedures are ASMFC, ASMFCL, and ASMFCLG, respectively, for the older 'IFOX00' assembler.)

Sample JCL to assemble, link, and execute an assembler program is included below if you choose to use these procedures. You will have to change the JOB statement to comply with your shop's standards. If you don't understand the changes necesary, further study of JCL is advisable before going much further with assembler language.

To use the JCL in Fig. 1.1 with the older assembler, change the procedure name 'ASMHCLG' to 'ASMFCLG' and everything should work fine.

Figure 1.1   Sample JCL to assemble, link-edit, and execute an assembler language program.

```
//jobname           JOB  (parameters for your shop)
//ASSEMBLE          EXEC  ASMHCLG
//ASM.SYSIN         DD  *
PROGNAME CSECT
*      (The program source normally goes here. For
*      this example, the following three statements will
*      be used.)
            LA     15,0                          SET REG 15 TO ZERO
            BR     14                            RETURN TO MVS
            END    PROGNAME                      END OF PROGRAM
/*
//GO.SYSUDUMP   DD    SYSOUT = *
//
```

The program in Fig. 1.1 doesn't really do anything. In fact, though, it's the same as a famous IBM MVS utility program which you have probably used — IEFBR14. All this program does is set the condition code (the RETURN-CODE special register in COBOL) to zero, then returns control to MVS.

Now key in the program in Fig. 1.1. Modify the JOB statement to follow your shop's standards. Submit the JCL.

Under MVS, when you get the job output back, you should have the JCL listing for the program, the assembly listing, and the linkage editor listing. (I'll discuss how to read the assembly listing later.) You should have condition codes of zero in the JCL listing for the ASM, LKED, and GO steps.

If you don't get condition codes of zero, check the data you keyed in and make sure that it follows the JCL and program provided above exactly.

If you have a JCL error because the MVS is not being able to find the ASMHCLG procedure, try ASMFCLG. If that doesn't work, you should probably ask the installation's systems programmer what procedure should be used to assemble a program. At this stage, you need to locate someone who knows your shop standards and some assembler language.

To do this under VM/SP, use XEDIT to key in the program listed above. Do not key in any MVS JCL — that's anything with "//" at the beginning of each line. Save the file with whatever file name you prefer, and a file type of ASSEMBLE. (For our examples, we'll assume a file name of ASMPROG.)

After filing the program, enter the following command if you are using assembler H:

HASM ASMPROG

If you are using the older standard VM assembler, enter:

ASSEMBLE ASMPROG

(You would change "ASMPROG" to whatever you had chosen for a file name.) The assembly will complete shortly. If you get any messages with "ERROR" in them, you can guess what that means. Compare what you've keyed in to the sample program in Fig. 1.1 and correct the differences.

Your assembly listing will be in a file called ASMPROG LISTING, and the object deck will be in a file called ASMPROG TEXT. You may review the LISTING file if you desire via XEDIT.

To run the program once you have an assembly with no statements flagged, enter the following:

LOAD ASMPROG

followed by

START *

This will execute the program. Since it doesn't do anything, you should receive a normal VM READY message. If you still have errors, go compare what you've keyed in to Fig. 1.1 again.

We'll assume that everything eventually worked OK in both MVS and VM and that you were able to get the output successfully. (That's easy for us to say!) There — you've run your first assembly. You may now gloat for an appropriate period. Time's up!

If this program were actually to do something, we'd have to add some code for initialization and termination. Since you probably had more in mind for assembler language than just setting the condition code, we probably should go on to a program that has a little more processing in it. To do this, let's look at Fig. 1.2.

Figure 1.2   An assembler program.

```
//jobname           JOB    (parameters for your shop)
//ASSEMBLE          EXEC   ASMHCLG
//ASM.SYSIN         DD     *
PROGNAME            CSECT
          STM    14,12,12(13)              SAVE REGISTERS
          LR     12,15                     GET PROG ADDR
          USING  PROGNAME,12               ADDRESSABILITY
          B      AROUND                    GO AROUND LABEL
          DC     CL8'PROGNAME'             PROGRAM NAME
          DC     CL8'&SYSDATE'             DATE ASSEMBLED
          DC     CL6'&SYSTIME'             TIME ASSEMBLED
AROUND    EQU    *
          SPACE  1
*                  CHAIN SAVE AREAS
          ST     13,SAVEAREA+4             OLD SAVE AREA
```

Figure 1.2 (Continued)

```
            LA     2,SAVEAREA                    GET NEW ADDR
            ST     2,8(13)                       STORE NEW ADDR
            LR     13,2                          UPDATE REG 13
*           OPEN  FILES
            OPEN   (INFILE,INPUT,PRINTER,OUTPUT)
            PUT    PRINTER,HEADLINE              WRITE PAGE HDG
            SPACE  1
*           MAIN LINE PROCESSING
MAINLINE    EQU    *
            GET    INFILE,INAREA                 READ A RECORD
            MVC    DATA,INAREA                   MOVE TO PRINT
            AP     RECNUM,ONE                    ADD TO REC CNT
            OI     RECNUM+3,X'0F'                SET SIGN BITS
            UNPK   NUMBER,RECNUM                 MOVE TO PRINT LINE
            PUT    PRINTER,LINE                  WRITE PRINT LINE
            AP     LINECT,ONE                    ADD TO LINE COUNT
            CP     LINECT,P50                    AT PAGE END?
            BL     MAINLINE                      NO - CONTINUE
            ZAP    LINECT,ZERO                   RESET LINE COUNT
            PUT    PRINTER,HEADLINE              WRITE PAGE HDG
            B      MAINLINE                      PROCESS NEXT REC
            SPACE 1
*           END-OF-FILE ROUTINE.
ENDDATA     EQU    *
            PUT     PRINTER,ENDLINE              WRITE ENDING LINE
            CLOSE  (INFILE,,PRINTER)             CLOSE FILES
            L      13,4(13)                      GET OLD SAVE AREA
            RETURN   (14,12),RC=0                RETURN TO MVS
            SPACE 3
*           DATA AREAS
SAVEAREA DC     18F'0'                           PROG SAVE AREA
INAREA   DS     CL80                             INPUT DATA AREA
LINE     DC     C' '                             CARRIAGE CONTROL
         DC     C' RECORD '
NUMBER   DS     CL7                              RECORD NUMBER
         DC     C':'
DATA     DS     CL80                             DATA RECORD
         DC     CL36' '                          FILLER
HEADLINE DC     CL133'1 * * * RECORD LISTING * * *'
ENDLINE  DC     CL133'0 * * * END OF REPORT * * *'
LINECT   DC     PL2'0'                           LINE COUNT
RECNUM   DC     PL4'0'                           RECORD NUMBER
ZERO     DC     P'0'                             CONSTANT 0
ONE      DC     P'1'                             CONSTANT 1
```

Figure 1.2   (Continued)

```
P50         DC     P'50'                          CONSTANT 50
*                  DATA CONTROL BLOCKS
* Note! In the following five lines, the 'X's must be in position 72, and
*              the 'RECFM = ' and 'EODAD = ' must be in position 16, or
*              you will get assembly errors!
PRINTER     DCB    DDNAME = PRINTER,DEVD = DA,MACRF = (PM),      X
                   RECFM = FBA,LRECL = 133,BLKSIZE = 0
INPUT       DCB    DDNAME = INFILE,DEVD = DA,MACRF = (GM),       X
                   RECFM = FB,LRECL = 80,BLKSIZE = 0,            X
                   EODAD = ENDDATA
            END    PROGNAME                       END OF PROGRAM
/*
//GO.SYSUDUMP    DD  SYSOUT = *
//GO.PRINTER     DD  SYSOUT = *
//GO.INFILE      DD  *,DCB = BLKSIZE = 80
     Key in some data statements here...let your
     imagination run wild. No, not that wild.
/*
//
```

Now that you've reviewed the sample program in Fig. 1.2, key it in. The same notes about JCL and the cataloged procedure names apply here as they did in the first example. Go ahead and run the program after keying it in.

This program uses an additional facility of assembler — macro instructions. If you are running under VM, you should enter an additional command at this point:

GLOBAL MACLIB DMSSP CMSLIB OSMACRO

This makes the VM system macro libraries accessible to your CMS virtual machine. You may want to add this command to your PROFILE EXEC. (Make sure that you don't have other GLOBAL MACLIBs defined in your PROFILE EXEC first. If you do, add the DMSSP, CMSLIB, and OSMACRO macro libraries to your PROFILE EXEC if they are not already in it.)

By comparison, Fig. 1.3 shows the same program in COBOL. I will compare the two programs in later chapters. Since I will be referring to these two sample programs (Figs. 1.2 and 1.3) later in the book, you might want to mark their place with a paper clip, Post-It™ note, or some other bookmark.

Figure 1.3   **The COBOL program corresponding to the assembler**
program in Figure 1.2.

```
        IDENTIFICATION DIVISION.
        PROGRAM-ID. PROGNAME.
        REMARKS. SAMPLE PROGRAM IN COBOL.
        ENVIRONMENT DIVISION.
        CONFIGURATION SECTION.
        INPUT-OUTPUT SECTION.
        FILE-CONTROL.
            SELECT INFILE           ASSIGN TO UT-S-INFILE.
            SELECT PRINTER          ASSIGN TO UT-S-PRINTER.
        DATA DIVISION.
        FILE SECTION.
        FD   INFILE
            BLOCK CONTAINS 0
            RECORD CONTAINS 80 CHARACTERS
            RECORDING MODE IS F
            LABEL RECORDS ARE OMITTED
            DATA RECORD IS A-RECORD.
        01   A-RECORD.
            05   FILLER   PIC X(80).
        FD   PRINTER
            BLOCK CONTAINS 0
            RECORD CONTAINS 133 CHARACTERS
            RECORDING MODE IS F
            LABEL RECORDS ARE OMITTED
            DATA RECORD IS A-LINE.
        01   A-LINE.
            05   FILLER   PIC X(133).
        WORKING-STORAGE SECTION.
        77   LINECT   PIC S999   COMP-3   VALUE ZERO.
        77   RECNUM   PIC S9(7)  COMP-3   VALUE ZERO.
        77   ONE      PIC S999   COMP-3   VALUE 1.
        77   P50      PIC S999   COMP-3   VALUE +50.
        01   INAREA.
            05   FILLER  PIC X(80).
        01   PLINE.
            05   PLINE-CC     PIC X      VALUE ' '.
            05   FILLER       PIC X(8)   VALUE ' RECORD '.
            05   PNUMBER      PIC X(7).
            05   FILLER       PIC X      VALUE ':'.
            05   PDATA        PIC X(80).
            05   FILLER       PIC X(36) VALUE SPACES.
        01   HEADLINE.
```

Figure 1.3   (Continued)

```
                    05'HEADLINE-CC    PIC X       VALUE '1'.
                    05    FILLER    PIC X(133)
                          VALUE ' * * * RECORD LISTING * * *'.
            01    ENDLINE.
            05    ENDLINE-CC    PIC X       VALUE '1'.
            05    FILLER    PIC X(133)
                          VALUE ' * * * END OF REPORT * * *'.
         PROCEDURE DIVISION.
         A-SECTION SECTION.
         0100-OPEN-FILES.
                    OPEN INPUT INFILE.
                    OPEN OUTPUT PRINTER.
                    WRITE A-LINE FROM HEADLINE.
         0200-MAINLINE-PROCESSING.
                    READ INFILE INTO INAREA
                          AT END GO TO 0900-END-DATA.
                    MOVE INAREA TO PDATA.
                    ADD ONE TO RECNUM.
                    MOVE RECNUM TO PNUMBER.
                    WRITE A-LINE FROM PLINE.
                    ADD ONE TO LINECT.
                    IF LINECT > P50
                          THEN GO TO 0200-MAINLINE- PROCESSING
                          ELSE MOVE ZERO TO LINECT
                                WRITE A-LINE FROM HEADLINE
                                      GO TO 0200-MAINLINE-PROCESSING.
         0900-END-DATA.
                    WRITE A-LINE FROM ENDLINE.
                    CLOSE  INFILE  PRINTER.
                    GOBACK.
```

To run the program in Fig. 1.2 under VM, you must define the files used by the program. The CMS FILEDEF terminal does this, and corresponds to MVS JCL DD statements. We will assume that you call the program FIG12. To run the program in Fig. 1.2 under VM, enter the following statements after keying in the program:

```
FILEDEF PRINTER TERM
FILEDEF INFILE DISK ASMPROG ASSEMBLE A
LOAD FIG12
```

Followed by

```
START *
```

These statements allocate the output print file to your terminal, and the input file to the program listing we keyed in for the first example. When you run this, you should see the source program from Fig. 1.1 displayed on your CMS terminal. If you have errors, make sure that your program matches Fig. 1.2 exactly (except for the MVS JCL).

Appendix 5 shows an annotated assembly listing based on the program in Fig. 1.2.

1.4   REFERENCE MATERIALS YOU'LL NEED

Before going much further in assembler language, you should start locating some reference materials. These are manuals which you may need as references. You should not plan on actually reading most of these unless you have a severe and advanced case of insomnia.

The IBM manual order numbers current as of November 1989 are included at the end of this chapter.

First, you should have access to a JCL reference and JCL guide. You should already know how to use these manuals and where they may be found. For VM, you should have access to a CMS commands reference manual.

Second, you should obtain a reference summary card — the *yellow card* for MVS/SP or VM/SP and the *pink card* for MVS/XA. (The MVS/ESA version is light blue.) These are booklets which contain oodles of reference information for assembler programmers. A must! We'll refer to these collectively as the *yellow card* and it doesn't matter which one you have for our purposes.

Third is a classic manual which is very detailed and almost completely incomprehensible at first reading. (Once you get into it, though, it's just almost unreadable.) This is the "Principles of Operation" manual, sometimes nicknamed the "pooh" or "P of O". This has very complete and detailed descriptions of how the machine and its instructions actually work.

Fourth are the assembler language manuals. These include a language reference and a programmer's guide. The older OS/VS assembler language reference is probably easier to use as a reference than the assembler H manual. The programmer's guide manual is probably not absolutely necessary.

Fifth you will find the data management services and data management macro reference manuals useful later in the book as we discuss I/O processing differences.

Finally, the supervisor services manual covers several macro instructions that will be addressed later in the book.

If you are running under VM, you should plan on getting access to the above manuals in their MVS versions. This book will focus on the OS simulation of macros under VM. Special macros which are unique to VM/CMS will be discussed separately later.

Note that you do not need a personal copy of all of these manuals — just access to them for occasionally looking up fine points, exact descriptions, and things that you haven't seen before.

1.5 THINGS TO DO NOW

If you are reading this book to teach yourself something about assembler language at work, you should start finding out some of the following information before proceeding much further. Ideally, you should locate all of them before running your first program. Treat the following as a checklist, and make sure each of the items get done.

1. Find out what shop standards apply to the use of assembler language at your installation. Some organizations do not allow new programs in assembler without management approval, or restrict assembler programming to systems programmers. Even if your shop has no such restrictions, you should probably still talk to your manager about any informal rules.

2. What assembly JCL procedures should you use? The examples given in this chapter use standard IBM-supplied JCL. Your shop may mandate use of other procedures customized for your installation.

3. Where are the manuals you need?

4. Who is your systems programmer? Or who is your interface to systems programming? And who is the best assembler programmer at your installation? In other words, who can you go to for help with technical questions? (Don't make a nuisance of yourself!)

5. One important issue is the type of CPU which you are running on, and its operating system. This affects the use of instructions that are covered in this book. For example, IBM 4341 CPUs don't support the Branch and Save and Set Mode (BASSM) instruction. The instructions which may cause you problems are as follows:

BAS	Branch and Save
BASR	Branch and Save Register
BASSM	Branch and Save and Set Mode
BSM	Branch and Set Mode
IPM	Insert Program Mask

If you can find someone knowledgeable about your CPU, you might ask them if these are available on your machine. (If you use one of these and they are not installed, you will receive an 0C1 ABEND — an operation exception.) There are alternative instructions for each of these, and they will be discussed in the text.

6. Finally, what assembler language programs do you run in production? If you have access to any, these can present a source of reference material

and examples. They may also represent a source of confusion if they are too complex for your understanding. Finally, they also may represent a good excuse for learning assembler language.

1.6 RECOMMENDED MANUALS

Following are the official IBM titles and order numbers for reference manuals which you may need while reading this book. Both the MVS/XA and MVS/SP versions of manuals are listed. You may also use older versions of the MVS/SP manuals, or VS1 manuals, or others as appropriate to your installation.

Assembler Language and Instruction Set Manuals

"Assembler H Version 2 Application Programming: Guide," GC26-4037.
"Assembler H Version 2 Application Programming: Language Reference," GC26-4037.
"OS/VS-DOS/VSE-VM/370 Assembler Language," GC33-4010 (if using older assemblers).
"IBM System/370 Principles of Operations," GA22-7000 (if you are running MVS/SP or other operating systems).
"IBM System/370 Reference Summary," GX20-1850 (if you are running MVS/SP, VM/SP, or other operating systems).
"IBM System/370 Extended Architecture Principles of Operations," SA22-7085 (if you are running MVS/XA).
"IBM System/370 Extended Architecture Reference Summary," GX20-0157 (if you are running MVS/XA).
"IBM ESA/370 Principles of Operations," SA22-7200 (if you are running MVS/ESA).
"IBM ESA/370 Reference Summary," GX20-0406 (if you are running MVS/ESA).

Additional References: MVS

"MVS/ESA Application Development Macro Reference," GC28-1822.
"MVS/ESA Data Administration: Macro Instruction Reference," SC26-4506.
"MVS/ESA VSAM Administration: Macro Instruction Reference," SC26-4517.
"MVS/ESA JCL Reference," GC28-1829.
"MVS/Extended Architecture Data Administration: Macro Instruction Reference," GC26-4014 (MVS/XA).
"MVS/Extended Architecture JCL," GC28-1148.
"MVS/Extended Architecture Supervisor Services and Macros," GC28-1154 (MVS/XA).
"MVS/Extended Architecture VSAM Administration: Macro Instruction Reference," GC26-4016 (MVS/XA).
"OS/VS2 MVS Data Administration: Macro Instruction Reference," GC26-4057 (MVS/SP).
"MVS/370 VSAM Reference," GC26-4074 (MVS/SP).
"OS/VS2 MVS JCL," GC28-0692.

"OS/VS2 MVS Supervisor Services and Macros," GC28-1114 (MVS/SP).

Additional References: Sort

"DFSORT Application Programming: Guide," SC33-4035.
"DFSORT Planning and Installation," SC33-4034.

Additional References: COBOL Manuals

"IBM VS COBOL for OS/VS," GC26-3857.
"VS COBOL II Application Programming: Guide," SC26-4045.
"VS COBOL II Application Programming: Language Reference,"
GC26-4047.

Additional References: VM/SP Release 6[1]

"VM/SP Application Development Guide for CMS," SC24-5286.
"VM/SP Application Development Reference for CMS," SC24-5284.
"VM System Facilities for Programming," SC24-5288.

Additional References: VM/SP Release 5

"VM/SP CMS Macros and Functions Reference," SC24-5284.
"VM/SP CMS for Systems Programming," SC24-5286.
"VM System Facilities for Programming," SC24-5288.

---

1   Note that the manuals have the same order numbers for both release 5 and 6, but the titles are
different.

Comparing COBOL and Assembler Programs

In this chapter, we will look at some fundamental differences between COBOL and assembler programs. We will cover some of the items in an assembler language program listing. Additionally, we will show some pitfalls in coding assembler language statements which should be remembered.

2.1 ASSEMBLER STATEMENT TYPES

Assembler language statements fall into three categories.

The first, termed *instructions*, represents actual machine instructions which the 370 executes. Examples of instructions from the program in Fig. 1.2 include MVC (move characters) and AP (add packed). Machine instructions actually do something when your program runs.

The second, *assembler directives*, consists of special commands which the assembler does rather than the 370 CPU. Examples of assembler directives include SPACE (space lines on the listing — like SKIP in COBOL) and END (used to mark the end of the assembler program). Directives cause the assembler to do something when your program assembles rather than when it runs.

The final category, *macro instructions*, is a special set of groups of assembler directives and machine instructions which the assembler processes to yield further input to the assembler. Examples of macros include OPEN (open a file for processing) and GET (read a record). Macros are used to simplify programming of complicated or tedious sequences of several instructions. Requests for MVS and VM services are normally coded as macros. You may also write your own macros, which we will briefly cover in Chap. 22.

In contrast, COBOL's basic unit is the word, which is organized into clauses (Data Division) or statements (Procedure Division). Clauses and statements may be combined into sentences. One or more sentences may make up a paragraph, and one or more paragraphs may comprise a section.

The COBOL concept of clause is probably closest to the assembler concept of statement (instruction, directive, or macro). COBOL allows several clauses in one sentence — assembler's syntax allows only one instruction, directive, or macro per statement, as we'll see in the next section.

2.2 ASSEMBLER SYNTAX OVERVIEW

In this section, we review the basic elements of assembler language syntax. For further, more precise definitions of exactly how assembler syntax operates, you may also wish to see the assembler language reference manual. Assembler syntax more closely approximates the syntax of MVS JCL than any other language.

2.2.1 Assembler Statement Contents

Assembler input statements contain five separate items. These include:

1. An optional name or label. This corresponds to a COBOL file name, data name, or paragraph name in the Data and Procedure Divisions. Labels normally begin in the first position of the assembler statement. (See further notes on labels below.)

2. A required operation code. This identifies which machine instruction, assembler directive, or macro instruction is being coded. The operation code ('opcode') may begin anywhere after the end of the label field, as long as at least one blank separates the label from the opcode. By convention, this is normally coded starting in position 10 of the assembler statement.

3. Optional operands. These include the names of labels, self-defining values, and special code values in macro instructions. There may be any number of operands. They are separated by commas. Operands may begin anywhere in the assembler statement, as long as they are separated by at·least one blank from the end of the opcode. The first operand is normally coded starting in position 16 of the assembler statement.

4. Optional comments — anything you want, similar to the COBOL NOTE statement. Comments may begin anywhere following the operands, as long as at least one blank separates the last operand from the beginning of the comments.

5. An optional continuation indicator. This is a character other than a blank coded in the continuation position of the assembler statement. This is normally position 72. This tells the assembler that the assembler statement continues on the next line of input. Continued lines must begin in the designated continue position of the assembler statement. This is normally position 16. Nothing may appear in positions 1 through 15 of continued lines. Only the opcode is needed to have a valid assembler statement. However, almost every statement will also require operands, and comments are highly desirable.

2.2.2 A Note on Labels

Assembler H can process name fields of up to 63 characters. For certain cases only a length of 8 is allowed. The most common of these cases are the program name and any subroutine names. (Note that COBOL has a similar restriction, only using the first 8 characters if these names are longer than that.)

Many assembler programmers continue to use the older limit of 8 characters out of habit, along with an inbred suspicion of any newfangled doodads. (*Newfangled* in this case means anything developed after 1980.) You should use whatever you think best. If your programs have to be assembled at another shop, which may not have assembler H, then it is wisest to stick to the older limit of 8.

2.2.3 A Note on Columns

Assembler manuals refer to position 1 as the *begin column*, to position 71 as the *end column*, to position 72 as the *continuation indicator field*, and to position 16 as the *continue column*. Positions 73-80 are normally used for sequence numbers. The term *column* is slightly archaic, since most data processing installations use TSO, ISPF, CMS, or similar products from other vendors to update programs and JCL or EXECs from terminals. However, this reference to columns is a throwback to the times when the majority of programs were stored on cards and is not unique to assembler language. We will use both column and position at times.

2.2.4 Some Examples

Let's look at some sample assembler statements to show how the foregoing rules apply. First, a simple move instruction from the sample program in Fig. 1.2 (the column positions are not to scale):

```
Position
1         10    16                      40            72
          ⇓     ⇓                       ⇓             ⇓
          MVC   DATA,INAREA             MOVE TO PRT AREA
```

In this instruction, "MVC" is the opcode, "DATA" and "INAREA" are the operands, and "MOVE TO PRINT AREA" is a comment. There is no name in the label field (starting in position 1) and the statement fits onto one line (no continuation indicator in position 72). Next, an assembler directive with no comments:

```
Position
1         10    16                      40            72
          ⇓     ⇓                       ⇓             ⇓
          SPACE 3
```

The opcode is "SPACE" (this tells the assembler to skip lines on the assembly listing) and the only operand is "3". Now, another directive:

Position

1	10	16	40	72
⇓	⇓		⇓	⇓
	DC	C':'		

'DC' is the opcode and "C':'" is the operand. (DC defines a data item and initializes it.) Now for another one:

Position

1	10	16	40	72
⇓	⇓		⇓	⇓
	DC	C' RECORD '		

In this case, "C' RECORD '" is the operand. Note that the operand didn't end at the first blank field, since the single quotation marks at the beginning and end of the constant value (" RECORD ") tell the assembler that we are defining a character string which may contain blanks. (This is the same way that COBOL handles blanks in a VALUE clause with picture X.) Finally, a macro instruction which spans two source program lines:

Position

1	10	16	40	72
	⇓	⇓	⇓	⇓
PRINTER	DCB	DDNAME = PRINTER,DEVD = DA,MACRF = (PM),		X
		RECFM = FBA,LRECL = 133,BLKSIZE = 0		

In this example, "PRINTER" is the name, "DCB" is the opcode, and "DDNAME = PRINTER,DEVD = DA,MACRF = (PM),RECFM = FBA, LRECL=133,BLKSIZE=0" are six operands. Note the "X" in position 72, which tells the assembler that the statement spills over into the next line.

Before continuing on with other examples, a note on the examples given in the book should be considered. The examples are set in a proportional type face (Helvetica). This is in contrast to the type used with most mainframe printers and terminals, which are monospace fonts. In a monospace font, each letter has the same width. In a proportional font, some letters are wider then others — M versus I, for example. This allows us to put more information in less space in the book, but means that the individual characters will not line up vertically.

2.2.5 Missing Commas May Mean Comments Instead of Code

One important point about continuing a statement: Note that if you forget the comma at the end of the first line, the assembler treats all subsequent (continued) lines as comments. For example:

Position

1	10	16	40	72
PRINTER	DCB	DDNAME = PRINTER,DEVD = DA,MACRF = (PM)		X
		RECFM = FBA,LRECL = 133,BLKSIZE = 0		

In this case, the RECFM, LRECL, and BLKSIZE operands are ignored, since the assembler thinks that they are comments. Be careful of this — it tends to creep in when you are modifying an existing continued macro instruction, can cause all sorts of interesting problems, and (unlike JCL or EXECs) doesn't necesarily cause any error messages.

2.2.6 Two Commas to Omit an Operand May Add Bugs

Some other miscellaneous items should be mentioned here. First, it is sometimes necesary to leave out (omit) an operand. This can be done by coding two commas in a row:

```
Position
1          10    16                    40                72
           CLOSE (INFILE,,PRINTER)      CLOSE FILES
```

In this case, "(INFILE,,PRINTER)" are two suboperands of the "CLOSE" macro instruction. (We'll explain the difference between operands and suboperands in Chap. 22.) The assembler CLOSE macro corresponds to the COBOL CLOSE verb. Like the COBOL CLOSE, the assembler CLOSE macro may have some options. (These are coded in COBOL in the WITH clause.) If we wanted to code these, we would place them immediately after the file name, as follows:

```
           CLOSE (INFILE,REWIND,PRINTER,REWIND)
```

But we don't need to code the REWIND option in this case. The two commas between INFILE and PRINTER tell the assembler that an operand which might have been coded there has been omitted. However, unintended extra commas may lead to interesting bugs with no error messages during assembly. Be careful.

2.2.7 No Reserved Words

Another major difference between assembler and COBOL is the almost complete absence of anything like reserved words in COBOL. Instruction names may also be used as labels. Thus,

```
           BAL    R3,BAL                    LINK TO 'BAL' ROUTINE
```

is completely legal (assuming that 'BAL' is defined elsewhere in your program).

The corresponding COBOL statement would be

```
           PERFORM PERFORM.
```

This will generate an error message in COBOL. The ability to use any label is a nice benefit, especially since assembler uses things like A, B, C, D, START, END, and other useful labels as opcode names.

There is one possible case in assembler which could be compared to COBOL's reserved words. This is the special processing the assembler does when it detects the ampersand (&) character. The assembler will edit and change statements which contain an ampersand before it assembles them. (This is similar to the use of ampersand in JCL procs or EXECs for symbolic parameters, which you may already know.) How this works is best covered in the macro section later in the book. For the present, avoid coding ampersands until later.

If you absolutely need to include an ampersand, code two in a row. The assembler will convert these to one ampersand and assemble the statement. (This is similar to how COBOL handles two single quotes in a row within a VALUE clause for picture X data.) For example, code

```
DC      C'BARTLES && JAYMES'
```

to generate BARTLES & JAYMES™.

2.2.8 Allowed Characters

Like COBOL, assembler language places certain restrictions on the character set used for labels and so forth. For labels, the allowable characters are A-Z, 0-9, and the special characters "$", "#", and "@". In addition, the underscore character ("_") may be used in most labels in Assembler H. Unlike COBOL, assembler names may not begin with a decimal digit. If you customarily name your paragraphs something like 0900-END-JOB, this may represent an awkward change in thinking. To make it easier, you may convert these to a valid assembler name by adding an alphabetic character at the front and changing the dashes to underscores. This would make the assembler label something like C0900_END_JOB. This approach has the advantage of making your labels almost the same as in COBOL. Many assembler programmers will not like such labels.

A good point to consider here, though, is why you used the digits at the beginning of the paragraph name. The most usual purpose of these was to allow a programmer looking at the COBOL program listing to know in which direction to go to find that paragraph. In a large COBOL program, this is a big help.

Assembler programmers never developed that habit. They don't need to have something in the label to tell them where that label is. The reason is that the assembler listing automatically tells them where the label is. We'll cover this in more detail when we go over the assembler listing in Sec. 2.4. (The assembler puts the address of each label referred to by a branch instruction in the ADDR1 column. By looking at this value, and comparing it to the current LOC value, you can determine whether the label precedes or follows the current location.)

Since you should get in the habit of using the ADDR1 and ADDR2 fields to locate labels to be a productive assembler programmer, inclusion of digits to locate a label as you may do in COBOL is probably a habit to avoid in assembler.

2.3 COBOL's DIVISIONS VERSUS ASSEMBLER

As we mentioned in Chap. 1, assembler does not provide a rigorous organization akin to COBOL's divisions. As part of this book, we will go through what you code in COBOL and show how you might code the same thing in assembler. This addresses the line-by-line conversion of a program from COBOL to assembler, but we also need to have a program layout in which to put the converted code.

To provide that, let's look at what information we usually code in COBOL divisions. (We'll ignore some of the details at this point, but they will be covered in later chapters.)

COBOL division	Information provided
IDENTIFICATION	Program name, program description (comments)
ENVIRONMENT	File names, file processing options
DATA	File descriptions, working storage, external record and data descriptions (LINKAGE and SORT sections)
PROCEDURE	Actual instructions.

It is possible to code an assembler program and have all the code in approximately this sequence. However, most assembler language programs follow a sequence closer to the following:

Program name

Program description (comments)

Actual instructions

Working storage

File descriptions, file names, file processing
    options (in Data Control Blocks — DCBs)

External record and data descriptions (in
    Dummy Sections — DSECTs)

Future examples in the book will follow this program layout. Note that you don't need to follow this layout in your own programs. Your own shop assembler programming standards (if any) should be your guideline.

Programs written under the DOS (Disk Operating System) or VSE (Virtual Storage Extension) operating systems usually have the file descriptions (DTFs) at the beginning of the program. This is not necesary in MVS or VM.

2.4 DECODING AN ASSEMBLER LISTING

Assembler listings differ from COBOL listings in that they provide information on one line which corresponds to what COBOL provides in a PMAP and in the cross reference. (If you haven't used one, a PMAP is a listing which shows exactly what assembler language statements were generated by the COBOL compiler by each COBOL verb. It is printed after the program listing and before the cross reference.)

Before going any further with this section, you should have one of the assemblies which you ran as examples while reading Chap. 1. (Refer to Appendix 5 if you don't.)

Turn to the first page of your assembler listing, or to the appendix. You will see some information at the top of each page that is similar to what you see in a COBOL compilation listing.

The first page of your listing should be titled *External Symbol Dictionary*, or something like that (commonly abbreviated "ESD"). The assembler version and release numbers and date and time of the assembly appear in the heading lines as well. This page has a list of all the program names, entry point names, and subroutine names the assembler found in the program. Unless you are dealing with a fairly complex program with many subroutines, you normally won't refer to this page.

The next page, and several subsequent pages in programs larger than a few statements, contain the listing of instructions, data, directives, and other items in your program. These pages will contain a subheading, which has column titles as follows:

LOC — This column contains the location, in hexadecimal, of the statement past the beginning of the program. (This is the same information provided in a COBOL PMAP or CLIST.)

OBJECT CODE — This covers three columns. Not all three will be filled in on every instruction. These contain the actual hexadecimal instruction code the assembler generated from the instruction or directive you coded. This is what you will see in memory in a dump.

ADDR1 — This column has the address in hexadecimal of the first operand in the instruction you coded. If the operand is a label, this will contain the location of that label past the beginning of the program. (This is what is printed in the LOC column where the label actually coded.) This provides you with a handy way of knowing where a label is in your program. By scanning the location column, you can find the label without knowing where it is and without referring to the cross reference.

ADDR2 — This column has the same information for the second operand.

STMT — This column has the statement number of this statement. This is like the statement number in COBOL. It will not necesarily match your input sequence one for one due to macros, copied code, and so forth.

SOURCE STATEMENT — This is the actual 80-byte assembler source program statement the assembler processed.

Understanding what's on the assembly listing is important if one is to become a productive assembler programmer. At this point, you should look at the ADDR1, ADDR2, and LOC columns for some instructions in your listing. If you are looking at the listing from the program in Fig. 1.2, try to use the listing as follows:

1. Locate the statement

```
LA      2,SAVEAREA
```

which is about six lines down from the start of the program. Find the ADDR1 column. Go through the listing until you find the entry in the LOC (location) column which matches that number. (Hint: the LOC value is ascending.) When you find it, what label is at the beginning of that source statement? (It had better be SAVEAREA.)

2. Locate the statement

      AP   RECNUM,ONE

several instructions later. Both the ADDR1 and ADDR2 columns should have a value printed there. Scan the program again until you find these addresses. They should have labels of RECNUM and ONE respectively. Try this a few more times until you're confident that you have the hang of it. Following the assembly instruction listing, there will be one or more pages labeled *RELOCATION DICTIONARY* (often called "RLD"). The RLD is used by the loader when it brings your program in for execution. You normally don't have to review this part of the assembly listing.

The assembler will normally then print a cross reference. (The assembler cross reference has more information than the COBOL cross reference.) This has several columns labeled as follows:

SYMBOL — The name of the field or instruction label, just like the name in a COBOL cross reference.

LEN — The assembler's computed length for the symbol. This is how many bytes long the assembler thinks the data area or instruction is. This doesn't always match the actual amount of storage generated. (We'll get into why later.)

VALUE — This may contain the location of the symbol, similar to what the assembly listing had in the ADDR1 and ADDR2 columns. It may also contain the actual value of the item for a special type of symbol called an equate (EQU).

DEFN — The statement number where the symbol was defined. If you accidentally use the same symbol twice in a program, the assembler will list them all in the cross reference and will flag the second and later definitions as duplicates.

REFERENCES — The statement numbers where this symbol was used in the assembly. Note that these refer to the number in the STMT column in the assembly, not to the LOC column. Several statement numbers may be printed on each line. Following the cross reference, the assembler also prints a literal cross reference, which is somewhat less useful. It follows the format of the first cross reference.

Should you receive any diagnostic messages, assembler provides the information about the errors in two places. First, a line containing

* * * ERROR * * *

is printed following the statement with the error. Second, a list of statement numbers containing errors is printed with the statistics which follow the cross reference. The actual error description usually prints following the statement in error with assembler H. With older assemblers, the error description is printed in the statistics section.

At this point, you should be comfortable reading an assembler listing. You should be able to locate labels in assembler programs by using the ADDR1 or ADDR2 and LOC columns. You should also have access to an assembler language programmer's manual to answer any questions you may have which this book doesn't cover.

2.4.1   Comment Abbreviations

In general, when explaining how a subroutine or particularly involved section of code works, it is best to do so with separate comments before the routine. These are coded with an asterisk ("*") in position 1.

However, it is also a good idea to include comments on most statements in an assembler language program. This usually makes the program much more readable and maintainable.

The problem that this creates is that the space available for comments on an assembler statement is limited. This leads to creative and well-meaning abbreviations. Unfortunately, the more creative the abbreviation, the more likely it will be misunderstood by future programmers.

To reduce this likelihood in this book, we will use a standard set of abbreviations within comments. These include the following:

Abbreviation	Meaning
ADDR	Address
CT	Count
LEN	Length
MSG	Message
PGM, PROG	Program
PRT	Print
REG	Register
RTN	Routine
RET	Return
RETCD, RC	Return code
THRU	Through
W/	With

2.5   ASSEMBLER FORMAT ESOTERICA

This is the first example of *esoterica* in a chapter in this book. This section covers a facility in assembler which is rarely used and which has no equivalent in COBOL. It is an assembler feature called the ICTL directive. It is not essential that you read this or understand it.

Future esoterica sections will cover similar items, or will cover advanced assembler techniques which have no real equivalent in COBOL.

2.5.1   Changing the Column Meanings

Assembler also has a unique facility to allow for different configurations of input source programs. This is an assembler directive called "ICTL." ICTL allows the programmer to redefine the begin, continue, and ending columns for program input. The default values are 1, 16, and 71 respectively. (The column following the ending column is automatically made the continuation indicator column.) If you see ICTL in a program you're reviewing or modifying, be sure you understand exactly what the new positions are. More important, be sure you understand why the original programmer used them. Unless you are both malicious (toward whoever has to maintain your code in the future) and masochistic (to put up with coding with ICTL), you probably should not use ICTL without a very good reason.

2.6   SUMMARY

This chapter introduced some differences in the format of assembler language when compared to COBOL. You should be aware of the various contents of an assembler statement — labels, opcodes, operands, and comments. You should know that you must code something in position 72 if you want to continue a statement over to the next line. You should know that continued statements must begin in column 16. You should also understand the rules for generating labels in the assembler you are using. You should be aware of the pitfalls of forgetting a comma when continuing a statement to the next line, and of coding an extra unintended comma. From this point onward in the book, we will begin a feature-by-feature comparison of COBOL and assembler language. We'll be referring back to the two sample programs in Figs. 1.2 and 1.3 which we introduced in Chap. 1.

Things to Do

1. Run an assembly of one of the sample programs shown in Chap. 1. Change the program to include one of the errors discussed earlier in this chapter and run the assembly again. Compare the outputs to see where the error information prints for your version of the assembler.

Identification Division in Assembler

We'll start with the first thing in a COBOL program — the Identification Division. This part of a COBOL program contains more comments than anything else. It has one important element — the actual program name that the linkage editor uses. We'll cover how we specify this in assembler, along with how to code comments in assembler as well.

3.1 CONTENTS OF THE IDENTIFICATION DIVISION

PROGRAM-ID is the first entry, and this entry provides the actual program name to the linkage editor. This is also the name by which other programs may call the program as a subroutine. The other entries in this division are as follows:

AUTHOR
INSTALLATION
DATE-WRITTEN
DATE-COMPILED
SECURITY
REMARKS

With the exception of DATE-COMPILED, these are all comments that don't generate any code.

3.2 PROGRAM IDENTIFICATION (CSECT, ENTRY, END)

The PROGRAM-ID of COBOL corresponds to the CSECT name in assembler. CSECT stands for *control section*, and identifies the beginning of a chunk of code and/or data to the assembler. CSECT has no operands, and the label is taken as the program name. The program name must begin with a letter or national character (A-Z, #, $, @), may contain decimal digits (0-9) in the second through eighth positions, and may not exceed eight positions in length. These rules are generally the same as COBOL's. COBOL allows several things in the program name which assembler does not. For example, COBOL will truncate a longer name, allow a program name in quotation marks, and will convert illegal characters to legal ones. In general, these COBOL features aren't used very much.

Thus, some valid names which meet these requirements for assembler language include

> BEGIN
> A00000
> $COST
> R1@ABEND

Conversely, some invalid names follow:

END-PROG	(Dash not allowed)
100BEGIN	(Can't start with numeric)
PROGRAMME	(Longer than 8 characters)
END_PROG	(Underscore not allowed in a program name)

Note, however, that the last two examples are valid as symbols inside the program under assembler H.

Referring back to the sample programs in Figs. 1.2 and 1.3 for program names, the COBOL program had

> PROGRAM-ID. PROGNAME.

The assembler program had

> PROGNAME CSECT

These two generate the same program name, PROGNAME. If you just start coding without putting a CSECT first, the assembler will generate one for you. This is called an *unnamed CSECT*. It will appear in linkage editor listings as a program name of $PRIVATE. This is sometimes referred to in IBM manuals as *private code*. You may also create this by coding a CSECT without a name field. In general, unnamed control sections are to be avoided.

3.2.1   Other Ways of Identifying a Program

Assembler provides another directive, START, which functions like CSECT in MVS. START follows the rules outlined for CSECT above, but allows an optional operand. This is the starting address of the program. For example,

PROGNAME START X'3E000'

This tells the assembler and linkage editor that this program is to be loaded into main storage at address 3E000 in hex. This technique was used in the DOS operating system when a relocating loader was not available. You may see this in older programs, especially when converting them from DOS. VM programs may also use this feature when written to execute in a discontiguous shared segment.

START also is only allowed for the first control section in a program. In general, CSECT is preferable to START in MVS. If your installation has programs which use START with a non-zero first operand, you should find out why.

Another way of identifying a program name for use as a subroutine is the assembler ENTRY directive. This has a corresponding COBOL verb,

ENTRY, which is used in the Procedure Division. We will discuss this later in the book. Some assembler programmers use this to identify the beginning of their program as well, especially within an unnamed CSECT.

3.2.2 The Assembler END Directive

While it has no exact corollary in COBOL, the assembler END directive may have a relationship to the CSECT which should be mentioned. END marks the end of the assembler source program. If you do not provide one, the assembler flags it as an error.

The END directive may also designate which instruction should get control first when the program runs. Thus, if you wanted an instruction in the middle or end of the program to receive control first, you could code its name as the operand of the END directive.

The reasons for doing this are not clear-cut. One reason is to organize your program in such a way that the instructions are not at the beginning of the program. This would be the case if you organized the program to have the data at the beginning, as COBOL does.

An END directive with no starting instruction or comments looks like the following:

```
1          10    16                                              72
           END
```

This is probably the preferred form.

Alternatively, you may specify the starting address for your program as the first operand as follows:

```
1          10    16                                              72
           END    PROGNAME
```

This is what was used in the sample program in Fig. 1.2.

3.3 COMMENTS IN GENERAL

Up to this point, assembler comments on an assembler statement following the opcode and operands were discussed. You may also code comment statements in assembler by coding an asterisk (*) before anything else. The asterisk is normally coded in column one. This form of comment is identical to the COBOL comment line. In COBOL, an asterisk placed in column seven causes the compiler to treat the entire line as comments.

You must take care not to accidentally place any character of comments in the assembler continuation indicator (position 72). Even though the line is comments, the assembler still checks the continuation indicator field. As a result, the statement following the comment line could be processed improperly. An error message might or might not be issued, depending on what was in the following statement.

This type of error may be detected more easily if a specific character is always used in the continuation indicator field. For example, if you always indicate a continuation with an X, it may be easier to detect an accidental continuation if you see any other character in column 72.

3.4 DATE-COMPILED AND THE ASSEMBLER SYSDATE

Since the assembler prints the assembly date on each page of the assembly listing, putting in a separate comment with the assembly date is probably unnecesary. However, one frequent requirement is to verify that an assembly listing matches a particular load module. (This arises when you need to be sure that you're debugging a dump from the right program listing, for example.) However, a simpler method is to create your own eye-readable indicator which you can readily locate in a dump. COBOL places an *eye-catcher* date near the beginning of the generated program.

To do the same thing in assembler, you may use two *system variable symbols*, which the assembler automatically provides. The first, called &SYSDATE, corresponds to the COBOL DATE-COMPILED feature. &SYSDATE may be used to generate a character constant containing the date. The date, 8 characters long, takes the form of MM/DD/YY, and is the same date as is printed on the assembly listing.

The second system variable symbol, called &SYSTIME, provides the 5-character time of the assembly. This takes the form of HH.MM, where HH is hours in 24-hour time (called military time or continental time). Thus, the assembler provides &SYSTIME of "20.15" for 8:15 P.M., and so forth. The assembler also prints this time on the assembly listing. Let's look at an example of how this is coded from the sample program from Fig. 1.2. The actual code related to the eye-catcher begins on the fifth line of the program (the "B   AROUND"):

```
PROGNAME CSECT
         STM    14,12,12(13)         SAVE REGISTERS
         LR     12,15               GET PROG ADDR
         USING  PROGNAME,12         ADDRESSABILITY
         B      AROUND              PAST EYECATCHER
         DC     CL8'PROGNAME'       PROGRAM NAME
         DC     CL8'&SYSDATE'       DATE ASSEMBLED
         DC     CL6'&SYSTIME'       TIME ASSEMBLED
AROUND   EQU    *
```

(The rest of the program continues from here.)

The first statement defines the control section PROGNAME. The next three lines are part of normal program initialization, which we will cover in more detail later. The "B   AROUND" branches past the actual eye-catcher text. B signifies branch and corresponds to the COBOL GO TO verb. The next three statements define character data areas (COBOL picture X) with lengths of 8, 8, and 6 bytes respectively. The first DC statement defines the program name. We could have added any further information we wanted here, such as version number, by making the character constant longer or defining another one.

The next DC statement defines the 8-byte system date. We code &SYSDATE to get this. The assembler changes the statement to contain the system assembly date value. The assembler will print the statement twice — once as we coded it, and once as it was modified and assembled. The next DC statement defines the time of the assembly using &SYSTIME. This example defines a 6-byte area, even though &SYSDATE takes only 5 bytes. The reason for this is that 370 instructions must be on even storage addresses. This will be discussed further on in the book.

Finally, the last part of the eye-catcher code is the statement "AROUND EQU *". EQU is an assembler directive which allows us to define a label without necesarily defining storage, among other things. This statement defines a label called AROUND, and defines it as the current storage location ("*"). The purpose of this statement is to have some location to branch around to avoid the data area we defined with the DC statements. You might think of "EQU *" as the equivalent of coding a paragraph name. It identifies a particular point in the program. Note that we could have put the eye-catcher anywhere in the program. However, it makes the most sense to have it as close as possible to the start of the program. This usually makes it easier to locate.

3.5 END DIRECTIVE ESOTERICA
As we discussed earlier, the END directive allows you to specify the address of the label in your program to receive control when your program is executed. This feature of the END statement means that you may introduce esoteric bugs by miscoding the END statement. For example, suppose you coded an END statement with the following comment:

```
END                          LAST CARD OF PROGRAM
```

Remember that assembler uses free-form input. Thus, the first operand of an instruction or directive is the first nonblank symbol following the opcode. In this case, the assembler will interpret "LAST" as the first and only operand. The fact that it is not in column 16 is ignored — it's free form input. "CARD OF PROGRAM" will be interpreted as comments.

If you don't have a label called "LAST" in your program, the assembler will generate an error message. This is the best thing that can happen.

If you do have a label called "LAST" in your program, the assembler will make sure that when your program runs, the first instruction executed will be at the label "LAST". If this is somewhere in the middle of your program, you will probably get an ABEND and dump. In any event, the assembly will not flag this as an error.

There are three ways to avoid this particular bug. The first is to always use an END card with no comments. The second is to always code the name of your first CSECT as the operand of the END directive. This may introduce bugs if you copy one assembler program to create another and change the CSECT name but not the END operand.

The third way is to tell the assembler that you have omitted the first operand. If you hark back to our discussion of omitted operands, remember that we did this by coding two commas in a row. For the END statement, just code one in the operand location (probably location 16), and you may then code anything you wish as comments. For example:

```
END    ,                        LAST CARD OF PGM
```

Note that the same bug may arise with any assembler directive which has an optional first operand. START is another example.

If you are completely confused by all of this, just code END cards with no comments and you won't have these problems.

3.6 SUMMARY

At this point, you should know how to define a program name with the CSECT directive. You should know how to end an assembler source program with the END directive. You should be able to code a line of comments successfully, avoiding continuation errors. You should be comfortable with the concept of system variable symbols, specifically &SYSDATE and &SYS-TIME.

Finally, you should feel comfortable that you can take a COBOL program ID division and convert it to the appropriate assembler language statements.

Things to Do

1. If you have a problem determining the version of a program that you are executing, you may be able to determine the link-edit date of the program by using the IBM-supplied MVS utility program AMBLIST (called HMBLIST in the VS1 operating system and IMBLIST in the MVT operating system). The appropriate IBM service aids manual shows how to determine this. ("MVS/Extended Architecture System Programming Library: Service Aids," GC28-1159, or "OS/VS2 MVS System Programming Library: Service Aids," GC28-0674.) Your systems programmer may have these manuals. The author is not aware of a corresponding VM utility program.

Environment Division in Assembler

This is a comparatively short chapter. It needs to be used in conjunction with Chap. 5 to learn how the assembler DCB corresponds to COBOL FDs. We'll introduce some of the information related to that topic here, and also discuss briefly some of the other Environment Division data which isn't covered in this book.

4.1 ENVIRONMENT DIVISION CONTENTS

In COBOL, the Environment Division contains all of the machine-specific information a program needs to run. (In theory, anyway.) The contents of this division generally fall into the following five categories:

1. File control data which we need in assembler (the SELECT...ASSIGN clauses, for example)
2. File control data which we need for random access VSAM disk processing (for example, the ACCESS MODE RANDOM and RECORD KEY clauses)
3. I/O data for miscellaneous special cases which we won't cover (SPECIAL-NAMES)
4. Miscellaneous data which COBOL treats as comments (SOURCE-COMPUTER)
5. Checkpoint/restart control information (RERUN clause)

We will be dealing with only the first two in this book.

The miscellaneous special cases for I/O involve cases such as on-line printers and punches, et cetera, and are not of general interest. (For those of you who may have a genuine need for this, refer to the discussion of the CNTRL macro in the data management manuals. You should have enough understanding after completing this book to handle this research on your own.)

The miscellaneous data which COBOL treats as comments can be handled with what you already know about comments.

The checkpoint/restart information is not of enough general interest to include here. It requires an understanding of the CHKPT macro instruction. (For those of you who have to have this information, refer to the appropriate IBM checkpoint/restart manuals listed at the end of this chapter. If you really have a need to use this facility, you are advised to read and fully understand the information in the IBM manuals. Again, you should have a good basis for understanding these manuals on your own after you have finished this book.)

With this classification in mind, let's examine the SELECT and ASSIGN clauses, along with some VSAM considerations.

4.2 FILE CONTROL DATA

COBOL puts information about file processing in both the Environment Division and the Data Division. In assembler, all information regarding a particular file is contained in a control block called a DCB (Data Control Block).

You should be familiar with the DCB from your JCL experience. In VM, the FILEDEF command options require the same information (e.g., LRECL). Assembler provides a way to specify all the information you put in JCL within the assembler program. We will cover this more thoroughly in the next chapter.

Within the Environment Division, the most important item at this point is the DD name for the file. This must match a DD name in the JCL, or a VM FILEDEF name, when the program runs. This is specified as part of the ASSIGN clause.

The COBOL ASSIGN clause takes the following form:

SELECT file-name
ASSIGN TO class[-device]-organization-name.

For example, in Fig. 1.3, the COBOL sample program, we coded

SELECT INFILE
ASSIGN TO UT-S-INFILE.

File-name in the above is the name we use inside the COBOL program when reading or writing the file. The options of the ASSIGN clause are:

Class DA for direct access, UT for utility (sequential access), and UR for unit record.

Device This is optional and specifies the unit number of device to be associated with this file. You probably don't code this, since it isn't required and means you may have to recompile your program if you change devices.

Organization is a one character value: S for sequential, D for direct access, R for direct access with rewrite or for relative access, I for indexed access.

Name The external name of the file (DD name).

The main item of importance to us now is the DD name. This will be specified as the DDNAME= operand of the corresponding DCB macro. (You would also refer to the other fields when converting a DCB on your own.)

The COBOL FILE STATUS clause does not have a direct equivalent in assembler. We will discuss how to get this type of information in Chap. 10.

The next chapter covers how to construct a DCB from the options normally specified in a COBOL FD and SELECT ... ASSIGN clause.

4.3 VSAM FILE CONTROL INFORMATION

A number of special clauses provide support in COBOL for the VSAM access method. (We'll discuss what an *access method* is in the next chapter.) Rather than attempt to cover all possible file processing options at once, we will also cover sequential access in the next chapter. Chapter 21 will deal with VSAM random access.

The Environment Division also has unique information for other disk direct access methods — BDAM and ISAM. These are not covered within this book, due to their slowly declining use. If you have a need to use these access methods, review the data management manuals after you complete this book.

4.4 ACCESS METHODS

This book will describe three access methods.

1. QSAM (Queued Sequential Access Method)
2. BSAM (Basic Sequential Access Method),A
3. VSAM (Virtual Storage Access Method)

We will spend most of our time on QSAM, show VSAM in some detail, and refer to BSAM occasionally.

We have been using the term *access method* without explicitly defining what it means. This is an instance of esoteric information which you don't necesarily need to know in detail to learn assembler.

An access method is a part of the I/O services in MVS. For our purposes, we can define it as the set of operating system programs and macro instructions to support data access for selected combinations of hardware and data organization. VM provides some access methods as part of its OS simulation, and it's important to know what is and is not supported.

There are three key ways in which access methods differ. These are as follows:

1. The I/O devices which they can use
2. The way in which they store data on those devices
3. The ways by which you can retrieve or store the data and control the devices

For example, the access method to write data on a tape (QSAM) doesn't allow you to control CAD/CAM design operations on an IBM 5080 terminal, which would be done by the BGAM access method (in the GAM/SP program product).

There are a lot of access methods in MVS, some of which are essentially obsolete. VM supports some of these. The MVS access methods include the following:

- The conventional sequential access set includes QSAM (Queued Sequential Access Method) and BSAM (Basic Sequential Access Method)
- Basic Partitioned Access Method (BPAM) is a variation of BSAM which allows access to members of libraries (partitioned data sets)
- Direct and indexed access methods for disk include Virtual Storage Access Method (VSAM), Basic Direct Access Method (BDAM), Basic Indexed Sequential Access Method (BISAM), and Queued Indexed Sequential Access Method (QISAM)
- Telecommunications access methods include Virtual Terminal Access Method (VTAM), Basic Telecommunications Access Method (BTAM), and Telecommunications Access Method (TCAM)
- Basic Graphic Access Method (BGAM) controls special IBM graphics terminals like the IBM 5080 and 3250

We will only cover QSAM, BSAM, and VSAM in this book. These are supported by VM through OS simulation, along with the BPAM and BDAM access methods. COBOL provides some support for many of the other access methods listed, but very few new applications are written using anything but QSAM, VSAM, and VTAM.

However, in MVS, you may still need to learn how to use the other access methods. One reason COBOL programmers want to learn assembler is to maintain existing systems with a high proportion of assembler language programs.

These large, complex older systems may have been written many years ago. As such, it is not uncommon to find assembler programs running that use the BDAM and ISAM access methods for disk files, or that use BTAM to interchange data with special terminal types that can't use VTAM, and so on.

A complete description of how to program in each of these access methods would take several books the size of this one. As such, we will cover only QSAM, BSAM, and VSAM, which should provide a good basis of knowledge to learn the others on your own. These are generally documented in the data administration manuals. The telecommunications and graphics access methods (VTAM, TCAM, GAM, and BTAM) have their own series of manuals.

4.5 SUMMARY

This chapter covered the COBOL Environment Division entries. These don't have direct equivalents in assembler in some cases, or address specialized situations which aren't frequently used.

The key elements in the Environment Division which apply to

The key elements in the Environment Division which apply to assembler are the DD name and access method selection information from the SELECT ... ASSIGN clauses.

If you need further information on the MVS checkpoint/restart function, refer to the following manuals:

"MVS/ESA Checkpoint/Restart User's Guide," SC26-4503.
"MVS/Extended Architecture Checkpoint/Restart User's Guide," GC26-4139
"MVS/370 Checkpoint/Restart User's Guide," GC26-4054.

Note that the CHKPT macro is not supported by VM OS simulation.

Things to Do

1. Review some COBOL application programs. Do any of them use the Environment Division features we haven't discussed, such as SPECIAL-NAMES?

Data Division in Assembler — File Section

This chapter will show how to convert a COBOL FD file description to an assembler DCB and will then introduce how data areas in assembler programs for the records that we read or write can be provided. Finally, some of the unique ways that COBOL processes records will be discussed, and the techniques that correspond to these in assembler will be shown.

We'll start this by going over the items in COBOL which we use to create the information needed to process a file in assembler.

5.1 SPECIFYING AN ACCESS METHOD

Assembler uses a Data Control Block (DCB) or Access Method Control Block (ACB) that corresponds to COBOL's FD. QSAM and BSAM use the DCB, and VSAM uses the ACB.

The DCB macro instruction has two operands which together specify the access method. These are the data set organization (DSORG) and the macro form (MACRF).

DSORG determines how the data is stored and accessed. This could be sequentially, directly, or in some other manner that is unique to a specific device (e.g., a terminal). For this book, we'll stick to physically sequential data-set organization. This is specified as DSORG=PS in the DCB.

MACRF specifies the macro instructions you use to retrieve or store records in the particular data set. Optionally, you may also specify macro instructions used to control the devices. For our examples, we'll start with the GET and PUT macros, which use MACRF=(GM) or MACRF=(PM) respectively.

For VSAM files, the AM operand allows us to specify the access method. For our examples in Chap. 21, we'll use AM=VSAM.

5.2 CONVERTING COBOL FDs TO ASSEMBLER DCBs

Now let's actually go through the conversion of an FD to a DCB. The DCB macro has oodles of operands. It is one of the largest macro instructions in MVS. The reasons behind this is that it must support many different access methods.

Fortunately for us, we have to worry only about a few operands in the case of QSAM. They also have direct corresponding values in COBOL in most cases. The operands, their meanings, and the corresponding COBOL values are as follows:

Operand	Meaning	COBOL source
Name	DCB name	FD name
BLKSIZE	Block size	FD BLOCK CONTAINS clause
LRECL	Record length	FD RECORD CONTAINS clause
RECFM	Record format	RECORDING FORMAT clause
DDNAME	JCL DD name or VM FILEDEF name	ASSIGN clause
DSORG	Data set organization	ASSIGN clause
DEVD	Device type	(See below)
MACRF	Macro form	(See below)
EODAD	End-of-input routine name	AT END clause of READ

Now let's convert one of the FDs from our sample program to a DCB. Here's the input FD:

```
FD   INFILE
     BLOCK CONTAINS 0
     RECORD CONTAINS 80 CHARACTERS
     RECORDING MODE IS F
     LABEL RECORDS ARE OMITTED
     DATA RECORD IS A-RECORD.
01   A-RECORD.
     05   FILLER   PIC X(80).
```

Here are the conversion steps to create the DCB.

1. The FD name can be used as the DCB name (the label on the DCB macro). If it were a longer name, like MASTER-FILE-IN, you could either convert it by changing the dashes to underscores (giving MASTER_FILE_IN) or by creating a shorter name with less than 8 characters (like MASTIN). To be compatible with older assemblers, you would have to select a shorter name. In this example, we have DDNAME=INFILE for our DCB.

2. The BLOCK CONTAINS 0 RECORDS converts directly into the DCB BLKSIZE operand. If you omit the BLOCK CONTAINS clause, COBOL assumes that the block size is equal to the record size. If you omit the BLKSIZE operand on a DCB, the DCB macro generates a value of zero.

Thus, if we have a BLOCK CONTAINS clause, we should just use the same value in the DCB, which gives us BLKSIZE=0 in this case. If your COBOL programs do not have a BLOCK CONTAINS clause, and you are sure that this is intentional, then set the BLKSIZE to the same value as the record length. (See the notes on BLKSIZE below.)

3. The RECORD CONTAINS clause should be used to set the LRECL value in the DCB. Thus, for our example, set LRECL=80. (See the notes later for variable-length records and how to determine the record length yourself).

4. At this point, we have to go outside the FD to get the rest of the information. As mentioned earlier, the ASSIGN clause contains the DD name. Thus, our DCB parameter should be DDNAME=INFILE.

5. The next parameter needed is the data set organization. In general, we can get this from the ASSIGN clause if desired. Other ways exist to get this, which will be covered shortly. For the examples in this book, physical sequential organization will be used. Thus, our DCB should contain DSORG=PS for this operand.

6. We must also specify a device type for the DCB macro. The DCB requires a device class rather than a specific device number. The DCB macro will generate various sizes of storage area depending on the device class specified. In general, specification of a disk device class is preferable. The disk device class generates the largest area (20 bytes) of any of the classes, and can be used with any class. This also allows the actual device-type selection through JCL. Following this precept, we will specify DEVD=DA for the DCB. (DA stands for *direct access*.)

7. As mentioned earlier, we must provide macro form information to indicate a specific access method. The simplest level of I/O in MVS uses QSAM via the GET and PUT macros. Since INFILE is an input data set, we will be using the GET macro to process it. Hence, our DCB should specify MACRF=(GM). Some options of QSAM are further discussed later on.

8. Finally, for input data sets, we must specify what address in our program should receive control when we come to the end of the file. This is a major difference from the COBOL approach, which allows this to be determined at every READ verb. (There are ways of doing the same thing in assembler which we'll also cover.) The DCB operand, EODAD, specifies the address of a routine. MVS will branch to that address when it determines that your program has reached the end of file. For our example, this routine is named ENDDATA, and our DCB is coded with EODAD=ENDDATA.

At the end of all these conversions, we have the following DCB:

```
INPUT      DCB   DDNAME = INFILE,DEVD = DA,MACRF = (GM),       X
                 RECFM = FB,LRECL = 80,BLKSIZE = 0,            X
                 EODAD = ENDDATA
```

Which corresponds to the original FD:

```
FD   INFILE
     BLOCK CONTAINS 0
     RECORD CONTAINS 80 CHARACTERS
     RECORDING MODE IS F
     LABEL RECORDS ARE OMITTED
     DATA RECORD IS A-RECORD.
```

There are other clauses in the COBOL FD, but they do not have any important meaning for us.

At this point, you should have a general understanding that we can directly convert a COBOL file description into a DCB macro. If you are not comfortable with this concept, try taking a sequential file FD and converting it to a DCB with the eight steps outlined above.

5.3   GETTING DCB INFORMATION FROM OTHER SOURCES

If you have a COBOL FD which you want to convert to a DCB, but which does not have all the information referred to above, you have several other ways of obtaining the information.

First, the TSO LISTD command will display RECFM, DSORG, BLKSIZE, and LRECL information for you. The same information is also included in option 3.2 of ISPF. The VM FILELIST or LISTDS commands also provide this information.

You may also run the MVS IEHLIST utility program with the LISTVTOC command and FORMAT option to get this information for data sets on disk.

A review of the COBOL program may also give you the information needed. The COBOL compiler DMAP option will map out all the record layouts in the data division, and you should be able to interpret this output to determine the record length.

For data sets on tape, you could dump the tape label and interpret the output with the aid of the tape labels manual. This should be a last resort, of course.

5.4   PROVIDING DATA AREAS FOR RECORDS

As in COBOL, you must provide data area descriptions for your records. This gets into the contents of the next chapter to some degree.

The assembler DS directive defines storage areas. It is appropriate to use it for data areas. Thus, our COBOL example in Fig. 1.3 had the following code after the FD entry for INFILE:

```
01   A-RECORD.
     05    FILLER    PIC X(80).
```

A corresponding definition for assembler would be:

```
INAREA     DS     CL80                          INPUT DATA AREA
```

Unlike COBOL, there are no references to the record data descriptions in the assembler DCB.

To more fully cover this topic, we have to be able to define individual data items as well as group items. Chapter 6 covers this.

5.5   OTHER QSAM PROCESSING ESOTERICA

QSAM has a number of other processing options which we won't fully cover in this text. There are many QSAM macros besides GET and PUT. QSAM also provides some other buffer processing options which are of interest to the COBOL programmer.

There are several QSAM macros which we can't fully describe. These macros include the following:

- CNTRL   Control a unit record device — may be useful for on-line printing
- FEOV   Force end of volume — causes a new tape to be mounted
- PUTX   Record update — similar to rewrite in COBOL
- PDAB   Parallel DCB access — improves performance when reading many DCBs to consolidate files
- PDABD   DSECT for above
- SETPRT Load FCB for printer — may be useful for on-line printing
- TRUNC   Truncate an output block — causes current block to be written with no more records
- XLATE   Translate between EBCDIC and ASCII — useful when processing tapes from other types of computers (e.g., DEC VAXes)

These macros are completely described in the data management macros manual. VM only documents support for FEOV and PUTX in the above list as of VM/SP release 6.

QSAM also provides other buffering techniques. Up to this point, we've discussed what is termed *move mode* processing. In this, each record is moved from the input buffer to the data area specified in the QSAM GET macro.

Another, more efficient method is *locate mode* processing. In this, QSAM just returns the address of the next record, rather than moving the record. This requires less storage, since we don't have to allocate an area to store the record. Probably more important is the fact that it uses less CPU time, since we don't have to actually move the record.

Using this technique requires an understanding of the assembler DSECT concept, which we will cover in detail in Chap. 7, on the LINKAGE SECTION. However, the important point about it at this time is that COBOL uses this technique when reading or writing sequential files. As a result, when you define a record layout with an 01-level following an FD, you are not really defining any storage.

5.6 NOTES ON BLKSIZE

Most COBOL programmers specify BLOCK CONTAINS 0 RECORDS in their FDs. Most assembler programmers specify BLKSIZE=0 in the DCB. This section presents some reasons why.

The way that MVS processes a DCB when it is opened allows information to be provided from three sources. Oversimplifying somewhat, these are the DCB itself, the data set label, and the JCL.

If information is provided both in the DCB and in JCL (or the label), MVS assumes that the information in the DCB is correct. As a result, if you specify a block size in the DCB (or the FD), it cannot be changed (overridden) through JCL.

Many data processing installations have programming standards which prohibit specification of block size in the FD. The reason behind this is that most computer operations staffs need to be able to relocate data sets from tape to disk, et cetera, and need to be able to change the block size to whatever is most appropriate for the device available. If the block size is coded in the FD or DCB, they can't do this.

Thus, unless you have a very good reason, you should code BLKSIZE=0 in your DCBs in assembler. The only exceptions which should be allowable are where the blocksize is specified by the MVS operating system (e.g., in the SNAP macro instruction) or in a U.S. government standard (e.g., MIL-STD-1840). Otherwise, use BLKSIZE=0.

For VM CMS disk files, BLKSIZE=0 is advisable. VM OS simulation will operate similarly to MVS when processing other files.

5.7 SUMMARY

In this chapter, we took the information found in a COBOL program describing a file and used it to create a corresponding DCB macro. We needed the information in both Chap. 4 and this chapter to complete this.

You should be comfortable with the process of creating a DCB from the same information you would use in COBOL.

Things to Do

1. If you are running under VM, obtain the current application development reference manual for your release of VM/SP. Review the supported OS macros and know where to look up what is and is not supported under VM OS simulation of the QSAM access method. (The chapter in that manual entitled "CMS Programming Interface" is helpful.)

Data Division in Assembler — Working Storage

In this chapter, we will show how assembler data definition types correspond to COBOL's data definitions. In addition, we will discuss how certain COBOL data definitions require both data and special instruction coding to implement. Finally, we will review the assembler data types which don't have reasonable facsimiles in COBOL.

After finishing this chapter, you should have enough information to convert the data division in a simple COBOL program to assembler.

6.1 IBM 370 DATA REPRESENTATION AND COBOL PICTURES

Before starting on the step-by-step comparison of how COBOL and assembler allow you to define data, let's go over the basic machine data formats.

In the IBM 370 architecture, the programmer can manipulate or control two main items — the contents of main storage and the contents of registers.

6.1.1 Main Storage

Main storage in the 370, like all computers, comprises groupings of bits. The basic storage element in the 370 is the byte. Each 370 byte contains 8 bits. You should already know both these terms. Bits are numbered left to right within bytes, zero through seven. Figure 6.1 shows the layout.

Figure 6.1 Layout of bits within a byte.

Bytes of main storage can be grouped into larger elements. The first of these, the word, or *fullword*, is composed of 4 bytes. This gives a 32-bit binary value. The leftmost bit — bit 0 of the word — is a sign bit. The remaining 31 bits make up the binary number. The maximum number which 31 bits will hold is 2,147,483,647. Figure 6.2 shows the layout of bytes in a fullword.

Figure 6.2   Layout of bytes in a fullword.

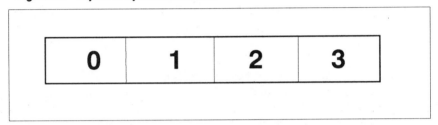

Binary arithmetic has a number of peculiarities which will be covered in Chap. 11.

Since the 31 bits in a fullword exceed the size needed for many common arithmetic operations, the IBM 370 architecture provides a smaller unit, the *halfword*. A halfword contains 2 bytes (16 bits), one of which is the sign bit. A halfword may not contain any number over 32,767.

Another, larger quantity is the *doubleword*. This is — you guessed it — two fullwords. It is used with floating-point operations, certain conversion instructions, and in storing the current clock value. The doubleword may be used for integer binary arithmetic with something called logical arithmetic, which we'll describe in Chap. 11.

Halfwords, fullwords, and doublewords should be aligned in main storage for best use. Basically, *alignment* means that the address of any of these units must be an even multiple of the length of the unit. Thus, halfwords (2 bytes long) must begin on even addresses. Fullwords (4 bytes long) must begin on addresses which are a multiple of 4. Doublewords (8 bytes) must begin on addresses which are a multiple of — can you guess? — 8 bytes.

Figure 6.3   Byte/halfword/fullword/doubleword relationship.

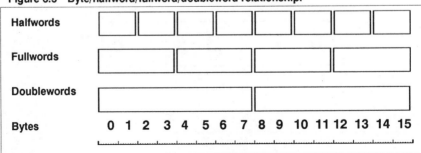

Figure 6.3 shows the alignment and relative storage allocations for halfwords, doublewords, fullwords, and bytes. The COBOL concept which corresponds to alignment is the SYNCHRONIZED attribute in the Data Division.

All IBM and all plug-compatible computers known to this writer that have been sold since the early 1970s have included a feature called *byte-oriented-operands*. This is an obscure way of saying that you don't have to align halfwords, fullwords, and doublewords. However, instructions execute a little faster if you do, so it's still a good idea. The ALIGN assembly option will also flag any misaligned data area uses.

In addition to binary arithmetic, the 370 architecture also supports *packed decimal* arithmetic. This is a special form of arithmetic where the data is stored as decimal digits (0-9) rather than as binary numbers. Packed decimal arithmetic operates between two fields in storage without the need for a register.

Finally, main storage is also used to store character values, with one character per byte.

6.1.2   Registers

The other main item which a programmer may manipulate is something called *registers*. These are essentially special places in the CPU in which you may do binary arithmetic. (Please note that this is a somewhat over-simplified explanation.) Registers are also used for addressing data, which we'll discuss in the next chapter.

Registers are termed as either general purpose registers, control registers, or floating point registers. Which type you use is determined by the instructions you code.

General purpose registers are 32 bits (one fullword or 4 bytes) long. There are 16 general purpose registers, numbered from 0 to 15. You may have seen them printed somewhere in a dump. These are the most commonly used registers. Figure 6.4 shows the relationship between the general purpose registers and storage.

Figure 6.4   Relationship of general purpose registers and storage.

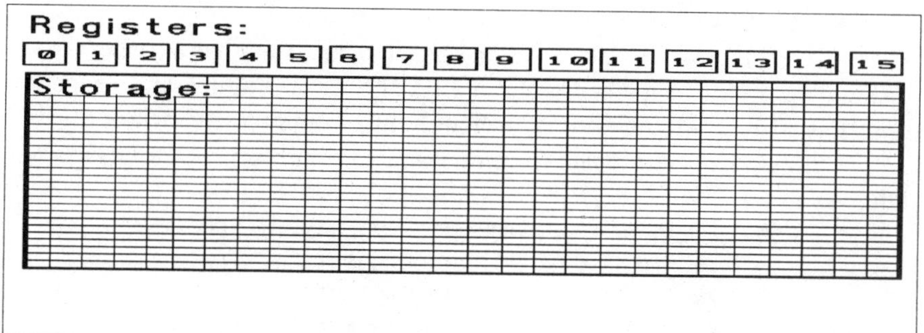

The 16 control registers are also 32 bits long. They are used to control the operation of the CPU and aren't directly accessible to application programmers. We won't be discussing these, but the reference summary contains a layout of their specific contents.

The floating point registers are either 64 bits (doubleword) or 128 bits (*quadword*) long. They may also perform 32-bit floating point arithmetic. We will not be covering floating-point arithmetic in this book.

The key thing to remember about registers is that they are not part of the CPU's main storage. You need special instructions to manipulate them.

6.2 ARITHMETIC (COBOL COMPUTATIONAL) DATA

COBOL stores numbers in either display or computational format. Display format is just a special case of character data, which we'll discuss later in this chapter.

If you think you know all you need to about how binary and packed decimal (COMP and COMP-3) numbers are stored, just skip to Sec. 6.3. COBOL defines several formats, including:

COMPUTATIONAL	Used for binary integer arithmetic
COMPUTATIONAL-1	Used for floating point arithmetic
COMPUTATIONAL-2	Used for floating point arithmetic
COMPUTATIONAL-3	Used for packed decimal arithmetic

Since we aren't covering floating-point arithmetic, we won't go into how these are defined and stored in assembler. The other two formats — COMP and COMP-3 — will be covered separately.

6.2.1 COMP Data

Computational usage in COBOL generates binary data. This means that the data must be stored as a halfword, fullword, or in some longer form. Assembler provides directives to do this.

COBOL, however, defines computational data in terms of how many digits are represented in the binary field. Additionally, COBOL defines the data as signed or unsigned through the PICTURE clause. There is no direct assembler corollary to the sign information, although there are ways of handling it as COBOL does.

COBOL creates halfword data fields if a data item has a PIC of S9(4) or smaller, and a usage of COMP. A PIC of 9(4) or smaller and usage of COMP also generate halfwords, although they are processed differently.

The appropriate fields from our sample program in COBOL are as follows:

```
77   LINECT      PIC S999  COMP-3  VALUE ZERO.
77   RECNUM      PIC S9(7) COMP-3  VALUE ZERO.
77   ONE         PIC S999  COMP-3  VALUE 1.
77   P50         PIC S999  COMP-3  VALUE +50.
```

The basic rule in COBOL is that up to 4 digits of COMP data are stored in a halfword, and that up to nine digits of COMP data are stored in a fullword.

Following this rule, cover the answer column below and try guessing what size storage area COBOL generates for the following working storage entries:

COBOL code		Generates (answer)
77 HALFWORD	PIC S9(4).	Halfword
77 FULLWORD	PIC S9(8).	Fullword
77 SHORTEST	PIC S9(1).	Halfword
77 FOOLWORD	PIC S9(3).	Halfword
77 FIVEDIGS	PIC S9(5).	Fullword

That shouldn't have been too difficult.

6.2.2 COMP-3 Data

The other most frequently used number representation is COMP-3, which generates packed data. Packed data comprises decimal digits and a specially coded sign. Since it only takes 4 bits to store a decimal digit, packed decimal data can store 2 digits per byte. The specially coded sign occupies the last 4 bits in a packed decimal number.

The valid signs for packed decimal digits are any of the hexadecimal digits from A through F. Packed decimal requires that the sign bits may occur only in the last 4 bits of the packed decimal number. If a sign occurs in any other position, the CPU will cause a data exception when you try to do arithmetic with the bad sign. (You probably know a data exception as an 0C7.)

Conversely, packed decimal digits must occupy all the digit positions except for the last, which must contain a sign. Again, the CPU causes a data exception if it detects a violation of this rule.

While any of the hex digits A through F may occur in the sign bits, generally only three of these — C, D, and F — are used. The digits C and F represent a positive sign, and D represents a negative sign. (A and E also represent positive signs, and B represents a negative sign.)

The CPU generates either a hexadecimal C or D following any packed decimal arithmetic operation. The presence of a hexadecimal F as a sign usually arises right after an input display-format (character) number is converted to packed decimal format.

If you refer to the "EBCDIC Code Table" section of the 370 reference summary, you will see that the characters zero through nine have hexadecimal representations of X'F0' through X'F9'. Take a moment to do this now.

(The 370 reference summary has a table of contents. You may find this listed under "EBCDIC Code Table" or just under "Code Table," depending on the version of the reference summary you use. The "EBCDIC" subheading under the "Graphics and Controls" column covers what we are looking at now. You may find it helpful to refer to Fig. 6.5, which shows the format of the reference summary code tables. We'll also discuss the format of this part of the reference summary in more detail in Sec. 6.6.7.)

When the CPU converts a number in character format to packed decimal format, it uses an instruction called PACK. PACK operates by taking the rightmost half of each byte to be packed and placing it in the corresponding digit position in the packed decimal number. (We'll go through this entire sequence when we talk about arithmetic, so this explanation is deliberately short.)

To generate the sign of the packed decimal number, PACK takes the leftmost half of the last character and copies it into the sign position. Since the character byte representations of all the decimal digits have a hexadecimal F in their left half, you receive a packed decimal sign of F when using PACK to convert an input field.

Conversely, when converting a packed decimal number (COMP-3) for display in COBOL as characters, you may have noticed that the rightmost digit may take on strange values. This arises because the sign bits of C or D, which the CPU generates, cause a digit to become a letter in the range of A-I or J-K when converted back. (Ending digits of zero generate an unprintable character.)

Since a packed decimal number holds two digits in each byte, a simple formula is necesary to calculate how long to make packed decimal fields. To store N digits, we need $(N+1)/2$ bytes. Conversely, if we have an N-byte field, it can store $(N*2)-1$ bytes. We have to add or subtract 1 to account for the packed decimal sign.

Following these rules, let's try a similar exercise to the one we did for binary digits. Cover the answer column on the right and try guessing how many bytes COBOL generates for the following working storage entries:

COBOL code		Generates
77 LINECT	PIC S999 COMP-3.	2 bytes: $(3+1)/2$
77 RECNUM	PIC S9(7) COMP-3.	4 bytes: $(7+1)/2$
77 ONE	PIC S9 COMP-3.	1 byte: $(1+1)/2$
77 FLAVORS	PIC S9(31)COMP-3.	16 bytes: $(31+1)/2$

And working the other way:

Storage area	Holds
3 bytes	5 digits: $(3*2) - 1$
1 byte	1 digit: $(1*2) - 1$
8 bytes	15 digits: $(8*2) - 1$
16 bytes	31 digits: $(16*2) -1$

6.2.3   Advantages of Both Types

Each of these two types of data have their own advantages and drawbacks.

Binary arithmetic is faster. If you have to perform a long string of calculations and can keep the numbers in registers as much as possible, you will normally see less CPU time used by binary arithmetic.

Binary arithmetic is also necesary when calculating or manipulating addresses (USAGE IS INDEX in COBOL). For this reason alone, you will use binary arithmetic frequently in some form.

On the negative side, binary arithmetic requires more conversions to get from character value to binary format. Thus, if you were reading in a series of numbers and adding them up, binary would probably take slightly longer. (But this is the type of processing that COBOL probably does better than assembler anyway.)

Packed decimal arithmetic is faster if you are making relatively few manipulations of many input numbers. Again, this is probably better done in COBOL.

Packed decimal allows a longer fixed-point number than does normal binary arithmetic — up to 31 digits. If you are calculating a number in the octillions — say, your total credit card debt — packed decimal arithmetic would usually be more straightforward. (Arithmetic with very large numbers requires *logical arithmetic* in binary, which is more complicated.)

Please note, however, that these relative efficiencies have little meaning when compared to other processing. If you are truly reading in a file and adding up one number from each record, the CPU time spent in reading the records would dwarf the CPU time used for all the arithmetic.

6.2.4   Storing Character Data

To round out our discussion of how data is stored, let's look at how normal character data is stored. This is what you define as PICTURE X, or numeric data with a USAGE IS DISPLAY clause.

In the 370, using the EBCDIC code set, each character takes 8 bits - 1 byte. Refer to the EBCDIC code table in the 370 reference summary to see exactly how this works. Conveniently, the 370 storage organization provides 8-bit bytes.

Since COBOL generates 1 byte of storage for each character or digit in a PICTURE clause when USAGE IS DISPLAY, you generate 1 byte of storage when you code one character in fields with PICTURE of X. The same applies to edited numeric fields.

Thus, for the COBOL PICTURE clauses below, COBOL will generate storage with the lengths shown for these examples. (All numeric pictures assume USAGE IS DISPLAY.)

PICTURE	Storage generated
X(10)	10 bytes.
9(5)	5 bytes.
ZZ,ZZ9	6 bytes — 5 for the digits and 1 for the comma.
S9(4)	4 bytes — the sign affects how the data is displayed, but not the length.
,,ZZ9	11 bytes.

A simple rule is that if it takes a position on a print line or on a terminal display, it usually takes 1 byte of storage.

6.3 GENERATING DATA IN ASSEMBLER

Now that we've beaten the ways to store numbers to death, let's look at what we code to define data in storage. Assembler provides two directives to do this: DS and DC. DS (Define Storage) allocates storage but doesn't put any initial value in it. DC (Define Constant) defines storage and puts an initial value on it. DS is used anytime that you would code a PICTURE clause in COBOL without a VALUE clause (i.e., a storage area with no starting value). DC, conversely, is used whenever you would have coded a VALUE clause in COBOL. We'll discuss DC first.

6.3.1 The DC Directive

The DC directive may have a name field, has an opcode of DC, and has two to four subfields as an operand. Examples:

```
1          10     16                                          72
TEN        DC     F'10'
HOWDY      DC     CL6'HELLO'
GOODBYE    DC     2CL3'BYE'
```

TEN, HOWDY, and GOODBYE are the names of the fields created by the three DC statements. The four subfields are as follows:

1. An optional duplication factor
2. A required type
3. An optional length
4. A required value

Let's look at what these examples generate, then discuss the four subfields.

The first DC statement operand, " F'10' ", specifies a type of F — a fullword of binary data — with a value of 10. This is equivalent in COBOL to:

```
77   TEN  PIC S9(8) COMP VALUE 10.
```

The second DC specifies a type of C — character — with the optional explicit length specified — L6 — and a value of HELLO. The COBOL equivalent is:

```
77 HOWDY  PIC X(6) VALUE 'HELLO'.
```

The final example specifies all four subfields. The type is again C (character data) with an optional explicit length of 3 bytes. The value of the constant is BYE. Finally, the optional duplication factor of 2 specifies that we want two of these. As a result, the assembler generates two copies of the constant, making the actual contents into BYEBYE. COBOL has no exact equivalent to the duplication factor. A possible COBOL equivalent to this DC statement is:

77 GOOBBYE PIC X(6) VALUE 'BYEBYE'.

Let's now discuss the subfields in some more detail.

The duplication factor tells the assembler how many of the fields we want. As such, it may serve the same function as the OCCURS clause in COBOL. (However, the rules in COBOL for using both VALUE and OCCURS prevent it from being identical.) Section 6.3.1.3 which follows discusses how to implement an OCCURS clause in more detail.

The type field defines the type of data we want to create. The assembler type field can be derived from a combination of the COBOL PICTURE and USAGE clauses. Assembler also supports several types of data which do not have a direct equivalent in COBOL.

The optional length factor lets us specify the length of a field explicitly for the assembler. This corresponds to the repetitive occurence value in a PICTURE clause, that is, the "4" in "PIC S9(4)". Unlike COBOL, the assembler will calculate the length of an item based on its type and value. Also unlike COBOL, the assembler length is always in bytes. COBOL's length for COMP and COMP-3 fields is in digits, and doesn't accurately reflect the number of bytes required.

The value subfield tells the assembler what specific data to generate in a field. This corresponds directly to the COBOL VALUE clause. The value is specified within single quotation marks (apostrophes). Unlike COBOL, the value must always be in quote marks, whereas the COBOL VALUE clause for a number (COMP or COMP-3) doesn't allow them.

Before doing a step-by-step discussion of converting COBOL data elements to assembler, let's discuss a few other similarities and differences between COBOL and assembler.

6.3.1.1   COBOL Equivalent Data Types

Assembler data types which have direct corresponding COBOL data types include the following:

1. Binary arithmetic values (assembler types of F and H)
2. Packed decimal arithmetic values (type of P)
3. Character (C, X)
4. Address pointer data type (type of A)

Table 6.1 shows how these correspond to COBOL data definitions, and is arranged by the assembler DC type.

Table 6.1 Assembler Data Types And COBOL Equivalents	
Type	**COBOL equivalent**
F	USAGE IS COMP, PIC S9(5) to PIC S9(9)
H	USAGE IS COMP, PIC S9(1) to PIC S9(4)
P	USAGE IS COMP-3, PIC S9(1) to S9(18)
C	USAGE IS DISPLAY, PIC X(1) to X(256) *(many other types of edited data fall into this category)*
X	USAGE IS DISPLAY, PIC X(1) to X(256), VALUE of LOW-VALUES or HIGH-VALUES *(plus many other types of edited data)*
A	USAGE IS INDEX *(type F may also be used)*

At this stage, we must skip over many of COBOL's other data types (such as edited data with floating dollar signs). These will be covered further in Chap. 13.

6.3.1.2 Padding and Truncation

Padding and truncation occur when the value supplied with the DC statement is smaller or larger than the length defined for the field in question. In general, assembler follows similar rules to COBOL when defining storage and initial values. (Processing is different.) Character values which are smaller than the field size being defined are padded with blanks on the right. Numeric values which are smaller than the field being defined are padded with zeroes on the left. (Padding will occur with 0 bits for binary arithmetic data and with 0 digits for packed decimal data.)

Data values which exceed the size of the field being defined result in an error, just as in COBOL. Thus, both " H'65536' " in assembler and " field-name PIC S9(4) COMP VALUE +65536." in COBOL generate errors.

6.3.1.3 Length Attribute and Duplication Factor

The assembler automatically calculates the length of DC items and associates it with the name of the DC (if any) as a length attribute. This value appears in the cross reference of the assembler. The assembler uses the length attribute to set up instructions, such as Move, which don't have a standard fixed length.

The length attribute is the same as the number of bytes generated by the DC statement unless a duplication factor is supplied. In this case, the assembler's computed length is the length before the duplication factor is applied.

In the case of our example, "GOODBYE   DC   2CL3'BYE' ", we supplied a length of 3. This is the assembler's length-attribute value.

However, since we also supplied a duplication factor of 2, the assembler generates two 3-byte constants for a total of 6 bytes.

The effect of this is that when we refer to GOODBYE in an instruction — such as Move Characters — which uses a variable length of data, the assembler will use the length attribute to decide how much data to move. In this case, we will move 3 bytes rather than 6.

Let's try an analogy to explain this further. It's sort of like going to a convenience store and asking for a six-pack of beer rather than asking for six beers. In this case, we are defining what we want — six beers in one container — just as in a DC statement.

However, when it comes time to move the beer from the can to the recipient stomach, you normally want to move only one beer, just as the assembler moves only one of the defined values. This sensible moderation is the inspiration for the assembler's use of the length attribute.

If this keeps up, you may need a beer soon yourself.

6.3.1.4 Doubleword Data Type

An additional assembler data type which we must have for certain operations is the doubleword. This has an assembler type of D and generates 8 bytes. There is no exact COBOL corollary, as a doubleword is used for both binary and floating-point operations. COBOL generates an 8-byte area if you code something like the following:

```
77  BIG-NUM   PIC S9(15) COMP.
```

6.3.2 The DS Directive

Just as the DC directive generates data fields with an initial value as in the VALUE clause in COBOL, the DS directive generates fields as when no VALUE clause is present in COBOL. Uses of DS are normally to create data items which will be filled in when the program runs, such as record I/O areas.

DS has the same syntax as DC. The value subfield is also allowed in DS, but has no effect on what's in the storage area defined. The DS descriptions state that the contents of the data area created with DS is unpredictable at run time.

DS allows a maximum length of up to 65,535 bytes. DC allows only up to 256 bytes.

DS is also used to define labels and for alignment. This use occurs when a duplication factor of 0 is specified. For example,

```
1          10    16
LABEL      DS    0H
```

defines a name field of LABEL, causes the assembler to align it on a halfword (even) boundary ("H"), and reserves 0 bytes of storage. This is a common technique in assembler programs to define the equivalent of COBOL paragraph names.

Additionally, the DS directive is commonly used to define group item names, again using the duplication factor of 0.

6.4   CONVERTING COBOL DATA DESCRIPTIONS TO ASSEMBLER

The step-by-step process to convert a COBOL data definition to its assembler counterpart follows.

6.4.1   Select the Assembler Data Type

Selecting the type can be accomplished by making these tests:

1. If USAGE IS INDEX, select assembler DC data type of A (a type of F may also be used).
2. If USAGE IS DISPLAY and the initial value is LOW-VALUES or HIGH-VALUES, select type of X.
3. Select type of C for all other cases of USAGE IS DISPLAY.
4. If USAGE IS COMP, and the number of digits in the PICTURE clause is four or less, select type H.
5. If USAGE IS COMP, and the number of digits in the PICTURE clause is 9 or less, select type F.
6. If USAGE IS COMP, and the number of digits in the PICTURE clause is 18 or less, either use two fullwords or select type D.
7. If USAGE IS COMP-3, select type P.

Other data types usually require editing, and will be covered in Chap. 13. These are usually generated in assembler as type C or X, however.

6.4.2   Determine the Length Subfield

Next, determine the length subfield (if any).

1. If USAGE IS DISPLAY, use the COBOL PICTURE clause length.
2. If USAGE IS COMP-3, calculate the number of bytes required using the formula in Sec. 6.2.2 above.

For types of A, D, F, and H, no length subfield is needed.

6.4.3   Determine the Duplication Factor

If the COBOL data area had an OCCURS clause, the number of times that the item occurred in COBOL should be taken as the duplication factor. For example, for the following COBOL data item:

```
        05    CTR-TAB PIC S9(4) COMP OCCURS 20 TIMES.
```

we would convert this to

```
        CTR_TAB DS   20H
```

6.4.4   Determine Value Subfield

If the COBOL data item has a VALUE clause, we must code a value subfield in a DC directive. If it does not, we should use a DS directive to just define the storage. Remember that the value clause goes inside single quote marks immediately following the type subfield, or length subfield if one is supplied.

6.4.5   Things To Do Now — Practicing Conversion

At this point, you have converted the data element from its COBOL form to an assembler equivalent. You now have enough knowledge to convert most 77-level items in working storage to assembler.

Before proceeding further, though, let's spend some more time looking at how COBOL generates data from PICTURE clauses. The easiest way to see what COBOL does is to compile a program with the DMAP option. (If you don't know how to do this, add " PARM.COB=DMAP" to your COBOL compile JCL's EXEC statement. Under VM, specify DMAP as an option for your compile on the CMS command line.)

For example, consider the following COBOL code:

```
WORKING-STORAGE SECTION.
77   FIELD-A      PIC S9(8) COMP  SYNC.
77   FIELD-B      PIC S9(4) COMP SYNC.
77   FIELD-C      PIC S9(8) COMP.
77   FIELD-D      PIC S9(8) COMP VALUE    +22.
77   FIELD-E      PIC S9(5) COMP-3.
77   FIELD-F      PIC S9(7) COMP-3 VALUE -5.
77   FIELD-G      PIC X(33) VALUE 'A CHARACTER CONSTANT'.
77   FIELD-H      PIC X(5).
01   A-GROUP-ITEM.
     05   FIELD-1   PIC X(30).
     05   FIELD-2   PIC X(5).
     05   FIELD-3   PIC S9(7) COMP-3.
```

If you were to compile this with the DMAP option, your compile would include output which looks something like the following fields:

INTRNL NAME	LVL	SOURCE NAME	BASE	DISP	DEFINITION	USAGE
DNM = 1-050	77	FIELD-A	BL = 1	000	DS 1F	COMP
DNM = 1-067	77	FIELD-B	BL = 1	004	DS 1H	COMP
DNM = 1-084	77	FIELD-C	BL = 1	006	DS 4C	COMP
DNM = 1-101	77	FIELD-D	BL = 1	00A	DS 4C	COMP
DNM = 1-118	77	FIELD-E	BL = 1	00E	DS 3P	COMP-3
DNM = 1-135	77	FIELD-F	BL = 1	011	DS 4P	COMP-3
DNM = 1-152	77	FIELD-G	BL = 1	015	DS 33C	DISP
DNM = 1-169	77	FIELD-H	BL = 1	036	DS 5C	DISP
DNM = 1-186	01	A-GROUP-ITEM	BL = 1	040	DS 0CL39	GROUP
DNM = 1-211	02	FIELD-1	BL = 1	040	DS 30C	DISP
DNM = 1-228	02	FIELD-2	BL = 1	05E	DS 5C	DISP
DNM = 1-245	02	FIELD-3	BL = 1	063	DS 4P	COMP-3

(Some fields are omitted from the actual COBOL output — for example, there are two "INTRNL NAME" columns.)

To see how the COBOL compiler does the data-field generation we'e been discussing, let's look at each of the fields in the working storage example and see what COBOL generated for them in the DMAP later. For example, the first entry was

    77 FIELD-A   PIC S9(8) COMP SYNC.

This generated the following in the DMAP (the heading is included for clarity):

INTRNL NAME	LVL	SOURCE NAME	BASE	DISPL	DEFINITION	USAGE
DNM = 1-050	77	FIELD-A	BL = 1	000	DS 1F	COMP

The "INTRNL NAME" field is COBOL's internal name for the data item, which doesn't matter for our purposes. "LVL" is the COBOL working storage level value — 77 for a 77-level item. "SOURCE NAME" is the name we gave the data item in our program — FIELD-A. The "BASE" and "DISPL" columns refer to the base register and displacement used to locate this field, which we'll get to explaining later.

Finally the "DEFINITION" column has something which should look familiar — the assembler language storage definition for this field. This is a define storage (DS) directive, specifying a type of fullword (F) and a replication factor of 1. The "USAGE" column gives COBOL's usage, which we had coded in the working storage section.

The "DS 1F" is COBOL's way of saying that this is a one-fullword binary field. An assembler programmer would normally code " DS F " instead.

We won't go over each line from the working storage example in gory detail, but let's look at a packed decimal data item:

    77 FIELD-E   PIC S9(5) COMP-3.

In the DMAP, this generates

INTRNL NAME	LVL	SOURCE NAME	BASE	DISP	DEFINITION	USAGE
DNM = 1-118	77	FIELD-E	BL = 1	00E	DS 3P	COMP-3

The " 3P " indicates a 3-byte packed decimal field — 3 bytes to hold 5 digits, as covered earlier. An assembler programmer would probably code " DS PL3 " instead.

At some point now, you should try converting the 77-level items of a COBOL program. A good way to test yourself is to do this with a COBOL program compiled with the DMAP option. Note that COBOL generates fields as a DS rather than as a DC, and has some other inconsistencies with how an assembler programmer would usually generate the data. However, it should provide enough information to give you a general idea of your understanding. If it isn't convenient for you to do this now, put something here to remind yourself to do this at work when you have the chance.

6.5 GROUP ITEMS

While individual data elements have been coded at this point, there is still another commonly used COBOL data type that hasn't been covered. This is how to define group items in assembler.

Group items in COBOL comprise any statement that has a level number other than 66, 77, or 88, which is immediately followed by a statement with a higher level number, and which does not have a PICTURE clause. Most 01 levels are group items.

Group items are most closely approximated in assembler by a DS declarative with a duplication factor of zero. This defines a storage area length without actually defining any storage. Thus, it's possible to refer to the group item with an assembler move statement and still have the individual fields defined as well.

For example, the following COBOL code:

```
05  P-DATE.
    10   P-MONTH     PIC 99.
    10   FILLER      PIC X      VALUE '/'.
    10   P-DAY       PIC 99.
    10   FILLER      PIC X      VALUE '/'.
    10   P-YEAR      PIC 99.
```

corresponds to the following assembler data definitions:

```
P_DATE     DS    0CL8
P_MONTH    DS    CL2
           DC    C'/'
P_DAY      DS    CL2
           DC    C'/'
P_YEAR     DS    CL2
```

P_DATE defines an 8-byte character data area, but because the duplication factor is 0, no storage is assigned. Thus, if we refer to P_DATE later in the program, we will be using an implicit length of 8 bytes.

In both assembler and COBOL, the length of a group item is the sum of its constituent fields. You should be able to compute this by adding up the fields.

Next, consider the series of statements from the working storage example shown earlier defining the 01-level:

```
01   A-GROUP-ITEM.
     05   FIELD-1   PIC X(30).
     05   FIELD-2   PIC X(5).
     05   FIELD-3   PIC S9(7) COMP-3.
```

This generated several statements in the DMAP:

INTRNL NAME	LVL	SOURCE NAME	BASE	DISPL	DEFINITION	USAGE
DNM = 1-186	01	A-GROUP-ITEM	BL = 1	040	DS 0CL39	GROUP
DNM = 1-211	02	FIELD-1	BL = 1	040	DS 30C	DISP
DNM = 1-228	02	FIELD-2	BL = 1	05E	DS 5C	DISP
DNM = 1-245	02	FIELD-3	BL = 1	063	DS 4P	COMP-3

The 01-level item named A-GROUP-ITEM generated " DS 0CL39 ". This was developed by adding up the lengths of the items making up the 01-level — 30 bytes, 5 bytes, and 4 bytes. The individual fields follow the rules we have discussed up to this point.

It would be a good idea to continue your conversion practice now using a COBOL program with a DMAP as a check on your answers. At this time, however, only try to convert the group items.

6.6 SPECIAL CASES OF COBOL DATA ITEMS

At this point, some remaining topics in COBOL data division conversion will be covered. Some of the topics don't occur in many COBOL programs, and you may wish to scan the topic subheadings and bypass those which aren't of interest.

6.6.1 Filler

One difference between COBOL's data definition rules and those for assembler lies in COBOL's requirement for a data name. This leads to COBOL's requirement for the FILLER data name to allow you to generate constant data (page heading titles, for example) without creating a new name.

Since assembler doesn't require a name field on a DC or DS statement, you can just leave the name off and have the same effect as the COBOL FILLER name field.

For example,

```
05    FILLER  PIC  X(50).
```

can be coded in assembler as

```
DS      CL50
```

and is functionally equivalent.

6.6.2 BLANK WHEN ZERO

BLANK WHEN ZERO allows a programmer to override the COBOL PICTURE clause when the data item has a value of 0. In this case, a numeric data item will contain spaces instead.

BLANK WHEN ZERO is really a procedural definition rather than a data definition. It tells the COBOL compiler what to do with the data in this field, rather than about the field itself.

As such, there is no assembler definition which corresponds to BLANK WHEN ZERO. Chapter 13 covers a way to implement this when editing fields.

6.6.3   JUSTIFIED

JUSTIFIED LEFT or JUSTIFIED RIGHT, like BLANK WHEN ZERO, tells the COBOL compiler how to display data rather than what the data field comprises. To do something like this in assembler requires instructions like Edit and Mark, which is also covered in Chap. 13.

6.6.4   SYNC

The COBOL SYNCHRONIZED option allows the COBOL programmer to specify alignment for binary fields (USAGE IS COMP). This is the usual practice for the assembler data types of F, H, and D. As such, it happens automatically in assembler data definitions.

However, it is possible to force generation of a fullword binary data item which is not aligned. This may be required if you have to define a field exactly as COBOL defined it to avoid the problem of *slack bytes*. The way that COBOL does this can be shown by referring to our working storage DMAP example:

FIELD-C   PIC S9(8) COMP.

This generated the following:

INTRNL NAME	LVL	SOURCE NAME	BASE	DISPL	DEFINITION	USAGE
DNM = 1-084	77	FIELD-C	BL = 1	006	DS 4C	COMP

Assembler also provides a directive which allows programmers to force the next statement to a specified halfword boundary. This is the CNOP — Conditional No Operation — directive. CNOP is the closest direct assembler equivalent to the SYNC clause.

CNOP has two operands and is coded as follows:

CNOP   byte,word

where *byte* specifies a byte relative to a doubleword, and *word* specifies the size of the alignment which should result. The customary values for byte are 0, 2, 4, and 6; those for word are 4 or 8.

You code CNOP by selecting the type of alignment you want — fullword or doubleword. These correspond to the values for *word* of 4 or 8. You then select where you wish to generate data relative to that type of alignment — this is coded as the number of *bytes* after that alignment, and may take the values 0, 2, 4, or 6.

Some examples of CNOP coding and the alignment that they generate are shown below.

CNOP Coding:	Generates:
CNOP 0,4	Start of a fullword
CNOP 0,8	Start of a doubleword
CNOP 2,4	Two bytes past the start of a fullword
CNOP 4,8	Four bytes past the start of a doubleword

We will use CNOP in some examples later in the book. Note that coding a DS statement with a duplication factor of zero is equivalent to coding CNOP with a first operand of zero. For example, " DS   0F " has the same effect as coding " CNOP 0,4 ".

6.7 SUMMARY

This chapter covered how the 370 CPU design stores data. Additionally, built on that was a look at how COBOL and assembler define data with the PIC clause and DC and DS directives, respectively. Finally, covered was a step-by-step conversion for some selected data types.

The next two chapters complete our discussion of the assembler equivalents to the COBOL data division, along with some unique assembler data definition features.

At this point, you are almost ready to begin coding. If you are itching to start writing programs, you may skip to Chap. 9 at this point, then come back and reread Chaps. 7 and 8 later.

Things to Do

1. If you haven't done so already, compile a COBOL program with the DMAP option, then look at how COBOL generates various types of data.

Data Division in Assembler — Linkage Section

Unless you have written subroutines in COBOL, or programmed in CICS using COBOL, you may not be familiar with the COBOL linkage section. While not as frequently used as other COBOL features, this concept is especially important in understanding the fundamental assembler concept of addressability.

In this chapter, we will review the COBOL linkage section and describe how it works. We'll then cover the assembler DSECT directive and how it describes data outside of your assembler program. A discussion of the COBOL DMAP, another place where COBOL approximates how assembler addresses data will follow. Finally, exactly how assembler addressability works will be covered.

For reference, a simple COBOL linkage section will be described. If you created one while reading Chap. 6, you may also want to have a COBOL program with a DMAP handy when reading this chapter.

7.1 COBOL LINKAGE SECTION

The COBOL linkage section differs from other Data Division entries in that it does not generate any storage. Instead, linkage section entries describe data outside of the COBOL program.

The original intent of this was to support passing data between a main COBOL program and a subroutine also written in COBOL. IBM also relies on it extensively in support of COBOL under CICS.

The linkage section is coded with the same rules as the working storage section. The only exception is that the VALUE clause is not permitted in the linkage section. (Since the data is somewhere else, the COBOL compiler couldn't generate an initial value anyway.) The linkage section is placed between the Working Storage Section and the Procedure Division.

In CICS OS/VS COBOL, the programmer normally maintains addresses by manipulating base linkage locator values. These are far more commonly called *BLL cells*. CICS passes the address of a COBOL program's own BLL cells as a parameter, allowing the program to set up the address of these data areas itself. The mechanics of this are beyond the scope of this book, but are discussed in further detail in the CICS application programmer's reference manual.

7.2 ASSEMBLER DSECT DIRECTIVE

Assembler provides a close equivalent to the COBOL linkage section with the DSECT (dummy section) directive. A DSECT is coded identically to a CSECT, except for the opcode. The label on the DSECT directive is called the DSECT name and will be used later.

To define a DSECT, code the DSECT directive followed by the data definitions which make up the data areas being described. The DSECT statement itself corresponds most closely to an 01 level in the COBOL linkage section. Examples of this in COBOL and Assembler follow.

COBOL

```
         LINKAGE SECTION.
         01   PARM-AREA.
         05   CUST-NAME    PIC  X(30).
         05   CUST-ADDR-1  PIC  X(30).
         05   CUST-ADDR-2  PIC  X(30).
         05   CUST-CITY-ST PIC  X(25).
         05   CUST-ZIP     PIC  9(5).
```

Assembler

```
PARM_AREA        DSECT
CUST_NAME        DS   CL30
CUST_ADDR_1      DS   CL30
CUST_ADDR_2      DS   CL30
CUST_CITY_ST     DS   CL25
CUST_ZIP         DS   CL5
```

In COBOL, an individual entry in the linkage section is terminated by another 01 (or another 77-level) entry. In assembler, a DSECT is terminated by

- another DSECT (i.e., a DSECT with another name),

- a CSECT, or

- the assembler END statement,

among others. Since a DSECT doesn't reserve any storage area — it just defines what it looks like — it's easy to accidentally code a DS or DC statement in a DSECT which you meant to put elsewhere. To avoid that, this writer suggests that DSECTs should be grouped at the end of the assembler source program. In this way, the program's actual data and external data can be separated safely.

Just coding the DSECT statement is not enough, however. The assembler also has to be told how and when to address the data in the DSECT. To do this, we must load the address of the data into a general purpose register, then tell the assembler which register has the address of the data defined in the DSECT. Assembler provides the USING directive to do this.

The USING directive is coded as follows:

USING *base address,base register 1,base register 2,...*

No label is used. The *base address* signifies a label or location for which you are setting up a base register. This is the name field of the DSECT. It is also used for other purposes which we will cover later. The *base register 1* operand specifies a general purpose register, 1 through 15, which you have loaded with the address of the base address. (General purpose register 0 can't be used as a base register.)

A base register lets you have access to only 4096 bytes of data. Thus, if your data area is longer than 4096 bytes (4K), you must provide another base register. This is the *base register 2* operand. If the data area exceeds 8192 bytes in length (8K), you will need to provide another base register, and so on, for each additional 4K.

The whole process of defining a base register is called *establishing addressability*. You have *addressability* to a data area after you've provided a USING directive for that area. COBOL does all this setup automatically. However, the PROCEDURE DIVISION USING ... clause is similar in some regards to the assembler USING directive.

When you are through accessing a DSECT data area, you may need to use the base register you specified for other purposes. To do this, assembler provides the DROP directive, which tells the assembler to stop using a given base register. DROP is coded with the base register or base registers as the only operand(s). We can't provide a good example of this whole process here, but Chap. 14 will include one.

7.3   OTHER COBOL ADDRESSABILITY EXAMPLES

You may already be familiar with some other COBOL addressability methods. COBOL establishes its own sets of base registers for the record areas in the file section and in the working storage section. If you have ever debugged a COBOL program dump and located data in the working storage section, you've gone through the same process the assembler does with addressability. If you haven't, this section will cover some of the points in doing this.

If you refer to a COBOL program with a DMAP and CLIST or PMAP, you will notice in the DMAP listing that COBOL includes a column headed "BASE". Below this, you will see values like "DCB=01" or "BL=3" and so forth. The entries with "BL=" followed by some number are defining the base register to be used for that particular data area.

There is another column in the DMAP listing headed "DISPL". This is the displacement of the data item past the base register. When looking at a dump, you take the value in the base register, add the displacement, and you have the address of the data item in storage. (The displacement is in hexadecimal, as will be the base register contents.)

To provide a specific example of this, let's look at the following COBOL linkage section:

```
LINKAGE SECTION.
77   LINK-FLD-1 PIC X(5).
01   A-LINK-GROUP-ITEM.
     05 LINK-FLD-2 PIC XXX.
     05 LINK-FLD-3  PIC X(8).
```

These are referred to in the COBOL program by coding:

```
PROCEDURE DIVISION USING  LINK-FLD-1
                          A-LINK-GROUP-ITEM.
```

The " PROCEDURE DIVISION USING " is analogous, in this case, to the assembler language USING directive. The DMAP generated for this would look something like

INTRNL NAME	LVL	SOURCE NAME	BASE	DISPL	DEFINITION	USAGE
DNM = 1-262	77	LINK-FLD-1	BLL = 3	000	DS 5C	DISP
DNM = 1-282	01	A-LINK-GROUP-ITEM	BLL = 4	000	DS 0CL11	GROUP
DNM = 1-312	02	LINK-FLD-2	BLL = 4	000	DS 3C	DISP
DNM = 1-332	02	LINK-FLD-3	BLL = 4	003	DS 8C	DISP

(As in the examples in Chap. 6, some additional information provided by COBOL is left out of this simplified layout. The additional information differs depending on the COBOL compiler you are using. If you are looking at your own DMAP, however, you should be able to find all of these columns.)

Note that there are two BLL values listed in the "BASE" column. The first is for the individual 77-level item LINK-FLD-1. The second covers the fields in the 01-level A-LINK-GROUP-ITEM. In assembler, these would be separate DSECTs.

Now let's look at the base and displacement values for the last entry, LINK-FLD-3. The "BASE" column indicates that base linkage locator cell (a long-winded COBOL name for a base register) number 4 was assigned to A-LINK-GROUP-ITEM and all the fields in it. LINK-FLD-3 has a "DISPL" (displacement) column value of 003, which says that it is 3 bytes past the start of A-LINK-GROUP-ITEM.

To find out which base register has been assigned, you need to go further in the COBOL DMAP listing to a section titled "MEMORY MAP." Base register addresses may be found in three places in this part of the listing, depending on whether the data is in the file section, working storage, or the linkage section. Within this, you will find a subheading titled "REGISTER ASSIGNMENT". (It's just about at the end of this section.)

You should see values like

REG 6   BL = 3

or something similar. This is supposed to tell us that the COBOL program will use general purpose register 6 to address the data which has "BL=3" as a base register. ("BL" stands for base locator.) This particular example covered the working storage section in our sample COBOL program from Chap. 1. You will have one BL value for each 4K of working storage.

For the linkage section, you must look for an entry called "BLL CELLS". This is where the base linkage locator for items received as parameters will be located. There will be one entry in this for each 77-level or 01-level in your linkage section. You will have to look at a dump to find out the exact values.

Figure 7.1 Locating COBOL working-storage fields in a dump.

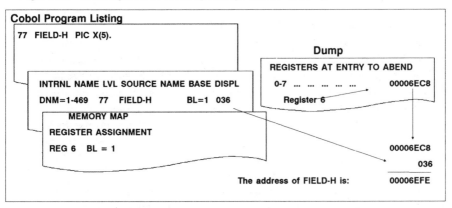

For FDs, COBOL generates a separate section of DCB addresses, which are also listed in the memory map. Similar to the linkage section's BLL cells, they are created in the order of the FDs in your file section.

The BL cells, BLL cells, and DCB addresses are all 4 bytes long. The BL values are usually loaded into a register when your COBOL program executes. VS COBOL II uses the term BLF cells (Base Locator for File) instead of DCB addresses.

Finding the information in a dump is complicated by the need to go through the addressability calculations to find the BLL cells or DCB address cells. These are kept in a COBOL control block called the *Task Global Table* (TGT). Register 13 usually points to this in a COBOL program. We could go much further in this description, but this is supposed to be a book on assembler.

If you have a dump produced by your COBOL program, try working through this calculation to find individual working storage entries. Use the DMAP to find out the base register and displacement for an individual field.

Next, find the actual base register assigned further on in the DMAP listing. Then, find the register contents when the program abnormally ended. Finally, add the displacement value to the register contents. This will give you the address of the individual data item in the dump. Figure 7.1 gives an overview of this process.

If you haven't done this before, it will be very productive for you to learn how to do it before going any further. There is a fuller description of this process in the COBOL programmer's guide. You should also be able to find a senior programmer, project leader, or systems programmer who knows how to do this and can walk you through the process. (It's much easier to understand how this works with a small program.)

If you know how to do this, proceed further in this chapter. If you don't, or feel hazy on how it works, try practicing it before proceeding. In this writer's experience, it's not too difficult to get a dump.

7.4 ASSEMBLER ADDRESSABILITY

Having confused you with the preceding descriptions of how COBOL handles data addressability, let's now complete the transformation of your brain to oatmeal by discussing how the assembler handles addressability.

This is a fundamental assembler concept. It does not have any effective equivalent in COBOL other than the description we just gave. You may need to reread this section more than once. Please do not feel inadequate if you don't understand the concept for a while — in this writer's experience, even very good, experienced programmers often have trouble understanding fully how this works.

As we mentioned earlier, the USING statement tells the assembler which base register to use to get to a particular data area. This is only part of the story. The assembler actually needs a base register to get to any label, whether it's inside our program or not. This applies to both data and instruction labels. And if we don't have a USING directive, we have to provide the base register as one of the instruction operands in most cases.

Because of this, we have to supply a USING statement to run almost any program. The reasons behind this have to do with the way IBM designed the 370 computer instructions.

7.4.1 The 370 Instruction Formats

The 370 has several instruction formats. IBM originally included five formats in the 360 computer design, and has added to those formats ever since. The five original formats, which cover the majority of instructions, follow:

1. **RR**—Register-to-Register, covering operations between two general purpose or floating point registers only

2. **RX**—Register-to-Indexed Storage, covering opcodes where one operand is a register and the other is a storage location

3. **RS**—Like RX, but with multiple register operands

4. **SI**—Storage Immediate, where one operand is in storage and the other is a byte in the instruction itself

5. **SS**—Storage-to-Storage, where both operands are storage locations (such as in a move instruction)

We will discuss one of these — the RX format — in some detail. You may want to refer to Fig. 7.2 while going through this discussion.

At this point, you should locate a section in your 370 reference summary called "Machine Instruction Formats." This is a chart depicting the layouts of the various instruction types. Find the "RX" entry on this.

Next, look at your assembly of the assembler program from Fig. 1.2. The fifth statement should be " B AROUND ". This line should read

LOC	OBJECT CODE	ADDR1 ADDR2	STMT	SOURCE STATEMENT
	...			
000006	47F0 C020	00020	5	B AROUND

(Lines 1 through 4 are omitted from the above.) Now hold your place in both the 370 reference summary and the program listing while we go over the 370 CPU addressability.

7.4.2   How the Machine Gets to Data

The 370 design uses a *base and displacement* form of addressing. This means that the machine adds together a base address value with a displacement to find out where a field really is. This is exactly what we did when we went through the COBOL DMAP and added the DMAP displacement to the base register contents. (This sum is called the *effective address*.)

This way of doing things is more efficient than keeping the entire data address in the instruction, since the base and displacement take up 2 bytes while the actual effective address takes 4 bytes (in MVS/XA) or 3 bytes (in MVS/SP). (MVS/ESA uses a 4-byte address plus an additional *access register* for effective addresses.)

The way the machine stores the base and displacement requires 4 bits to store the base register number. (Four bits can hold a value from 0 to 15 in binary.) The 370 uses a 12-bit displacement. Twelve bits hold a number from 0 to 4095. (This is why we need one base register for every 4K of data or program.)

Adding the 4 bits and 12 bits together, we arrive at a requirement for 16 bits — 2 bytes — to store a base and displacement address.

If you look at the 370 reference summary now, you'll find sections in the RX format description labeled Opcode, R1, X2, B2, and D2. Opcode is the actual operation code, and is 8 bits — 1 byte — long in this format. The next field — R1 — specifies a register which is one of the operands. The X2 field is used to specify an index register, which we'll cover when we talk about table handling.

Finally, the B2 and D2 fields are the base and displacement values for the instruction. These are 4 bits and 12 bits long, and are located in bits 16—19 and 20—31, respectively, of the instruction.

7.4.3 How the Assembler Generates a Base Register

Now let's turn to the listing. The object code columns for the " B AROUND " should have contained

        47F0 C020

If we decode this into the RX instruction format, we have

Opcode: **47**
R1:   **F**
X2:   **0**
B2:   **C**
D2:   **020**

Figure 7.2 compares the generated object code to the RX machine instruction format as it is described in the reference summary.

Figure 7.2   Decoding an RX-format instruction.

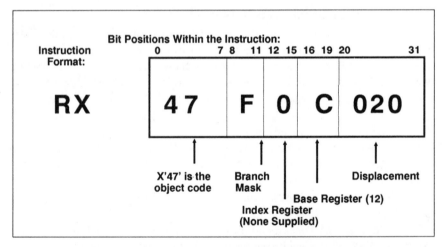

How did the assembler get from " B AROUND " to "47F0 C020" ? We'll skip the first part for now, but let's look at the B2 and D2 fields. B2 was the base register and had a value of hexadecimal C, or decimal 12. Where did we get 12 as a base register? From the " USING PROGNAME,12 " in statement 4. By telling the assembler that 12 was our base register for the area starting at PROGNAME, we caused the assembler to generate hexadecimal C — 12 — in the B2 field of that instruction. If you follow this on through the program, you'll see that almost every B2 or B1 field throughout the program has a value of C in the generated object code. If you change the USING statement, you will see the new base register propagated through all the base register fields in the object code.

How about the "020" part in the D2 field? Well, if you find the label that was referenced in the branch instruction AROUND, it should have a location value of 000020. This is where the value of 020 arose.

If you scan the program, you'll see a similar pattern for all the other branch instructions. (Find the instruction " BL MAINLINE ", for example.)

For any assembler program, you will always be able to find this relationship between USING statements and the actual base register the assembler generates.

At this point, you should have a general understanding of how addressability works. You should understand the relationship of what you specify in a USING statement to what the assembler generates. You should be comfortable with the idea of effective address and base and displacement. If you aren't, try rereading the chapter. It especially helps to understand the COBOL base and displacement usage in the DMAP.

To practice this further, go through the decoding process with other instructions. For instance, the MVC, AP, and CP instructions are all SS-format instructions. You may find it informative to follow those to the data fields they are using.

7.4.4   Assembler Addressability Esoterica

Now let's cover some finer points on addressability. These are items which you won't need to understand immediately. However, you will probably find them in advanced assembler language programs you may maintain in the future.

7.4.4.1   Multiple Base Registers

One common problem is that 4K is too short for many programs or data areas. As a result, assembler programmers often need to specify more than one base register for their program or data areas. You do this by specifying the additional base registers as operands following the first base register specification. We discussed the format for this in Sec. 7.2.

You must also make certain that your additional base registers, like your first, have contents which reflect their relative order in the USING statement. To do this, you must add 4096 to the first base register's contents to get the right value for the second, add 4096 to the second to get the proper value for the third, and so on.

Assembler provides many ways to do this. One which we will use in this book is the LA (Load Address) instruction. This allows you to add up to 4095 to an address in a register, among other things. Since we have to add 4096, we have to use two LA instructions to do this. For example:

```
USING  PROGNAME,12,11
LA     11,4095(,12)
LA     11,1(,11)
```

This code assumes that you have the address of PROGNAME already in register 12, which our sample program does. The first LA instruction adds 4095 to the address in register 12 and puts the result in register 11. The second LA instruction adds 1 to the address in register 11 and puts the result into register 11. One plus 4095 equals 4096, and that is the amount we needed to add. We'll explain the exact syntax of the LA instructions in more detail later in the book.

Why don't we just use some other instruction which just adds a value of 4096 instead of using two LA instructions? We could do that. However, the add instructions need a variable from storage. To get to storage, we need addressability. We can't have addressability until we have set up the base register contents successfully. As a result, it's safer to use two LA instructions to set up the second and subsequent base register contents.

7.4.4.2 Explicit Base Registers

The assembler doesn't always require a USING statement. You may, instead, provide the base register explicitly by coding the base register number into the operands. The official syntax for addresses is a displacement number followed by a base register number in parentheses. For RX format instructions, an optional index register is available. In this case, the format is a displacement, followed by an open parentheses, the index register number, a comma, the base register number, and a closing parentheses.

For the RX format instructions, this is formally specified as follows, using the LA instruction as a model:

```
LA     R1,D2(X2,B2)
```

where

LA = the opcode
R1 = the first operand register
D2 = the displacement associated with the second operand
X2 = the optional second operand index register
B2 = the second operand's base register

Let's look at one of the LA instructions from the previous subsection:

```
LA     11,4095(,12)
```

In this case, the values are:

R1 = 11
D2 = 4095
X2 = Omitted (nothing between the left parentheses and the comma)
B2 = 12

Another example is the STM (Store Multiple) instruction in the sample program in Fig. 1.2. This was coded as

> STM   14,12,12(13)

In this case, 12(13) specifies a displacement of 12 bytes past the address in register 13.

You normally code references to data areas using labels rather than by explicitly coding a base register. You must, however, do this when (1) you haven't established a base register yet, or (2) are accessing data outside your program for which you don't have a DSECT or other addressability. (This second case applies to what we're doing in the STM above.)

7.4.4.3 Miscellaneous Addressability Notes

This section lists some additional addressability points which don't fall into the preceding categories. It also covers some nuances which affect MVS/ESA addressability.

You can't use register 0 as a base register. If you do, the 370 CPU assumes that you want no base register and are accessing data in the lowest 4K of the CPU.

For all operating systems except MVS/ESA, the X2 and B2 (index and base registers) are essentially interchangeable for RX format instructions. You may wish to code the LA instructions as we have coded them, but you could also have coded one as " LA 11,4095(12) ". Since the comma inside the parentheses is omitted, the assembler assumes that 12 is the index register operand and that the base register is omitted. The instructions execute the same way in MVS/SP, VM/SP, MVS/SA, and VM/XA, but the effect on MVS/ESA is entirely different. We will discuss MVS/ESA addressability in Chap. 17.

This syntax note does not apply, however, to SS (storage-to-storage) format instructions. In these, a length should be coded in the syntactical location where we coded the index register earlier. If we code something like

> AP   FIELD,0(2)

the assembler interprets the " 0(2) " part as a displacement of 0, a second operand length of 2, and — you may have guessed this — no base register.

This will force you to use an address in the lowest 4K of the CPU. Since you probably don't have valid packed decimal data in low storage, your program will probably get an 0C7 or 0C4 ABEND at this point. If you're lucky, that is. If not, and there happens to be a valid packed decimal number there, you will have unpredictable results.

So when coding explicit base registers with storage-to-storage instructions, such as Add Packed, be careful to code both an explicit length and an explicit base register. Or you may have some unusual and elusive problems.

7.5 SUMMARY

Several fundamental assembler concepts have been covered in this section. These include addressability, establishing a base register with the USING directive, the format of 370 instructions, and how base registers affect the instruction code that the assembler generates.

How to use these concepts to find data in a COBOL program dump have also been briefly covered. The explanation given here, in conjunction with other COBOL manuals, should also help you in debugging COBOL programs.

This has been a lot of material discussed under the guise of the COBOL linkage section. However, the linkage section is the closest thing COBOL has to assembler addressability.

If you understand that you need a base register and a USING statement to run an assembler program, you have enough to proceed on. If you understand the concept of finding data in a dump, it's a big plus.

Things to Do

1. If you didn't do it during the discussion earlier, locate a COBOL program listing with a DMAP and a dump from an execution of that program, and go through the DMAP evaluation we covered in this chapter.

2. If you want to learn more about COBOL internal control blocks, get one of the following manuals:

   "VS COBOL II Application Programming: Debugging," SC26-4049.

   "OS/VS COBOL Compiler and Library Programmer's Guide," SC28-6483.

Handling Other DATA DIVISION Features

In this chapter, our comparison of COBOL's data division to assembler language data definition features will be complete. The following COBOL-related topics will be covered:

- COBOL REDEFINES and the Assembler ORG directive
- 88-level names and the Assembler EQU directive
- 66-level names

Following these, some assembler data definition features which don't have direct equivalents in COBOL will be addressed. These are things which you may not see used frequently, but are included to ensure a complete coverage.

8.1 THE COBOL REDEFINES CLAUSE

The COBOL REDEFINES clause lets programmers compile and describe a data area more than once. The easiest way to conceive of this in assembler is to think of it as assembling the same area twice. There are two or three ways to accomplish this.

The first is for those cases where you merely want a larger field as a faster way of referring to several smaller ones. Defining another group item allows a simple way of doing this. Simply define another group item (a DS directive with a duplication factor of zero) at the appropriate point.

A second case arises when you want to redefine several fields into several other fields of differing sizes. Assembler provides a way of doing this by reassembling the area. This method uses the ORG directive, which resets the origin value (the starting location) of the next assembled statement. (ORG stands for *origin*.) ORG has one operand — the address where the assembler should begin assembling next.

A short example of the COBOL REDEFINES clause and the assembler code which corresponds to it follows:

```
01   SOME-FIELDS.
     05   MONTH-TAB PIC X(36) VALUE
     'JANFEBMARAPRMAYJUNJULAUGSEPOCTNOVDEC'.
     05   MONTH-NAME  REDEFINES MONTH-TAB PIC X(3)
          OCCURS 12.
```

In assembler,

```
SOME_FIELDS    DS    0CL36
MONTH_TAB    DC    C'JANFEBMARAPRMAYJUNJULAUGSEPOCTNOVDEC'
              ORG    MONTH_TAB
MONTH_NAME    DS    12CL3
              ORG
```

The second ORG statement, with no operand, tells the assembler to go back to assembling at the location it was using before the previous ORG statement. Since both our original and redefined fields were the same length, we actually don't need it. However, it's best to always pair an ORG directive using a blank operand to reset the location counter with the ORG that originally redefines the area. This prevents accidental redefinitions later on.

A third way of doing something in assembler which corresponds to the COBOL REDEFINES is to use the assembler EQU directive. EQU — *equate* — defines a symbol and its value to the assembler. EQU has many uses and will appear several times in this book. In the example above, EQU could have been used by coding the following instead of the last three lines of the example (the ORG directives and the MONTH_NAME definition):

```
MONTH_NAME EQU    MONTH_TAB,3,C
```

This tells the assembler to define a symbol (MONTH_NAME) which has the same address as MONTH_TAB, which has a length attribute of 3, and a type of C (character). (We will present a fuller discussion of EQU later in this chapter.)

Of the three ways discussed in this subsection that approximate the COBOL REDEFINES, the first two are most common.

An important point when redefining areas in assembler is why you are redefining at all. If you wish to create different sized fields in the same storage area that is used by other fields, the ORG directive is probably appropriate.

However, if you are redefining an area because you want to get at one type of COBOL data as another type, you should probably find a different way to do this in assembler. An example of this is redefining a COMP field as character to get a 1-byte binary value. Assembler permits manipulation of any type of data with any instruction, and this type of redefinition isn't needed. In general, make sure that you really need to redefine storage before doing it.

8.2   88-LEVEL DATA ITEMS

88-level items define conditions rather than data. As implemented, 88-level items require only a VALUE clause.

Assembler language has no direct corollary to the 88-level condition name. There are ways of approximating the same function in assembler. 88-levels define both data (the value to be compared) and how that data affects processing (i.e., the way COBOL uses condition names in IF statements). Because of this, we will discuss the definition of data similar to

COBOL 88-level condition names here. The IF statement in assembler is covered in Chap. 12 on branching and control.

Assembler language can very closely approximate the case of a condition name with a one-character VALUE clause. The EQU directive provides a way to do this. We discussed EQU previously as a way of redefining storage. EQU can also define a symbol unrelated to storage, which is close to the idea behind COBOL condition names. The assembler will substitute the value you code for the EQU operand whenever it finds the EQU symbol.

Let's go through an example to show how this can work. Below is a COBOL working storage item with three condition names defined for it, along with the procedure division code to reference one of the conditions.

```
77  PROCESSING-MODE  PIC X    VALUE '0'.
    88  START-OF-JOB          VALUE '0'.
    88 MIDDLE-OF-JOB          VALUE '1'.
    88 END-OF-JOB             VALUE '2'.
    IF    END-OF-JOB
          THEN GO TO 0900-END-JOB.
```

Some similar code in assembler,

```
PROCMODE DC   C'0'    PROCESSING MODE
STARTJOB EQU  C'0'    INITIALIZATION MODE
MIDJOB   EQU  C'1'    MAINLINE PROCESSING
ENDJOB   EQU  C'2'    TERMINATION PROCESSING
         CLI  PROCMODE,ENDJOB   ARE WE AT END OF JOB
         BE   ENDPROC      YES - GO PROCESS
```

We will have to defer the explanation of the CLI (Compare Logical Immediate) and BE (Branch Equal) until Chap. 12, but this may give you the general idea.

Condition names with multiple conditions (multiple VALUE clauses) or with the THROUGH option require more work to implement in assembler. Very complex multiple conditions may also use the TRT (Translate and Test) instruction and branch tables, which we will cover in Chap. 20.

8.3 66-LEVEL DATA ITEMS

COBOL provides another less frequently used way of defining group items. This, the 66-level item, lets programmers define an area which redefines previous data areas. Unlike the REDEFINES clause, the 66 level specifies a beginning and ending field name. This allows programmers to define new data items which span different levels.

If you aren't familiar with the COBOL 66 level, we will provide a simple example below. It would be best for you to refer to the COBOL language manuals for a complete explanation.

The assembler implementation of 66-level items, like REDEFINES, relies on the ORG directive. Since assembler does not have a concept of levels for data items as does COBOL, you can implement a 66-level type of data item by merely specifying the first data item to be covered by the renamed field as the operand of the ORG statement.

The following is an example of a 66-level item in COBOL, followed by the equivalent code in assembler:

01	A-GROUP.		
	05	FIELD-G1	PIC X(20).
	05	GROUP-G2.	
		10 FIELD-G2	PIC X(2).
		10 FIELD-G3	PIC X(2).
		10 FIELD-G4	PIC X(2).
	05	FIELD-G5	PIC X(10).
	66	FIELD-66 RENAMES FIELD-G3 THROUGH FIELD-G4.	

```
A_GROUP      DSECT
FIELD_G1     DS    CL20
GROUP_G2     DS    0CL6
FIELD_G2     DS    CL2
FIELD_G3     DS    CL2
FIELD_G4     DS    CL2
FIELD_G5     DS    CL10
             ORG   FIELD_G3
FIELD_66     DS    CL14   (FIELD_G3 + FIELD_G4 + FIELD_G5 = 14)
```

8.4 SPECIAL ASSEMBLER DATA TYPES

This section covers several assembler language features which have no direct corollary in COBOL. You may treat all of these as esoterica, but you may wish to note where they are for later study. You may have to maintain programs in the future which use these assembler features.

8.4.1 Multiple Values in a DC Directive

For certain types of assembler language constants, you may define multiple values in one DC directive. This is valid with all data types except character data. The method of doing this is to code the multiple values within the same set of quotation marks, separated by commas. (Since the comma is just another piece of data in character constants, it can't be done with data of type C.)

Here's an example:

```
PRIMES      DC    F'1,2,3,5,7,11,13,17,19,23,29,31,37,41,43'
```

The data here is the set of the first 15 prime numbers. What this directive defines is 15 fullwords (type F) with values of one, two, three, five, and so on. This may be most useful when defining tables and initializing the entries to varying initial contents.

This is handy, but can introduce an unintentional error. If you code

PACK10K   DC   P'10,000'

It may look as though you are generating a packed decimal number of ten thousand. In fact, you are generating a packed value of ten followed by a packed value of zero.

8.4.2 Providing an Explicit Length in a DC Directive

Assembler automatically determines the length of DC values based on the type and value supplied. Thus, type F always generates four bytes (a fullword), type H always generates two bytes (a halfword), and so on. For variable-length data, such as character or packed decimal fields (type C and P), the assembler calculates the length based on the value supplied. Thus, " DC C'HI' " generates a 2-byte character field with a value of "HI". " DC P'100' " generates a 2-byte packed decimal field. (Refer back to Sec. 6.2.2 if you don't understand how we got a length of 2 bytes.)

In certain cases, however, you may need to define a different sized field. In this situation, you may specify the explicit length subfield and create a different sized field than the assembler would, even when the field should be a fixed length.

For example,

SHORTONE DC   FL1'1'

This generates a 1-byte binary field with a value of hexadecimal 01.

The assembler ignores the normal alignment for the type and starts the field at the next available location in your program. Putting that another way, the type F has an implicit alignment as if the COBOL SYNC clause were specified. Adding the explicit length subfield means that the field is not *synchronized* like COBOL.

Use of explicit lengths requires special ways of getting and storing the data, which may involve the IC/STC or ICM/STCM instructions (Insert/Store Characters or Insert/Store Characters Under Mask, respectively). We will mention this in Chap. 11 on arithmetic.

8.4.3 Large Duplication Factor Values

The DS directive allows you to define up to 65,535 bytes when defining character (type C) and some other forms of data. You may also specify a duplication factor on both DC and DS statements of up to 65,535.

When defining a very large area, it is preferable to use a long length subfield rather than a large duplication factor. The reason for this lies in the current assembler implementation. When the assembler encounters a duplication factor, it uses the duplication factor value as a loop counter. Conversely, a length value is handled as one operation. Thus,

BIGFIELD   DS   CL65535

will assemble faster than

```
BIGFIELD    DS      65535C
```

If you submit assemblies of large programs, and wait for the assembly output, you will appreciate the difference. This implementation has been true in the assembler for the last twenty years.

8.4.4   Defining Binary Data — Type B

One assembler data type which has no direct COBOL equivalent is binary data. Assembler allows you to define the value of individual bits with the B type of data. For example,

```
        DC      B'11000001'
```

defines the bit pattern for the EBCDIC coding of the letter A.

You may see this used in assembler programs, particularly for MVS parameter lists. You may also see multiple bit-level switches defined in this way. The TM and OI/NI/XI instructions (Test Under Mask and OR/AND/Exclusive OR Immediate) allow you to do this type of manipulation.

The normal reason given for using binary switches is that it saves storage. Unless you are dealing with a field which is reproduced thousands of times, the savings are usually not enough to justify the additional programmer time.

Binary data is padded on the left to form a complete byte. You may define multiple bytes with B type data. If you provide fewer than 8 bits (or less than a multiple of 8 bits), the assembler pads your value on the left with 0 bits.

8.4.5   The EQU Directive

We referred to EQU previously in this chapter. EQU, which stands for *equate*, defines a label which means something other than a label on a data definition or instruction. There is no real exact equivalent for EQU in COBOL, although the 88-level items and the SPECIAL-NAMES clause have some resemblance to EQU.

EQU allows up to three operands. It requires a label and at least one operand. The general form of EQU is

```
        label    EQU    value,length,type
```

The label is a name which you will use elsewhere in your program to refer to whatever you code as the *value* operand. The *length* operand specifies an optional length you wish to assign. It may not exceed 65,535. Finally, the *type* operand specifies the type of data or element you are defining.

Without getting into gory details of each of these operands, let's present a few common uses of EQU which will be used in this book.

One frequent use of EQU is to define labels — the equivalent of paragraph names or field names in COBOL. We saw an example in our discussion of the REDEFINES clause earlier. Use of EQU which is equivalent to defining a paragraph name in COBOL is

```
LABEL       EQU    *
```

The '*' indicates the current location in the program. You may wish to read it as 'here'. We can then use the name LABEL as an operand of a branch instruction (like a GO TO) or as part of a branch and link (like a PERFORM). Chapter 12 will provide descriptions of these instructions.

Another common use of EQU is to provide a label to refer to registers. The primary benefit of this is that a label defined by EQU will appear in the assembly cross reference. Normal references to a register will not. Large assembly programs frequently have to reuse general purpose registers for several purposes. A cross reference of register uses is crucial in this case. For example,

```
R7          EQU    7
```

defines the label "R7" as equivalent to the value 7. When we use the label in an instruction, for example,

```
        L       R7,COUNTER2
```

the assembler will automatically substitute '7' for 'R7', so the instruction assembles normally. However, the use of R7 will also show up in the assembly cross reference.

The older 'macro level' version of CICS used this technique extensively. Use of many CICS data areas required that the assembler programmer define the register to use through an EQU directive specifying a CICS-mandated name, for example,

```
TCTTEAR     EQU    4
```

to address the CICS terminal control table terminal entry.

Even if you write only very short assembler programs on your own, this use of EQU is very highly recommended.

Another use of EQU is to compute the length of a collection of fields. For example,

```
START       DS     CL77
FLD2        DS     3C
CTR3        DS     F
CTR4        DS     PL1
LENGTH      EQU    *-START
```

The "*-START" tells the assembler to subtract the address of START from the current address. The result of the subtraction will be assigned a name of LENGTH. We can then code

```
LENVAL      DC     H'LENGTH'
```

LENVAL will contain a halfword value of 85, the difference between START and the location where we coded the EQU defining LENGTH.

The EQU directive has many other uses, and you may see many of these if you maintain many assembler programs.

8.4.6 Address Constants

The assembler has three types of data which define addresses. These are similar in concept to the COBOL USAGE IS INDEX, but have many more uses.

If you have used COBOL in CICS and are familiar with the concept of BLL cells, you will have already dealt with address values. The three types follow:

1. Address constants: Type A — to generate the address of Something in your program. This is the closest to COBOL USAGE IS INDEX

2. External address constants: Type V — to generate the address of something outside your program. Used in subroutine linkage. No direct COBOL equivalent.

3. Short address constants: Type Y — are a holdover from the allegedly good old days when CPUs were smaller. They generate a 2-byte address field and can't be used for addresses over 32K (32,767).

These are sometimes called Acons or Adcons, V-cons, and Y-cons, respectively.

Address constants differ from other DC types in that the nominal value is supplied in parentheses rather than within quotes. For example,

        DC   A(PROGNAME)

generates the address of our program in the sample in Fig. 1.2.

When the MVS program loader brings our program into storage, it automatically finds all the address constants which need to be modified and makes them contain the actual address. (The assembler lists all the fields in a program that will be modified by the MVS loader in the *relocation dictionary* (RLD) which we mentioned in Chap. 2.) V-type address constants work the same way, but refer to subroutines or data items outside your program.

Y-type address constants are sometimes found in DOS programs. Their use should be avoided in MVS programs. You may still find them in VM programs. At this stage of the IBM mainframe family development, you can't do much in 32K.

8.4.7 S-type Address Constants Are Probably Trouble

Another holdover from programming in smaller CPUs is the S-type address constant. This generates a base and displacement type of address. We will cover this concept at several later points in the book.

S-type address constants are usually found when an assembler programmer wants to modify an instruction. The closest COBOL equivalent to this is the ALTER verb.

If you liked ALTER, you will love instruction modification. Most COBOL programmers hate it. If you see an S-type address constant in an assembler program you have to maintain, proceed carefully.

8.4.8 Zoned Decimal Type

Assembler provides a data type — zoned decimal — which corresponds very closely to the COBOL definition of data with USAGE IS DISPLAY and PIC 9. This is assembler type Z data — zoned decimal. This generates character data and operates just like type C character data, but the assembler allows you to code only the digits 0 through 9 in a Z type constant.

Since you can move any type of data into the field when your program actually runs, the Z type of data definition is more valuable for documentation than for anything else. You may also see it used for certain limited numeric validation.

This writer has found it to be of little value.

8.4.9   Q Type

Assembler provides a data type, "Q", and two directives — DXD and CXD — which support a special type of PL/I language storage allocation. A Q-type constant supplies what is termed a *pseudo register*. DXD and CXD stand for Define External DSECT and Cumulative length of External DSECTs, respectively.

These apply to a form of PL/I storage called "CONTROLLED EXTERNAL". For further details on this, refer to a PL/I programmer's guide.

8.4.10   Scale and Exponent Modifiers

Assembler provides a scaling function which is used like the length modifier. Scaling only applies to binary (halfword, fullword) and floating-point constants. For binary numbers, it specifies a power of 2 by which the number is to be multiplied to determine the actual constant. Scaling is specified by coding an "S" followed by a decimal number. The number represents the power of 2 (positive or negative) to which the value is to be raised. For example,

```
DC      HS4'22'
```

causes the value of 22 to be converted to binary (giving hexadecimal 0016), then multiplied by 2 to the fourth power (decimal 16 or hexadecimal 10), giving a final value of decimal 352 (or hexadecimal 0160).

Scaling can be used along with the length modifier, so we could code something like " DC HL1S2'7' ", which generates a 1-byte binary value of decimal 28 or hexadecimal 1C.

Assembler also has an exponentiation factor, coded like the length and scaling modifiers, which does something similar. Scaling and exponentiation are more applicable to scientific programming, and will not appear again in this book.

8.4.11   Multiple Location Counters

Assembler H provides a directive, LOCTR, which allows the programmer to have multiple location counters. (LOCTR stands for *Location Counter*.) This technique is helpful when generating complicated Control Section (CSECT) structures. The intent behind it is to allow data or instructions to be included at one place in the program source, but cause the generated code or data to be built in a different physical sequence in the object program.

LOCTR is coded with a label, which specifies the location counter that the assembler is to use. The programmer names these. The first location counter in a CSECT uses the CSECT name.

Another way of doing the same thing is to assemble the various groups of code or data as separate CSECTs, which accomplishes the same aim. You are probably more likely to see this latter method used.

This technique is helpful when generating a table which has both an index and variable-length entries. A common example of this is the CICS terminal control table at CICS release 1.7 or earlier. In this type of table, an index — of terminal names in the case of CICS — is assembled in one area and the information relating to that terminal (such as terminal type, current operator, number of transactions, and so forth) is assembled at another. (Note that your installation may dynamically create the terminal-control table entries, so this may not apply to your installation. However, other CICS tables are assembled in the same way, and may provide a similar example.)

This technique requires a fair amount of experience with assembler, but is commonly used for these situations.

8.4.12 Generating Multiple Types on One DC Directive

In addition to generating multiple values of the same type on one DC statement, you may also generate multiple constants of different types on the same DC statement. The DC statement allows you to code multiple operands, separated by commas following each value subfield except the last. For example, a table of Irish names follows:

```
IRISH       DC       H'6',CL10'MURPHY'
            DC       H'7',CL10'O''NEILL'
            DC       H'4',CL10'MAYO'
            DC       H'9',CL10'MULROONEY'
```

In this example, we generate a halfword value which contains the actual length of the name, followed by a 10-byte character constant which contains the actual name.

This technique is fairly frequently used when generating a table of commands or keywords which you want to compare to some input.

Note also the two apostrophes in a row to generate the single quote mark in " O'NEILL ".

8.4.13 Generating Bit-level Fields with a DC Directive

Assembler allows you to generate fields shorter than 1 byte. To do this, specify a length subfield with a value of less than one. For example,

```
            DC       FL0.4'5'
```

generates a 4-bit field with a value of hexadecimal 5.

The assembler automatically starts the next statement on a byte boundary, so you can't define several bit-level fields in several DC statements to create 1 byte. However, you may combine multiple definitions on one DC statement to create several bit-level fields in one or more bytes. For example, let's code the date as it is carried in an IBM PC:

DC   HL0.7'09',HL0.4'7',HL0.5'4'

This generates a 7-bit field with a value of binary 0001001, followed by a 4-bit field with a value of binary 0111, followed by a 5-bit field containing binary 00100. This generates a 2-byte binary number.

The date coded in this way is July 4, 1989. The first 7-bit number is the year (past 1980). The second 4-bit quantity is the month. The third, 5-bit quantity is the day of the month.

This type of coding requires special instructions — the shift instructions — to do arithmetic or otherwise use the bit-length fields. The value of this type of coding is that it saves storage. For example, months in the Gregorian calendar only go from 1 to 12, which can be stored in 4 bits.

Use of this type of data storage can generate extremely condensed records. It can also generate extremely complicated programs. As a rule of thumb, you need to have several million occurences of a small value to make this type of compression worth the effort. (This should be determined based on occurrences, not records. If you have small numbers ten times in a file with 500,000 records, that would represent five million occurrences.)

In general, this is an advanced technique which requires some experience with assembler before its use.

8.5 SUMMARY

The preceding three chapters have compared the COBOL data division entries to their closest assembler language counterparts. We have covered a lot of material.

The data division is a very large part of your COBOL programs. Understanding how data is laid out is probably half the task in learning a programming language.

At this point, we are ready to begin programming in assembler, and the next chapter starts that.

Things to Do

1. If you have access to assembler programs used in production at your installation, look for examples of ORG, A-type address constants, Y-type address constants, and S-type address constants.

2. Do the assembler programs at your installation use EQU to define register names?

Overview of the Procedure Division in COBOL

We've finally reached the point where we can start coding. This chapter introduces how COBOL's Procedure Division corresponds to assembler language code. As part of this, we will discuss some general items to consider when writing assembler code.

Following this chapter, we will cover how to write assembler language in several specific areas. Chapter 10 covers basic I/O processing in assembler for sequential files. Chapter 11 then discusses how to do arithmetic computations in assembler. Chapter 12 will show you how the COBOL IF statement options can convert to assembler.

Chapter 13 goes over how COBOL's MOVE verb can be translated into one of several assembler equivalents. Chapter 14 will cover how to write subroutines, which is also important to understand the standard MVS calling sequence.

At this point, a variety of special topics are covered. These include table handling, the COBOL DISPLAY and ACCEPT verbs, VSAM file processing, how to use the IBM sort program in assembler for internal sorts, and the COBOL EXAMINE and TRANSFORM verbs.

Additionally, some assembler special techniques which don't have good approximations in COBOL will be discussed. These include the macro language facility and how to use the exit facility of many MVS services.

More use will be made of *esoterica* sections in the remaining chapters. Many of these present functions which are rarely used, but which are vital for certain special situations. This section may be reviewed or bypassed as needed, depending on your mood.

9.1 PROGRAM MODIFICATIONS

From this point onward in the book, we will be modifying the code in Fig. 1.2 as we learn more about assembler. If you have not already keyed in this program, you should do this now.

9.2   ASSEMBLER PROGRAM INITIALIZATION

MVS requires that programs running under it follow a specific set of rules. These rules apply to how a program initializes itself, what rules it follows while running, and how it terminates. The rules for initiation and termination will be covered here, then discussed in Chap. 14 (on subroutine linkage) in greater detail.

Program initialization under MVS requires that the program do the following:

1. Save all the registers at the time it starts
2. Establish its own base register
3. Provide its own register save area
4. *Chain* the save areas by storing addresses

We will examine each of these requirements in turn, then look at the code in Fig. 1.2 as an example. Many programmers use the term *housekeeping* to cover these steps.

9.2.1   Save All Registers

The first instruction in almost every MVS program is as follows:

      STM   14,12,12(13)

This instruction — Store Multiple — operates like a COBOL MOVE instruction in that it puts a copy of registers into storage locations. The first two numbers — 14 and 12 — specify the first register and the last register to store. "14,12" tells the CPU to store registers 14 through 12. The CPU automatically *wraps around* from the last register (15) to the first (register 0) when the first register to store is a higher number than the last register to store.

Thus, this instruction places a copy of the contents of register 14 into the storage location specified by the last operand — "12(13)". (We'll explain more about this operand later.) The STM instruction then stores the next register (15) into the fullword following where register 14 went, or 16(13). STM then stores the next register — register 0 at this point — into the next 4 bytes of storage, then stores register 1 into the following 4 bytes, and so forth.

At the end of the instruction, fifteen registers have been stored: registers 14, 15, 0, 1, 2, 3, 4, 5, 6, 7, 8, 9, 10, 11, and 12 in that order. The original contents of the registers are still there, since this works like a COBOL MOVE.

STM is used fairly often to store sequences of registers. " STM 4,6 " stores registers 4, 5, and 6, for example. The cases where you store registers tend to be for use in internal program subroutines, similar to a COBOL PERFORM. Chapter 13 will discuss STM in more detail.

9.2.2 Establish Own Base Register

As Chap. 7 discussed, we have to have a base register for our program. We have two ways to do this. The first uses the program address provided as part of the MVS standard program linkage conventions. The second uses specific instructions to obtain an address within our program.

The first way relies on the program address, which is always provided when a program begins execution in MVS. When your program starts, register 15 contains its address. The normal practice is to load register 15 into another register, then use that register as a base register.

The code to do this is

```
LR      12,15
USING  PROGNAME,12
```

This assumes that the CSECT name is PROGNAME. If it is not, the CSECT name should be coded in place of PROGNAME.

The second way relies on 370 instructions which provide the address of the next instruction in your program. These are the BASR (Branch and Save Register) and BALR (Branch and Link Register) instructions. These instructions are used for program linkage. They place the address of the next instruction into a register. (You specify the register as the first operand.) These instructions then branch (go to) the program location specified as the second operand.

A side effect of these instructions is that they will not branch if the second operand (the *branch to* address) is zero. They will, however, still put the address of the next instruction into the first operand register. As such, they are frequently used to set up the program base register.

The instructions to do this are

```
BASR   12,0
USING  *,12
```

You will see the BALR instruction used in place of the BASR. The instructions are logically equivalent in MVS/SP and in MVS/XA when running in 24-bit addressing mode. The BASR will also operate properly in 31-bit addressing mode, and is preferable for new programs. Many assembler programmers continue to use the BALR instruction out of habit.

You will see both ways of setting up a base register used, and both are equally valid. Be sure, however, not to mix up the USING statements of one method with the other. You will have problems.

9.2.3. Provide Own Save Area

MVS also requires that you provide your own save area. A save area is eighteen fullwords (72 bytes) long. It is used by other programs or operating system services to save your program's registers when they do work on your behalf. The save area name in our sample program is SAVEAREA.

9.2.4   Chain Save Areas

As part of providing our own save area, we must put its address into register 13. MVS conventions require that register 13 point to a save area when many system services are used. We also must set up the address of our save area into the save area we use, and vice versa. The code to do this is as follows:

```
*              CHAIN SAVE AREAS
               ST     13,SAVEAREA+4          STOREOLD  ADDR
               LA     2,SAVEAREA            GET NEW SAVE ADDR
               ST     2,8(13)              STORE NEW ADDR
               LR     13,2                 UPDATE REG 13
```

We will explain this process in more detail in Chap. 14. For now, just do it this way.

9.3   REGISTER USAGE CONVENTIONS

When your program is running, it has to follow a set of rules regarding how registers are used. Specifically, certain registers have defined uses.

Registers 0, 1, 14, and 15 will be used by various MVS macros and services. The GET macro for I/O is an example of this. Register 13 must always contain the address of your save area.

As a result of these operating system usages, you should not use any of these registers as base registers. This leaves registers 2 through 12 as potential base registers. Which should you use? Register 2 is not advisable for use as a base register. The TRT (Translate and Test) instruction modifies it during use.

Any one of registers 3 through 12 are thus possible. This writer recommends the use of register 12. This leaves ten registers available as pairs of registers. Having pairs of registers available simplifies coding of certain types of instructions, such as BXLE, CDS, CLCL, or MVCL. These will be covered in later chapters.

Register 3 is also commonly used. When choosing a specific register, you should leave others available as base registers in case your program exceeds 4K in length. You should also use as few registers as possible in your program. This simplifies matters when your program gets larger, since it leaves more registers available as future base registers. Running out of base registers is a common assembler language maintenance problem.

9.4   PROGRAM TERMINATION

When ending, your program must essentially go through the reverse of the sequence followed when starting up. This means that you must do the following:

- Set the address of the old save area (the one you used at the start of the program) into register 13
- Restore the previous contents of registers 14 through 12

Finally, your program must return (branch back) to the address originally supplied in register 14. We'll cover this in more detail in Chap. 14.

9.5 SUMMARY

Your program has to follow the rules we've outlined in this chapter. These cover things which COBOL has done for you without any specific actions on your part.

Following program initialization, you normally set up your COBOL program by opening any files you are using and printing headings for reports. We'll start on this process in the next chapter.

Things to Do

1. If you have access to assembler programs at your installation, review their housekeeping. How do they generally set up base registers? How do they handle the save area? Do they employ proper save area chaining?

Introductory I/O in Assembler

This chapter covers I/O operations with QSAM for sequential files. We will discuss how to open and close a DCB, along with the GET and PUT macros used to read and write records respectively.

The topic of I/O deserves a book or two by itself, so we must naturally skip many items. The esoterica section covers several techniques. One of these, testing for a successful OPEN macro, is highly recommended as a coding practice. Most of the techniques discussed here operate equally well under the OS simulation of VM.

10.1 HOW TO OPEN A DCB

COBOL provides several options on the OPEN verb, all of which correlate directly to options in assembler. Most COBOL OPEN concepts convert easily into assembler. Table 10.1 lists COBOL OPEN verb options and the corresponding OPEN macro keyword.

Table 10.1 COBOL OPEN Options and Assembler Equivalents	
COBOL item	**Assembler equivalent**
OPEN verb	OPEN macro
INPUT option	INPUT keyword
OUTPUT option	OUTPUT keyword
I/O option	UPDAT keyword
EXTEND option	EXTEND keyword
REVERSED option	RDBACK keyword
WITH NO REWIND	LEAVE keyword

The syntax of the assembler OPEN macro deserves some explanation. An example of an OPEN macro is

        OPEN   (INFILE,INPUT,PRINTER,OUTPUT)

The syntax of this statement differs from any example we've given up to this time. This example opens a DCB named INFILE for input, and another DCB named PRINTER for output. The OPEN macro, however, has only one operand. This is the list of DCBs to open and their associated processing options. Each DCB may have one or two options. If the processing option for the DCB is omitted, a default of INPUT is assumed. If two options are provided, they must be in parentheses.

Some examples may clarify this. First, opening a single DCB for output,

        OPEN   (PRINTER,OUTPUT)

PRINTER is the DCB name. Next, opening a single DCB for input and using the default,

        OPEN   INFILE

Since there is only one DCB, and no options are specified, the parentheses may be dropped. Note, however, that

        OPEN   INFILE,INPUT

may cause an error, since the assembler assumes that INPUT is the name of another DCB to be opened.

As a final example, opening a DCB for *extend* processing (like DISP=MOD in JCL) and requesting that the tape not be rewound at end of file follows:

        OPEN   (HISTTAPE,(EXTEND,LEAVE))

HISTTAPE is the DCB name. The EXTEND option is like output, but only adds to the end of the existing data on the file. The LEAVE option tells MVS or VM to leave the tape positioned at the end (i.e., no rewind). Note that both of these are in parentheses, which tells the assembler that these are a *sublist* providing multiple values for a single parameter. (If the parentheses were omitted, the OPEN macro would assume that LEAVE was another DCB name, probably causing an error.)

The first option for each DCB corresponds exactly to a COBOL option, as listed in Table 10.1. The second OPEN options are best thought of as things you would normally specify in the COBOL CLOSE verb. These options include the following:

- REREAD, which repositions the data set to be read again
- LEAVE, which doesn't rewind tape data sets
- DISP, which specifies that the option in the JCL DISP parameter determines what happens (the default)

In general, it's more common to specify tape positioning in the CLOSE macro, so the second option isn't used very frequently.

10.2   HOW TO READ RECORDS

The COBOL READ verb's options allow a straightforward conversion to the assembler GET macro. The macro format in assembler, however, allows the use of only one of the two formats of the COBOL READ in one program. Additionally, the COBOL READ AT END clause may require a slightly different approach.

COBOL lets you specify where the next record goes in one of two ways. The first, by coding only the file name following the READ verb, causes COBOL to get the address of the next record. You may then access the record by using the field names in one of the 01-level group item descriptions following that file name FD.

The second way, used by coding the INTO clause, causes COBOL to move the next record into the 01-level you specify. In this case, COBOL gets the address of the next record, then moves it to the field.

Both of these approaches have direct equivalents in assembler. The first, called *locate mode* processing, causes the QSAM access method to return the address of the next record in register 1 following a GET macro. This is how COBOL processes records. The second, *move mode*, requires that you specify (as an operand of the GET macro) the name of the field to receive the next record.

We'll cover move mode processing first, as it's somewhat simpler.

10.2.1   Move Mode GET Processing

This form of the GET macro is specified by coding the macro format operand in the DCB. This is coded as MACRF=(GM) to specify the GET macro (G) and the move mode (M). The actual GET macro is coded with the DCB name as the first operand, and the data area which is to receive the next record as the second operand. For example,

```
        GET     INFILE,RECIN
```

specifies a DCB name of INFILE and a receiving field of RECIN. (As you'll remember from Chap. 5, the DCB corresponds to the COBOL FD.)

Move mode is the simplest way to process an input file, but adds the overhead of actually moving the data record. Unless you have a huge file, though, you won't see much difference in the CPU time actually used.

10.2.2   Locate Mode GET Processing

Use of locate mode processing — also referred to as "GET-locate" or "PUT-locate" — imposes several requirements on an assembler program. The program must do the following:

1. Specify MACRF=(GL) in the DCB.
2. Provide a DSECT to describe the records (this corresponds to the COBOL 01 level).
3. Save the address from register 1 in another register to provide addressability to the record fields.

If you skipped Chap. 7, you may wish to also skip this topic until you read it.

Since locate mode requires several changes, we'll show them below. These are changes needed from the sample program in Fig. 1.2 to convert the INFILE DCB to use GET-locate as follows:

MAINLINE	EQU	*	
	GET	INFILE	READ A RECORD
	LR	11,1	SAVE ADDR IN R11
	USING	INDSECT,11	ADDRESSABILITY
	MVC	DATA,INAREA	MOVE TO PRINT
INPUT	DCB	DDNAME = INFILE,DEVD = DA,MACRF = (GL), X	
		RECFM = FB,LRECL = 80,BLKSIZE = 0, X	
		EODAD = ENDDATA	
INDSECT	DSECT		
INAREA	DS	CL80	INPUT DATA AREA

The first segment of code reads the next record. We then save the address of the record into register 11. (Remember that register 1 is changed by many MVS and VM services, and shouldn't be used as a base register.) The USING statement tells the assembler that whenever it encounters a reference to the fields which comprise the INDSECT dummy section, it should use register 11 as the base register. Finally, we move the data from INAREA to the field called DATA, just as we did in the original example.

The middle segment of code shows the revised DCB. The only difference is in the MACRF operand.

The last segment of code shows the added dummy section called INDSECT. This is followed by the field descriptions for each field. (This is just like an 01-level record description.) This should be placed at the very end of the program, just before the actual END directive.

GET-locate processing has the drawback of requiring an extra register during the program's execution. However, this technique saves the CPU time needed to move the entire record. As such, GET-locate is an advisable technique when processing a large number of records. It also does not require extra storage for an area in your program. This isn't usually a major savings unless the records are very large.

10.2.3 The AT END Clause

There is no exact equivalent to the AT END clause with QSAM processing. The DCB macro provides an operand, EODAD, which is used to specify the name of a routine. QSAM branches to this routine when it detects end-of-file for the particular DCB.

Our example program in Fig. 1.2 shows how this works. The DCB specifies " EODAD=ENDDATA ". When we code

```
GET    INFILE,INAREA
```

with this, it is (sort of) equivalent to the COBOL code
> READ INFILE INTO INAREA
> AT END GO TO ENDDATA.

As such, this is equivalent to having the same GO TO destination in each READ verb for a particular file throughout a COBOL program.

Under MVS, if you don't provide an EODAD routine, you will receive a 337-04 ABEND when your program reads to end of file. If you issue a GET macro after the end of file, you will receive an 001-5 ABEND. Under VM, expect message DMS104 or DMS120.

10.3   HOW TO WRITE RECORDS

The PUT macro provides basic record writing services in assembler. It does not provide equivalent functions for the COBOL printer control clauses.

As with the GET macro, PUT provides move mode and locate mode processing. Move mode corresponds to coding a COBOL WRITE verb with the FROM clause. For example,

> PUT   PRINTER,ENDLINE   WRITE ENDING LINE

corresponds to coding

> WRITE A-LINE FROM ENDLINE.

in COBOL. (A-LINE would have to be the name of an 01-level record following the PRINTER FD.)

Locate mode processing with PUT corresponds to locate mode with GET, with the added nuance that you must issue an extra PUT macro to get the first buffer address. Thus, you normally issue PUT following the OPEN for the DCB, followed by loading the address of the first buffer into whatever register you've chosen for the base register. Put-locate is not widely used, in the author's experience.

As mentioned above, assembler does not provide exact corrollaries to the COBOL clauses BEFORE ADVANCING, AFTER ADVANCING, or AT END OF PAGE. To provide this printer control, most assembler programmers use a recording format that uses ANSI control characters (e.g., FBA)[1]. Table 10.2 shows the correspondence between COBOL AFTER ADVANCING values and the corresponding ANSI control characters. You use these by placing them in the first byte of each print line, and are probably familiar with them already. (The sample program in Fig. 1.2 provides examples if you are not.)

---

1   ANSI stands for American National Standards Institute; FBA means Fixed, Blocked, with ANSI control characters.

Table 10.2 COBOL AFTER ADVANCING VALUES and ANSI Control Characters		
COBOL clause **Control character**		**Remarks**
AFTER ADVANCING PAGE	'1'	Skip to channel 1 (new page)
AFTER ADVANCING C01	'1'	Skip to channel 1 (new page)
AFTER ADVANCING C02	'2'	Skip to channel 2
AFTER ADVANCING C03	'3'	Skip to channel 3
AFTER ADVANCING C04	'4'	Skip to channel 4
AFTER ADVANCING C05	'5'	Skip to channel 5
AFTER ADVANCING C06	'6'	Skip to channel 6
AFTER ADVANCING C07	'7'	Skip to channel 7
AFTER ADVANCING C08	'8'	Skip to channel 8
AFTER ADVANCING C09	'9'	Skip to channel 9
AFTER ADVANCING C10	'A'	Skip to channel 10
AFTER ADVANCING C11	'B'	Skip to channel 11
AFTER ADVANCING C12	'C'	Skip to channel 12
AFTER ADVANCING 1 LINES	' '	Space 1 line
AFTER ADVANCING 2 LINES	'0'	Space 2 lines
AFTER ADVANCING 3 LINES	'-'	Space 3 lines

Table 10.3 shows the corresponding values for the BEFORE ADVANCING clause. This must be used with 370 machine control characters. You specify these by coding "M" rather than "A" in the RECFM operand of the DCB macro. For example, " RECFM=FBA " specifies ANSI control characters and " RECFM=FBM " specifies machine control characters.

Machine control characters are less frequently used than ANSI control characters, but you may still encounter them when maintaining older assembler programs.

There are also several other commands available when using RECFM=FBM. You may find these by referring to the list in the 370 reference summary under "Printer Channel Commands."

The final clause of the WRITE verb — AT END-OF-PAGE — may be simulated in assembler with the PRTOV macro. Like the CNTRL macro alluded to in Chap. 4, this won't be covered in this book. However, you should have enough information to research this on your own after finishing this book.

Table 10.3   COBOL BEFORE ADVANCING VALUES and 370
Machine Control Characters

COBOL clause	Control character	Remarks
BEFORE ADVANCING PAGE	X'89'	Skip to channel 1 (new page)
BEFORE ADVANCING C01	X'89'	Skip to channel 1 (new page)
BEFORE ADVANCING C02	X'91'	Skip to channel 2
BEFORE ADVANCING C03	X'99'	Skip to channel 3
BEFORE ADVANCING C04	X'A1'	Skip to channel 4
BEFORE ADVANCING C05	X'A9'	Skip to channel 5
BEFORE ADVANCING C06	X'B1'	Skip to channel 6
BEFORE ADVANCING C07	X'B9'	Skip to channel 7
BEFORE ADVANCING C08	X'C1'	Skip to channel 8
BEFORE ADVANCING C09	X'C9'	Skip to channel 9
BEFORE ADVANCING C10	X'D1'	Skip to channel 10
BEFORE ADVANCING C11	X'D9'	Skip to channel 11
BEFORE ADVANCING C12	X'E1'	Skip to channel 12
BEFORE ADVANCING 1 LINES	X'09'	Space 1 line
BEFORE ADVANCING 2 LINES	X'11'	Space 2 lines
BEFORE ADVANCING 3 LINES	X'19'	Space 3 lines

10.4   HOW TO CLOSE A DCB

The CLOSE macro closely follows the options available in COBOL. Table 10.4 lists the COBOL CLOSE verb clauses, along with the closest assembler equivalent CLOSE macro option. The CLOSE macro options normally only apply to magnetic tape files.

MVS provides another macro, FEOV, which provides some of the COBOL CLOSE verb options. FEOV (Force End Of Volume) causes the current tape to be ended, after which MVS continues with the next tape specified in the JCL. For files on disk, FEOV causes MVS to start writing data to or reading data from the next disk extent. (VM does not completely support the FEOV macro in its OS simulation.)

FEOV normally is only used when you need to position data on specific reels of a multivolume tape file. As such, it most closely emulates the CLOSE REEL or UNIT options. You code the FEOV macro with only one operand, the name of the DCB representing the file.

Assembler provides no direct equivalent to the COBOL WITH LOCK option.

MVS does provide a similar feature. This is the **FREE** option of the CLOSE macro. This allows you to specify that the file in question be released for use by other jobs. As such, it corresponds most closely to the JCL feature of FREE=CLOSE. (Refer to the explanation in the JCL manual if you aren't familiar with this.)

If you don't provide any options, the default is DISP. This tells MVS to do whatever was specified in the JCL DISP parameter.

Table 10.4 COBOL CLOSE Clauses and Assembler Equivalents	
COBOL clause	**Assembler equivalent**
REEL	FEOV macro
UNIT	FEOV
NO REWIND	LEAVE option of CLOSE or OPEN
FOR REMOVAL	Normal CLOSE macro
WITH LOCK	No direct equivalent

There is no clearly equivalent VM service to allow us to implement the CLOSE WITH LOCK option.

The TYPE=T parameter in assembler is discussed in the following section.

10.5   ESOTERICA
This section covers some additional techniques which may prove useful, but which aren't essential for writing typical assembler language programs. You may bypass this section if you are experiencing cranial capacity checks (i.e., your brain is full).

10.5.1   How To Test For a Successful OPEN
If you're ever bothered by those pesky MVS IEC130 messages (you know, the ones that say "DD STATEMENT MISSING"), you should know that you can avoid them in assembler. A similar situation occurs in VM indicated by the DMS036 message. Avoiding these is a good idea, since you also avoid those 0C1 or 0C4 ABENDs which endear you so much to the operations staff.

You may test if a DCB has been opened successfully in two ways. One way uses an instruction called Test Under Mask (TM) along with a DSECT supplied by MVS and VM in the DCBD macro. The other uses a service added by VSAM to provide a return code in register 15. The first is included in our example program in Figure 1.2. The second will be shown in Chap. 21.

The first method requires code like the following:

```
OPEN  (dcb_name,option)
LA    R1,dcb_name            GET DCB ADDR
USING IHADCB,R1              ADDRESSABILITY
TM    DCBOFLGS,X'10'         TEST GOOD OPEN
BZ    error_routine          OPEN FAILED - ERR
```

The OPEN macro is no different from any others we've discussed up to this point. The LA (Load Address) instruction computes the effective address of the DCB and puts it in register 1. (We could have used any register.) The USING statement tells the assembler that we want to use register 1 as the base register for a DSECT called IHADCB.

IHADCB is a dummy section created by a macro called DCBD. It provides labels for all of the fields in the DCB. In this case, we're using the DSECT to look at something inside our program — the DCB — rather than to look at something outside our program, such as parameters passed to a subroutine or records passed with GET locate processing, as we have previously discussed.

The TM (Test Under Mask) instruction which follows tests a bit — the one specified by the X'10' operand. The BZ (Branch if Zero) after the TM will branch (go to) an error routine if the bit is off. The sequence of instructions (LA, USING, TM, and BZ) thus tests for a successful open and branches to the error routine if it is not. (MVS and VM set the bit to 1 if the OPEN macro is completed okay. It is named DCBOFOPN.)

For this process to work, we must also create the IHADCB DSECT. To do so, we should code a DCBD macro. This should be placed at the end of the program, along with any other DSECT statements. The DCBD macro has two operands. The first is the device type(s) to be described by the DSECT — the DEVD operand. The second is the data set organization — the DSORG operand. An example of a DCBD follows:

```
DCBD  DEVD = (DA,TA),DSORG = (QS,BS)
```

(Unlike the DCB macro, you may specify multiple values for DEVD and DSORG.) The DA and TA operands tell the DCBD macro to define the unique DCB field names for direct access and for tape devices. The QS and BS operands specify that the DCBD macro should provide the unique DCB field names used with the QSAM and BSAM access methods. (DSORG=PS will cover both, and is often coded instead.)

The DCBD macro will define the field called DCBOFLGS which we tested with the TM instruction. It also provides several other useful pieces of information. One of these is the length of the record you just received with a GET macro. If you are processing fixed-length records (RECFM=FB), this is usually not too important. For variable-length or undefined formats (RECFM=VB or RECFM=U), this may be handy.

You may also modify fields in the DCB, such as the DD name or EODAD routine address, by using the fields defined in the DCBD macro (see Sect. 13.7.3). In a slight way, the DCBD provides access to some of the same information COBOL provides through the FILE STATUS clause.

The second technique for determining if an OPEN has been successfully completed is to test the value of register 15. This is where MVS and VM normally provide return codes from macro service requests. The code to use this technique, which applies to VSAM only, would look like the following:

```
OPEN   (acb_name,option)
LTR    R15,R15                          TEST RET CODE
BNZ    error_routine                    OPEN FAILED - ERR
```

The LTR (Load and Test Register) tests the value in register 15 to determine if it is positive, negative, or zero. (The convention used in both MVS and VM is that a return code of zero indicates a successful operation.) The BNZ (Branch if Not Zero) branches (goes to) the error routine if the contents of register 15 were not zero. Of these two methods, the second is newer and probably more preferable. However, it only works when used with VSAM.

You may wish to review what's produced by the DCBD macro. It creates about twenty pages of output, and you may not wish to look at it each time you assemble the program. Assembler language provides a directive — PRINT — which controls what appears in the assembler listing. PRINT has three operands.

The first, coded as ON or OFF, tells the assembler whether to print the listing (ON) or not (OFF). You may provide as many PRINT statements as desired within a program. IBM-supplied CICS programs often will specify PRINT OFF for large copied sections.

The second operand of PRINT, coded as GEN or NOGEN, specifies whether the generated code should be printed (GEN) or not (NOGEN). Macro instructions like DCB or DCBD generate a lot of print lines. Many assembler programmers prefer to not to print these, since they rarely need to look at them.

The third operand tells the assembler how much generated data to print in the listing. This is coded as DATA or NODATA. Except in special situations, you rarely need to show this generated data.

The assembler's default settings for the PRINT directive are " PRINT ON,GEN,NODATA ". To avoid printing the DCBD listing, code the following in your program:

```
PRINT  ON,NOGEN
DCBD   - operands -
```

You may move this statement in front of the DCB macros if you don't want to print the output from those macros either.

10.5.2   The TYPE = T Option of CLOSE

TYPE=T is an option which applies only to the BSAM access method. BSAM, like all basic access methods, processes blocks of data rather than records, and requires that your program wait for I/O to complete. BSAM also allows you to change directions when reading a data set (forward or backward). You may still have code at your shop which reads a tape both forward and backward, but this is becoming increasingly rare.

Since you could switch from writing a data set forward to reading it backward with BSAM, MVS provides a service which allows you to complete a tape data set without completely closing the file. This is the temporary close (TCLOSE) service of the CLOSE macro, specified with the TYPE=T operand. CLOSE TYPE=T uses a separate supervisor call (SVC) — 23 rather than 20 for the normal close.

CLOSE TYPE=T causes MVS to write the trailer labels for a tape data set. MVS then positions the data set as specified in the CLOSE macro option. So, if you were reading a data set forward, and specified the REREAD option in CLOSE, BSAM would rewind the tape. If you specified LEAVE, BSAM would leave the tape at the end in preparation for reading it backward.

CLOSE TYPE=T also causes information for a disk data set to be updated. MVS keeps this information in a Data Set Control Block (DSCB), which corresponds to a tape label. You can get a formatted dump of a DSCB with the IEHLIST utility program.

Coding TYPE=T when closing a QSAM data set has no effect. CLOSE TYPE=T is supported by VM OS simulation.

10.5.3   Updating In Place with the PUTX Macro

The COBOL REWRITE verb allows you to replace a record which you have previously read. The PUTX macro provides the corresponding service for sequential files in assembler.

PUTX requires the locate mode of GET. To use PUTX, you must generally do the following:

1. Change the OPEN macro to reflect a processing option of UPDAT.
2. As mentioned, you must use the locate mode of GET. This requires the DCB to contain a MACRF parameter of MACRF=(GL,PL).
3. Add a DSECT to describe the input records (if you aren't already using GET locate).
4. Add the logic necesary to change the input record's data as appropriate.

Some segments of code which illustrate these changes follow. (The rules indicate code which is in separate sections of the program.)

	OPEN	(IOFILE,UPDAT)	
MAINLINE	EQU	*	
	GET	IOFILE	GET NEXT RECORD
	LR	11,1	PUT ADDR IN R11
	USING	RECDESC,11	ADDRESSABILITY
* The logic necesary to update the records would go here			
	PUTX	IOFILE	UPDATE REC
	B	MAINLINE	GET NEXT RECORD
IOFILE	DCB	DDNAME = TEXTFILE,DEVD = DA,DSORG = PS, X	
		MACRF = (GL,PL),EODAD = ENDDATA	
RECDESC	DSECT		
* The individual field descriptions would follow here			

Use of PUTX applies to any program which modifies only a portion of the records in a sequential file. Performance will usually be better than creating a separate, modified file if less than a fifth of the records are rewritten. Space requirements, of course, are halved, since no second copy of a file is created.

PUTX may only be used with sequential files on disk. Chapter 21 covers rewriting records in VSAM files. PUTX is supported by VM OS simulation.

10.5.4   Reading Multiple Files with the PDAB Macro
The PDAB macro provides improved performance for some special situations and has no equivalent in COBOL. The PDAB macro generates a special control block — the Parallel Data Access Block — which provides a list of Data Control Blocks.

The GET macro has an operand, TYPE=P, which specifies that a request for a record is through a PDAB rather than a DCB.

When this technique is used, QSAM examines each of the DCBs in the PDAB list. QSAM then returns the next available record from whichever DCB has records ready.

The advantage of this lies in the ability to overlap I/O operations much more heavily. In normal MVS QSAM processing your program will wait whenever you issue a GET macro and there are no records available in a buffer. With the PDAB technique, your program only waits when none of the listed DCBs have data available.

Effective use of this technique requires a special situation. This is where you must read in several files, each containing the same types of records, which are all processed together. An example might be reading in four files of weekly transactions and sorting them together to produce a monthly transaction report by account.

In the case of COBOL, each of the four files would be read in sequence. (This would happen if each were given a separate FD, or if they were concatenated via JCL and read in through the same FD.)

With the PDAB technique, the four files could be read in parallel, with QSAM reading one while your program was processing records from the next file. As a result, this technique can provide substantial improvements in performance for this type of job.

You should refer to the data management services manuals for more information on PDAB. It is not supported by VM OS simulation.

10.5.5   The COBOL FILE STATUS Clause

Assembler has no direct equivalent to the COBOL FILE STATUS clause. COBOL assembles a variety of information to provide the file status information. Table 10.5 lists some COBOL FILE STATUS clause values and the corresponding actions in assembler. Table 10.6 shows the same information for VSAM files.

Table 10.5 FILE STATUS Values and Assembler Equivalents		
COBOL File Status	COBOL Meaning	Assembler Equivalent
00	Successful I/O	None needed
10	At end of file	ABEND 337 or 001
30	Permanent error	SYNAD exit or ABEND 001
34	Boundary violation (sequential file)	VSAM RTNCD/ FDBK2
90	Other errors (no further info)	Depends on situation
92	Logic error	Depends on situation
96	No file ID	No DD statement: Message IEC141 at OPEN, 0C4 or 0C1 for GET/PUT

In reference to Table 10.6, errors for VSAM processing are returned in a combination of register 15 and in various control block fields. The table lists errors which are reported in the Request Parameter List (RPL) FDBK field, along with a few errors which are passed back in the Access method Control Block (ACB) ERROR field. (The ACB-related errors arise as part of OPEN for a VSAM file.) Chapter 21, which covers VSAM, provides further information.

Table 10.6   FILE STATUS Values and Assembler Equivalents
For VSAM Processing

COBOL File Status	COBOL Meaning	Assembler Equivalent: R15:	RPL FDBK :
00	Successful I/O	0	0
02	Duplicate Key	8	8
10	At end of file	8	4
20	Invalid key	8	16, 24, or 192
21	Sequence error	8	12
22	Duplicate key (when not allowed)	8	8
23	No record found	8	16 / 32
24	Boundary violation (indexed or relative)	8	Varies[1]
30	Permanent error	12	Varies[2]
34	Boundary violation (sequential file)	8	Varies, e.g. 192
90	Other errors (no further info)	—	Varies
91	Password Failure	8 or 12	ACB[3]
92	Logic error	8	Varies, e.g. 44
94	No record pointer for sequential access	8	88
95	Invalid/incomplete file information	8 or 12	ACB[4]
96	No file identification	8 or 12	ACB[5]
97	Open successful, file verified	0	0

1   For example, the RPL return code/feedback area may contain a value of 192.
2   Return codes of 4 through 24 may be present depending on the operation attempted and the location of the error.
3   This error will be reported at the time of OPEN in the ACB rather than in an RPL — the ACB ERROR field will contain a value of 152.
4   This may also be an OPEN error — ACB ERROR code will vary, e.g., 160.
5   OPEN error — ACB ERROR will contain 128.

10.6 SUMMARY

This chapter has presented an overview of I/O processing in assembler. You should feel comfortable that you can code the OPEN, GET, PUT, CLOSE, and DCB macros based on the information you've read so far.

Things to Do

1. If you have access to assembler programs at your installation, review the I/O macros used in them. Do any of them use macros besides OPEN, CLOSE, GET, PUT, and DCB?

2. Do these programs test for successful completion of the OPEN macro as discussed above?

3. If you are running under VM, review the VM-unique I/O macros described in Appendix 4 (Sect. A4.1).

Arithmetic

In this chapter, we'll learn how the four basic arithmetic verbs in COBOL — ADD, SUBTRACT, MULTIPLY, and DIVIDE — have corresponding instructions in assembler. To implement these, we'll cover the assembler instructions for packed decimal and binary arithmetic.

11.1 FOUR COBOL VERBS VERSUS FIFTEEN INSTRUCTIONS

Where COBOL has only four straightforward arithmetic operations, assembler provides fifteen instructions. (We're excluding some instructions which we'll mention in the esoterica section.) The reason for this difference lies in a major difference between the two languages, which will show up in most of our comparisons from here on in.

In COBOL, you only have to code the arithmetic operation, without regard to how the individual fields are defined. For example, the statement

ADD BATCH-TOTAL TO GRAND-TOTAL.

causes the COBOL compiler to

- Figure out how each of the two data fields are stored.

- Determine the most effective instruction to use to add the two numbers together.

- Generate that instruction.

- Generate any conversion instructions to get from one format to another.

To see what this involves, try looking at what COBOL generates in a PMAP when you add two numbers with different USAGE clauses together.

By comparison, in assembler you must do this analysis yourself and select the specific, most efficient instructions yourself. This isn't as bad as it may sound, and becomes second nature after some practice.

The specific reason why assembler provides 15 arithmetic instructions lies in the 370 CPU's need to provide specific instruction types based on the type of data being used. There are four basic arithmetic instruction formats as follows:

1. Binary arithmetic on 32-bit (fullword) numbers in general purpose registers

2. Binary arithmetic involving a 32-bit (fullword) number in a register and a 32-bit (fullword) number in working storage

3. Binary arithmetic involving a 32-bit (fullword) number in a register and a 16-bit (halfword) number in working storage

4. Packed decimal arithmetic between two numbers in working storage

Each of these four basic arithmetic types requires its own set of the four basic arithmetic functions (add, subtract, multiply, and divide). As a result, there are 15 arithmetic instructions. (There should be 16, but no Divide Halfword instruction is provided. This may make sense later.)

The instruction opcodes, their names, and the type and length of data they operate on are shown in Table 11.1.

Table 11.1   Arithmetic Instructions in Assembler Language

Opcode	Instruction name	Data locations	Data length
AR	Add Register	Registers	Fullword
SR	Subtract Register	Registers	Fullword
MR	Multiply Register	Registers	Fullword
DR	Divide Register	Registers	Fullword
A	Add	Register/Storage	Fullword
S	Subtract	Register/Storage	Fullword
M	Multiply	Register/Storage	Fullword
D	Divide	Register/Storage	Fullword
AH	Add Halfword	Register/Storage	Halfword
SH	Subtract Halfword	Register/Storage	Halfword
MH	Multiply Halfword	Register/Storage	Halfword
AP	Add Packed	Storage	Variable
SP	Subtract Packed	Storage	Variable
MP	Multiply Packed	Storage	Variable
DP	Divide Packed	Storage	Variable

At this point, we'll describe how one set of these — Register-to-Register arithmetic — works in some detail. Register-to-storage arithmetic is very similar, and will be discussed next for both its fullword and halfword forms. Finally, we'll discuss the packed decimal, storage-to-storage arithmetic format, and some of its unique requirements. At the end of the chapter, the esoterica section will outline several unique and infrequently used arithmetic methods.

11.2   REGISTER-TO-REGISTER BINARY ARITHMETIC

Binary arithmetic has some nuances which don't necesarily show up when doing arithmetic on binary fields in COBOL. We'll discuss these, then cover how the instructions actually process numbers. You may find it useful to look at App. 1, which covers the binary and hexadecimal number systems, before continuing.

11.2.1 Characteristics of Positive Binary Arithmetic

Binary arithmetic has two advantages. The first is that, from an electrical engineering standpoint, it's simpler and cheaper to implement than arithmetic in other number bases. The second advantage is that it is invariably the fastest form of arithmetic on a computer.

To get this speed, binary data must be standardized in its representation and in its length. This standardization is part of what makes binary arithmetic faster. In the IBM 370 design, binary arithmetic is performed with 31-bit quantities. The addition of a sign bit makes 32 bits, or one IBM 370 fullword. Each general purpose register has 32 bits. The layout of these is shown in Fig. 11.1.

Figure 11.1   Register bit positions.

The sign bit is bit 0. This has a value of 0 if the binary number value is positive. It has a value of 1 if the binary number is negative. Bits 1 through 31 are the binary number. Bit 1 is called the *most signficant bit* (MSB) and bit 31 is called the *least significant bit* (LSB). Bit 31 represents a value of 1, bit 30 represents a value of 2, bit 29 represents a value of 4, and so on up to bit 1, which represents a value of 1073741824.

The largest positive number which can be contained in a general purpose register (i.e., in a fullword) is 2147483647. The largest negative number which can be held is -2147483648.

When data is stored as a halfword, the halfword also retains a sign bit, along with fifteen bits for the binary number. The range of values which can be held in a halfword in storage is from positive 32757 to negative -32768.

The IBM 370 provides for both signed and unsigned arithmetic on binary data. We'll only be discussing signed arithmetic in detail.

11.2.2 Two's-Complement Arithmetic

At this point, we have to look at how the IBM 370 handles negative numbers. The IBM 370 uses what's called *two's complement* arithmetic for negative numbers.

The concept behind complement arithmetic is that adding the opposite of a number is the same as subtracting. If you hark back to high school algebra, you may remember the algebraic rule that adding a negative number was the same as subtracting a positive number of the same magnitude.

What the 370 does in complement arithmetic is to store negative numbers in such a way that, when they are added to a binary number, it has the same effect as subtracting the number. The 370 forms a two's complement of a number by the following steps:

1. Invert all the bits in the number (make the 0 bits into 1 bits, and the 1 bits into 0 bits)
2. Add one

Figure 11.2 shows how this works. If the result of a subtraction exceeds 32 bits, the leftmost bits are discarded into the "bit bucket."

Figure 11.2   Subtraction with two's-complement arithmetic.

Let's subtract 23 from 47 in two's complement. First, decimal 47 is hex X'0000002F'. Decimal 23 is hex X'00000017'.

Convert X'00000017' to binary: 00000000000000000000000000010111

Invert the bits: 11111111111111111111111111101000

Add 1:   00000000000000000000000000000001

Result (X'FFFFFFE9'):   11111111111111111111111111101001

Now add the result to 47 in binary:

Positive 47 =   00000000000000000000000000101111

Negative 23 in 2's complement =   11111111111111111111111111101001

Add together to get a result of: 100000000000000000000000000011000

But, since our result is 33 bits long, and the register size is only 32 bits long, the leftmost bit (a one) is discarded, giving our actual result of: 00000000000000000000000000011000

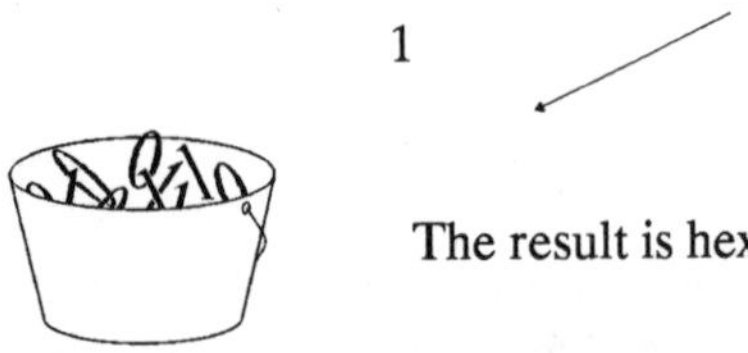

The result is hexadecimal X'00000018' — decimal 24.

When you code a subtraction instruction, the 370 converts the number to be subtracted into two's complement form, then adds it. As a result, you normally don't have to worry about complementing the number yourself. You may wish to be able to when debugging, however.

Some other details about two's complement notation are worth mentioning here:

- The two's complement of zero is zero.

- There is no negative zero.

- The absolute magnitude of the largest possible negative number is 1 greater than the absolute value of the largest possible positive number.

The reason for this last nuance is that zero takes one of the possible combinations of bits making up the positive numbers.

11.2.3 Overflow

One condition which applies to arithmetic both in COBOL and in assembler is the possibility of overflow. This happens whenever the result of arithmetic is too large to fit into the field which is to receive the result. COBOL signals this to the programmer by executing the ON SIZE ERROR clause, if one is provided.

The 370 CPU sets a corresponding indicator, called the *condition code*, when an overflow happens. We will discuss this in Chap. 12, when we cover branching.

This condition is more of a concern in assembler, however, since assembler doesn't provide some of the error messages and other information that COBOL does. For example, there is no warning message regarding truncation from the assembler. As such, you must design your arithmetic field sizes to accommodate the largest possible result.

11.2.4 Add Register

Having put the discussion of binary arithmetic behind us, let's look at the instructions which actually do it. The first is Add Register, with an opcode of AR. AR adds the binary number in the general-purpose register specified as the second operand to the contents of the register specified as the first operand. It then stores the result in the first operand register.

For example:

        AR   R1,R2

adds the value in register 2 to the value in register 1 and puts the result in register 1.

AR also sets the condition code to indicate if overflow occurred, and to indicate as well if the result was positive, negative, or zero.

Remember that, logically, the second operand does something to the first operand — generally the reverse of COBOL. Thus, if we had

        ADD A TO B.

in COBOL, the corresponding assembler instructions would be

        AR   B,A

(assuming that A and B were equated to registers elsewhere in the program).

11.2.5 Subtract Register

SR (Subtract Register) is similar to AR, with the obvious distinction that it subtracts rather than adds. The CPU performs subtraction by forming the two's complement of the number in the second operand register and adding that to the first operand register.

The second operand register is not modified in this sequence. The number in the second operand register is copied to a work area within the CPU's adder hardware, then manipulated to produce the two's complement, then actually added to the contents of the first operand register.

For example, given the following register contents:

Register 1 = X'00000012'   (Decimal 18)
Register 2 = X'00000004'   (Decimal 4)

The instruction

        SR   R1,R2

produces the following results:

Register 1 = X'0000000E'   (Decimal 14) (18 - 4)
Register 2 = X'00000004'   (Decimal 4) (unchanged)

SR also sets the condition code to indicate if overflow occurred, and also to indicate if the result was positive, negative, or zero.

11.2.6 Multiply Register

Multiply Register (MR) is more difficult than AR or SR because it involves three registers rather than two. The reason for this is that when multiplying two numbers together, you produce a result which is potentially as long as the two numbers put together.

Since we are multiplying two 31-bit numbers, the result can be as long as 62 bits. So, to prevent a likely overflow, the 370 requires that you specify a pair of registers as the first operand. The second operand is still a single register.

The two registers must be an *even-odd* pair of registers. This means that the two registers start with an even-numbered register — 0, 2, 4, 6, 8, 10, 12, or 14. The second register is always the odd-numbered register following the even-numbered register — 1 if 0 were specified, 3 if 2 were specified, and so forth. The odd-numbered register is not coded in the instruction, but it is implicit in the instruction.

The multiplication produces a 63-bit result. Along with the sign bit, this takes up two registers. For example, given the following register contents:

Register 1 = X'0000000A'   (Decimal 10)
Register 2 = X'00000017'   (Decimal 23) (see note)
Register 3 = X'00000008'   (Decimal 8)
The instruction

        MR   R2,R1

produces the following results:
Register 1 = X'0000000A'   (Decimal 10) (unchanged)
Register 2 = X'00000000'   (High-order part of result)
Register 3 = X'00000050'   (Low-order part of result)
Product = X'0000000000000050'   (Decimal 80)

Note: Another nuance of MR is that the even-numbered register doesn't participate in the multiplication — it's only there to receive half of the result. Because of this, the even register doesn't have to have any special preparation before the MR. In our example, the actual contents of register 2 — hex X'17', or decimal 23 — had no effect. Register 2 could have held any value in this example without affecting the product.

Another example of MR follows:

        MR   R1,R2

This is not a valid instruction. The first operand must specify an even-numbered register.

MR does not set the condition code.

11.2.7   Divide Register

DR (Divide Register) is even more complex than MR. Many experienced assembler programmers still have to refer to the manual to get everything set up right. If you find this discussion confusing, at least you have company.

DR uses the even-odd register method to contain the 64-bit dividend. Another single register holds the divisor. Divide operations produce two results — the quotient and the remainder. (The dividend is what's being divided, not a result. This conflicts with the more common, and inexact, usage of *dividend* as a distribution of part of a company's earnings. Per-share dividends, as used in financial markets, are actually quotients.)

In COBOL, keeping these four items separate did not present a big problem. The DIVIDE verb syntax provided separate clauses for the quotient and remainder. For example:

        DIVIDE A INTO B GIVING C REMAINDER D.

In this case, you easily determine that the data field named C will contain the quotient, and D the remainder.

In assembler, however, the processing for the divide operation is more like "divide a doubleword in two registers by a fullword in another register and place the remainder and quotient into the original doubleword."

In practice, what this means is that the original 64-bit (doubleword) value is divided and replaced by a 32-bit remainder and a 32-bit quotient.

An even-odd register pair holds the original (dividend) doubleword. After the divide operation, the even-numbered register holds the remainder. The odd-numbered register holds the quotient. For example, given the following register contents:

Register 3 = X'00000007'   (Decimal 7)
Register 4 = X'00000000'   (First half of dividend)
Register 5 = X'00000050'   (Second half of dividend)
Doubleword = X'0000000000000050' (Decimal 80)

the instruction

        DR   R4,R3

produces the following results:

Register 3 = X'00000007'   (Decimal 7) (unchanged)
Register 2 = X'00000003'   (Remainder – decimal 3)
Register 3 = X'0000000B'   (Quotient – decimal 11)

    DR does not set the condition code. However, certain conditions, like dividing by zero, cause an 0CB ABEND.

11.3   REGISTER-TO-STORAGE ARITHMETIC

The register-to-register instructions covered up to now have corresponding register-to-storage forms. These process both fullword and halfword data. We'll discuss fullword data in this section and cover halfword data starting in Sec. 11.4.

    Both the RR and RS forms of these instructions deal with data in registers. In the RS form, however, the second operand is always a fullword (or halfword) in storage. The first operand is still a register, or an even-odd register pair.

    Note that we've ignored the trivial detail of how we actually get the data into the registers. To do this, we use what are called *load* and *store* instructions. Chapter 13 covers these.

11.3.1   Add

Add — opcode A — operates exactly like the AR instruction, with the exception of the second operand. The second operand is a fullword in storage, usually created with a DC or DS statement with a type of F.

    The following shows an example of the Add instruction:

Register 1 = X'0000000C'   (Decimal 12)

Assume we have a data field coded as:

FOUR   DC   F'4'   (Hex value = X'00000004')

The instruction

        A   R1,FOUR

produces the following results:

Register 1 = X'00000010'   (Decimal 16) (12 + 4)
FOUR contains Hex X'00000004'   (Decimal 4) (unchanged)

A also sets the condition code, as in the AR instruction.

11.3.2   Subtract

Subtract, which has the operation code of S, operates like the SR instruction. An example of SR follows. Given the following initial values:

Register 3 = X'00000012'   (Decimal 18)

FIVE   DC   F'5'   (Hex value = X'00000004')

The instruction

        S   R3,FIVE

produces the following results:

Register 1 = X'0000000D'   (Decimal 13) (18 - 5)

FOUR contains Hex X'00000004'   (Decimal 4) (unchanged)

Subtract also sets the condition code.

11.3.3   Multiply

Multiply operates like MR and has the opcode M. For example, given the following starting values:

TWENTY   DC   F'20'   (Hex value X'00000014')

Register 6 = X'00000FFF'   (Decimal 4095) (see note)

Register 7 = X'00000004'   (Decimal 4)

The instruction

        M   R6,TWENTY

produces the following results:

TWENTY contains Hex X'00000014'   (Decimal 20) (unchanged)

Register 6 = X'00000000'   (High-order part of result)

Register 7 = X'0000003C'   (Low-order part of result)

Product = X'000000000000003C'   (Decimal 60)

Note: As with MR, the even-numbered register doesn't participate in the multiplication, it is only used to store the left half of the product.

As with MR, the following is not a valid instruction:

        M   R7,TWENTY

because the first operand must specify an even-numbered register.

Multiply does not set the condition code.

11.3.4   Divide

Divide — opcode D — operates like DR. For example, given the following initial values:

SIX   DC   F'6'   (Hex value X'00000006')

Register 8 = X'00000000'   (First half of dividend)

Register 9 = X'00000048'   (Second half of dividend)

Doubleword = X'0000000000000048'   (Decimal 72)

The instruction

        D   R8,SIX

produces the following results:

SIX contains Hex X'0000006'	(Decimal 6) (unchanged)
Register 8 = X'00000000'	(Remainder − zero)
Register 9 = X'0000000C'	(Quotient − decimal 12)

Divide does not set the condition code.

11.4   HALFWORD REGISTER-TO-STORAGE ARITHMETIC

Halfword arithmetic operates much like the fullword register-to-storage arithmetic we've just discussed. The differences revolve around the length of the storage operand — 2 bytes — and how this is converted to a fullword.

Figure 11.3 shows the bit configuration for a halfword. As in a fullword, bit 0 is the sign bit, with positive indicated by a 0 sign bit and negative by a 1 sign bit. Bits 1 through 15 are the binary number, with bit 1 being the most signficant bit and bit 15 the least significant bit. Bit 15 represents a value of 1, bit 14 represents a value of 2, bit 13 a value of 4 and so on up to bit 1, which represents a value of 16384.

Figure 11.3   Halfword bit layout.

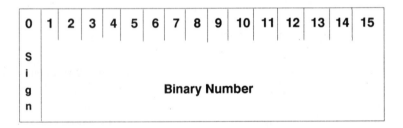

The 370 processes halfword instructions in the following sequence:
1. Fetch the halfword from storage.
2. Convert it to a fullword by propagating the sign bit.
3. Complete the operation in the same way as the corresponding fullword register-to-storage operation (i.e., add, subtract, multiply).

Propagating the sign bit means that the CPU adds 16 bits, all the same as the halfword's sign bit from storage. This has the effect of keeping the arithmetic value of the number the same in both forms. (See Chap. 13.)

Halfword arithmetic has only three instructions — AH, SH, and MH. No DH is supplied. If DH were provided, you might wind up with an instruction which had both the quotient and remainder in the same register. We will, however, write a macro instruction to simulate a divide halfword instruction in Chap. 22.

The Load Halfword and Store Halfword instructions are used to move data to and from registers. These will be covered in Chap. 13.

What determines when you would use halfword versus fullword arithmetic? The primary concern is the magnitude or size of the numbers your program will be processing. Since halfwords are limited to 32K, they are most appropriate for values which obviously can't exceed that. For example, the number of days in a month never exceeds 31, and the number of hours in a day never exceeds 24. Halfwords would be an appropriate choice for variables of that type.

By comparison, there are 86400 seconds in a day, and that would not be an appropriate use for halfword data fields.

Additionally, you should normally avoid halfwords when you intend to do a lot of division, since that isn't supported with the halfword data format.

11.4.1 Add Halfword

Add Halfword — op code AH — operates like the Add instruction. The second operand must specify a halfword rather than a fullword.

For example, with the following starting values:

NINE	DC	H'9'	(Hex value X'0009')

Register 6 = X'00000003'   (Decimal 3)

Executing the instruction

        AH   R6,NINE

presents these values:

NINE contains Hex X'0009'   (Decimal 9) (unchanged)

Register 6 = X'0000000C'   (Decimal 12)

Add Halfword sets the condition code.

11.4.2 Subtract Halfword

Subtract Halfword, which has the op code SH, executes like the Subtract instruction with the exception of the second operand length.

For example, given these initial contents:

ELEVEN	DC	H'11'	(Hex value X'000B')

Register 8 = X'00000032'   (Decimal 50)

The instruction

        SH   R8,ELEVEN

causes these results:

ELEVEN contains Hex X'000B'   (Decimal 11) (unchanged)

Register 8 = X'00000027'   (Decimal 39)

Subtract Halfword sets the condition code.

11.4.3 Multiply Halfword

Multiply Halfword (MH) differs from the fullword M and MR instructions by only requiring one register rather than two. It also has some pitfalls which we'll cover after looking at an example.

Given the following starting values:

THIRTEEN	DC	H'13'	(Hex value X'0000000D')

Register 9 = X'00000003'   (Decimal 3)

Executing

MH   R9,THIRTEEN

produces the following results:

THIRTEEN still holds hex X'0000000D'   (Decimal 13) (unchanged)

Register 9 = X'00000027'   (Decimal 39)

Unlike M/MR, either even- or odd-numbered registers may be used. Only one register is required. Like M/MR, the condition code is not set.

Unlike M/MR, MH may produce an overflow result. This can't be detected, though, since the condition code is not set. The product of a 15-bit number and a 31-bit number (ignoring the sign bits) is up to 46 bits long. Since the result is placed into a general purpose register, truncation may occur. Also, the rightmost 32 bits are placed in the register. This means that the sign may not reflect the algebraic relations of the original multiplier and multiplicand. Thus, you may get a negative result by multiplying two positive numbers together if they are too large.

When writing a program doing serious mathematical calculations, you should probably stick to fullword arithmetic. However, Multiply Halfword works fine for many programming requirements, such as calculating the offset into a table. For this reason, many assembler programmers prefer MH since it requires only one register.

11.5 PACKED DECIMAL STORAGE-TO-STORAGE ARITHMETIC

Packed decimal arithmetic is intuitively much simpler than binary arithmetic. Many assembler programmers prefer it because of this. Using packed decimal (COMP-3 in COBOL) in assembler requires more planning than with COBOL, however.

11.5.1 Representation of Packed Decimal Numbers

If you remember our discussion of packed decimal data in Chap. 6, packed decimal stores numbers as sequences of 4-bit decimal digits. A 4-bit sign at the end of the sequence completes the number. Figure 11.4 shows the format of a 5-digit, 3-byte packed decimal number. The data shown corresponds to a value of positive 337.

Assembler requires that you select correct sizes for packed decimal arithmetic. If this is not done, you will have inaccurate results. This requirement for packed decimal arithmetic isn't helped by how the assembler processes these fields. Where COBOL at least prints a warning message when truncation may arise, assembler is silent. The assembler assumes that if you coded it, you must know what you're doing.

Unlike binary representation, packed decimal allows both a positive and negative zero.

Packed decimal arithmetic uses an instruction called Zero and Add Packed (ZAP) to move data from one field to another. We'll cover this in Chap. 13.

Figure 11.4   Format of a packed decimal number.

Bits	0 1 2 3 4 5 6 7	0 1 2 3 4 5 6 7	0 1 2 3 4 5 6 7

Digits	1	2	3	4	5	Sign

Bytes	1	2	3

Data in hex	0	0	3	3	7	C

11.5.2   Add Decimal

The opcode for this instruction is AP. Add Decimal adds the contents of the second operand to the first operand and places the result in the first operand field. If the first operand is too short to contain the result, the condition code is set to indicate that overflow occurred.

All of the digits and signs of both operands are checked for validity. If an incorrect value is found, a data exception occurs, eventually causing an 0C7.

No registers (except base registers) are used with Add Decimal, or any other packed decimal instruction. As an example, consider the following fields:

```
NINETY9     DC      PL3'99'                 (Hexadecimal X'00099C')
NINETEEN    DC      PL2'19'                 (Hexadecimal X'0019C')
```
When we execute

```
            AP      NINETY9,NINETEEN
```
we get:

NINETY9   Hexadecimal X'00118C'   (Decimal 118)
NINETEEN   Hexadecimal X'0019C'   (Unchanged)

Now let's look at another example where we improperly select the field size:

```
INNINGS     DC      P'9'                    (Hexadecimal X'9C')
BASES       DC      P'4'                    (Hexadecimal X'4C')
```

When we do

AP   INNINGS,BASES

we get:

INNINGS   Hexadecimal X'3C'   (Decimal 3)
BASES   Hexadecimal X'4C'   (Unchanged)

Nine plus four is thirteen, but is truncated to a result of three. The condition code would be set to indicate overflow.

11.5.3 Subtract Decimal

The Subtract Decimal instruction — opcode SP — operates just like the Add Decimal instruction, but the sign of the second operand is reversed. (This is similar to the complementing operation discussed in the binary arithmetic subtraction instructions.)

As an example of SP, consider the following:

MIDFIELD   DC   P'50'   (Hexadecimal X'050C')
PENALTY   DC   P'10'   (Hexadecimal X'010C')

When we execute

SP   MIDFIELD,PENALTY

the fields become:

MIDFIELD   Hexadecimal X'040C'   (Decimal 40)
PENALTY   Hexadecimal X'010C'   (Decimal 10)

Now let's look at an example where the result is negative rather than positive. Assume these starting values:

HATTRICK   DC   P'3'   (Hexadecimal X'3C')
SHUTOUT   DC   P'0'   (Hexadecimal X'0C')

When we execute

SP   SHUTOUT,HATTRICK

we get:

HATTRICK   Hexadecimal X'3C'   (Decimal 3) (unchanged)
SHUTOUT   Hexadecimal X'3D'   (Decimal negative 3)

The condition code reflects the result of the operation.

11.5.4 Multiply Decimal

Multiply Decimal — opcode MP — requires the same scaling and sizing planning as the other packed decimal instructions. The basic rule is to define the result (product) as long as the multiplier and multiplicand combined. However, unlike the preceding packed decimal instructions, you may get an 0C6 or 0C7 ABEND if the fields aren't properly sized.

For example, suppose we wished to multiply these two packed decimal fields together:

LENGTH   DC   PL2'100'
WIDTH   DC   PL2'100'

To properly do the multiplication, we would need to define another field as follows:

```
AREA        DC      PL4'0'
```

Since LENGTH and WIDTH are each 2 bytes long, AREA should be at least 4 bytes long.

To actually do the operation, we would need to move one of the two numbers into the field called AREA with the ZAP instruction referred to earlier:

```
ZAP     AREA,LENGTH
MP      AREA,WIDTH
```

At the conclusion of this, AREA would contain hexadecimal X'0010000C'. LENGTH and WIDTH would be unchanged.

This approach may seem to make the resulting field (AREA in this case) too long. However, the MP instruction does not set the condition code. To guard against undetected overflow, MP makes a "dry run" of the instruction execution. If the second operand (multiplier) is not greater in length than the first operand, the MP instruction causes a specification exception (0C6). If there are not enough leading zeroes in the first operand to hold the second operand, the MP instruction causes a data exception (0C7).

Enough leading zeroes means enough to hold the entire second operand. So, for a 3-byte second operand, there must be at least six leading zeroes (3 bytes worth).

As an additional limit, the second operand may not be longer than 15 digits (8 bytes) or a specification exception (0C6) will occur. An MP of negative zero by positive zero yields a result of negative zero.

11.5.5 Divide Decimal

Divide Packed (opcode DP) requires similar field sizing to MP. DP is much more complex, however, and many assembler programmers must refer to the principles of operations manual to code it. The complexity of Divide Packed comes from the way in which three of the mathematical quantities in the divide operation are handled.

Four numbers participate in a divide operation: the dividend, divisor, quotient, and remainder. Divide packed puts three of those into the same field: the dividend, quotient, and remainder. So, in addition to the sizing needed for MP, you must also calculate the lengths of the quotient and remainder, which together replace the dividend.

An example is probably the easiest way to explain this. Given the following starting values:

```
INNINGS    DC      PL5'9'              (Hex X'000000009C')
BASES      DC      PL2'4'              (Hex X'004C')
```

Remember that 9 divided by 4 produces a quotient of 2 and a remainder of 1. When we execute

DP   INNINGS,BASES

the fields are changed to:

INNINGS becomes hexadecimal X'00002C001C'

BASES stays hexadecimal X'004C'

Note that the INNINGS field now holds two packed decimal numbers rather than one. The first, the quotient, is in the first 3 bytes of INNINGS (the hexadecimal X'00002C' part). The second, the remainder, is in the last two bytes of INNINGS (the hexadecimal X'001C' part).

As a result of two numbers being placed where one was originally kept, you must go through some special operations to extract these results. We will cover these as part of Chap. 13.

11.5.6   Scaling in Packed Decimal Arithmetic

The COBOL compiler automatically handles certain aspects of mathematical calculations for you. One of these is the positioning of the decimal point. To accomplish this in assembler, we have to do some additional planning.

For example, consider the following COBOL calculation:

77	BATTING-AVERAGE	PIC 9V999 USAGE COMP-3.
77	TIMES-AT-BAT	PIC 9(5) USAGE COMP-3.
77	TOTAL-HITS	PIC 9(5) USAGE COMP-3.

DIVIDE TIMES-AT-BAT INTO TOTAL-HITS GIVING
BATTING-AVERAGE.

This presents some problems with what we've learned up to this point. All the arithmetic operations we've covered have applied to integer arithmetic. Here, however, we must calculate a fractional result. (The happy result of a hitter with a batting average of 1.000 is the only exception.)

If we redefine the fields given above in assembler, and supply some initial values, we have

BATTING_AVERAGE	DC	PL6'0'	(Hexadecimal X'00000000000C')
TIMES_AT_BAT	DC	PL3'99'	(Hexadecimal X'00099C')
TOTAL_HITS	DC	PL3'21'	(Hexadecimal X'00021C')

Note that we had to redefine BATTING-AVERAGE as 6 bytes rather than the three needed to hold the possible number of digits.

Now, if we just compute the batting average as we have in the examples up to now, we would code

ZAP   BATTING_AVERAGE,TOTAL_HITS
DP   BATTING_AVERAGE,TIMES_AT_BAT

after which BATTING_AVERAGE would contain hexadecimal X'00000C00021C'.

The result we want is 21 divided by 99, or 0.212. Instead we got 0, with a remainder of 21.

To get the number we want from the division, we need to change the relationship of the numbers to change the relative position of the implied decimal point. The way to do this is to introduce the same number of trailing zeroes as we want of positions to the right of the decimal point.

For our example, we want 3 digits to the right of the decimal point. Thus, we have to add three trailing zeroes to the value in TOTAL_HITS. This has the effect of making it 21.000, rather than 21.

The easiest way to do this is to use the MP instruction. So, let's add a field with a value of 1000 to get three trailing zeroes as follows:

```
BATTING_AVERAGE DC   PL6'0'      (Hexadecimal X'00000000000C')
TIMES_AT_BAT    DC   PL3'99'     (Hexadecimal X'00099C')
TOTAL_HITS      DC   PL3'21'     (Hexadecimal X'00021C')
THREE_DIGITS    DC   PL3'1000'   (Hexadecimal X'01000C')
```

And let's redo our instructions:

```
ZAP   BATTING_AVERAGE,TOTAL_HITS
MP    BATTING_AVERAGE,THREE_DIGITS
DP    BATTING_AVERAGE,TIMES_AT_BAT
```

After the ZAP instruction, BATTING_AVERAGE contains hexadecimal X'00000000021C'. After the MP instruction, it contains hexadecimal X'00000021000C'. Finally, after the DP instruction, it contains hexadecimal X'00212C00012C'.

Thus, we finally have our desired quotient — 0.212 — and a remainder of 12. Note that we still have to remember where the implied decimal point is — something that COBOL did for us.

When it becomes time to print or display the number, we can use the Edit instruction to properly position the decimal point for output. We'll discuss this in Chap. 13.

11.5.7   Decimal Arithmetic Summary

This brings to a close our discussion of arithmetic in both binary and packed decimal forms. You may feel that the arithmetic in assembler is more complex than what you desire. That's partly true.

Arithmetic in assembler offers a few additional features. For example, you can define 31-digit fields with packed decimal arithmetic in assembler. COBOL limits you to 18 digits. For some situations, this is absolutely necessary.

For most typical programming chores, however, there is no major performance advantage when using assembler. Certain types of array or table processing are often more efficient in assembler. In most cases, though, you will be able to code extensive calculations faster and easier in COBOL than in assembler.

11.6 ARITHMETIC ESOTERICA

As with other assembler features, there are several unique facilities available in assembler which may not have a direct equivalent in COBOL. Conversely, one COBOL feature which has no direct assembler equivalent is the CORRESPONDING option for the ADD and SUBTRACT verbs.

11.6.1 Using Shift Instructions

A common assembler technique is to use the shift instructions rather than a multiply or divide when dealing with binary numbers.

All CPUs have some form of shift instruction. Shifts are used to manipulate data in registers and allow the programmer to deal with units of information in sizes other than byte, halfword, or fullword. Shift instructions have three possible attributes in the 370 design:

Direction:	Left or Right	(Movement of bits)
Size:	Single or Double	(Number of registers, 1 or 2)
Type:	Algebraic or Logical	(How sign bit is handled)

Shifts have two operands: The first operand specifies a register or even-odd register pair, and the second operand specifies the number of bits to shift. Thus, " SLL 7,10 " specifies a shift left logical of register 7 for 10 bits.

Bits shifted out of a register are lost — they go into the "bit bucket". In double shifts, bits shifted out of one register will go into the other depending on the direction of the shift.

The condition code is not set for logical shifts, but is for algebraic shifts. *Logical* shifts process all 32 (or 64) bits as data; *algebraic* shifts do not process the sign bit. The specific shift instruction op codes are:

SLL	Shift Left Logical
SRL	Shift Right Logical
SLDL	Shift Left Double Logical
SRDL	Shift Right Double Logical
SLA	Shift Left Algebraic
SRA	Shift Right Algebraic
SLDA	Shift Left Double Algebraic
SRDA	Shift Right Double Algebraic

Left shifts have the effect of multiplying by a power of 2; right shifts divide by a power of 2. Shifts are often used in place of the more CPU-intensive Multiply or Divide instructions. Figure 11.5 shows how the SLL instruction can be used to multiply a number in a register by 4.

Double right shifts permit the remainder to be extracted into the odd-numbered register. Thus, " SRDA 6,3 " has the effect of dividing the number in register 6 by 8 (2**3). " SRL 3,29 " positions the "remainder" from that right shift to the low-order bit positions of register 7. (29 = 32 bits minus 3 already shifted.)

In general, you should stick to the binary instructions we've covered up to this point. However, if you come across these in programs you are maintaining, you will have some idea what they do.

Figure 11.5 Example of Shift Left Logical.

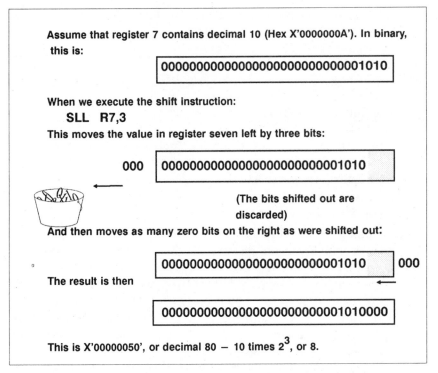

Assume that register 7 contains decimal 10 (Hex X'0000000A'). In binary, this is:

00000000000000000000000000001010

When we execute the shift instruction:

SLL   R7,3

This moves the value in register seven left by three bits:

000   00000000000000000000000001010

(The bits shifted out are discarded)

And then moves as many zero bits on the right as were shifted out:

00000000000000000000000001010   000

The result is then

00000000000000000000000001010000

This is X'00000050', or decimal 80 — 10 times 2^3, or 8.

There is also a packed decimal shift instruction — SRP, or Shift and Round Decimal. SRP shifts a number within its own storage area.

The first operand specifies the field to be shifted. The second operand is the number of positions to shift, in the range of +31 to -32. A positive number is treated as a left shift, and a negative number as a right shift. A value of 0 causes no shift.

Only the low-order 6 bits of the second operand value are considered. The second operand format is D2(B2), so the shift amount can be specified in a register.

The third operand of SRP is a rounding value used with the right shifts only. A rounding value of 5 provides normal rounding, 0 (zero) provides truncation of the shifted digits, and 9 will force the next higher number. The rounding digit is added to the leftmost of the digits which are shifted out.

For example, "   SRP   FLDA,3   " will shift the packed decimal number in FLDA 3 digit positions to the left (equivalent to multiplying by 1000). As such, this may be used instead of MP when setting up numbers as we did for the batting average calculation above.

Some second operand values and their actions include the following:

1 =	left 1 digit =	multiply by 10
2 =	left 2 digits =	multiply by 100
31 =	left 31 digits =	clears field
32 =	right 32 digits =	clears field
62 =	right 2 digits =	divide by 100
63 =	right 1 digit =	divide by 10

A shift value of 31 or 32 is equivalent to " ZAP FLDA,=P'0' " or " SP FLDA,FLDA ".

In addition, an older instruction, Move with Offset (opcode MVO) was commonly used to perform packed decimal shifts. In general, the 370 SRP instruction is preferable to this.

COBOL uses SRP when moving COMP-3 fields which have different implied decimal point locations.

11.6.2   Using SRDA with Binary Divide Operations

One nuance of binary divide operations is that the instruction deals with a 64-bit signed quantity rather than 32 bits. An imprecise coding technique, which normally works correctly, frequently arises when we need to divide a fullword value by some other number. The following code is an example:

```
L      R3,DIVIDEND          NUMBER TO DIVIDE
SR     R2,R2                SET REG 2 TO ZERO
D      R2,DIVISOR           DIVIDE BY DIVISOR
```

This works just fine with positive numbers. If DIVIDEND happens to be a negative number, though, this code generates an incorrect result.

The reason behind this is that the divide instruction expects a 64-bit number. What this code does is to provide a 32-bit number (in register 3) preceded by 32 bits of zeroes.

If DIVIDEND is negative, it needs to be preceded by 32 bits of ones to properly follow two's complement rules. The SRDA — Shift Right Double Algebraic — instruction can accomplish this. It will properly set up the second register for a divide for both positive and negative cases.

The code to use SRDA looks like the following:

```
L      R2,DIVIDEND          NUMBER TO DIVIDE
SRDA   R2,32                SHIFT = 64-BIT NUM
D      R2,DIVISOR           DIVIDE BY DIVISOR
```

SRDA is the only correct way of setting up for the DR or D instructions if the dividend may be negative.

11.6.3   Logical Arithmetic

Logical arithmetic in the IBM 370 means unsigned binary arithmetic, that is, 32-bit numbers versus 31-bit signed numbers as in algebraic (regular) arithmetic. Logical arithmetic does not provide for negative numbers. Only absolute values may be manipulated. Logical arithmetic allows for computation with very large binary numbers.

Add, subtract, and comparison instructions are provided in register-to-register and register-to-storage formats. Uses for these instructions are strictly for arithmetic of binary numbers longer than 31 bits. They are not frequently used. The logical arithmetic instructions and their closest equivalent op codes are:

Op Code	Instruction Name	Equivalent Op Code
AL	Add Logical	A
ALR	Add Logical Register	AR
CL	Compare Logical	C
CLR	Compare Logical Register	CR
SL	Subtract Logical	S
SLR	Subtract Logical Register	SR

Logical arithmetic may also be used to add or subtract without overflow. Thus, " ALR   R2,R3 " is equivalent to " AR   R2,R3 ".

COBOL uses these instructions when processing COMP numbers with picture clauses in the range of S9(9) to S9(18).

11.6.4   Vector Operations Explanation

We will not cover the 51 floating-point instructions in this book. The IBM 3090 also has an optional vector processing feature which adds 93 instructions.

Vector processing allows one instruction to do the same operation to all the entries in an array. In some ways, it is similar to the CORRESPONDING option in COBOL, but not identical. Vector processing is more efficient for many highly mathematical processes, such as processing geological field data in petrochemical companies.

All of the vector instructions have names like Vector Multiply and Add and opcodes like VMAD. They may be easily identified, since the opcodes all begin with the letter V.

If you want to find out more about these, refer to the IBM manual *IBM System/370 Vector Operations*, form number SA22-7125.

11.7   SUMMARY

At this point, you should understand the representation of positive and negative numbers in both packed decimal and binary formats. You should also understand what each of the 15 main arithmetic instructions do, and know when to use each.

We have covered four COBOL verbs in this chapter — ADD, SUB-TRACT, MULTIPLY, and DIVIDE. You may have chosen not to use these verbs in your own coding, selecting the COMPUTE verb instead. However, the structure of COMPUTE is composed of these four arithmetic operators. You should be able to convert a COBOL COMPUTE verb to its equivalent assembler form with the items we have covered in this chapter.

Things to Do

1. If you have located a production assembler program from your shop, look through it to see if you can understand the arithmetic operations from what you've learned in this chapter.
2. Look for uses of the esoterica in production programs. The shifts and MVO are fairly common.
3. Look for a D or DR binary divide instruction. How is the setup of the first operand even-odd register pair performed? Do they use SRDA? Is there a test for a possible negative value?

Branching and Control

If you aren't familiar with these terms, branching refers to the transfer of control within a program. GO TO and PERFORM provide branching facilities in COBOL.

Control refers to conditional branching, or controlling branching based on comparisons or other indeterminate conditions (i.e., which instruction gets control next). COBOL provides the IF statement for this purpose.

In this chapter, we will learn what assembler facilities correspond to these COBOL facilities. Additionally, we'll look at how some other COBOL facilities have assembler equivalents.

12.1 DIFFERENT CONCEPTS IN PROGRAM CONTROL

COBOL provides many clauses in the language which are executed only under certain conditions. The THEN or ELSE clauses of IF are the best example. Other common examples include the AT END clause of the READ verb and the ON SIZE ERROR of arithmetic statements.

In assembler, there is no similar automatic bypassing of instructions. The programmer is responsible for testing for each of the conditions which may occur, and for providing an instruction to transfer control to the appropriate instructions.

COBOL provides several branching verbs, including the following:

- GO TO
- IF
- PERFORM
- EVALUATE (VS COBOL II)
- EXIT
- STOP
- ALTER

While the last three don't actually transfer from one part of the program to another, they still affect the operation of the others. There are also reasonably convenient assembler equivalents to these.

The verb with the most direct assembler equivalent is GO TO. The assembler branch instructions provide a one-to-one correspondence with GO TO.

The COBOL IF statement has a reasonable set of equivalents in assembler. However, several instructions are usually required to fully match the functions of COBOL's IF statement. The assembler comparison instructions, and the 370 condition code must also be included in that evaluation.

The COBOL PERFORM has a similar, but not direct equivalent in the assembler Branch and Save instruction. The assembler implementation of this function requires that the programmer consider certain linkage instructions.

EXIT, a COBOL feature associated with PERFORM, provides termination processing for performed paragraphs or sections, or for complete programs. EXIT is optional in COBOL, but is equivalent to a mandatory function for PERFORM-like logic in assembler.

STOP is classified as a procedure branching statement in COBOL, and will be discussed with the others here. While not used as frequently as the other statements, STOP is similar to EXIT in its assembler implementation.

Finally, the ALTER statement provides a unique — some would say dreaded — method of changing the flow of control in a COBOL program. The assembler equivalent is equally difficult to maintain, but will be discussed for completeness.

The subsections which follow will describe the assembler equivalents for these COBOL verbs in the above order. A basic introduction to each will be given. The esoterica section will then cover some of the more complex options in COBOL and what assembler language programming techniques apply to them.

12.2   GO TO AND THE ASSEMBLER BRANCH INSTRUCTION
The assembler equivalent of GO TO is the Branch instruction (opcode B). Where you might code something like

        GO TO READ2.

In assembler, you would code

        B   READ2

Logically, the branch instruction works just like GO TO in COBOL.

12.3   THE COBOL IF STATEMENT IN ASSEMBLER
The COBOL IF has no single equivalent instruction in assembler. You may simulate the effect by coding multiple instructions.

There are many ways to code the equivalent of an IF statement in assembler. We'll discuss several here, but you will have to evaluate each situation and code the most efficient test — that's programming.

The general approach we'll discuss here is to assume that you have some program logic which can be expressed as

```
IF    condition
THEN    then_ part
ELSE    else_ part.
```

In assembler, selection of the *then_part* logic or the *else_ part* logic requires a conditional branch instruction. Prior to taking the branch, you must also code some instruction — usually a comparison — which sets the condition code to indicate the outcome of the instruction. Thus, we can generally code COBOL IF-statement logic in assembler as something like:

```
        Comparison
        B_NOT_TRUE ELSE0001
        then_ part
        B        END_IF_0001
ELSE0001    EQU    *
        else_ part
END_IF_0001 EQU   *
```

What this says is that you should code a comparison, and branch to a label (ELSE0001) at the *else_ part* of your logic if the comparison is not true. If the comparison is true, fall through to the *then_ part*, then branch around the *else_ part* to the end of the IF statement logic (END_IF_0001). If we were to flowchart this, it would look like Figure 12.1.

The labels ELSE0001 and END_IF_0001 could be any desired labels. Use of a 4-digit suffix lets you use the same labels without having to think up new meaningful names.

Indenting in assembler is okay, since assembler follows a free-form syntax. Some programmers begin their opcodes earlier than in the normal position (10), which allows them more levels of indenting. Other programmers may find this irksome.

Figure 12.1   IF-THEN-ELSE sequence.

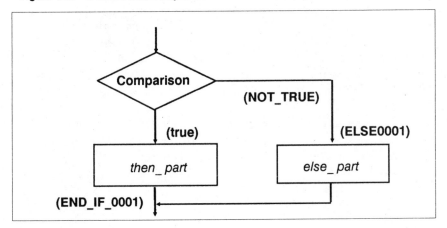

The remainder of this section will cover the comparison instructions in the 370. Before going over those in detail, though, we must first explain their primary output — the 370 condition code.

12.3.1 The Condition Code

To do any conditional branching (i.e., IF statements), you must create a condition which can be evaluated as true or false. The CPU then branches if the condition is true.

However, many instructions have more than two possible outcomes. For example, arithmetic instructions have four possible outcomes: the result may be positive, negative, or zero, or there may be an overflow if the result is too big for the receiving field (COBOL SIZE ERROR).

Many computers handle this situation by providing several separate true-false flag bits which may be tested individually. As an example, the Intel 8086 (IBM PC architecture) has a 16-bit flags register, with separate bit settings for the conditions of overflow, zero, sign (positive/negative), carry, and auxiliary carry, among others.

The 370 approaches this by providing one central flag for all conditions, called the *condition code*. The condition code may take one of four values, 0 through 3. The condition is kept as a 2-bit number, with particular types or classes of results keyed to one of these values.

For example, a condition code of 0 means that the result was 0 following an arithmetic operation. The same condition code of 0 following a comparison instruction means that the first and second operands were equal. Other instructions have other meanings for condition code 0.

Thus, arithmetic instructions can have four general classes of results: zero, positive, negative, or overflow (result too large for receiving field). Addition and subtraction instructions of all types (binary, packed decimal, floating-point) all set these four condition codes.

Similarly, comparison instructions may have three results: the first operand may be greater than, equal to, or less than the second operand.

See the 370 reference summary (the yellow card) for a list of instructions and condition codes. The condition code is kept in the PSW, in bits 18-19 in EC mode and 34-35 in BC mode. (*EC mode* is used with all virtual storage operating systems, e.g., MVS/ESA, MVS/XA, and MVS/SP. *BC mode* was used with much older systems (e.g., OS/MVT), and may be provided to VM CMS virtual machines, depending on how your account's directory is defined.)

To put the condition code to work, the 370 provides one branch instruction: Branch on Condition (opcode BC). BC tests the current condition code against a *branch mask* coded as an operand of BC. If the branch mask and the condition code match, the branch is taken. If the code and the mask do not match, no branch is taken.

The branch mask is a number, 0 through 15, which is matched to the results of a preceding instruction as expressed in the condition code. The 4-bit mask is used to specify which of the four possible code values should cause a branch. This also allows for multiple conditions and negative (not) conditions to be more easily specified.

The assembler assigns a particular value to each of the 4 bits in the mask. These, in turn, specify one of the four possible condition codes. A condition code of 0 is tested by coding a mask value of 8. A condition code of 1 is tested by coding a mask value of 4. Condition codes 2 and 3 are tested by coding 2 and 1 in the mask, respectively.

Figure 12.2 shows the relationship between the branch mask and the PSW condition code.

Figure 12.2   BC mask and condition code.

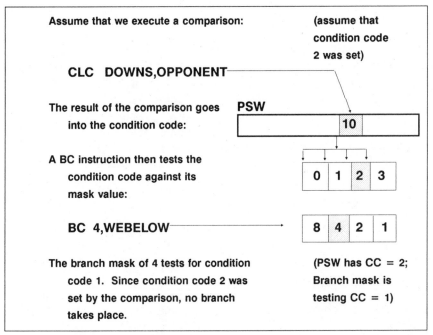

You may test for several conditions at the same time by adding the appropriate mask values. For example, a mask value of 12 tests for condition codes 0 (mask value 8) and 1 (mask value 4).

As another example, a branch mask of 7 after an addition instruction means to branch if the condition code is 1 ("4" bit) or 2 ("2" bit) or 3 ("1" bit). This corresponds to conditions of result negative, result positive, and overflow. This is equivalent to branching if the result was not 0.

As another example, assuming that the condition code was currently 1, the following instruction would branch to LOW:

```
BC    4,LOW
```

and would branch to a label in your program called LOW.

There is also an RR-format version of the Branch on Condition instruction, with an opcode of BCR.

12.3.2   An Easier Way of Branching

If your eyelids have been getting heavier and heavier while reading through the preceding discussion of the condition code and the BC instruction, you will be relieved to know that there is an easier way to do it. The assembler provides several *extended mnemonics*, which it automatically translates into the appropriate BC instruction and branch mask for you.

For example, assume that we wish to branch to a label called HIGH if the condition code is 2 (high). Thus, instead of coding

```
BC    2,HIGH
```

we could code

```
BH    HIGH
```

and get exactly the same effect.

Some of the extended mnemonics are listed in Table 12.1. A full list is shown in the assembler language reference manual and in the 370 reference summary. Note that all of these have opposite forms, indicated by adding an 'N' following the 'B' in the mnemonic name. For example, "BNE" means "Branch Not Equal" and is the opposite form of "BE".

Table 12.1   Some Extended Mnemonic Codes and Meanings

Mnemonic	Meaning	BC code
B	Branch (always)	15
BH	Branch if 1st operand is high	2
BL	Branch if 1st operand is low	4
BE	Branch if 1st and 2nd operands equal	8
BZ	Branch if result is zero	8
BM	Branch if result is negative (minus)	4
BP	Branch if result is positive	2
BO	Branch if result overflowed	1

In addition to the mnemonic forms shown in Table 12.1, there are also RR-format equivalents for the BCR instruction. These are indicated by coding an "R" at the end of the extended mnemonic. The most common of these is BR (Branch Register) which corresponds to the "B" (Branch) extended mnemonic.

Most assembler programmers use these opcodes rather than coding a BC instruction. Extended mnemonics are usually OK, but don't work following all instructions.

For example, instructions called Test and Set (opcode TS) and Exclusive Or (XC) don't set the condition code in a way to logically match the extended mnemonic BO, which might reasonably be used with them. As a result, you should only use these following arithmetic, or comparison instructions for now.

Also, not all instructions set the condition code. (For example, Multiply and Divide instructions don't set the condition code.) Refer to the 370 reference summary to find out which ones do.

12.3.3   Comparison Instructions

As we mentioned earlier, you normally provide some kind of comparison instruction at the beginning of an IF-type structure in assembler language. The IBM 370 architecture provides several types of comparison instructions. These vary based on the type of data being compared. They all begin with the letter "C", for compare.

You may often choose more than one comparison instruction to develop a specific test. Table 12.2 shows a matrix of data types. For each combination of data types, a preferred instruction or set of instructions is shown. In addition, the instructions necesary to get one of the fields into the same format as the other is shown.

For example, if you wanted to compare a packed decimal field to a fullword binary field, you would need to use a Convert to Decimal (CVD) instruction to get one operand changed from binary to packed decimal. After doing that, you would use the Compare Decimal (CP) instruction to actually compare the fields.

There may be more than one likely way of programming other comparisons. For example, when comparing a fullword binary (type F) value to a halfword binary value (type H), you will have to have one of the values in a register. To do this comparison if both values are in storage, you could load the halfword into a register with an LH instruction, then do a fullword compare (C) to the fullword. If the fullword operand is already in a register, then only a Compare Halfword (CH) instruction is needed.

Table 12.2, unfortunately, must refer to instructions which we haven't completely covered yet.

12.3.3.1   Compare

The Compare instruction — opcode C — compares the value in a register to a fullword of data in storage. For example, given the following values:

Register 2: Hexadecimal X'00000011' (decimal 17)

```
DOZEN        DC       F'12'                          (Hex X'0000000C')
```

After the execution of

      C   R2,DOZEN

the condition code would be 2 (first operand high). The Compare instruction is used only to compare binary numbers.

Table 12.2   Comparison Instructions for Various Data Types

Data types:	Fullword binary	Halfword binary	Packed decimal	Character field	Group item
Fullword binary	L plus C or CR	CH or LH + C	CVD + CP	CVD + UNPK + OI + CLC	N.A.
Halfword binary	LH + C or CH	LH plus CH	LH + CVD + CP	LH + CVD + UNPK + OI + CLC	N.A.
Packed decimal	CVB + C or CR	CVB + CH	CP	UNPK + OI + CLC	N.A.
Character field	PACK + CVB + C/CR	PACK + CVB + CH/CR	PACK + CP	CLC	CLC or CLCL
Group item	N.A.	N.A.	N.A.	CLC or CLCL	CLCL

12.3.3.2 Compare Halfword

Compare Halfword (CH) copies a halfword of data from storage, expands it to a fullword, and compares the resulting fullword to the the value in the first operand register. Like LH, CH expands the halfword to a fullword by copying the sign bit into the extra leading 2 bytes to make a fullword. This maintains the proper positive or negative value of the original halfword number. (See Fig. 13.2 in the next chapter for some idea of how this works.)

For example, with the following initial contents:

Register 3: Hexadecimal X'00000003' (decimal 3)

STOOGES   DC   H'3'   (Hex X'0003')

After executing

      CH   R3,STOOGES

the condition code would be 0 (the values of the fields are equal).

As with the LH instruction, you must ensure that you do not accidentally have a mismatch between the compare instruction used and the type of data actually in storage. This would arise when using CH to compare with a field defined as type F, or when using the C instruction with a field defined as type H.

For example, given the following fields:

```
MUSKETEERS DC   H'3'
MUSES       DC   F'9'
```

the first compare halfword below is valid — the second will not give proper results.

```
        CH    R4,MUSKETEERS        VALID COMPARISON
        CH    R4,MUSES             BAD COMPARISON
```

The comparison to MUSKETEERS is identical to our previous examples of CH and is proper. The second CH will assemble correctly, but will always compare to the leftmost 2 bytes of the fullword at MUSES. Since MUSES had an initial value of 9, the leftmost 2 bytes would be zeroes. Thus, this comparison would be incorrect — but would work properly some times. This bug — confusing fullword and halfword operands — is not uncommon.

12.3.3.3 Compare Register

Compare Register — opcode CR — performs a compare operation on two fullwords, both of which are in registers. It operates like the Compare instruction with the exception of the second operand location.

For example, with these initial contents:

Register 8: Hexadecimal X'00000028' (Decimal 40)
Register 9: Hexadecimal X'00000036' (Decimal 54)

After executing

```
        CR    R8,R9
```

the condition code would be set to 1 (first operand low).

12.3.3.4 Compare Logical

The Compare Logical (CLC) operation has several forms. The CLC opcode is for comparison between two fields in storage of the same size. CLC does not pad either operand with blanks when the sizes differ.

CLC is a storage-to-storage instruction and compares from 1 to 256 bytes. The comparison proceeds left to right, bit by bit. CLC should only be used to compare character fields or group items.

It should not be used to compare binary or packed decimal numbers. The reason for this is that positive and negative numbers will not compare properly when using CLC.

As an example, with the following starting values:

```
MINUS    DC    CL6'MINUS'
MINUTE   DC    C'MINUTE'
```

After executing

```
        CLC   MINUS,MINUTE
```

the condition code would be 1 (first operand low).

As discussed before, the CLC instruction only compares correctly with equal-length fields. CLC compares the number of bytes that are in the first operand. If the second operand is longer, not all of the bytes will be compared. This is in sharp contrast to the COBOL practice of comparing as though the shorter field were padded with blanks.

If the first operand is longer than the second operand, CLC will compare for as many bytes as are in the first operand. In this case, the ending bytes of the first operand will be compared to whatever follows the second operand in storage. This normally does not produce the desired comparison result.

Two examples will show how this works. First, the case where the first operand is longer than the second operand:

```
MONTH     DC     C'MAY'
CLINIC    DC     C'MAYO'
```
After executing
```
CLC    MONTH,CLINIC
```
the condition code would be 0, indicating that the two operands were equal. Because MONTH is only 3 bytes long, only the first 3 bytes of CLINIC are considered, hence the incorrect comparison (by COBOL standards).

The next example covers the situation where the first operand is longer than the second operand. Given the following initial contents:

```
PLUGGED   DC     CL6'NICKEL'
CUT       DC     CL4'NICK'
CIRCLE    DC     C'CIRCLE'
```
When executing
```
CLC    PLUGGED,CUT
```
the condition code would be set to 2 (first operand high). This happens to be correct, since we are comparing the 6- byte value "NICKEL" to the 6 bytes in storage containing "NICKCI" (beginning at the label CUT). However, if the fields were coded as:

```
PLUGGED   DC     CL6'NICKEL'
CUT       DC     CL4'NICK'
SQUARE    DC     C'SQUARE'
```
The condition code would be set to 1 (first operand low). This is not the case.To avoid this type of problem, you should always make sure that you are comparing fields of equal length.

12.3.3.5   Immediate Form of Compare Logical

The 370 also provides the Compare Logical instruction in the Storage Immediate, or SI format. The opcode for this is CLI, usually referred to by assembler programmers as *Compare Logical Immediate*. The second operand for CLI is a 1-byte constant contained in the instruction itself. Thus, CLI provides a comparison with a 1-byte operand which you code in the instruction.

As an example, given the following initial values:

CD_NAME   DC   C'COMPACT DISK'

After executing

    CLI   CD_NAME,C'C'

the condition code would be set to 0 (first and second operands are equal).

Note that CLI always compares only 1 byte. The length of the first operand doesn't matter. Thus, CLI is only equivalent to COBOL statements like

    IF   CD-NAME = 'C'

if CD-NAME is defined as PIC X.

12.3.3.6 Comparing Packed Decimal Fields

As discussed previously, CLC is not appropriate for comparing packed decimal fields. It doesn't handle different length fields, and the sign is not processed properly. To compare these as numbers, the 370 provides the Compare Decimal instruction (opcode CP).

CP handles fields of variable lengths and performs the proper comparison. It takes the sign into account, and a negative packed decimal number will compare as lower than a positive one. Both the first and second operands must be valid packed decimal numbers, or a data exception (MVS 0C7) will occur.

If the operands differ in length, CP will process the comparison as though the shorter operand was padded with leading zeroes. In doing so, it acts more like a COBOL IF statement comparison.

As an example, assume that you have the following beginning values of:

OLDER1 DC   PL3'3083'   (Hex X'03083C')
NEWER1 DC   PL4'3090'   (Hex X'0003090C')

After executing

    CP   OLDER1,NEWER1

the condition code would be set to 1 (first operand low).

You may find instances of assembler language programs with CLC used in place of CP. This only works if both fields are the same length and only when comparing positive numbers. You should usually replace these with CP.

12.4   PERFORM IN ASSEMBLER

Implementing the equivalent of PERFORM in assembler usually requires use of the Branch And Save (BAS) instruction or its older equivalents. BAS is similar, but not directly equivalent to the COBOL PERFORM. As when implementing any other COBOL-like function in assembler, several steps need to be considered.

Most COBOL programmers tend to separate PERFORMed paragraphs from other codes. However, COBOL is unique among computer languages in allowing the programmer to execute a paragraph or section as both in-line and out-of-line code.

We'll discuss how to implement "PERFORMed" code in assembler. We shall refer to this type of code as *internal subroutines*. (Also, we'll capitalize PERFORM when referring to the actual COBOL verb, and express it in lowercase when referring to the concept.)

So, how do we execute an internal subroutine? And how does that differ from COBOL PERFORM? In general, to execute a subroutine, you need to:

1. Know the address of the subroutine (not a big deal if it's in your own program)
2. Be able to tell the subroutine where the data is
3. Be able to tell the subroutine how to branch back to the right place in your program
4. Ensure that the subroutine will restore the context in which it was originally executing (i.e., not have any unknown side effects and restore appropriate register contents)

Let's look at how we can do all of these things.

For the first requirement, if you're using a subroutine inside your own program, you'll be referring to a label which you've already defined in your program. No problem.

Second, if the data is all inside your program, the subroutine should be able to get to your own labels. Again, no problem.

If, however, your subroutine deals with data whose address may vary — a specific entry in a table, for instance — you need to plan how to pass the correct address. Usually, a register is used for this.

For the third requirement, the internal subroutine needs to know how to branch back to the point in your program which invoked it. To do this, we need a new series of instructions.

Branch And Save provides us with a branch instruction which remembers where it was used. BAS is coded as:

```
BAS    register,label
```

BAS does two things. The first is to load the address of the next instruction (the one following the BAS) into the register specified in the instruction. The second is to branch to the second operand, just like the B opcode. (Note that some IBM CPUs do not support this instruction; in that case, you should use Branch and Link - opcode BAL.)

By convention, register 14 is most frequently used as the first operand register. Other registers may be used, although register 0 is a poor choice since you can't branch back using that. We'll use register 14 for all of our examples in this book.

BAS by itself does not provide a complete equivalent to PERFORM. The internal subroutine must also do some work. First, it must save the *return address* set up by BAS. (Use ST to save it during the subroutine.) Second, it must branch back to that address. The BR opcode is commonly used to do this.

An example of BAS follows. This shows an internal subroutine being used to print a new page heading line and update the page number. Assume that the BAS instruction is located at address X'00109000':

	BAS	R14,NEWPAGE	WRITE PAGE HDG
	MVC	P_REC,RECORD_IN	MOVE TO PRINT
NEWPAGE	EQU	*	PAGE HEADING RTN
	ST	R14,NEWPAGER	SAVE CALLER'S R14
	PUT	SYSPRINT,HEADING	WRITE HDG LINE
	AP	PAGENUM,ONE	ADD 1 TO PAGE CT
	UNPK	HEADPAGE,PAGENUM	UNPACK INTO HDG
	OI	HEADPAGE+3,X'F0'	SET SIGN BITS
	L	R14,NEWPAGER	GET RET ADDR
	BR	R14	BRANCH BACK
NEWPAGER	DS	F	SAVE RET ADDR

(The other data areas are not shown.) After execution of the BAS instruction, register 14 will contain hex X'00109004' — the address of the MVC instruction. (BAS and all other RX-format instructions are 4 bytes long.) Since BAS branches to the second operand address, the next statement executed would be the Store of register 14 following the NEWPAGE label.

At the end of the NEWPAGE internal subroutine, the Load instruction gets the address that BAS originally put into register 14. The BR opcode which follows will branch back to whatever address is in register 14, which points to the MVC instruction following the BAS.

Some notes are appropriate here on saving the return address. Some internal subroutines don't modify the register used with the BAS instruction. As a result, they don't need to save and restore it. However, our NEWPAGE routine used the PUT macro, which changes register 14. As a general rule, it's best to save the return address anyway, since future changes to the program may affect the contents of the register.

Another use of the BAS instruction is to establish a base register. BAS has a companion RR-format opcode, BASR, in which the second operand is a register number rather than a label. One of the nuances of the register form of BAS is that it will not branch if the second operand is register 0, but will still store the address of the next instruction in the first operand register.

This side effect is widely used to determine where a program actually is in storage, and hence to establish a base register. For example,

```
BASR   R12,0
USING  *,R12
```

This puts the address of the next instruction into register 12. The USING directive tells the assembler that register 12 has that address and can be used as a base register.

12.4.1 The Branch and Link Instruction

While we've used BAS for our examples, and will use it predominantly in this book, almost all of the assembler programs you may see or maintain don't use BAS. Most use an instruction called Branch And Link. Why do they use BAL, and why does this book tell you to use BAS?

The answer to the first question lies in the history of the IBM 370 architecture. In 1964, the only linkage instruction originally provided with the System/360 was Branch and Link. (It has two opcodes, BAL and BALR for the register form.) Thus, historically, BAL was the only linkage instruction assembler programmers learned.

IBM added the Branch and Save instruction in the late 1960s. Branch and Save works like BAL, but stores a 31-bit address rather than 24-bit address. BAS was originally developed for the TSS (Time Sharing System) operating system in the late 1960s, was then provided in some 360s and early 370 machines, and finally put in most 370 CPUs. Since all the assembler programmers (except the very few who worked with TSS) only knew about BAL, few bothered to use BAS.

This situation changed in the 1980s, when IBM announced the MVS/XA operating system. XA, like TSS, uses 31-bit addressing. BAL works differently in the 24-bit and 31-bit addressing modes.

The answer to the second question, then, is that we use BAS in this book because it is preferable for IBM's newer operating systems. This may cause a lot of resistance from older, more experienced assembler programmers, who are still in the habit of using BAL. However, all future assembler programs should use BAS rather than BAL to avoid inconsistencies between the two addressing modes.

If your CPU does not have the Branch and Save instruction installed (e.g., some 4341s), you will receive an operation exception (MVS 0C1). In this case, you should use Branch and Link.

Branch and Link has some other side effects which are discussed in the esoterica section. BALR, the register form of BAL, is often used to establish a base register as was discussed with BASR. It may normally be replaced by BASR.

12.5 EXIT AND RETURNING FROM SUBROUTINES

The COBOL EXIT verb, marking the end of a section of performed code, may or may not cause a branch to be taken. EXIT, in its normal usage, will cause control to go back to the PERFORM statement which invoked the section or series of paragraphs. If EXIT is encountered by falling through (i.e., no PERFORM), it performs no operation.

There is no corresponding identical function in assembler. The second method of using EXIT — allowing code to fall through — is, in some ways, antithetical to the concept of internal subroutines.

The function of EXIT is normally performed by branching back to the invoking section of the program. This is done by restoring the return address and branching back. For example:

```
        L       R14,CLEAR14             GET RETURN ADDR
        BR      R14                     BRANCH BACK
```

This is from our earlier example.

Should you really need to both use a section of code as an internal subroutine, as well as execute it by falling through, there is a coding technique to do so. This is to set up the address of the instruction immediately following the subroutine and then execute the subroutine in the normal program flow.

As an example, let's do this with the NEWPAGE subroutine used earlier. To accomplish this, we will use the Load Address (LA) instruction, which will be covered in Chap. 14. Only the first and last lines have been added to the original routine:

```
        LA      R14,PAGEDONE            LA PAST 'NEWPAGE'
NEWPAGE EQU     *                       PAGE HEADING RTN
        ST      R14,NEWPAGER            SAVE CALLER'S R14
        ...     ...    ...
(body of routine not shown)
        L       R14,NEWPAGER            GET RETURN ADDR
        BR      R14                     BRANCH BACK
PAGEDONE EQU    *                       'FALL-THROUGH' ADDRESS
```

The LA instruction puts the address of the label 'PAGEDONE' into register 14. When 'NEWPAGE' is done, it restores that as the return address. When using this technique, you must also set up any variables used in the internal subroutine.

12.6   THE COBOL STOP VERB

COBOL defines the STOP verb as a control instruction, and we will cover it here for that reason. However, it really covers two functions which are covered in other chapters.

The more common use of STOP — to terminate the current program's execution — is discussed with the assembler RETURN macro in Chap. 14. This covers the use of subroutines, which is closer to the normal COBOL use of STOP.

The alternative use of STOP — to issue a message to the operator and halt execution of the program until receiving a response — is covered in Chap. 16. This discusses the assembler WTOR macro.

12.7   ALTER AND ASSEMBLER STATEMENT MODIFICATION

Many programmers have the widely held view that the ALTER verb is difficult to maintain and should be avoided. This view is not without some justification. Unfortunately for those holding that view, there is a directly corresponding technique in assembler. It is also difficult to maintain.·

The ALTER verb's function is closely related to a form of the GO TO verb, which is coded

```
PARAGRAPH-NAME.
GO TO.
```

This is then modified by coding

```
ALTER PARAGRAPH-NAME TO PROCEED TO PARAGRAPH-2.
```

This makes the original code act as though it had been coded

```
PARAGRAPH-NAME.
GO TO PARAGRAPH-2.
```

The assembler technique has a component which is similar in intent to the above format of GO TO. This is the assembler NOP (No-Operation) directive. It is more commonly called *No Op*. NOP is coded like a normal branch instruction, with the first operand being the statement you want to eventually branch to. For example:

```
LABEL NOP                          ROUTINE2
```

The NOP directive generates the equivalent of a " BC 0,ROUTINE2 ". If not modified, No-Operation does absolutely nothing. . . just like certain managers. . . .

The equivalent of the ALTER verb can then be simulated with the Move Immediate (MVI) or the Or Immediate (OI) instructions. Showing this with MVI, you would code

```
MVI    LABEL + 1,X'F0'
```

This has the effect of changing the NOP instruction at LABEL into an unconditional branch instruction. It does this by overlaying the branch mask of the instruction with the hex X'F', which causes a branch to be taken no matter what the condition code value is.

You may also see this technique used with the S-type address constant. In this case, the code would be something like

```
MVC    LABEL + 2(2),NEWADDR
```

Where the second operand is defined as

```
NEWADDR    DC      S(ROUTINE3)
```

The S-type address constant defines an address in base-and-displacement form. This is how assembler puts operand addresses in instructions. This has the effect of changing the original NOP to

```
LABEL      NOP     ROUTINE3
```

This technique is generally difficult to maintain since the program listing doesn't accurately reflect the program that actually runs. You should avoid coding using this technique. However, you may run across it in some older assembler programs, and should be aware of what it is doing.

12.8 ESOTERICA

The techniques presented in this section cover COBOL techniques and how to implement them in assembler, as well as certain infrequently-used instructions and techniques.

12.8.1 Compound IF Statements

The examples presented earlier only covered simple COBOL comparisons, that is, only one condition tested in the IF statement. Obviously, more complex comparisons occur often.

The type of connectives — AND, OR, NOT — determine how the compound test is coded. When testing multiple conditions connected by ANDs, you should code each separate test to branch to the *else_ part* if the condition is false. When testing conditions separated by ORs, you should code each test to branch to the next test if it is false, and to branch to the *then_ part* if true. NOT inverts the type of branch — you would code BNE if testing for an equal condition originally.

Let's work through two examples of this. Assume we have the following COBOL code, and that the variables A, B, C, and D are defined as PIC X:

```
IF  A > B  AND  C > D
THEN then_ part
ELSE else_ part.
```

Assuming that we've defined A, B, C, and D as " DS C ", we could code this in assembler as:

```
              CLC    A,B                    COMPARE A TO B
              BNH    ELSE_PART              A NOT HIGH = ELSE
              CLC    C,D                    COMPARE C TO D
              BNH    ELSE_PART              C NOT HIGH = ELSE
THEN_PART EQU    *
              then_ part
              B      END_IF
ELSE_PART EQU  *  else_ part
END_IF    EQU    *
```

Let's try another example with the OR connective. Assuming the same definitions as before:

```
IF  A > B  OR  C > D
THEN then_ part
ELSE else_ part.
```

In the AND connective example, we were able to immediately branch to the *else_ part* of the statement if either test was false. With the OR connective, we must code the program to make another test if the first part of the OR test was false. For example,

```
              CLC    A,B                    COMPARE A TO B
              BH     THEN_PART              HIGH = THEN PART
              CLC    C,D                    COMPARE C TO D
              BNH    ELSE_PART              NOT HIGH = ELSE
THEN_PART EQU    *
              then_ part
              B      END_IF
ELSE_PART EQU    *
              else_ part
END_IF    EQU    *
```

For complex tests, you may wish to flowchart the test before doing it in assembler.

12.8.2   Implementing PERFORM VARYING in Assembler

Assembler provides three instructions for automatic table handling loops. We will discuss these in Chap. 15. However, the following is provided if you wish to control execution of an internal subroutine with logic similar to that of PERFORM with the VARYING option.

Assume that we have a COBOL variable defined as

```
77   LOOP-CTR          PIC S9(3) COMP-3.
```

And assume that we have the following COBOL code:

```
PERFORM  ROUTINE1 VARYING LOOP-CTR FROM
         1 BY 1 UNTIL LOOP-CTR  10.
```

To do this in assembler, we need to break this loop into several parts, then code each of the parts as follows:

1. Initialize the variable (VARYING LOOP-CTR FROM 1)
2. Invoke the internal subroutine (PERFORM ROUTINE1)
3. Increase the variable (BY 1)
4. Test for loop termination (UNTIL LOOP-CTR 10)

Let's define our loop variable as follows:

```
LOOP_CTR   DS    PL2
ONE        DC    P'0'
TEN        DC    P'10'
```

Our equivalent of the PERFORM VARYING would look like the following:

```
*              INITIALIZE THE LOOP VARIABLE
               ZAP    LOOP_CTR,ONE
*              INVOKE THE INTERNAL SUBROUTINE
CALLIT    EQU    *
               BAS    R14,ROUTINE1
*              INCREMENTING THE VARIABLE
               AP     LOOP_CTR,ONE
*              TEST FOR LOOP TERMINATION
               CP     LOOP_CTR,TEN
               BNH    CALLIT
```

Loops normally involve manipulation of a table. In this case, the loop counter variable (LOOP_CTR in this example) provides an index into the table. The assembler BXLE or BXH instructions provide a more direct method for doing this.

Another variation of PERFORM, the TIMES option can be implemented in a similar way. In fact, the preceding example is equivalent to

```
PERFORM ROUTINE1 10 TIMES.
```

in COBOL. You must ensure that the loop counter variable is not modified during the loop's execution.

12.8.3   GO TO DEPENDING ON — The Branch Table Technique

COBOL provides a variation of the GO TO instruction which corresponds to the CASE structure of other languages (e.g., PASCAL). In CASE, a variable specifies which of a set of enumerated routines should be executed. The VS COBOL II EVALUATE verb is very similar to the PASCAL CASE statement.

COBOL's DEPENDING ON option for GO TO provides a less structured, but similar function to CASE. To use this, you must have a variable, such as

```
77 PROCESS-TYPE  PIC 9 COMP.
```

In the procedure division, you then code something like the following:

```
GO TO    ROUTINE1
         ROUTINE2
         ROUTINE3
         DEPENDING ON PROCESS-TYPE.
```

This is equivalent to coding

```
IF PROCESS-TYPE = 1
     THEN GO TO ROUTINE1.
IF PROCESS-TYPE = 2
     THEN GO TO ROUTINE2.
IF PROCESS-TYPE = 3
     THEN GO TO ROUTINE3.
```

If PROCESS-TYPE contains a value other than 1, 2, or 3, control passes to the next instruction in the COBOL program.

Assembler programmers use a coding technique called *branch tables* to achieve a similar result in assembler. The variable must be a multiple of 4 (4, 8, 12, and so forth).

The branch table depends on a property of branch instructions which is not immediately obvious. Branch instructions in the RX format have a length of 4 bytes. You may use this property to arrange branch instructions in sequence to provide a table of branch instructions. The variable, being a multiple of 4, can then be used as an index into this table of instructions.

Unlike COBOL, however, assembler has no automatic range checking. Thus, you should also code instructions to verify that the value of the variable is valid. An example should clarify this.

Assuming we have a variable defined as

PROCTYPE DS   H

which has values of 1, 2, or 3, we can simulate a GO TO DEPENDING ON with code like the following:

```
            LH    R1,PROCTYPE        GET VARIABLE
            CH    R1,=H'1'           TEST LOWER LIMIT
            BL    NOBRANCH           < 1 - NO BRANCH
            CH    R1,=H'3'           TEST UPPER LIMIT
            BH    NOBRANCH           > 3 - NO BRANCH
            MH    R1,=H'4'           MULTIPLE OF 4
            B     BTAB(R1)           USE AS BTAB INDEX
BTAB        B     NOBRANCH           0 = NO BRANCH
            B     ROUTINE1           1 = ROUTINE1
            B     ROUTINE2           2 = ROUTINE2
            B     ROUTINE3           3 = ROUTINE3
NOBRANCH EQU      *                  NO BRANCH TAKEN
```

The LH gets the variable PROCTYPE into a register. The two CH instructions and the BL/BH instructions perform a range check, ensuring that the value is between 1 and 3. The MH converts the value from PROCTYPE to the corresponding multiple of 4. The " B BTAB(R1) " branches to the label BTAB, and is indexed by the value in register 1.

Thus, if register 1 contains 4, this would branch to BTAB+4. This is the " B ROUTINE1 " instruction. If register 1 contained 8 or 12, one of the other two branches would get control.

This technique is best used where there are a large quantity of possible processing options, selected by a code ranging from 1 (or 0) to some higher number with few or no gaps. If there are fewer than five choices, a branch table is probably overkill.

However, there are many instances where MVS tailors its processing to allow efficient use of branch tables. For example, MVS utility programs and macros give return codes as a multiple of 4. This allows the return code to be used immediately as the index into a branch table. We will also use the branch table technique when discussing the Translate and Test (TRT) instruction later in the book.

There are many other ways of coding a branch table. However, whenever you see a branch instruction which uses an index register (like " B BTAB(R1) "), you are probably dealing with a branch table.

12.8.4 Other Compare Instructions

Assembler provides a number of other comparison instructions which you may see used in special situations. These are listed here for completeness, but are not usually needed outside of the special situations listed with them. The "Principles of Operation" manual contains more complete descriptions of these operations.

12.8.4.1   CLCL

Compare Logical Long — opcode CLCL — provides a comparison function which most closely approximates COBOL comparisons. It is similar to the Move Long — MVCL — instruction discussed in the next chapter.

CLCL operates like the CLC opcode. However, it allows operands up to 16 million bytes in length. Like COBOL, CLCL will compare different sized fields by considering the shorter field to be padded with a fill character. Unlike COBOL, the programmer selects the fill character value. CLCL also identifies the first byte where a difference occurs between the two operands.

CLCL has two primary drawbacks. First, CLCL requires four registers. Second, CLCL is the most confusing of the comparison instructions.

An example of CLCL follows. (A full description of the setup is given later in the description of the MVCL instruction.) Assume the following two fields:

```
OPERAND1  DC      CL5'HELLO'
OPERAND2  DC      CL4'HELP'
```

Also assume that OPERAND1 is at address hex X'00112000' and that OPERAND2 is at address hex X'00112005'. The following sequence of code shows the setup and execution of CLCL:

LA	R2,OPERAND1	1ST OPERAND ADDR
LH	R3, = H'5'	1ST OP LENGTH
LA	R4,OPERAND3	2ND OP ADDR
LH	R5, = H'4'	2ND OP
ICM	R5,8, = C' '	FILL CHAR (BLANK)
CLCL	R2,R4	COMPARE

At the completion of the operation, the condition code is 1 (first operand low). Register 2 would contain hex X'00112003' and register 4 would contain hex X'00112008'. (These are the addresses of the first unequal bytes in each operand.)

CLCL is best used in three situations. The first is when comparing equal-length fields which are longer than 256 bytes. The second is when comparing unequal-length fields and when a COBOL-like comparison is required. The third is when the address of the first unequal byte(s) must be found. Use of CLCL outside of these situations is probably not needed.

12.8.4.2   CLM

The Compare Logical under Mask instruction, opcode CLM, provides a way of comparing individual bytes in a register to fields in storage. CLM is coded with three operands. One is the register containing the byte or bytes to be compared. Another is the storage location holding the bytes to be compared against. The final operand is a *mask* value from 0 to 15, which specifies the bytes to be compared.

Setup and use of CLM is similar to that for the ICM and STCM instructions discussed later in this book (Sect. 13.7.3). CLM is not frequently used, and the special situations requiring it rarely arise.

12.8.4.3 CL/CLR

The CL and CLR opcodes provide a Compare Logical function with one or both operands being in a register. They are coded like the C and CR opcodes. However, the leftmost bit in the register is not considered to be a sign.

CL and CLR may be used when comparing character data in a register, when comparing numbers in *logical* arithmetic as previously discussed, and when comparing absolute values. In most other cases, C or CR are preferable.

12.8.4.4 CDS

The Compare and Swap instructions — opcodes CS and CDS — provide a way of simultaneously comparing a register to a field, then setting the field to a third value.

These instructions are normally only applicable to specialized multitasking situations. They ensure that a field is not changed incorrectly by two different tasks which use the same storage area. While called *compare* instructions, their real function is to make sure that a field hasn't been changed by another program before your program updates it. They could also be called *Store if Unchanged*.

CS and CDS are most frequently required in programs which use the MVS ATTACH macro. The VTAM access method also uses these instructions fairly widely. This is an advanced technique with no real COBOL equivalent. You should refer to the "Principles of Operation" manual for a more detailed discussion.

12.8.5 Manipulating the Condition Code

Occasionally you may need to compare a variable, change it, and then branch based on the original comparison. At other times, you may find a need to force the condition code to contain a specific value. Assembler provides two instructions which make this feasible. Note that this is an infrequently used technique.

The condition code can be extracted and manipulated with the BALR and shift instructions, or by the IPM (Insert Program Mask) instruction in MVS/XA. The SPM (Set Program Mask) instruction can be used to set the value of the condition code.

SPM (Set Program Mask) is used to set the *program mask* field and condition code field of the PSW. Refer to the PSW layout on the 370 reference summary (the *yellow card*).

Setting a program mask bit to 1 will cause fixed-point binary overflow conditions to abnormally end and get a dump. This also works for packed decimal overflow and floating-point exponent underflow and significance conditions. Normally, these bits are set to 0.

This allows SPM to force a dump on arithmetic significance errors. This technique is not frequently used, since it is easier to check for an overflow condition code.

However, of more interest, SPM can also be used to set a condition code. BALR will store bits 32-63 of the BC mode PSW into a register, and SPM can then be used to set that condition code back. Thus, if you make a comparison, do a BALR, and then do something else which changes the condition code (e.g., arithmetic), you may use SPM to store back the original condition code and branch based on the original comparison.

This approach won't work in MVS/XA, since the condition code and the other information aren't kept in the PSW in the same format. As a result, all CPUs capable of running the MVS/XA operating system have an additional instruction — Insert Program Mask. IPM gets the condition code, program mask, and instruction length code and stores them into a register in the same bit positions as BALR.

Use of this technique is not recommended in most situations. If you are writing programs which will execute on more than one type of IBM computer, you run the risk of having the wrong instruction to get the condition code. BALR won't work properly for this in 31-bit addressing mode. IPM isn't available on many CPUs (e.g., 4341s), and will cause an 0C1 ABEND if used on these. However, if you see SPM in a program, this technique is probably being used.

12.9 SUMMARY

This chapter has discussed two fundamental concepts. The first is the condition code. The second is the use of special instructions — the compare instructions — to manipulate the condition code.

If you are comfortable with these two concepts, you should be able to program tests and branching easily.

Things to Do

1. If you have been able to locate production assembler programs at your shop, review the comparisons. Are they understandable?
2. For compound tests, are the designs of tests understandable? If you find one or more that don't seem to make sense, why? Can you flowchart the test to make it more understandable?
3. Do any of your production programs have comparisons of fields over 256 bytes in length? Would CLCL be better in these cases?
4. Do you find instances of the logical binary comparisons (CL, CLR)? Is there a reason for this?

Data Movement

Moving data from one field to another takes only one verb in COBOL: MOVE. The MOVE verb handles both individual fields and group items or records. The COBOL compiler determines exactly what conversions, filling, realignment, and other processing is needed and performs whatever is required without any additional programmer involvement.

Moving data in assembler requires more thought. Basically, assembler provides instructions which cover movement of various forms of data, along with instructions to handle conversion from one form to another. Assembler programmers must determine which of these apply to a particular move operation, then code them properly for the specific fields involved.

In practice, moving data requires less analysis than might be expected from the preceding description. If both the sending and receiving fields are of the same form (e.g., both are packed decimal), then only one of two instructions should be used for the move operation. If the fields are of different forms, one of six instructions which convert the form of the data is appropriate.

Table 13.1 lists various combinations of data and the instructions which apply to these combinations for moving data.

COBOL doesn't differentiate between binary data in a register and in storage. Binary data is defined as USAGE COMP. COBOL will move it into or out of registers as needed.

In assembler, we need to have binary data in registers to do any arithmetic operations with it. Thus, two types of binary data are defined in Table 13.1 — binary data in storage and binary data in registers.

Now each of the data movement instructions will be covered in detail. We'll start with the binary data movement instructions.

13.1 MOVING BINARY DATA INTO REGISTERS

Assembler provides four instructions to move ("load") data into registers. These (and their opcodes) are as follows:

1. Load (L)
2. Load Halfword (LH)
3. Load Multiple (LM)
4. Load Register (LR)

Each of these will be discussed in a separate subsection.

Table 13.1 Assembler Instructions for Data Movement

Sending Field Format (USAGE)	Receiving Field Format				
	Binary (storage)	Binary (register)	Packed-decimal	Character (numeric)	Edited character
Binary (storage) (COMP)	MVC*	L,LH, LM	L+CVD	L+CVD+ UNPK	L+CVD+ ED
Binary (register) (COMP)	ST,STH, STM	LR	CVD	CVD+ UNPK	CVD+ ED
Packed-decimal (COMP-3)	CVB+ST	CVB	ZAP	UNPK	ED
Character (numeric) (DISPLAY)	PACK+ CVB+ST	PACK+ CVB	PACK	MVC*	PACK+ ED

* = MVC instruction may be used if the fields are the same length. If not, then:
- L+STH moves a fullword to a halfword
- LH+ST moves a halfword to a fullword
- PACK+UNPK may be necesary to move different-sized character numeric fields

Note 1: To move group items, use either MVC or MVCL.

Note 2: To move edited fields to unedited fields, first create a single numeric field (i.e., no commas, decimal points, et cetera) with MVC instructions,then use the appropriate instructions to get from character numeric data to other forms.

13.1.1 Load

The Load instruction (opcode L) moves (copies) a fullword of data from storage into a register. For example, given the following values,

Register 2: Hexadecimal X'0000001B' (Decimal 27)

YEAR DC F'1991'   (Hexadecimal X'000007C7')

After the execution of

                L   R2,YEAR
the results would be:
Register 2: Hexadecimal X'000007C7' (Decimal 1991)
YEAR: Hexadecimal X'000007C7' — unchanged

13.1.2 Load Halfword

Load Halfword (LH) copies a halfword of data from storage, expands it to a fullword, and puts the result into the register specified as the first operand. LH expands the halfword to a fullword by copying the sign bit 16 times into the extra leading 2 bytes in the fullword. This preserves the positive or negative attribute of the original halfword number. Figure 13.1 shows how this works in two steps.

Figure 13.1 Operation of Load Halfword.

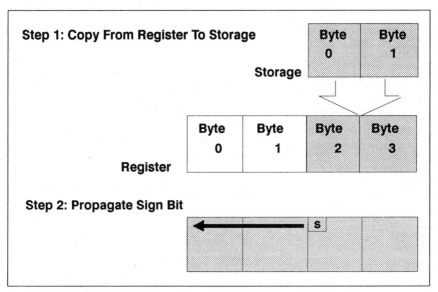

An example is shown below. Given the following starting values:
Register 3: Hexadecimal X'00000022' (Decimal 34)
MARCH DC H'3'   (Hexadecimal X'0003')
After executing
                LH   R3,MARCH
the register and sending field would contain:
Register 3: Hexadecimal X'00000003' (Decimal 3)
MARCH: Hexadecimal X'0003' — unchanged
        Here's another example, showing how this works with a negative number:
Register 4: Hexadecimal X'00000055' (Decimal 85)

PROFITS DC H'-44'   (Hex X'FFD4')
After executing

      LH   R4,PROFITS

the register and sending field would contain:

Register 4: Hexadecimal X'FFFFFFD4' (Decimal -44)

PROFITS: Hexadecimal X'FFD4' — unchanged ·

A bug which sometimes crops up when using both halfword and fullword arithmetic is a mismatch between the load instruction used and the type of data defined in storage (i.e., using LH with a field defined as type F, or using L with a field defined as type H).

This type of bug shows itself in two ways, both indicating some type of math problem. When using LH to load a fullword, you will usually receive zero as a result. When using Load to access a halfword, you will usually receive wildly enlarged values.

If you have a problem with binary arithmetic and are using both halfword and fullword data items, time spent verifying that the load instruction types match the data used usually proves worthwhile.

13.1.3   Load Multiple

Load Multiple — opcode LM — was already discussed in Chap. 9, introducing the Procedure Division. The concept behind the Load Multiple and Store Multiple instructions is that a range of registers is loaded or stored with one instruction. Coding a Load Multiple produces the same result as coding a series of Load instructions, but does the data movement with only one instruction.

An example of Load Multiple follows.

Assuming the following starting values:

Register 5: Hexadecimal X'0000003C' (Decimal 60)

Register 6: Hexadecimal X'00000026' (Decimal 38)

Register 7: Hexadecimal X'00000014' (Decimal 20)

CENTURY   DC   F'19'   (Hexadecimal X'00000013')
DECADE   DC   F'80'   (Hexadecimal X'00000050')
YEAR   DC   F'9'   (Hexadecimal X'00000008')

After the execution of

      LM   R5,R7,CENTURY

the results would be:

Register 5: Hexadecimal X'00000013' (Decimal 19)

Register 6: Hexadecimal X'00000050' (Decimal 80)

Register 7: Hexadecimal X'00000008' (Decimal 9)

CENTURY: Hexadecimal X'00000013' — unchanged

DECADE: Hexadecimal X'00000050' — unchanged

YEAR: Hexadecimal X'00000008' — unchanged

LM is appropriate for use in any situation where you need to set up several adjoining registers — for a loop, for example.

LM is the first instruction we've presented which has more than two operands. For unknown reasons, the assembler terms the middle operand the "R3" operand. The leftmost operand is termed the "R1" operand, and the rightmost operand is termed the "B2" operand. This usually doesn't matter, except when referring to formal instruction descriptions in the principles of operations or assembler reference manuals.

If the second register coded — the middle, or "R3" operand — is a lower value than the first operand, the LM instruction will *wrap around*. This loads the registers in the sequence from the first operand register up to register 15, then from register 0 up to the register specified as the "R3" operand. The most common example of this is " LM   R14,R12,12(R13) ", which loads registers 14 through 12. Putting it another way, this example loads every register except register 13.

If you code the same number for both the "R1" operand and the "R3" operand, only that register is loaded, and the LM instruction operates like a Load instruction.

13.1.4   Load Register

Load Register — opcode LR — operates like the Load instruction, but moves (copies) data from another register rather than from storage. The sending register's contents are not changed.

For example, given the following initial contents:
Register 8: Hexadecimal X'00000104' (Decimal 260)
Register 9: Hexadecimal X'00000046' (Decimal 70)
After the execution of
        LR   R8,R9
the contents would be:
Register 8: Hexadecimal X'00000046' (Decimal 70)
Register 9: Hexadecimal X'00000046' (Decimal 70 — unchanged)

Load Register is unique in that it cannot ABEND. No possible set of data can cause it to fail, short of a machine check (i.e., the CPU isn't working).

13.2   MOVING BINARY DATA BACK TO STORAGE

To complement the four Load instructions, assembler provides three instructions to move ("store") data from registers into storage. These (along with their opcodes) are as follows:

1. Store (ST)
2. Store Halfword (STH)
3. Store Multiple (STM)

There is no Store instruction corresponding to Load Register. The following subsections cover each of the Store instructions.

13.2.1 Store

The Store — opcode ST — instruction moves (copies) a fullword of data from a register into storage. This instruction does the opposite processing to the Load instruction. The following example assumes these starting contents:

Register 10: Hexadecimal X'00000038' (Decimal 56)

YEAR   DC   F'1990'   (Hexadecimal X'000007C6')

After the execution of

        ST   R10,YEAR

the results would be:

Register 10: Hexadecimal X'00000038' (Decimal 56 — unchanged)

YEAR: Hexadecimal X'00000038'

13.2.2 Store Halfword

Store Halfword (STH) operates like the opposite of Load Halfword. However, where Load Halfword propagates the sign bit, Store Halfword just stores the low-order 2 bytes of the register, as shown in Fig. 13.2.

Figure 13.2   Operation of Store Halfword.

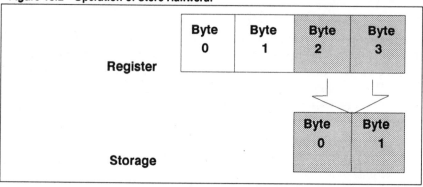

Note that if using Store Halfword with a number larger than 32767, an incorrect value results. A number in the range of 32768 to 65535 stores a negative number instead. A number above 65535 will either store a negative number or an incorrect value.

This happens because Store Halfword just copies the values in the two rightmost bytes in the register. Whatever happens to be in bit 16 — the leftmost bit of byte 2 — becomes the sign bit.

The bottom line to this is that you must avoid halfword arithmetic if the values may exceed 32767.

Now, let's see an example of normal operation of Store Halfword. Assume the following initial values:

Register 11: Hexadecimal X'0000004B' (decimal 75)

STRIKE   DC   H'10'   (Hexadecimal X'000A')

After executing

STH   R11,STRIKE

the contents would be:

Register 11: Hexadecimal X'0000004B' (Decimal 75 — unchanged)

STRIKE: Hexadecimal X'004B'   (Decimal 10)

For a second example, let's show what happens when we store a value greater than 32767. Assume the following starting contents:

Register 12: Hexadecimal X'000186A0'   (Decimal 100000)

SALARY   DC   H'29000'   (Hexadecimal X'000A')

After executing

STH   R12,SALARY

the contents after this instruction would be:

Register 12: Hexadecimal X'000186A0' (Decimal 100000 — unchanged)

SALARY: Hexadecimal X'86A0'   (Decimal negative 31072)

If you don't want your SALARY to inadvertently become a negative number, use a fullword instead.

13.2.3   Store Multiple

Store Multiple (STM) operates like the Store instruction, but stores multiple registers. As such, it acts like the opposite of Load Multiple described previously. The range of registers is specified as in Load Multiple.

Store Multiple is normally the first executable instruction in a program. Its use to save the caller's registers was described in Chap. 9.

The following is an example of Store Multiple. (Figure 13.3 shows a diagram of this example.) Given the following initial contents:

Register 14: Hexadecimal X'00000001' (Decimal 1)

Register 15: Hexadecimal X'00000002' (Decimal 2)

Register 0: Hexadecimal X'00000003' (Decimal 3)

FIRST   DC   F'0'   (Hexadecimal X'00000000')
SECOND   DC   F'0'   (Hexadecimal X'00000000')
THIRD   DC   F'0'   (Hexadecimal X'00000000')
FOURTH   DC   F'0'   (Hexadecimal X'00000000')

After executing

STM   R14,R0,FIRST

the contents would be:

Register 14: Hexadecimal X'00000001' (Decimal 1 — unchanged)

Register 15: Hexadecimal X'00000002' (Decimal 2 — unchanged)

Register 0: Hexadecimal X'00000003' (Decimal 3 — unchanged)

FIRST: Hexadecimal X'00000001'

SECOND: Hexadecimal X'00000002'

THIRD: Hexadecimal X'00000003'

FOURTH: Hexadecimal X'00000000' — unchanged

Note that the field named FOURTH was not changed. This is because the sequence of registers 14 through 0 is only three registers.

Besides its use at program initialization, STM is also used whenever you must save several registers in sequence.

Figure 13.3   Operation of Store Multiple (STM R14,R0,FIRST).

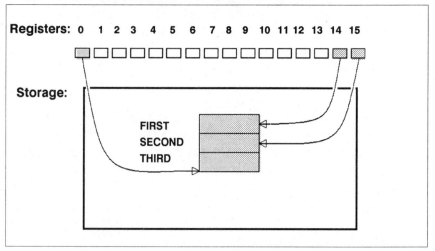

13.3   MOVING CHARACTER DATA AND GROUP ITEMS

Assembler provides two instructions for moving data fields or group items: Move and Move Long. These instructions differ in the field length they can process. Move processes from 1 to 256 bytes of data. Move Long processes up to 16 million bytes. The coding requirements of the two instructions are quite different. The instructions are often referred to as *Move Character* and *Move Character Long*.

Additionally, assembler provides a Move instruction used only for moving 1-byte literals. This is usually referred to as *Move Immediate* and will also be discussed in this subsection.

13.3.1   Move

The Move instruction — opcode MVC — provides data movement capability similar to the COBOL MOVE verb. However, MVC accurately emulates only the COBOL MOVE of equal-sized fields. MVC does not pad the receiving field with blanks in case of a field size mismatch.

MVC is a storage-to-storage instruction and moves from 1 to 256 bytes. Like the Load and Store instructions, and like the COBOL MOVE, it copies rather than moves the data.

An example of MVC follows. For the examples of the Move instructions in this subsection, only printable character data will be used. The hexadecimal equivalents in these examples will be not provided. However, MVC and the other move instructions move whatever data is present, regardless of content.

Given the following initial values:

```
MONTH      DC     CL5' '
MARCH      DC     C'MARCH'
```

After executing the following,

```
      MVC   MONTH,MARCH
```

the fields would contain:

MONTH: C'MARCH'
MARCH: C'MARCH'   (unchanged)

As mentioned earlier, the MVC instruction accurately simulates only a COBOL MOVE of equal-length fields. MVC moves as many bytes as are in the first (receiving) operand. If the second operand is longer, not all of the bytes will be moved. (This is the same way COBOL handles a MOVE of a longer field to a shorter.)

If the first operand is longer than the second operand, MVC still moves as many bytes as are in the first operand. In this case, MVC will move whatever fields follow the second operand, which normally produces erroneous output. (COBOL will pad the receiving field with blanks in this situation.)

Two more examples may help clarify this. First, an example of moving a longer field to a shorter one. Assume the following starting values:

```
MONTH       DC     CL5' '
SEPTEMBER DC       C'SEPTEMBER'
```

After executing the following,

```
      MVC   MONTH,SEPTEMBER
```

the fields would contain:

MONTH: C'SEPTE'
SEPTEMBER: C'SEPTEMBER'   (unchanged)

Since MONTH was 5 bytes long, only the first 5 bytes of SEPTEMBER were moved.

Our next example shows movement of a shorter field to a longer one. Given the following initial contents:

```
MONTH      DC     CL5' '
MAY        DC     C'MAY'
JUNE       DC     C'JUNE'
```

After executing

```
      MVC   MONTH,MAY
```

the contents would be:

MONTH: C'MAYJU'
MAY: C'MAY'   (unchanged)
JUNE: C'JUNE'   (unchanged)

Since MONTH was 5 bytes long, but MAY was only 3 bytes long, the next 2 bytes following the contents of MAY were moved. This provided 5 bytes of data, which was required by the field length of MONTH.

We can avoid this situation by providing an explicit length. An explicit length is provided by coding the number of bytes you wish to move in parentheses following the first operand. For example with these starting values,

```
MONTH      DC     CL5' '
JUNE       DC     C'JUNE'
```

After executing

```
MVC    MONTH(4),JUNE
```

the contents would be:

MONTH: C'JUNE '

JUNE: C'JUNE' (unchanged)

If you do not code an explicit length, the assembler moves the number of bytes computed as the implicit length from the data definition (DC or DS statement).

Explicit lengths are commonly used, but have some pitfalls. If you change the length of a data item, you must also change whatever explicit length references you have made to that data item.

You may also use a technique called *relative addressing*. This is specified by coding a numeric value following a plus sign after the first operand. Relative addressing tells the assembler that you do not want to move data to the first byte of the operand, but to some area past the first byte. (You may also specify bytes before the first byte of an operand by coding a minus sign rather than a plus sign.)

For example, the following is a program segment to create a character string from three others. Assuming the following starting values:

```
NEWYEAR    DC     CL15 ' '
JANUARY    DC     C'JANUARY'
FIRST      DC     C'1'
YEAR       DC     C'1992'
COMMA      DC     C','
```

After executing

```
MVC    NEWYEAR(7),JANUARY
MVC    NEWYEAR+8(1),FIRST
MVC    NEWYEAR+9(1),COMMA
MVC    NEWYEAR+11(4),YEAR
```

the result would be:

```
NEWYEAR    DC     CL15'JANUARY 1, 1992'
JANUARY    DC     C'JANUARY'              (unchanged)
FIRST      DC     C'1'                    (unchanged)
YEAR       DC     C'1992'                 (unchanged)
COMMA      DC     C','                    (unchanged)
```

When using relative addressing, you should almost always code both an explicit length and the relative address offset. The reason for this is that if you do not provide the explicit length specifying the number of bytes you want to move, the assembler will move the total field length. This normally leads to unintentional overlays.

If you see a statement like " MVC   FIELD+3,BLANKS ", it is almost invariably an error.

Another assembler feature which you will frequently use is the literal facility. Assembler literal values are similar to the COBOL literal facility. Literal values in assembler are identified by coding an equals sign ("=") before the literal value. The literal value itself may be any value you could code as an operand of a DC directive.

For example, the COBOL statement:

MOVE 'HELLO' TO GREETINGS.

is equivalent to

MVC   GREETINGS, = C'HELLO'

(assuming that GREETINGS is 5 bytes long in both cases).

Literals are placed at the end of your program by the assembler. You may also control where they go by coding the LTORG directive.

13.3.2   Move Long

Move Long (MVCL) was added to get around the 256-byte limitation of the MVC instruction. It also provides for different-length sending and receiving operands and padding, and works more like the COBOL MOVE verb than MVC does. MVCL has several major differences when compared with MVC, however.

MVCL is an RR-format instruction rather than the SS-format of MVC. MVCL uses two even-odd register pairs. It moves up to 16 megabytes in one instruction.

To process this size of movement, along with providing for different-length fields, two lengths must be provided — one for each field. Two addresses are also required — one for each field. Finally, a fill character must be specified. This goes into the same register as the sending field length. Figure 13.4 shows the arrangement of this information in the registers.

As with MVC, movement proceeds left to right. Lengths are decremented after each byte is moved. Addresses of sending and receiving fields are raised by one after each byte is moved. If the length of the receiving field (R3 in the above example) goes to zero, the MVCL operation terminates.

If the sending field length becomes zero (the length in R5 in our example), the fill character is moved to all the remaining receiving field bytes. At the end of the operation, the address registers (R2 and R4 in Fig. 13.4) will point to the end of the sending and receiving fields plus 1 byte.

Unlike MVC, MVCL sets the condition code. It shows the length of the relationship (equal, first operand shorter than second operand, or first operand longer). Unlike MVC, overlap of operands is not allowed, and no movement takes place. This sets condition code 3 and no movement occurs.

Figure 13.4   Register setup for MVCL.

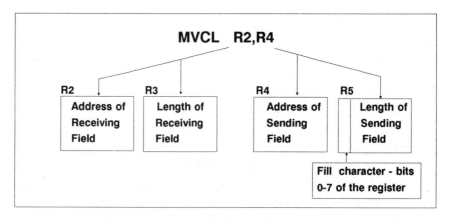

The following is an example of MVCL where both operands are the same length. Assume starting values as follows:

```
FROM      DC    CL13'SENDING FIELD'
TO        DC    CL13'RECEIVES DATA'
```

Assume that FROM begins at hexadecimal address 130000 and that TO begins at hexadecimal address 13000D. Also assume that registers 4, 5, 6, and 7 contain zeroes.

The MVCL instruction requires that four registers be set up. The code to do this and to move the fields is as follows:

```
LA      R6,FROM
LH      R7, = H'13'
LA      R4,TO
LH      R5, = H'13'
MVCL    R4,R6
```

The LA instruction (Load Address) puts the address of a field into the register specified. We will discuss it in more detail in Chap. 15. In this case, it would put hex X'00130000' in register 6 (the address of FROM). It would also put hex X'13000D' in register 4 (the address of TO).

The MVCL instruction would move the data and modify the registers. At the end of the process, the values would be

FROM: C'SENDING FIELD' (unchanged)

TO: C'SENDING FIELD'

Register 4: Hex X'0013000D' (address of FROM plus 1 byte)

Register 5: Hex X'00000000' (receiving length goes to zero)
Register 6: Hex X'0013001A' (address of TO plus 1 byte)
Register 7: Hex X'00000000' (sending length goes to zero)

Now for another example. In this example, the receiving operand will be shorter than the sending field. Given beginning contents of

```
SHORTONE  DC    CL6'PINCAY'
LONGONE   DC    CL12'ABDUL-JABBAR'
```

Assume that SHORTONE is at hexadecimal address 200000 and that LONGONE starts at hexadecimal address 190000. Again, assume that registers 4 through 7 contain zeroes.

The MVCL instruction and its register setup is

```
      LA    R6,LONGONE
      LH    R7, = H'12'
      LA    R4,SHORTONE
      LH    R5, = H'6'
      MVCL  R4,R6
```

Following the MVCL, the resulting values would be

SHORTONE: C'ABDUL-'

LONGONE: C'ABDUL-JABBAR' (unchanged)

Register 4: Hex X'00200006' (SHORTONE ending address plus 1 byte)

Register 5: Hex X'00000000' (receiving length goes to zero)

Register 6: Hex X'00190006' [address of LONGONE plus the number of bytes moved (6)]

Register 7: Hex X'00000006' [sending length (12) minus number of bytes moved (6)]

In the preceding two examples, MVCL operated just like MVC. Now let's look at an example where it operates differently. In this case, the second (sending) operand will be shorter than the first (receiving) operand.

Given these starting values:

```
NEWYEAR   DC    CL15'***************'
JANUARY   DC    CL7'JANUARY'
```

Assume that NEWYEAR starts at hexadecimal address 180000 and that JANUARY is located at hexadecimal address 18000F. Again, assume that registers 4 through 7 contain zeroes.

The MVCL and register setup is as follows:

```
      LA    R6,JANUARY
      LH    R7, = H'7'
      LA    R4,NEWYEAR
      LH    R5, = H'15'
      ICM   R7,8, = C' '
      MVCL  R4,R6
```

The ICM (Insert Characters under Mask) instruction is a special form of Load instruction which only moves 1 byte into the register in this case. We are using ICM to set up the fill byte with this instruction. (ICM is explained later in this chapter.) The resultant values after the MVCL would be

NEWYEAR: C'JANUARY '

JANUARY: C'JANUARY' (unchanged)

Register 4: Hex X'0018000F' (NEWYEAR ending address plus 1 byte)

Register 5: Hex X'00000000' (receiving length goes to zero)

Register 6: Hex X'00180016' (ending address of JANUARY plus 1 byte)

Register 7: Hex X'40000000' (sending length goes to zero. The fill
              character is unchanged.)

Note that the fill character was propagated into the last 8 bytes of the receiving field.

    One final example of MVCL is appropriate to describe a function which it does better than any other instruction. This is clearing a large area to some preset value. For example, if a field is defined as " LARGE DS CL2000 ", the following instructions would clear it to binary zeroes:

```
LA    R6,0
SR    R7,R7
LA    R4,LARGE
LH    R5, = H'2000'
MVCL  R4,R6
```

This is equivalent to

    MOVE LOW-VALUES TO LARGE.

in COBOL. Note that the " SR R7,R7 " sets register 7 to 0 by subtracting it from itself.

    MVCL is best used when dealing with areas over 256 bytes long. Areas less than that size are generally best processed with MVC.

    A common problem with MVCL is incorrect specification of the length, causing large areas of a program or data area to be overlaid or access exceptions (0C4s). The address and length registers will usually be updated with the addresses of the sending and receiving bytes if a program check or other abnormal end occurs and these should be checked when debugging. The value in these may tell you which length or address was wrong.

    It is advisable to test for overlap and for excessive field length, if using addresses or lengths provided by another program.

    MVCL is unique in Move instructions in that it sets the condition code. Condition codes of 0, 1, and 2 indicate that the first operand was equal in length to, shorter than, or longer than the second operand. Condition code 3 indicates that there was an overlap in the first and second operands and that no movement took place. This should be treated as an error. You can code " BO ERROR " to do this, for example, if your routine is named ERROR.

13.3.3   Move Immediate

The 370 architecture provides a class of instructions — the Storage Immediate, or SI format — in which the second operand is a 1-byte constant contained in the instruction itself. The MVI opcode provides a move function with a 1-byte operand which you code in the instruction.

An example of MVI follows. Given the following initial contents:

```
DARING      DC      CL5'FEATS'
```
After executing
```
          MVI     DARING,C' '
```
the resulting contents would be:

DARING: C' EATS'

You may also code the first operand with relative addressing. For example, if we had instead coded:
```
          MVI     DARING+2,C'E'
```
the result would have been:

DARING: C'FEETS'

(This assumes the same starting contents as in the first example.)

MVI is used frequently to set up 1-byte values. It is also used with a feature of the MVC instruction termed *destructive overlap*. This occurs when all or part of the first operand overlaps all or part of the second operand.

Overlaps means that they share the same storage area. In COBOL, the result of an overlapping move is termed unpredictable. In assembler, you can set up the data definitions and the move instruction to control what happens.

The most common use of this feature is in clearing print lines to blanks. For example, assuming starting values of
```
LINE1       DC      CL133'?????????????????WHATEVER'
```
(The actual contents of LINE1 don't matter.) When we execute
```
          MVI     LINE1,C' '
          MVC     LINE1+1(132),LINE1
```
the MVI statement moves a blank to the first byte of LINE1. The MVC statement moves 132 bytes of data (the explicit length in parentheses) from the area starting at the first byte of LINE1 (the second operand) to the area starting at the second byte of LINE1 (LINE1+1).

The MVC operation proceeds left to right, byte by byte. The first byte moved is the blank we put in LINE1 with the MVI. It is moved to the second byte of LINE1.

The second byte moved is the second byte of LINE1. It originally held something else, but now contains the blank we just moved into it. So, the second byte's contents are copied into the third byte of LINE1. This process continues through the rest of the line. Figure 13.5 shows the first part of this process.

Figure 13.5   Using destructive overlap to clear a field.

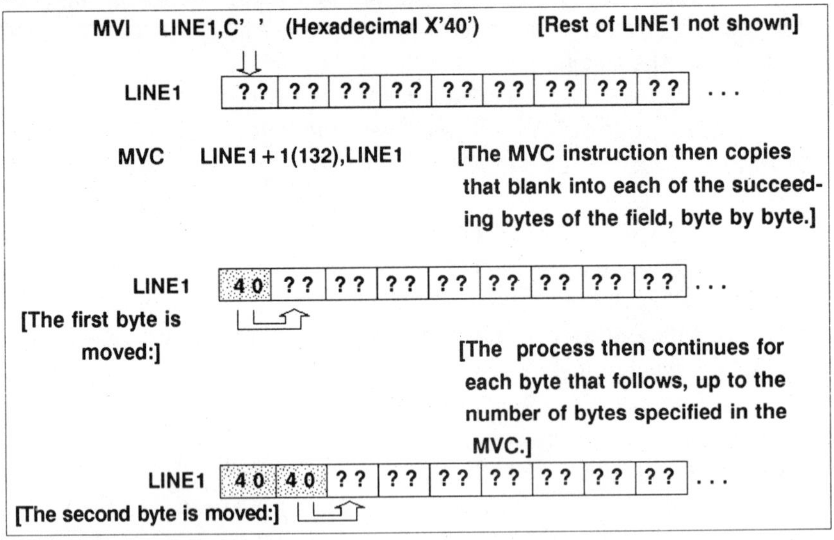

13.4   MOVING PACKED DECIMAL FIELDS

Moving packed decimal fields presents certain problems. MVC will only work satisfactorily if both fields have the same length. For the other two cases, MVC will either add extraneous bytes or not move the entire number. Either of these will result in an invalid packed decimal number, and will produce an 0C7 on the next arithmetic operation on the moved field.

To handle this case, the 370 architecture provides an instruction called Zero and Add Packed (opcode ZAP). ZAP behaves more like a packed decimal arithmetic instruction than a data-movement instruction, but provides a data-movement function.

ZAP is coded with a first and second operand. The second (sending) operand must be a valid packed decimal number or an 0C7 will occur. The contents of the first (receiving) operand don't matter. ZAP sets the contents of the first operand to a valid packed decimal zero. (This is all 0 bits with a sign of hexadecimal X'C'.) ZAP then adds the contents of the second operand to the first operand in the same way as the Add Packed instruction does.

If the second (sending) operand is shorter than the first (receiving) operand, ZAP will pad with leading zeroes. If the first operand is shorter than the second operand, the packed decimal number is truncated. (These follow the same rules as COBOL.)

Three examples follow showing each situation. The first covers the case where both operands are the same length. Assuming the following beginning values

| RECEIVE | DC | PL3'407' | (Hex X'00407C') |
| SEND | DC | PL3'1000' | (Hex X'01000C') |

After executing

ZAP   RECEIVE,SEND

the contents would be:

RECEIVE: Hex X'01000C'

SEND: Hex X'01000C' (unchanged)

The next example covers the case of a shorter sending operand. Assuming the following initial contents:

| RECEIVE2 | DC | PL2'5' | (Hex X'005C') |
| SEND2 | DC | PL1'9' | (Hex X'9C') |

After the following instruction executes

ZAP   RECEIVE2,SEND2

the resulting fields would hold:

RECEIVE2: Hex X'009C'

SEND2: Hex X'9C' (unchanged)

The final example covers the situation where truncation must occur. In this example, the sending field length exceeds that of the receiving field. Given the following initial contents:

| RECEIVE3 | DC | PL2'5' | (Hex X'005C') |
| SEND3 | DC | PL3'12345' | (Hex X'12345C') |

Following the execution of

ZAP   RECEIVE3,SEND3

the results would be:

RECEIVE3: Hex X'345C'

SEND3: Hex X'12345C' (unchanged)

Note that the first 2 digits are truncated, just as COBOL does in the same situation.

In normal execution, ZAP sets the condition code to indicate the resulting value (zero, positive, or negative). It would set a condition code of 3 to indicate overflow in the last example.

13.5 CONVERTING FROM AND TO BINARY AND PACKED FORMS

Another area which poses the same type of problems that ZAP addresses is *radix conversion*. The radix of a number is the base (2, 10, or 16) of the number. Putting it another way, radix conversion is what we do when moving a decimal item to a binary field, when moving an external (character) field to a packed decimal field, or when moving such fields in the other direction.

The 370 provides four radix conversion instructions:

1. *Pack* converts a number from EBCDIC (character) form to packed decimal form.

2. *Unpack* converts a packed decimal field to a character field.

3. *Convert to Binary* converts a packed decimal field to a binary number in a register.

4. *Convert to Decimal* converts a binary number in a register to a packed decimal field.

Each of these will be covered in a separate subsection below. Figure 13.6 shows the complete conversion flow from input to output. You may wish to refer back to it while you read the individual instruction descriptions.

This figure shows the coversions necesary to take an input character field, convert it to binary, convert it back to packed decimal after performing arithmetic with it, and finally convert it back to displayable form. Assume that we have the following data areas defined for Fig. 13.6:

RECAREA	DS	0CL80	(Input record area)
FIELDIN	DS	CL3	(Input field)
	DS	CL77	(Filler)
PACKWORK	DS	PL8	(Packed decimal work area)
RECOUT	DS	0CL133	(Output record area)
	DC	C' RESULT IS:'	(Constant − label output)
FIELDOUT	DS	CL4	(Output field)
	DC	CL118' '	(Filler)

The processing steps to get FIELDIN, add 10 to it, and display the output are shown in Fig. 13.6. Assume that FIELDIN contains character C'147'. The instructions in the figure are doing the following:

Instruction	Effect/Description
PACK PACKWORK,FIELDIN	Converts from character to packed decimal
CVB R3,PACKWORK	Converts from packed decimal to binary and puts result in R3
CVD R3,PACKWORK	Converts contents of R3 back to packed decimal
UNPK FIELDOUT,PACKWORK	Converts from packed decimal to displayable characters
OI FIELDOUT + 23,X'F0'	Sets sign bits on in result
PUT SYSPRINT,RECOUT	Prints output line

We will be discussing each of these instruction types now.

Figure 13.6   PACK/CVB/CVD/UNPK data flow.

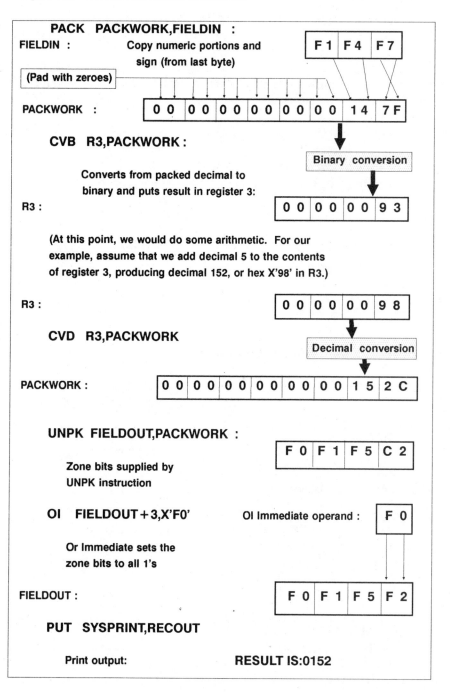

PACK PACKWORK,FIELDIN :

FIELDIN :   Copy numeric portions and   F 1 | F 4 | F 7
                   sign (from last byte)

(Pad with zeroes)

PACKWORK :   0 0 | 0 0 | 0 0 | 0 0 | 0 0 | 0 0 | 1 4 | 7 F

CVB R3,PACKWORK :

                                                       Binary conversion

          Converts from packed decimal to
          binary and puts result in register 3:
R3 :   0 0 | 0 0 | 0 0 | 9 3

(At this point, we would do some arithmetic. For our
example, assume that we add decimal 5 to the contents
of register 3, producing decimal 152, or hex X'98' in R3.)

R3 :   0 0 | 0 0 | 0 0 | 9 8

CVD R3,PACKWORK

                                                       Decimal conversion

PACKWORK :   0 0 | 0 0 | 0 0 | 0 0 | 0 0 | 0 0 | 1 5 | 2 C

UNPK FIELDOUT,PACKWORK :

                                                       F 0 | F 1 | F 5 | C 2

          Zone bits supplied by
          UNPK instruction

OI   FIELDOUT+3,X'F0'   OI Immediate operand :   F 0

          Or Immediate sets the
          zone bits to all 1's

FIELDOUT :   F 0 | F 1 | F 5 | F 2

PUT SYSPRINT,RECOUT

          Print output: RESULT IS:0152

13.5.1 Pack

The Pack instruction has an opcode of PACK. It is a SS-format instruction. Pack changes the format of the second operand from character (also called zoned decimal) to packed decimal.

The Pack instruction moves the digit parts of each byte into the packed decimal number it is creating in the first operand. The sign for the packed decimal number is taken from the zone bits of the last byte of the second operand.

The result from the Pack instruction is produced as though the instruction processed from right to left. By doing this, the instruction preserves the numeric value of the original character-format number.

Additionally, if the receiving operand is shorter than needed, the high-order (left) digits will be truncated. In this way, PACK operates like the COBOL MOVE verb. Similarly, PACK provides leading 0 digits when the sending field has fewer digits than the receiving field.

Figure 13.7 shows how the Pack instruction processes a 5-byte field. Figure 13.6 showed PACK in sequence with the other radix conversion instructions.

Figure 13.7   PACK of a five-byte field.

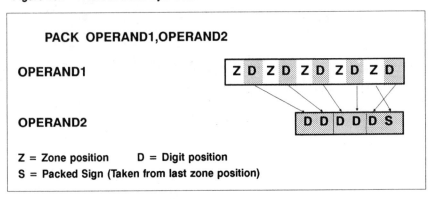

An example of PACK with the initial contents follows:

CHARIN	DC	C'333'	(Hexadecimal X'F3F3F3')
PACKOUT	DC	PL4'0'	(Hexadecimal X'0000000C')

After executing

        PACK   PACKOUT,CHARIN

the resulting field contents would be:
CHARIN: Hex X'F3F3F3' (unchanged)
PACKOUT: Hex X'0000333F'

Note that the assembler generated a sign for the packed field of X'C' in PACKOUT. However, when we issued the PACK, the sign became X'F'.

This is because the Pack instruction copies the sign from the second operand.

Because PACK does not do any checking or computation with the data in the second operand — just a special form of data movement — invalid data can be packed successfully. However, later instructions will normally receive an 0C7 ABEND when processing this data.

The reason for this is that, in EBCDIC, most letters and a few special characters will convert into a valid packed decimal digit. The letters A-Z and certain special characters (blank, dash, ampersand, and slash) will pack properly. The capital letters will also provide a valid sign.

However, all other special characters will produce invalid digits. Additionally, all lowercase letters and all special characters will produce an invalid sign.

This unfortunately means that you may pack invalid data, yet have it process successfully. It is only when an invalid digit or sign is produced that an 0C7 occurs. However, an ABEND may not be as bad as continuing to process invalid information "successfully." As a result of this, a numeric test is strongly advised before packing a field. (Chapter 20 covers this.)

13.5.2 Unpack

Unpack — opcode UNPK — converts from packed decimal to zoned decimal. The digits and sign are copied, unchanged, from the second (packed) operand to the first (zoned) operand. As part of the data movement, valid zone bits are placed in each byte but the rightmost.

As with PACK, there is no validity check for the packed digits or sign. Processing is done as though it were processed right to left, from the low-order to the high-order digit. As with PACK, UNPK provides truncation or zero filling as appropriate. Figure 13.8 shows the data movement for an UNPK.

Here is an example of UNPK, starting with the following values:

```
PDAYS      DC     PL2'365'                (Hex X'365C')
DAYS       DC     CL3' '                  (Hex X'404040')
```

After executing

```
          UNPK   DAYS,PDAYS
```

the values would be:

PDAYS: Hex X'365C' (unchanged)

DAYS: Hex X'F3F6C5' (character C'36E')

Note that the ending digit in DAYS is the letter E rather than the number 5. This introduces another problem when processing packed decimal numbers — producing proper displayable output.

The reason for the letter rather than the number at the end lies in the copying of the sign from the packed decimal number. While the 370 accepts any of the hex digits A through F as valid signs, it produces only hex C or D as the sign when doing arithmetic.

Figure 13.8   UNPK of a five-digit field.

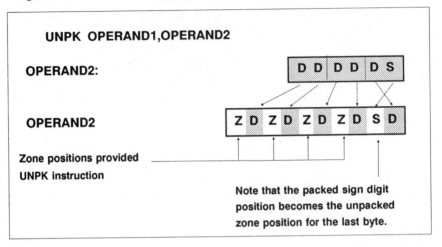

As such, assembler programmers have to do something to correct the sign before displaying or printing the number. There are several common techniques for doing this, none of which have any major advantage over the others. The method we will use in this book is to use the OR instruction.

The instruction to be used is the SI format of OR. The opcode for this is OI, usually called *Or Immediate*. OI is one of twelve *logical instructions*. These implement Boolean — binary — logic, hence the term logical.

The logical instructions, named And, Or, and Exclusive Or, provide ways of setting individual bits on or off. For our problem with the sign bits, we need to set certain bits on (to 1 instead of 0).

The Or instruction processes bytes of data one bit at a time. OI will look at each bit in the first operand and at the corresponding bit in the second operand. It will set the bit in the first operand to a 1 if the bit is set to 1 in either the first operand OR the second operand. (Hence the name of "Or" for this process.)

Since Or sets a bit on whenever it finds a 1 in the second operand, and leaves the bit unchanged if it finds a 0, we can use it to set specified bits on.

The way in which we can do this is to code an OI instruction following each UNPK. The second (immediate) operand for this should be hexadecimal X'F0' — all the zone sign bits on and all the digit bits off. The first operand for the UNPK should be the last byte of the unpacked field.

The following shows how this is done with the data from our UNPK example. After the UNPK, our result was

DAYS   DC   CL'36E'   (Hex X'F3F6C5')

By executing

OI   DAYS + 2,X'F0'

the result would be:

DAYS: Hex X'F3F6F5' (character C'365')

which is what we originally wanted.

The way in which the OI instruction works may be clearer if we work the processing out in binary:

Last byte of DAYS in binary: 11000101   (Hex X'C5')
Immediate operand of OI in binary: 11110000   (Hex X'F0')
Result in binary: 11110101   (Hex X'F5')

To specify the last byte of the unpacked field, code a relative address of the unpacked field plus one less than the field length. Thus, for a 3-byte field, we code " OI field + 2,X'F0' ". For a 4-byte field, we code " OI field + 3,X'F0' ", and so on. We will see further examples of OI and the logical instructions later.

13.5.3 Convert to Binary

Convert to Binary — opcode CVB — changes the second operand from packed decimal to binary format, then puts the resulting binary number into the register specified as the first operand.

The packed decimal number is always 8 bytes long. It is customarily coded as a doubleword and aligned as a doubleword, which is not necesary, but may improve performance on some CPUs. The binary number produced by CVB is always a fullword.

The digits and sign of the packed decimal number must be valid, or an 0C7 ABEND will result. The maximum number which can be converted is positive 2147483647 or negative 2147483648. If the packed decimal number is outside this range, a decimal divide (0CB) ABEND will occur.

For example, given the following initial values:

NODRINKS   DC   PL8'1920'   (Hex X'000000000001920C')
Register 4: zeroes

After execution of

CVB   R4,NODRINKS

the contents would be:

NODRINKS DC   PL8'1920' (Hex X'000000000001920C' — unchanged)
Register 4: Hex X'000007E4'

13.5.4 Convert to Decimal

Convert to Decimal — opcode CVD — works like the opposite of CVB. A fullword binary number in a register is converted to its packed decimal equivalent. The result is placed in an 8-byte field in storage.

Here is an example of CVD, assuming the following starting values:

Register 5: Hex X'00000E00'

BIGNUM   DC   PL8'0'   (Hex X'000000000000000C')

After executing

CVD   R5,BIGNUM

the contents would be:

Register 5: Hex X'00000E00' (unchanged)

BIGNUM: Hex X'000000000003584C'   (Decimal 3584)

13.6   EDITING PACKED DATA

The 370 provides two instructions for editing packed decimal data. These are the Edit and the Edit and Mark instructions — opcodes ED and EDMK respectively. While the two instructions do not provide a one-to-one match with COBOL numeric editing options, they come quite close.

The ED and EDMK instructions are very powerful and can do a lot of processing in editing. They are also very complex. We will not describe the complete set of facilities for ED and EDMK, but will show how some COBOL-like editing tasks can be done using them.

Certain COBOL editing facilities are specified by the COBOL PICTURE clause. The specific PIC clause features to be described include the following:

- Zero suppression (Z)
- Digit positions (9)
- Comma insertion
- Decimal point insertion
- Asterisk fill (*)
- Credit symbols (+, -, CR, DB)
- Slash insertion (/)
- Blank insertion (B)
- Floating dollar sign ($)

Before going through each of these in detail, let's cover the Edit instruction. (The Edit and Mark instruction is identical, with one exception.)

13.6.1   The Edit Instruction

The ED instruction converts packed decimal fields to edited output. It operates similarly to UNPK, but adds many features for more control of the output field appearance.

ED requires a special field setup in the receiving field. The programmer must define an *edit pattern*, which tells the ED instruction how to process the data. The edit pattern in turn describes how various options like zero suppression are used.

The edit pattern (also commonly called an *edit mask*) includes five pieces of information:

1. Which character replaces leading zeroes (e.g., blank, dash, et cetera). This is called the *fill character*, and is in the first byte of the edit pattern.

2. Where the edited numeric digits go in the output field. This is specified by including bytes containing a special *digit selector* code which tells the 370 to unpack a digit there.

3. Which formatting characters must be included, such as commas, decimal points, et cetera. These are called *message bytes*.

4. Where the ED instruction should stop suppressing leading zeroes, if desired. This is specified with a special *significance starter* byte.

5. Which sign control is required, if any. This specifies the message bytes used to indicate if the number is negative — CR, for example.

The 370 ED instruction also processes some other information in the edit pattern. Reviewing the principles of operation for this will be left as an exercise for the reader.

Using the ED instruction essentially depends on learning how to code edit patterns. Edit patterns are the closest thing to a COBOL PIC clause in assembler. They must, however, be coded as hexadecimal constants (DC with type of X). The edit pattern should have the same number of digits as the source packed decimal field.

To edit a packed decimal field, the edit pattern must first be moved into the output field. The ED instruction then specifies the output field as the first operand and the packed decimal field as the second operand.

The hexadecimal code for the digit selector is X'20'. The hexadecimal code for the significance starter is X'21'.

Table 13.2 shows a group of COBOL PICTURE clause values, their corresponding edit masks, and other information.

An edit pattern is usually planned in the following sequence.

- First, determine the size of the packed field you are editing.

- Second, determine the fill character desired (usually blank).

- Third, determine the formatting characters needed, if any.

- Fourth, determine where you wish zero digits to begin printing even if no nonzero digits occur first.

- Fifth, determine if a credit symbol is needed.

To create the edit mask, code a DC directive with a type of X (hexadecimal), and code as the value as follows:

- The fill character

- The digit positions, interspersed with the hex values of the formatting characters

- Determine where zeroes should begin printing, even if no nonzero characters have been found. Change the preceding digit selector to a significance start.

Table 13.2 COBOL PICTURE Clauses and Assembler Edit Masks			
Source COBOL field	PICTURE clause	Edit mask value	Output field length
PL5	ZZZ,ZZZ,ZZ9	X'402020206B2020206B202120'	CL12
PL2	ZZ9	X'40202120'	CL4
PL3	ZZ,ZZ9	X'4020206B202120'	CL7
PL4	Z,ZZZ,ZZ9	X'40206B2020206B202120'	CL10
PL3	ZZ,ZZ9-	X'4020206B20212060'	CL8
PL3	ZZ9.99	X'402021204B2020'	CL7
PL3	**,***	X'5C20206B202020'	CL7

- Finally, when enough digit selectors have been coded to contain the packed decimal field, code the credit symbol in hex if any is needed. What could be simpler?

This is not quite as involved as it sounds, and many of the decisions you have to make are instinctive for COBOL programmers. Let's go through creating an edit mask. Assume that we have a field called HANGERS which is defined as PL6. To plan out the edit mask:

First, determine the size of the packed field you are editing: 6 bytes or 11 digits.

Second, determine the fill character desired: blank (X'40').

Third, determine the formatting characters needed: We'll use a COBOL PIC of ZZ,ZZZ,ZZZ,ZZ9: three commas.

Fourth, determine where you wish 0 digits to begin printing even if no nonzero digits occur first: Only on the last byte.

Fifth, determine if a credit symbol is needed: no.

To code the edit mask, code a DC directive with a type of X (hexadecimal):

```
EDMASK    DC    X'
```

and code as the value:

- The fill character (blank)

```
EDMASK    DC    X'40
```

- The digit positions, interspersed with the hex values of the formatting characters (using the COBOL PIC as a guide)(see Fig. 13.9).

- Determine where zeroes should begin printing, even if no nonzero characters have been found. Change the preceding digit selector to a significance start (see Fig. 13.9).

- When enough digit selectors have been coded to contain the packed decimal field, code the credit symbol in hex if any is needed. (Not applicable to our example. Note that we have to add the ending quote mark to make EDMASK a valid constant, though.)

Our final result is:

```
EDMASK     DC      X'4020206B2020206B2020206B202120'
```

Figure 13.9   COBOL picture conversion to edit mask.

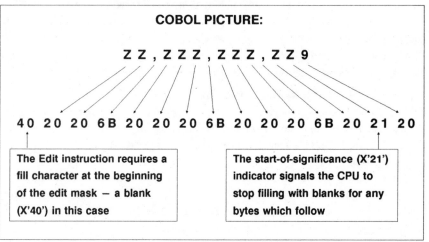

Let's continue our example by actually editing the field. While it's permissible to code the edit pattern directly in the output area, the more common practice is to code the edit pattern as a separate field and move it into the actual output field just before editing.

Assume the following fields and starting values:

```
FIELDOUT   DS      CL15' '                       (actual displayed output)
EDMASK     DC      X'4020206B2020206B2020206B202020'
HANGERS    DC      PL6'1000000'                  (Hex X'00001000000C')
```

Assume we execute

```
           MVC     FIELDOUT,EDMASK
           ED      FIELDOUT,HANGERS
```

the resulting values would be:

```
FIELDOUT: C'    1,000,000'  (Hex X'404040404040F16BF0F0F06BF0F0F0')
```

(HANGERS and EDMASK would be unchanged.)

The MVC instruction above moved the edit mask into the actual output field. Note that we need to do this in any case where we are printing or displaying the same line or screen more than once.

To select another fill character, just code the hexadecimal value for that in the first byte of the edit pattern. You can do this "on the fly" with an MVI instruction. For example, " MVI EDMASK,C'*' " changes the fill character in the edit mask we created earlier to an asterisk.

You may also need to provide other formatting characters than the commas we have used as examples up to this point. You may do this by just coding the desired characters like any other message byte. One example in Table 13.2 shows this with a decimal point. You may also code hex X'40' as a message byte, which corresponds to the COBOL PIC clause value of B.

Another common case is the need to edit a date in the form MMDDYY into the form MM/DD/YY. The packed field needed to hold this must be defined as PL4, which contains 7 digits. The edit mask for a date is then:

DATEMASK DC   X'402120206120206120206120'

This mask has a significance starter as the first digit position. This causes 0 dates to display as " 00/00/00". Note also that this takes 10 bytes to display.

13.6.2   The Edit and Mark Instruction

EDMK follows the same general conventions as the ED instruction, but adds a feature. It tells you where the first significant character appeared in the edited field. EDMK places this address in register 1.

If no significant bytes are found, EDMK does not change register 1. This calls for some special planning to avoid misuse of an incorrect address.

The primary use for EDMK is to place a floating dollar sign. The following is an example of this. Assume the following initial values:

```
CASHMASK  DC      X'5C20206B2020204B2020'
AMOUNT    DC      PL4'12345'
OUTFIELD  DS      CL10
```

Also assume that register 1 contains zeroes, and that the address of OUTFIELD is hex X'00180000'. After executing

```
            MVC     OUTFIELD,CASHMASK
            EDMK    OUTFIELD,AMOUNT
```

the values would be:

OUTFIELD: C'****123.45' (Hex X'5C5C5C5CF1F2F34BF4F5')

Register 1: Hex X'00180004'   (address of the '1' in '****123.45')

We may now use the address in register 1 to insert the floating dollar sign. If we now execute

```
            SH      R1, = H'1'                      SUBTRACT ONE
            MVI     0(R1),C'$'                      MOVE DOLLAR SIGN
```

the resulting values will be:

OUTFIELD: C'***$123.45' (Hex X'5C5C5C5BF1F2F34BF4F5')
Register 1: Hex X'00180003'   (address of the byte before
the '1' in '****123.45')

EDMK requires one check before its use. If the sending packed decimal field contains zero, register 1 will not be affected. To avoid modifying data at another (unknown) address, you should check that the address is valid. There are three main options:

1. Set up a valid address in register 1 with the Load address instruction before you execute the EDMK.

2. Test the value in the sending packed decimal field for zero before editing.

3. Test the condition code after the EDMK instruction for zero after editing.

Most assembler language books recommend the first alternative. This is workable, but probably not desirable in the real world.

The primary reason for doing floating dollar sign insertion is to prevent alteration of a check amount. If the check has a zero amount, printing "****$.00" may not be as desirable as printing "**VOID**", or something similar. For this reason, testing for zero with the second or third options may be better alternatives.

The second and third approaches also are the best techniques to implement the COBOL BLANK WHEN ZERO clause.

Also note that if a start-of-significance indicator in the edit mask is detected before a nonzero digit in the second operand, register 1 will not be changed.

13.7 MOVE ESOTERICA

This section covers fifteen additional instructions which may be of some value in special situations, along with UNPK and relative addressing.

13.7.1 Special Move Instructions

Assembler provides three additional move instructions (MVN, MVZ, and MVO) which assist in editing and packing operations. A special backward move (MVCIN) is available as a special feature on IBM 4300 series machines only. Finally, there are three special move instructions — MVCS, MVCP, and MVCK — used for moving data between different jobs in MVS.

The MVN (Move Numerics) and MVZ (Move Zones) instructions are coded and operate exactly like MVC. However, they only work on half of each byte. Neither changes the condition code. Up to 256 bytes may be processed by MVN or MVZ.

MVN copies the rightmost 4 bits of each byte in the sending field to the rightmost 4 bits of each corresponding byte in the receiving field. The leftmost 4 bits of each byte in the receiving field are not changed. The length of the receiving field determines the length of move. Figure 13.10 shows the data movement for this instruction.

Figure 13.10   MVN instruction data flow.

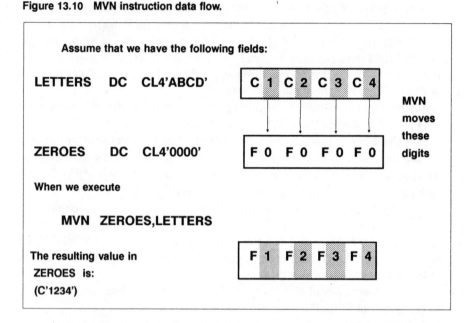

MVZ copies the leftmost 4 bits of each byte in the sending field to the leftmost 4 bits of the corresponding byte in the receiving field. The rightmost four bits of bytes in the receiving field aren't changed. It works the same as MVN, but affects the other half of the byte. Figure 13.11 shows an example of this.

Figure 13.11 MVZ instruction data flow.

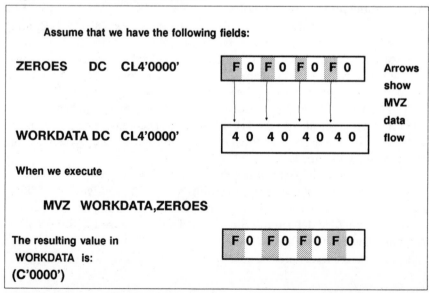

MVN and MVZ may be used wherever it may be appropriate to fiddle with the left half (zone portion) or right half (numeric portion) of bytes in storage. Both may be used to put hex 'F' zone bits in a field prior to PACK or following UNPK. This is sometimes used to ensure that blank fields on input don't cause a data exception, but is an unsatisfactory measure when compared to a real numerics test.

MVO (Move with Offset) acts more like a packed decimal instruction than a character instruction. It copies bytes from the sending field to the receiving field and places them adjacent to (to the left of) the rightmost 4 bits in the receiving field (the last half of the last byte). The sending and receiving fields may have different lengths, up to a maximum of 16 bytes.

If the receiving field is longer than the sending field, as many extra leading zeroes as necesary are placed in the receiving field. If the sending field is longer than the receiving field, movement stops when the receiving field is filled with the rightmost byte contents from the sending field (i.e., truncation).

MVO is mainly used to shift packed decimal numbers an odd number of digits. The MVN instructions can be used to *shift* a packed decimal number any even number of bytes. In general, the SRP instruction is preferable to both of these. Figure 13.12 shows an example of MVO. You would normally follow the MVO in Fig. 13.12 with an MVZ to move a hex 0 into the last digit's position, e.g., " MVZ   WORKDATA+3(1),=X'00' ".

Figure 13.12 MVO instruction data flow.

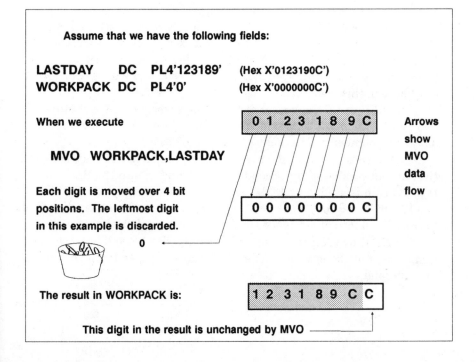

MVCIN (Move Inverse) is provided as an optional feature on the IBM 4300 series. It operates like an MVC, but movement proceeds from the high address (right end) of the second operand. This has the effect of reversing the letters in the sending field and placing them in the receiving field.

Uses of this instruction are to reverse the order of characters. This allows them to be set up for a right-to-left scan with the Translate and Test (TRT) instructions. Due to the comparative rarity of this instruction, its use is not advised. The same effect is possible with a special setup for the Translate (TR) instruction (see Chap. 20).

Three additional special move instructions provide for special data transfer capabilities among address spaces in the MVS operating system. Use of these requires special authorization, and you probably won't see these in very many programs. The three instructions are as follows:

1. MVCK — Move with Key
2. MVCP — Move to Primary
3. MVCS — Move to Secondary

13.7.2 Special Load Instructions

Assembler provides four special load instructions — LPR, LNR, LCR, and LTR — which move data like the LR instruction, but also manipulate the data.

LTR (Load and Test Register) is more of a comparison instruction than a data movement instruction. It copies the fullword in the second operand register into the first operand register. Unlike LR, however, LTR also sets the condition code based on the value of the fullword. The same register may be specified for both operands.

Uses for LTR are to test for a value in a register without coding a storage reference. For example, " LTR R2,R2 " provides the same condition codes as "C R2,=F'0' ". LTR is often coded to test return codes from subroutines or operating system service requests, and will be used for this elsewhere in this book.

LCR (Load Complement Register) operates like LR, but stores the two's complement of the second operand value into the first operand. Thus, a negative number will be made positive, and vice versa.

LPR (Load Positive Register) operates similarly, but loads the (positive) absolute value of the second operand number into the first operand register. LPR is used in COBOL to store data items with USAGE of COMP and PIC 9(4) or 9(8). This is necesary to change potentially negative fields to store them into an unsigned (no S in the picture clause) data item.

LNR (Load Negative Register) is similar to LPR, but loads the two's complement of the absolute value of the second operand number into the first operand.

All of these instructions set the condition code to indicate a zero, negative, positive, or overflow result. Overflow is only possible when complementing the maximum negative number (-2**31 or -2,147,483,648).

Uses for LCR/LNR/LPR are primarily in algebraic computations where absolute positive or negative values or the negative value of a number are needed.

13.7.3 Character Load Instructions

The 370 includes four instructions which insert (load) or store character data into registers. These are used whenever you need to work with arithmetic quantities of other than a fullword or halfword. Also, these are used when dealing with data structures that have multiple fields in a fullword.

The four instructions provided (and their opcodes) are as follows:

1. Insert Character (IC)
2. Store Character (STC)
3. Insert Characters under Mask (ICM)
4. Store Characters under Mask (STCM)

We will discuss them in that order.

The L, ST LH, and STH opcodes provide the functions of moving 32-bit and 16-bit binary values between registers and storage. The IC (Insert Character) and STC (STore Character) instructions provide a similar service, but allow the movement of 8-bit values (1 byte).

IC works like the L or LH opcodes, but only affects the rightmost byte in the selected register. Bits 0 through 23 of the register are not affected, and bits 24-31 are copied from the specified byte in storage to the low-order byte of the register. The condition code is not changed. Figure 13.13 shows an example of the IC instruction.

IC and STC allow the use of 1-byte unsigned binary fields to hold values between 0 and 255 (the largest number possible in 8 bits). The register must be set to zero before the IC fetches the 1-byte counter from storage. STC will store back the 1-byte counter. Some limit check may be useful to ensure that the counter value does not exceed 255 before storing it back.

To use a 1-byte signed counter (values from -128 to +127), code (assuming COUNTER is a 1-byte counter) as follows:

```
IC      1,COUNTER
SLL     1,24
SRA     1,24
```

to set up the value in register 1.

IC and STC were used in the 360 era to store counters or flags in the leftmost byte of a word which held an address in the rightmost 3 bytes. This practice is still common, but should be avoided in new programs. The 31-bit

Figure 13.13   IC instruction data flow.

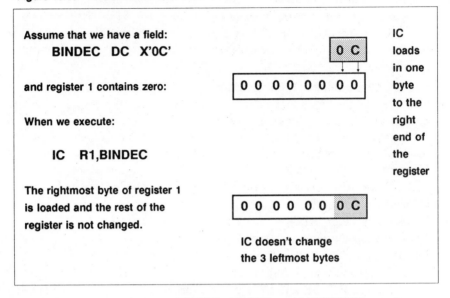

addressing requirements of MVS/XA, VM/XA, and MVS/ESA are incompatible with this practice. The 370 introduced the ICM, STCM, and CLM instructions which may be preferable to IC and STC for some applications.

*   *   *   *   *

ICM (Insert Characters under Mask) is an enhancement to the IC instruction which allows multiple bytes to be inserted into a register. ICM operates like IC, but adds a 4-bit mask field to specify which bytes will be inserted. The 4 bits of the mask correspond to the 4 bytes of a register.

If a bit is 1, a byte is moved from storage into the corresponding byte in the register. Movement into the register is controlled by the mask as follows:

Mask bit value:	8	4	2	1
Register byte:	0	1	2	3
Bits:	0-7	8-15	16-23	24-31

Movement from storage proceeds left to right through the second operand address. The condition code indicates what type of data was loaded (zero bits, leftmost bit 1, or nonzero and leftmost bit 0). Various settings of the mask give effects similar to the following:

ICM R2,1,FLDA =   IC R2,FLDA
ICM R2,3,FLDA =   LH R2,FLDA   (3 = 2 + 1)
ICM R2,15,FLDA =   L   R2,FLDA   (15 = 8 + 4 + 2 + 1)
Any mask value from 0 to 15 is valid. (Note that the sign bit is not propagated, so the middle example is not exactly like a Load Halfword.)

Figure 13.14 shows an example of ICM, explaining its use in an earlier example of MVCL.

Figure 13.14   ICM instruction data flow.

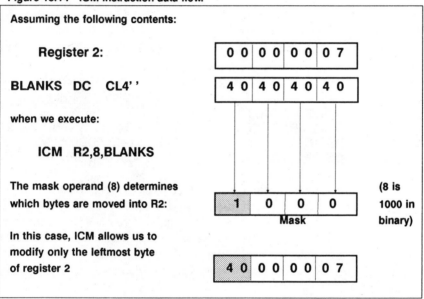

Assuming the following contents:

Register 2:   `0 0 | 0 0 | 0 0 | 0 7`

BLANKS DC CL4' '   `4 0 | 4 0 | 4 0 | 4 0`

when we execute:

ICM R2,8,BLANKS

The mask operand (8) determines   (8 is
which bytes are moved into R2:   `1 | 0 | 0 | 0`   1000 in
                                         Mask   binary)

In this case, ICM allows us to
modify only the leftmost byte
of register 2   `4 0 | 0 0 | 0 0 | 0 7`

STCM (Store Characters under Mask) is identical in coding and processing to ICM, but data transfer proceeds from the register to storage.

STCM is useful when you need to change an address in a control block which is defined as " AL3 ". This is a definition of a 24-bit address, and couldn't hold an address above the 16MB storage line.

STCM is useful in implementing a COBOL facility which we didn't cover in Chap. 10. This was the AT END clause of the READ verb. Our earlier presentation discussed use of the DCB EODAD parameter to provide the address of an AT END routine.

With STCM, however, we can dynamically change the address we originally provided in the DCB macro for the EODAD parameter. To do this, we must modify a field called "DCBEODA", which is defined as " AL3 ".

(If you want to look at this, you will find this field in the section of the DCBD macro listing called "Foundation Extension", at offset X'20' in the DCBD macro expansion. Note that there is also a field called "DCBEODAD" defined as a 4-byte address — this is not what we need to modify!)

Assume that we have the following COBOL code:

READ IN-FILE AT END GO TO ROUTINE-2.

Assume that IN-FILE and ROUTINE-2 are defined elsewhere in the program. Also assume that we have a DCB called INFILE, a record area called REC1 for this, and a routine called in ROUTINE2 in our assembler program which correspond to these. The corresponding assembler code for this, using the STCM instruction to set up the AT END address, would be as follows:

```
LA      R0,ROUTINE2        GET 'AT END' ROUTINE ADDR
LA      R1,INFILE          GET DCB ADDRESS
USING   HADCB,R1           ADDRESSABILITY
STCM    R0,7,DCBEODA       STORE NEW 'AT-END' ADDR
DROP    R1                 END DCB ADDRESSABILITY
GET     INFILE,REC1        READ A RECORD
```

This sets the equivalent of " EODAD=ROUTINE2 " in the DCB. Note, however, that this setting will stay the same for the rest of your program's execution unless you change it again. If you use this technique, you should probably change the "at-end" address each time you issue a GET macro. This adds code, but avoids the problem of using the wrong "at-end" routine if you have more than one at different points in your program's logic.

13.7.4   Relative Addressing with Packed Division

When we discussed the Divide Decimal (DP) instruction in Chap. 11, we glossed over the steps needed to extract the quotient and remainder from a larger field. To do this, we must use the technique of relative addressing. However, relative addressing with packed decimal instructions requires slightly different coding, since the packed decimal instructions have two length values, one each for the first and second operands.

We will illustrate how to use relative addressing with the UNPK instruction. However, other packed decimal instructions — e.g., ZAP — follow the same rules.

Our example of DP from Chap. 11 used the following fields:

```
INNINGS    DC     PL5'9'
BASES      DC     PL2'4'
```

and divided with the following instruction:

```
DP     INNINGS,BASES
```

To access the quotient and remainder values in INNINGS, we can use one of two techniques. The first is to redefine the dividend with the quotient and remainder fields broken out, such as:

```
INNINGS    DS    0CL5
QUOT       DS    PL3
REM        DS    PL2
```

With these definitions, the quotient can be used via the label QUOT, and the remainder with the label REM. No special coding in the instructions is needed.

The second approach is to use relative addressing to access the quotient and remainder. To do this, we need two pieces of information:

1. The offset of the number we want to unpack (i.e., how far past the start of the field)

2. The length of the number we want to unpack.

For packed decimal division, these are easy to calculate if we know the length of the dividend and the divisor. In the case listed above, INNINGS was five bytes long, and BASES was two bytes long. This meant that the quotient would be 3 bytes long - the length of the dividend (5 bytes) minus the length of the divisor (2 bytes). Since the quotient begins at the left end of the original dividend field, the offset to get to it is zero.

Similarly, the remainder will always be as long as the divisor — 2 bytes in this case. The offset to the remainder will be the same as the length of the quotient — 3.

With this information, it is now easy to unpack the quotient and remainder into other displayable fields. Assuming that we wish to display the quotient in a field called COMPLETE, and the remainder in a field called PARTIAL, the code to do so looks like

```
UNPK   COMPLETE,INNINGS + 0(3)     OFFSET 0, LEN 3
UNPK   PARTIAL,INNINGS + 3(2)      OFFSET 3,LEN 2
```

Note that we would still need to use OI to set the zone bits. When coding this type of addressing, make certain that a length is provided where needed. For the packed decimal instructions — AP, CP, DP, MP, MVO, PACK, SP, UNPK, and ZAP — this means that you must code a length on the second operand, as shown above. If the second length is omitted, you will process whatever the full length of the original field is, and probably receive a data exception (0C7) or incorrect results.

13.8 SUMMARY

This chapter has presented many instructions whose primary purpose is to do the same thing as the COBOL MOVE verb. The reason behind this number of instructions is the need to deal with many different data formats (character, packed decimal, binary) at the machine level.

While many instructions have been presented here, a few account for most of the MOVE-like functions in most assembler programs. These key instructions are

L, LH, LM, LR	Register load instructions
ST, STH, STM	Register store instructions
MVC, MVI	Character movement instructions
ZAP	Packed decimal move instruction
PACK, UNPK, CVB, CVD	Radix conversion instructions

If you feel that you have a good grasp of these instructions, you have gotten the key elements from this chapter.

Some of the other instructions are worth study, but won't be as frequent as the other instructions. The MVCL, IC, STC, and LTR instructions are probably the most common of the other instructions covered.

Things to Do

1. If you have access to any production assembler programs at work, look for old uses of instructions which have been superceded by newer instructions. Some particular examples follow:

MVC loops	Should be MVCL
MVO packed decimal shifting	Should be SRP
IC and shifts for fields shared with addresses	Should be avoided

2. If your organization uses an assembler language program to print dollar amounts on checks — do they use EDMK? Would "**VOID**" be preferable?

Subroutines and Save Areas

In this chapter, how to write a subroutine in assembler language will be covered. To illustrate this, an example of an assembler language subroutine which gets information not available in COBOL will be presented.

14.1 WHY USE SUBROUTINES?

Program design in assembler language has some special considerations. Pure structured programming is difficult to achieve, due to the constant requirement for branches. While special macro instructions may provide something like structured programming, a more common technique for improving the maintainability of assembler programs is modularity. This is most commonly achieved with extensive use of internal subroutines and external subprograms.

Subroutines and subprograms reduce the size of program segments. This simplifies development by only designing and debugging the same code once. This also simplifies maintenance by doing similar processes in one place. Finally, they reduce the total amount of code needed to do a given task.

The terms *subroutine* and *subprogram* are often used interchangeably. To be absolutely specific, we will use *subroutine* to indicate a subsection of a program which does some specific task. *Subprogram* will refer to a small program which does a specific task, but which is assembled separately from the program which uses it. Subprograms are typically not executed by themselves.

Strictly speaking, this chapter is intended to cover subprograms.

Another important reason to use subprograms is to avoid coding an entire large program in assembler. By moving the unique functions into subprograms, a large COBOL program can perform unique processing when necesary in assembler, but keep the bulk of the program in a more maintainable form. This point may be an important one when you need to convince your management that assembler is justified for a particular task.

14.2   ELEMENTS OF WRITING AND USING SUBPROGRAMS

Certain things must occur for a program to call a subprogram and get processing done on its behalf. These are as follows:

1. The calling program must allow the subprogram to find and update the data involved.
2. The calling program must be able to find the subprogram.
3. The calling program must be able to transfer control to the subprogram.
4. The subprogram must save and restore the context in which it was called (i.e., save registers).
5. The subprogram must be able to transfer control back to the calling program.

We will also use the term *main program* for the calling program, and *called program* for the subprogram. The term *linkage* refers to both the act of transferring control to a subprogram and to the setup needed to do this. *Arguments* refer to individual data elements passed from a main program to a subprogram.

The following subsections describe how each of these requirements are met. For most of this chapter, we will be describing how COBOL programs use subprograms if the COBOL compiler's NODYNAM option is selected (usually the default).

14.2.1   Finding the Data

For the subprogram to be able to find and update the right fields, the calling program must provide addresses of the parameters. (There are some other ways of doing this, using commonly addressable areas, but they are more frequently used in languages other than COBOL — for example, COMMON data in FORTRAN.)

MVS conventions require that this is done using a series of four-byte addresses called a *parameter list*. Each data element referred to by the list is called an *argument*. The process of setting up this address list and providing it to the subprogram is called *parameter passing*.

You may already be familiar with the concept of a parameter list if you know the USING option of the PROCEDURE DIVISION statement in COBOL. (If you aren't familiar with this, we'll explain it in the esoterica section later.)

To set up the parameter list, we have to provide the addresses. We may either have the assembler do this for us, by coding address constants, or we may build the list ourselves, by using the Load Address instruction. (We'll cover the Load Address method later.)

Address constants were mentioned earlier in Chap. 8. They are data items which are similar to COBOL USAGE IS INDEX fields. If you have coded COBOL under CICS, BLL cells provide another good example.

The type of the address constant determines how the assembler, linkage editor, and MVS program loader provide the address.

A-type address constants, often called *A-cons* or *adcons*, are used to generate an address of another field or label. Adcons are normally 4 bytes long, but the length may be modified. You code them as

LABEL   DC   A*(field-name)*

where *field-name* refers to either a data address or a program label address. Adcons normally refer to addresses within your program (but see the discussion of EXTRN later for an exception to this).

To create a parameter list, we should code it as a series of A-type constants. For example, assume that we wanted to have a parameter list with three entries. The first is a DCB for an input file. The second is a field in storage called "DATASET". The third is a fullword called "STATUS". To create this, we would code as follows:

```
PARMLIST  DC     A(INFILE)              DCB ADDRESS
          DC     A(DATASET)             DATA SET NAME
          DC     A(STATUS)              RETURN CODE
```

This generates three 4-byte addresses. The MVS program loader will make sure that these contain the proper virtual storage addresses when the program is brought into main storage.

The MVS linkage conventions require that we provide the address of this parameter list to the subprogram when we give it control. The expected way of doing this is to provide the address in register 1. Thus, we normally code the following before passing control to the subprogram:

```
          LA     R1,PARMLIST            GET PARM ADDRS
```

Figure 14.1   Operation of Load Address instruction (in 24-bit addressing mode).

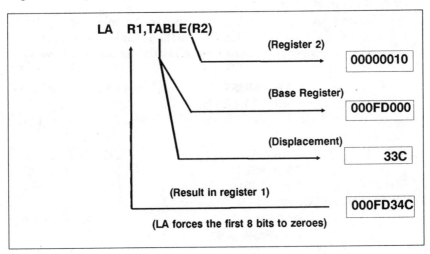

Figure 14.2   Operation of Load Address instruction (31-bit mode).

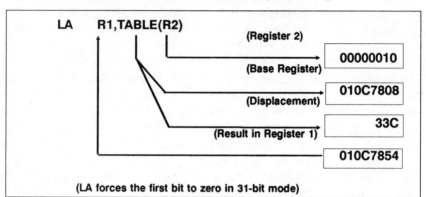

Figure 14.1 shows how the Load Address instruction works in 24-bit addressing mode. Figure 14.2 shows how LA works in 31-bit addressing mode.

The MVS linkage conventions are set up in such a way that there is no difference between the way you code a main program and a subprogram. Main programs may also have parameters — the PARM option of the MVS JCL EXEC statement or the parameters on the CMS START command provide this.

The coding given above for PARMLIST is acceptable, but not strictly what MVS requires in a parameter list. MVS specifies that the first bit of the last fullword in the parameter list must be set to 1. In COBOL, the number of parameters is fixed by the count of field names in the USING clause. However, MVS linkage conventions allow a subprogram to process a parameter list without knowing the length, and to verify that the right number of parameters are provided.

The first bit of the last fullword in our example's parameter list would be in the address of STATUS. The method that this book encourages is to use the Or Immediate instruction to set the bit on. Thus, we would code:

```
        LA    R1,PARMLIST                GET PARM ADDRS
        OI    PARMLIST + 8,X'80'
```

to set the bit on. To make this a little more understandable, we might code our parameter list as

```
PARMLIST  DC    A(INFILE)                DCB ADDRESS
          DC    A(DATASET)               DATA SET NAME
LASTPARM  DC    A(STATUS)                RETURN CODE
```

and set the bit on by coding

```
        LA    R1,PARMLIST                GET PARM ADDRS
        OI    LASTPARM,X'80'
```

You may see older programs which generate the bit along with the parameter list. In our example, this might be done by coding:

```
PARMLIST   DC    A(INFILE)            DCB ADDRESS
           DC    A(DATASET)           DATA SET NAME
           DC    X'80',AL3(STATUS)    RETURN CODE
```

This approach won't work with XA or ESA, since it only allows a 24-bit (AL3) address for the last parameter. This makes it impossible to have a data area above the 16-megabyte address limit of older operating systems.

You may still generate the last bit on through use of bit-length constant coding, but other programmers who will have to maintain the program later will probably understand the OI method more easily.

Other languages use different methods of passing parameters. For example, FORTRAN functions may pass data directly in register 0 rather than through parameter lists. FORTRAN also provides the COMMON area facility, which is addressed in assembler through the COM directive. COBOL internal subroutines may rely on register contents rather than in a parameter list. Programs written in the older CICS macro level use registers 12 and 13 to pass the addresses of control blocks. These methods are all valid, but may limit use of other software not written to these unique linkage conventions.

The OS/VS COBOL subroutine library includes many examples of subprograms with nonstandard linkage. One common example of this in COBOL is use of the Task Global Table (TGT) to pass common information. These subroutines are documented in the IBM manual "IBM OS/VS COBOL Subroutine Library Program Logic," manual number LY28-6425. This writer advises against use of anything other than standard linkage.

14.2.2 Finding the Subprogram

The assembler, linkage editor, and the MVS program loader provide services to get a subprogram included with your main program. To do this, the main program must somehow specify the subprogram's name, and must tell MVS where to put the address of the subprogram.

You specify that you wish to use a specific subprogram by including its name in an address constant of type V, or by specifying it in an assembler EXTRN directive. You get the address in an address constant of type A or V.

The preferred way to access data or programs outside of your own program is with the V-type address constant (sometimes called *V-cons*). They are similar to A-type constants in size and coding. The assembler automatically assumes that a name in a V-con refers to an address outside of your program.

Another way of specifying that a name refers to a subprogram or to data outside of your program is with the EXTRN linkage directive. EXTRN is coded as

```
EXTRN name
```

where *name* is an 8-byte or shorter program name. The linkage editor keeps track of these symbols. (Refer to the "External Symbol Dictionary" at the beginning of an assembly listing.)

Once you have defined a name with EXTRN, you may refer to it either via A-type or V-type address constants.The function of EXTRN overlaps with that of V-type address constants. We will use V-type constants rather than EXTRN throughout the rest of this book. However, you may see EXTRN used in programs you maintain.

Once you assemble a main program, the linkage editor will merge the subprograms with it to make an executable program, or load module. The linkage editor listing will show all the subprograms included in the load module if the LIST or MAP options are specified.

By convention, you place the address of the subprogram into register 15 before calling it. Thus, to call the subprogram "GETDSN", we would need to define its address by coding

```
SUBPROG    DC    V(GETDSN)
```
and set it into register 15 by coding
```
           L     R15,SUBPROG
```

14.2.3   Transferring Control to the Subprogram

Having gotten the address of the subprogram and specified the addresses of the parameters, we now need to give it control so it can execute. We do this with the Branch and Save instruction discussed in Chap. 12. The normal way of doing this is by coding

```
           BASR   R14,R15
```
using the address we previously loaded into register 15. You may see older programs which use " BALR R14,R15 ", but this is not preferable due to the 24-bit addressing limitation of BALR.

Before doing this, we must have done all the other setup discussed up to this point. The complete set of code to invoke the GETDSN subprogram is thus

```
           LA     R1,PARMLIST          GET PARM ADDRS
           OI     LASTPARM,X'80'       SET ON LAST BIT
           L      R15,SUBPROG          GET SUBPGM ADDR
           BASR   R14,R15              CALL 'GETDSN'
```
The data areas to support this are
```
SUBPROG    DC    V(GETDSN)         .
PARMLIST   DC    A(INFILE)            DCB ADDRESS
           DC    A(DATASET)           DATA SET NAME
LASTPARM   DC    A(STATUS)            RETURN CODE
```
and the above are all we need to do to call the routine.

Having explained all the specific details on how we call the subprogram, we'll now show a simpler way of doing it. MVS provides a macro (CALL) which does all of the setup and data area generation listed above.

The CALL macro has three parameters. The first is the name of the subprogram we want to execute. The second is the name (or names) of the parameters we want to pass to the subprogram. This name or set of names is coded inside parentheses. The final parameter (VL) is a keyword which tells the CALL macro to set on the first bit of the last word in the parameter list. Our example above would be coded

CALL   GETDSN,(INFILE,DATASET,STATUS),VL

The CALL macro is similar to the COBOL CALL verb. Our example above would be coded in COBOL as

CALL GETDSN USING INFILE, DATASET, STATUS.

The CALL macro will handle most cases of subprogram usage. There are some cases where it won't. For example, if you don't know the names of the arguments, you can't generate the parameter list with the CALL macro.

The Load Address instruction (opcode LA) provides a way to create the parameter list dynamically. Load Address provides a special arithmetic operation that calculates an address from a base, displacement, and index register if supplied. Figure 14.1 showed how Load Address operates.

Load Address does not use the first bit or first 8 bits in the calculation, depending on the addressing mode. No overflow is signalled. LA cannot ABEND.

Load Address performs a three-way addition to create a single number containing a virtual address of some area in storage. Load Address works differently in 370 (e.g., MVS/SP, VM/SP) and XA modes. The diagram in Fig. 14.1 showed how the address is calculated for a 24-bit addressing mode. (For Fig. 14.1, assume that TABLE is defined as DS 12F, that the base register is 12 and it contains hex X'000FD000', that the displacement of TABLE is hex X'33C', and that register 2 contains hex X'00000010'.)

Figure 14.2 then showed how to do this in a 31-bit addressing mode. (Assume the same initial values as in Fig. 14.1, except that the register 12 contains hex X'010C0000'.)

We can use LA to build or modify the parameter list when we can't do that via A-type address constants. For example, if we wanted to call GETDSN with a different DCB named PRINTER, and return the data set name in a field called PRINTDSN, we might code our example as follows:

```
LA      R1,PRINTER          OTHER DCB ADDR
ST      R1,PARMLIST         STORE AS 1ST PARM
LA      R1,PRINTDSN         OTHER AREA ADDR
ST      R1,PARMLIST+4       STORE AS 2ND PARM
LA      R1,PARMLIST         GET PARM ADDRS
OI      LASTPARM,X'80'      SET ON LAST BIT
L       R15,SUBPROG         GET SUBPGM ADDR
BASR    R14,R15             CALL 'GETDSN'
```

The data areas to support this are the same as used previously. If we need to make many modifications to the parameter list, it would be better to give each entry a name rather than coding "PARMLIST+4", et cetera.

Note that there is one more requirement that we handle at the beginning of our main program — providing a save area. The next section covers that.

14.2.4   Saving and Restoring Context

MVS and VM require that each subprogram not destroy the registers used by the calling program. To do this, subroutine conventions require that each program provide a *save area* where the called program may save the registers while it runs. The called program then sets the registers back before returning to the calling program.

By convention, register 13 should always point to a save area when you call another program or use any MVS macro. Most programmers interpret this to mean that register 13 must always point to a save area. This is not strictly true, but is a good rule to follow anyway. (Not all macros change your registers, for example.)

We saved the registers and provided a save area as part of our program initialization. The code to do this looked like

```
          STM    14,12,12(13)              SAVE REGISTERS
and

*                CHAIN SAVE AREAS
          ST     13,SAVEAREA+4             OLD SAVE AREA PTR
          LA     2,SAVEAREA                NEW SAVE AREA
          ST     2,8(13)                   NEW SAVE AREA PTR
          LR     13,2                      UPDATE REG 13
and
SAVEAREA  DC     18F'0'                    PGM SAVE AREA
```

The STM instruction actually saved registers 14, 15, and 0 through 12. Register 13 is not explicitly saved. We save and restore register 13 through the process labeled *chain save areas* above.

The save area is 18 fullwords (72 bytes) long. Its layout is shown in Fig. 14.3.

The process of chaining save areas sets up the *old save area* and *next save area* addresses so that the save areas may be linked. This relationship is shown in Fig. 14.4.

Figure 14.4 shows the relationship after program A calls program B, and program B calls program C. In the figure, "OSA" indicates the old save area address, and "NSA" indicates the next save area address.

Figure 14.3   Save area layout.

Word 1:	Used by PL/I Language
Word 2:	Address of Old Save Area
Word 3:	Address of Next Save Area
Word 4:	Register 14
Word 5:	Register 15
Word 6:	Register 0
Word 7:	Register 1
Word 8:	Register 2
Word 9:	Register 3
Word 10:	Register 4
Word 11:	Register 5
Word 12:	Register 6
Word 13:	Register 7
Word 14:	Register 8
Word 15:	Register 9
Word 16:	Register 10
Word 17:	Register 11
Word 18:	Register 12

Figure 14.4   Save area chaining.

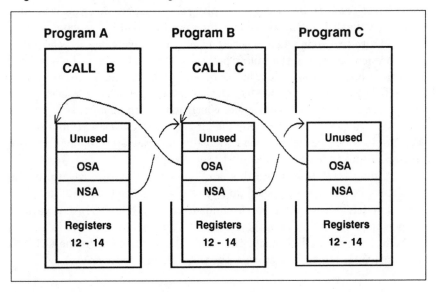

The calling program thus provides a save area into which the subprogram saves registers using the STM instruction. Both main programs and subprograms use the same linkage conventions in MVS, and both must provide save areas before calling another subprogram or using MVS services.

To restore the context, we must essentially reverse the process. Where we use an STM instruction to save the registers, we must use an LM instruction to restore the old register contents. Where we placed our save area address into register 13 at the beginning of the subprogram, we must now set the previous save area address into register 13. Also, we must do these things in reverse order from how they were done initially.

The code needed to actually perform this is

```
L      13,4(13)                OLD SAVE AREA PRT
LM     R14,R12,12(R13)         GET OLD REGS
```

At this point, the registers have the same contents as when the subprogram received control.

14.2.5 Transferring Control Back

Having completed our work, and restored the registers to their contents when the subprogram started, we now must give control back to the calling program. We do this by branching back to the address in register 14. We can do this with

```
BR     R14                     RET TO CALLER
```

and this is sufficient for returning control.

However, for completeness, we need to consider two other things. The first is to provide a return code. COBOL supports this via the RETURN-CODE special register, and you may provide this value when you give control back. If writing a main program in assembler, you may also wish to set the JCL condition code, which is controlled in the same way.

The return code value is set by placing a binary value in register 15 before branching back to the calling program. This may be done by using the LA instruction to set a specific value, or by using " SR R15,R15 " to set register 15 to 0. This must be done between the LM instruction, which resets the register contents, and the BR R14 instruction, which actually returns control.

Things get a little more complex if you wish to set a variable return code. To do this, you have to load the value into register 15, then restore register 14 and registers 0 through 12 separately.

A simpler method to do this, and one which handles several of the functions which we've described up to this point, is the RETURN macro.

The RETURN macro corresponds to the COBOL GOBACK verb. It also performs the function of the COBOL STOP verb when used in a main program. (The RETURN macro should not be confused with the COBOL RETURN verb, which is used with the COBOL sort feature.)

RETURN provides for three services. First is the restoration of the registers, which we do through the LM instruction. Second is setting the return code, if desired. Third is actually returning control to the calling program, which we did with the BR R14 instruction.

RETURN is coded with the registers to restore as the first operand and the optional return code specified via the RC= keyword. To return control with a 0 return code, write the RETURN macro as:

```
L       R13,4(R13)              OLD SAVE AREA PTR
RETURN (14,12),RC=0            RET TO CALLER
```

Note that we must have register 13 pointing to the old save area before executing the RETURN macro. If this isn't done, you will probably get into a loop between the last subprogram call or use of MVS services and the RETURN macro itself.

If we wish to have a variable return code supplied by several routines, but still have a common exit from the program, we can do this by using a common return code variable and the RETURN macro. Assuming that we have a halfword variable called RETCODE, we can code

```
LH      R15,RETCODE             GET RETURN CODE
L       R13,4(R13)              OLD SAVE AREA PTR
RETURN (14,12),RC=(15)         RET TO CALLER
```

The "RC=(15)" tells the RETURN macro that register 15 contains the return code. (The parentheses specify a register rather than the actual value. Thus, "RC=15" specifies a return code of 15, and "RC=(15)" specifies that the return code is in register 15.)

MVS has certain other conventions regarding return codes. Any value that fits into register 15 is valid as a return code, as long as both the calling and called program understand what it signifies. However, the step initiator and terminator logic in MVS only saves and reports a 12- bit value. This leads to a generally accepted range on return codes from 0 to 4095. In VM, return codes are reported back in the CMS READY message.

If you don't set the return code in a main program, both MVS and VM use whatever is in the rightmost 12 bits of register 15. This will be part of your program's beginning address, and will make no sense whatsoever. If you've ever seen nonsense condition codes in JCL listings, this is usually the cause.

Another MVS convention is that return codes are generally a multiple of 4. This allows their use with the branch table technique previously discussed. If only multiples of 4 are used, this results in only 1024 possible return code values. This should still be adequate for most needs.

VM conventions in the past have allowed return codes which aren't multiples of 4. However, newer VM commands tend to follow the same convention as MVS does. In both MVS and VM, a return code of 0 indicates successful completion.

The second item which we should consider for completeness is a little-used technique called *save area tagging*. If you have ever seen an MVS dump — not unlikely, if you've gotten this far into the book — you may remember a section of the dump called the *save area trace*. This lists the save areas, using the next and previous save areas to print all the save areas used by a main program and all its subprograms.

This is a useful debugging tool with programs that call many subroutines. This allows you to see the flow of control through the various subprograms up to the point of the ABEND.

Unfortunately, however, the save area trace may be misleading. If program A calls subprogram B, and subprogram B in turn calls subprogram C, there will be three save areas in the save area trace (plus one other provided by MVS to start program A). If subprogram C completes, giving control back to subprogram B, and B then ABENDs, the save area trace includes one save area too many.

If you are following the save area chain yourself in a dump, this leads to wasted debugging time or misleading results.

To avoid this, MVS provides for save area tagging. To do this, you set on the leftmost bit of the fourth word of the save area (the word which holds register 14). This tells the dump printing routines to stop printing further save areas.

You may do this yourself with the OI instruction, or you may specify it in the RETURN macro. To do this, you code a "T" as the second operand of RETURN, like this:

```
          RETURN  (14,12),T,RC = (15)          RET TO CALLER
```
You may use this under VM as well.

14.3   EXAMPLE OF A SUBPROGRAM IN ASSEMBLER

To put together all of the subprogram coding techniques we've discussed up to this point, let's look at a specific subprogram. This is the 'GETDSN' subroutine, which provides the data set name of a specified file. This subroutine works under both MVS and VM.

'GETDSN' requires three parameters. The first is an FD for which the data set name is desired. Second is a 44-byte area into which the data set name is placed. The third parameter is a binary fullword into which a return code is placed. (This is somewhat redundant, since you can also test the COBOL RETURN-CODE special register.) From COBOL, we provide the data by coding as follows:

```
FD    INFILE     and related parameters
...
77    IN-DSNAME          PIC X(44).
77    DSN-RETURN-CODE PIC S9(8) COMP.
...
```

and we invoke the subroutine by coding

```
CALL 'GETDSN' USING INFILE,
    IN-DSNAME,
    DSN-RETURN-CODE.
IF DSN-RETURN-CODE = ZERO
    THEN  MOVE IN-DSNAME TO HEAD-DSN
    ELSE  MOVE '*UNKNOWN*' TO HEAD-DSN
    DISPLAY 'GETDSN RETURN CODE:',
    DSN-RETURN-CODE.
```

(HEAD-DSN is an area used to print the data set name.)

GETDSN provides three return codes. Zero means successful completion, in line with normal conventions. Four means that an error occurred trying to get the data set name. Eight means that the FD was already open and that GETDSN will not attempt to get the data set name.

GETDSN uses an MVS macro called RDJFCB (Read Job File Control Block). VM also supports this through OS simulation. RDJFCB takes as input a DCB (FD), and provides the the data set name along with a large amount of other information about the file in a 176-byte storage area. To provide the address of the storage area, you must modify the DCB macro. While possible, it's probably not usually desirable to modify the DCB (FD) in a COBOL program, so GETDSN uses its own dummy DCB and copies in the DD name from the COBOL program.

A full explanation of RDJFCB and modifying the DCB is outside the scope of this book. However, with this background, you should be able to understand the subroutine itself, which is shown as Fig. 14.5.

Figure 14.5   The GETDSN subroutine and its associated JCL.

```
The numbers in brackets refer to notes which follow the listing.
//JOBNAME JOB  your usual JOB statement
//ASSEMBLE  EXEC ASMHCL
//ASM.SYSIN DD  *
GETDSN    CSECT
[1]       STM   14,12,12(13)           SAVE REGISTERS
          LR    R12,R15                GET PGM ADDRESS
          USING GETDSN,R12             ADDRESSABILITY
          SPACE 1
*         CHAIN SAVE AREAS
          ST    R13,SAVEAREA+4         OLD SAVE AREA PTR
          LA    R2,SAVEAREA            NEW SAVE AREA PTR
          ST    R2,8(R13)              SET NEW SAVE PTR
          LR    R13,R2                 UPDATE REG 13
          SPACE 1
*         GET PARAMETERS
[2]       LM    R2,R4,0(R1)            LOAD PARM ADDRS
```

Figure 14.5   (Continued)

```
        USING  IHADCB,R2                          DCB DSECT
[3]     TM     DCBOFLGS,X'10'                     TEST GOOD OPEN
        BO     OPENERR                            ALREADY OPEN: ERR
        LA     R5,FAKEDCB                         POINT TO OUR DCB
[4]     MVC    DCBDDNAM-IHADCB(8,R5),DCBDDNAM   DD NAME
        RDJFCB (FAKEDCB)
        LTR    R15,R15                            TEST GOOD RET CD
        BNZ    BADREADJ                           NOT ZERO - ERROR
[5]     MVC    0(44,R3),JFCBAREA                  MOVE DATA SET NAME
        SPACE 1
*       END OF SUBPROGRAM.
GOBACK  EQU    *
[6]     LH     R15,RETCODE                        GET RET CODE
        ST     R15,0(R4)                          GIVE RC TO CALLER
        L      R13,4(R13)                         GET OLD SAVE AREA
        RETURN (14,12),RC = (15)                  RETURN TO MVS
        SPACE 1
*       ERROR WHEN OPENING A FILE. END WITH RETURN CODE 8.
OPENERR EQU    *
        MVC    RETCODE, = H'8'                    SET UP BAD RET CD
        B      GOBACK                             RETURN TO CALLER
        SPACE 1
*       ERROR IN RDJFCB MACRO. END WITH RETURN CODE
*       FROM REGISTER 15 AFTER RDJFCB MACRO.
BADREADJ EQU   *
        STH    R15,RETCODE                        STORE RET CODE
        B      GOBACK                             RETURN TO CALLER
        SPACE 3
*       DATA AREAS
SAVEAREA DC    18F'0'                             PGM SAVE AREA
RETCODE DC     H'0'                               RET CODE VALUE
        SPACE 3
*       DATA CONTROL BLOCKS
FAKEDCB DCB    DDNAME = FAKENAME,DEVD = DA,MACRF = (E),     X
               LRECL = 0,BLKSIZE = 0,                       X
[7]            EXLST = EXITLIST
        CNOP 0,4      ALIGN TO FULLWORD BOUNDARY
EXITLIST DC    X'87',AL3(JFCBAREA)      EXITLIST
JFCBAREA DS    CL176      JOB FILE CONTROL BLOCK PUT HERE
[8]     SPACE 3
*       DATA CONTROL BLOCK DUMMY SECTION (IHADCB)
        PRINT  ON,NOGEN
        DCBD   DEVD = DA,DSORG = PS
        SPACE 3
```

Figure 14.5   (Continued)

```
*              REGISTER EQUATES
R0             EQU   0
R1             EQU   1
R2             EQU   2
R3             EQU   3
R4             EQU   4
R5             EQU   5
R6             EQU   6
R7             EQU   7
R8             EQU   8
R9             EQU   9
R10            EQU   10
R11            EQU   11
R12            EQU   12
R13            EQU   13
R14            EQU   14
R15            EQU   15
               END   GETDSN                    END OF PROGRAM
/*
//LKED.SYSLMOD  DD   DSNAME=TSOUSER.PDS.LOAD(GETDSN),
//                   DISP=SHR                   [9]
```

Notes to Fig. 14.5:

1. Note that the subprogram uses the same linkage conventions as any main program.
2. The LM instruction loads the three parameter addresses into registers 2, 3, and 4.
3. Refer to Chap. 10 for an explanation of the TM to determine if the file is open and the IHADCB DSECT.
4. In a convoluted way, this moves the DD name from the caller's FD (referred to as "DCBDDNAM" in the second operand) to the DD name field in our fake DCB. Register 5 contains the DCB address. "DCBDDNAM-IHADCB" tells the assembler to use the difference between the two labels IHADCB and DCBDDNAM as the displacement amount.
5. This moves the data set name from our program (in JFCBAREA) to the caller's area. Register 3 points to the caller's data set name area from the earlier LM.
6. At this point, we get the return code value, without regard to where it was set.
7. The " EXLST=EXITLIST " operand of the DCB tells MVS where to find the address of the area to get the JFCB.

8. The "X'87',AL3(JFCBAREA)" defines this as the end of the parameter list; the "7" part identifies this as the address of the JFCB area. Note that the DCB contains many 24-bit addresses, and hence can't be above the 16-megabyte address line.
9. You should replace "TSOUSER.PDS.LOAD" with the name of a valid load library where subprograms are kept at your installation.

Also, you would not key in the MVS JCL (the statements starting with "//") under VM.

To use this subroutine in one of your own COBOL programs, you may have to change your COBOL program's link edit step MVS JCL. If your installation has a standard library where subroutines are kept, you may link GETDSN into that library by changing the LKED.SYSLMOD DD statement noted in Fig. 14.5. (Such libraries are usually identifiable as concatenations to the SYSLIB DD statement in the linkage editor step of your COBOL compile procedure.)

If you do not have access to such a library, you may still link edit GETDSN into the same load library as your COBOL main program. Then, when you compile your COBOL main program, add the following overrides to the linkage editor step:

```
//LKED.SYSIN  DD  *
 INCLUDE  SYSLMOD(GETDSN)
 NAME     progname(R)
```

Note that you should code the actual name of your COBOL program rather than *progname* as shown in the above example. Also, this assumes that your COBOL compile JCL has a step name of LKED. If your shop has numerous changes from the IBM-supplied COBOL compile JCL, you may need to research this further.

The RDJFCB macro has many other uses and provides additional information. For example, the member name specified (if any) is provided in the 8 bytes following the data set name. There is a mapping macro, called IEFJFCBN, located in an IBM-supplied library called SYS1.AMODGEN (or possibly SYS1.MODGEN). VM does not supply this macro. You may find it worthwhile to locate this and review the other data supplied by the RDJFCB macro. You may need the assistance of your installation's systems programmer to locate this.

VM will return a data set name field for RDJFCB made up of the VM disk identification fields. This will include the 8-byte file name, 8-byte file type, and 2-byte file mode. For example:

```
ASMPROG ASSEMBLEB2
```

Note that there is no spacing between these three fields, and that the file type and file mode have run together in the above example.

You may wish to insert some spaces in the name if you are running this under VM. You can do this by changing the statement

[5]   MVC   0(44,R3),JFCBAREA MOVE DATA SET NAME

which was identified by note [5] in the figure. This statement should be
replaced by

MVI	0(R3),C' '	SET CALLING PGM
MVC	1(43,R3),0(R3)	AREA TO BLANKS
MVC	0(8,R3),JFCBAREA	MOVE FILE NAME
MVC	8(8,R3),JFCBAREA+8	MOVE FILE TYPE
MVC	16(2,R3),JFCBAREA+16	MOVE FILE TYPE

This causes the data set name to be stored back to the calling program as

ASMPROG ASSEMBLEB2

which is more readable.

14.4   THE COBOL DYNAM OPTION

Up to this point, we've assumed that you are including subroutines with
your COBOL main programs by using the linkage editor to make one big
load module with all the subprograms included. Figure 14.6 shows this link
editing process for MVS, and Fig. 14.7 shows how the main program calls
its subroutines after they are all link-edited together.

Figure 14.6   Overview of link edit process.

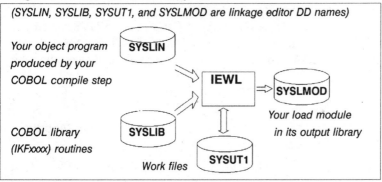

(*SYSLIN, SYSLIB, SYSUT1, and SYSLMOD are linkage editor DD names*)

Your object program SYSLIN
produced by your
COBOL compile step   IEWL ⇒ SYSLMOD

                                    Your load module
COBOL library SYSLIB   *in its output library*
(IKFxxxx) routines
                 Work files SYSUT1

Your installation may use another method of getting subroutines.
This is the COBOL DYNAM option.

If you aren't sure if your installation uses this, check a COBOL
compile listing. In the statistics section of the listing, there will be several
lines titled "Options in Effect." Scan these lines looking for either DYNAM
or NODYNAM. If you find NODYNAM, you may skip this section.

If you find DYNAM, it means that you will see a different way of
passing control to your subprograms. Rather than using the BALR instruction, or the CALL macro, you will be using another series of MVS macro

Figure 14.7   Relationship of main program to subroutines.

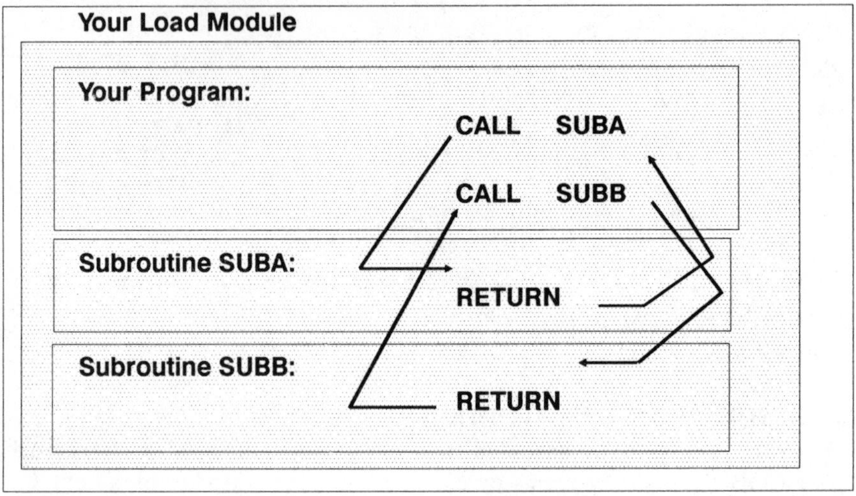

Your Load Module

Your Program:

CALL   SUBA

CALL   SUBB

Subroutine SUBA:

RETURN

Subroutine SUBB:

RETURN

instructions. These are the contents management macros, which are also simulated by VM.

The macro instructions included in this are LINK, LOAD, XCTL, and DELETE. LINK is similar to CALL in its operation, but the others represent entirely different services.

When you use the DYNAM option, COBOL causes MVS to bring in each subprogram separately when it is needed. With NODYNAM, both the main program and all subprograms needed are brought in at the same time.

Figure 14.8   Overview of LINK macro.

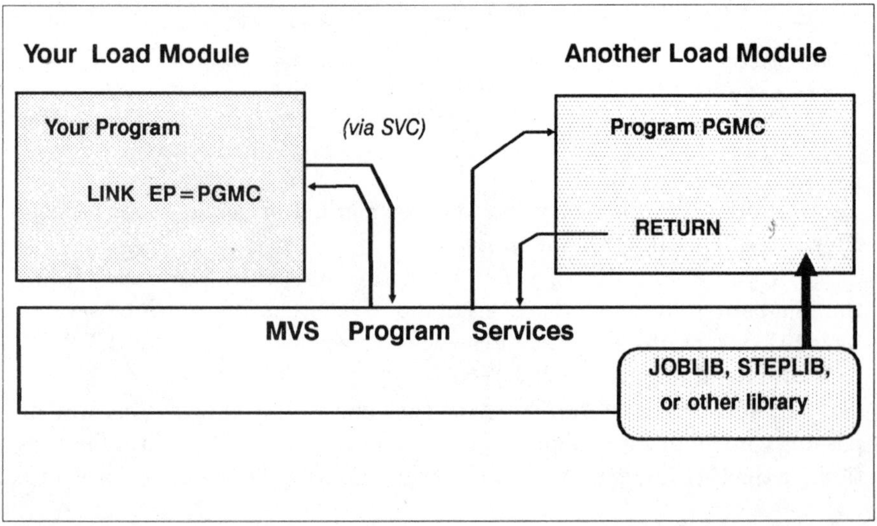

Your Load Module   Another Load Module

Your Program   (via SVC)   Program PGMC

LINK EP = PGMC

RETURN

MVS   Program   Services

JOBLIB, STEPLIB,
or other library

DYNAM may take less main storage, but NODYNAM will tend to require less disk I/O. Selection of one or the other options depends on the limiting factors at your installation more than anything else.

The LINK macro provides the service of bringing in the requested subprogram, and then transfers control to it much like CALL does. An example of LINK coded similarly to our CALL macro would be

```
LINK      EP = GETDSN,PARAM = (INFILE,DATASET,STATUS),VL = 1
```

Alternatively, you may put the address of the parameter list into register 1 before issuing the LINK macro. In this case, the PARAM and VL operands must be omitted. Figure 14.8 shows how the LINK macro operates.

The LOAD macro brings a program into main storage, and passes the address back to your program. The following will bring the GETDSN program into storage (assuming that it is in a STEPLIB or JOBLIB data set), but doesn't transfer control to it:

```
LOAD   EP = GETDSN
```

Register 0 contains the address of GETDSN after the LOAD completes. You could then use BASR to branch to it if desired.

The DELETE macro is sort of the opposite of LOAD. DELETE marks your subprogram as no longer in use. If no one is using a program, and MVS needs the space, it will reuse the main storage occupied by that program. The program normally stays put until that occurs, however. For example:

```
DELETE EP = GETDSN
```

Register 15 contains a return code following this macro's execution.

DELETE keeps count of how many requests have been made for a program. It won't make the main storage eligible for reuse until the number of deletes equals the number of requests for the program.

DELETE is similar in function to the COBOL CANCEL verb, although not identical.

XCTL (Transfer Control) operates sort of like a combination of LINK and DELETE. There is no real COBOL equivalent to XCTL. XCTL operates like LINK in that it passes control from your program to a subprogram. However, XCTL does NOT ever let your program get control again. After bringing in the specified program, XCTL issues a DELETE to remove yours if needed.

Use of XCTL requires special planning. For example, you may not pass parameters that are inside your own program, since your program's storage is no longer reserved. You also should not open any DCBs which the other program may need to use.

XCTL also requires that you set up the registers as though your program was about to return. You specify which registers are restored. For more information about XCTL, refer to the supervisor services and macros manual.

VM/SP also provides a macro, CMSCALL, which provides contents management services. This operates much like the LINK macro in MVS. The CMSRET macro provides a return service. CMSCALL provides a number of CMS-specific services and links to another program as well. For further details, refer to the VM application development reference.

14.5   INTERMIXING 24-BIT AND 31-BIT ADDRESSING IN MVS/XA

MVS/XA allows programs to run in two modes. The first, 24-bit or 370 mode, acts just like older versions of the MVS and VM operating systems. The second, 31-bit or XA mode, allows programs to access much larger amounts of main memory.

In general, putting programs or data in the area beyond the 24-bit addressing limit (16 megabytes) is a good idea. It may not be appropriate if the data must be accessed by a large number of existing programs which only run in 24-bit mode.

The 370 architecture provides several instructions and other facilities to support extended (31-bit) addressing. Assembler H and the DFP linkage editor also provide directives and services to support 31-bit addressing. We will discuss the instructions and directives in subsections 14.5.1 and 14.5.2.

In addition, many MVS and VM macros have additional operands to support 31-bit addressing. Due to space limitations, we cannot discuss all of these. However, many DCB-related functions (GET, PUT) will not operate properly in the 31-bit addressing mode.

The most frequent case which you will probably see is the need to get to a 31-bit mode subprogram from an existing 24-bit program. To do this, you must provide an intermediate program which switches from one mode to another and transfers and returns control in the appropriate mode. (This type of program is sometimes termed a *glue module*, since it holds two distinct types of programs together.)

14.5.1   Instructions for 31-bit Addressing

To take advantage of 31-bit addressing without rewriting all previously created programs, the IBM 370 CPU provides instructions which allow programmers to switch from one mode to another. These are the Branch and Save and Set Mode (BASSM) and the Branch and Set Mode (BSM) instructions.

14.5.1.1   Branch and Save and Set Mode (BASSM)

BASSM is used to switch from one addressing mode to another. It is an RR-format instruction. Operation of BASSM is conceptually similar to BASR and BALR. The CPU stores the right half (rightmost 32 bits) of the current PSW into the first operand (R1). The CPU then uses the second operand register's contents (R2) as a branch address.

The difference in processing between BASSM and BASR is in the effect on the addressing mode bit (bit 32) in the PSW. Both BASR and BASSM save the right half of the current PSW into the first operand register. However, BASR only updates the instruction address part of the PSW - bits 33 through 63. BASR does not update the addressing mode in the PSW and hence can only be used to transfer control among routines with the same addressing mode. (This discussion also applies to BAS, BAL, and BALR.)

BASSM, in addition to the processing listed above, also updates the addressing mode (bit 32) of the PSW. Thus, BASSM can be used to transfer control to programs running in a different addressing mode. To call a subroutine and change addressing modes, you would code

BASSM 14,15

instead of " BASR 14,15 ". There is some register setup required which we will show later.

14.5.1.2 Branch and Set Mode (BSM)

BSM is used to return back to a calling program which has used the BASSM instruction. It logically fills the role of the BR instruction when returning from a subroutine. However, it has some added features which allow other uses.

BSM is an RR-format instruction. The second operand register (R2) contains a branch address, just like the BR instruction. The difference in processing is that BSM replaces the addressing mode bit in the PSW in addition to the branch address. The first operand of BSM specifies a register (R1) which is to receive the current addressing mode.

To return control from a subroutine and to change the addressing mode back to the caller's addressing mode, code

BSM   0,14

This is logically equivalent to " BR 14 ". (This assumes that the calling program used " BASSM 14,15 to invoke our program.)

The first operand specifies a register which receives only the current addressing mode bit. This is placed in bit 0 of the register. The other 31 bits are not changed.

If the first operand is zero, the addressing mode bit is not stored. If the second operand is zero, the CPU does not branch. Thus, " BSM   7,0 " would put the current addressing mode bit into register 7. It would not branch anywhere, and control would fall through to the next instruction. Figure 14.9 shows the operation of 24-bit mode to 31-bit mode using the BASSM and BSM instructions.

14.5.2 Directives for 31-bit Addressing

To support the intermixing of 24-bit and 31-bit programs, the assembler and linkage editor provide new directives which specify how the program runs. These are the AMODE (Addressing Mode) and RMODE (Residence Mode) directives.

Figure 14.9   Linkage between 24-bit and 31-bit addressing modes.

Storage above 16MB address line (31-bit addresses)

Program PGMB

BSM   R14

Storage below 16MB address line (24-bit addresses)

Program PGMA

BASSM   R14,R15

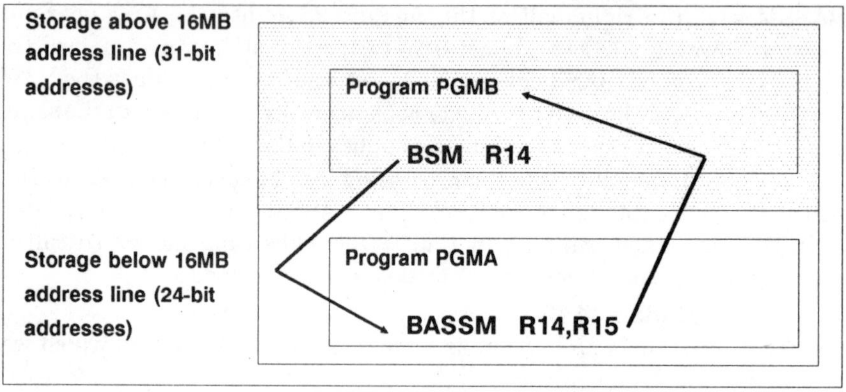

14.5.2.1   Addressing Mode Directive — AMODE

AMODE specifies how MVS/XA should set the PSW addressing bit when your program executes. The format for coding AMODE is

csect_name AMODE   24 | 31 | ANY

The csect_name is coded in the label position and must identify the name of your program's CSECT statement. (It may only be blank if you have an unnamed CSECT in your program.)

The addressing mode operand may be 24, 31, or ANY. These have the following meanings:

24 — This CSECT requires 24-bit addressing mode.

31 — This CSECT requires 31-bit addressing mode.

ANY — This CSECT is not sensitive to addressing mode.

The ANY option allows your program to run as a subroutine of programs in either 24-bit or 31-bit addressing modes.

14.5.2.2   Residence Mode Directive — RMODE

RMODE specifies where MVS/XA should load your programs. The coding format is

csect_name RMODE   24 | ANY

CSECTNAME is the name of your CSECT, as in the AMODE discussion above. The operands mean

24 — This program must be loaded at an address below 16 megabytes (i.e., below the 24-bit address limit).

ANY — This program may be loaded anywhere.

Note that both AMODE and RMODE default to 24 if not specified. RMODE ANY and AMODE 24 cannot be specified for the same control section. RMODE and AMODE can only be specified once for a control section.

14.5.3   Example of Switching Addressing Modes

Figure 14.10 is an example of how to switch from 24-bit addressing mode to 31-bit addressing mode and back within one program. The function of the code shown here is to use an MVS/XA macro, NUCLKUP, in 31-bit addressing mode. (The function of NUCLKUP is to locate a program in the MVS/XA nucleus. This allows us to call certain subroutines in MVS/XA which aren't otherwise easily accessible.) Note that The 'TRYLOOK' routine could have been an internal subroutine elsewhere in our program. The " O R7,=X'80000000' " sets the leftmost bit in register 7 to a 1. The BASSM instruction will then set this into the addressing mode bit of the PSW. ADDRFLD is a fullword defined elsewhere in the program.

The NUCLKUP macro is described in "MVS/Extended Architecture System Programming Library: System Macros and Facilities, vol. 2," manual number GC28-1151. You may have to see your systems programmer for this manual.

Figure 14.10   Switching between 24-bit and 31-bit addressing modes.

```
*          SET UP ADDRESSING MODE
           LA     R7,TRYLOOK           GET 31-BIT RTN ADDR
           O      R7, = X'80000000'    SET BIT 0 ON (XA MODE)
           BASSM R8,R7                 GO TO TRYLOOK RTN
           B      LOOKDONE             GO PAST 31-BIT CODE
*          LOOK UP A ROUTINE BY NAME - THIS PART RUNS IN
*          31-BIT MODE
TRYLOOK    EQU    *
           LA     R2, = CL8'IGC001 '   WAIT MACRO SVC NAME
           NUCLKUP BYNAME,NAME = (2),ADDR = ADDRFLD
           BSM    R7,R8                GO BACK  TO 24-BIT MODE
*          LOOKUP DONE - CONTINUE WITH OTHER PROCESSING
LOOKDONE           EQU                 *
```

14.5.4   VM AMODESW Macro

VM provides a macro instruction called AMODESW. This generates the code necesary to support intermixed 24-bit and 31-bit linkage.AMODESW has four general options which determine what it actually does. These are:

1. CALL — Call one program from another and switch addressing modes.
2. RETURN — Return back to a caller and restore the previous addressing mode.
3. QRY — Determine the current addressing mode.
4. SET — Set a specific addressing mode.

Each of these options involve other parameters, which we won't discuss here. Refer to the VM/SP application development reference for more details on AMODESW.

14.6   THE COBOL STOP AND STOP RUN FUNCTIONS

The assembler RETURN macro is most like the COBOL GOBACK verb. RETURN only passes control back to whatever program called it.

COBOL allows STOP RUN to be coded in either the main program or a subprogram, and it automatically ends the step. It is difficult to have a direct equivalent to this in assembler. (If DYNAM is used, it is more difficult.)

However, one way to simulate this is with the assembler EXIT macro. EXIT generates a special MVS service request which halts the current load module's execution. If your subprogram is link-edited with the program called in via the JCL EXEC statement, EXIT will act like a STOP RUN.

This may not be a desirable feature. The main COBOL program may need to perform certain termination routines to ensure file integrity.

You code EXIT as a macro with no operands. The assembler EXIT macro should not be confused with the COBOL EXIT verb, which has a completely unrelated function.

Under VM, code " SVC 3 " instead of " EXIT " to achieve the same result.

You should set register 15 to contain the desired return code in both operating systems before using EXIT.

14.7   SUBPROGRAM ESOTERICA

Some additional techniques are presented here which are slightly related to the general linkage topic of this chapter. The first of these, passing parameters to a main program, shows how to use the JCL EXEC statement PARM feature to pass information to a main program, and is fairly frequently used.

14.7.1   Passing Parameters to a Main Program (MVS)

You are probably familiar with the practice of passing parameter information through the JCL EXEC statement PARM operand. A main program (one specified on the EXEC statement) can access this data just as though it were passed to it as a parameter.

The format of the parameters passed is shown in Fig. 14.11. When the main program receives control, register 1 points to a fullword, which in turn points to a halfword containing the number of bytes of parameter data, followed by the PARM data itself.

You can do this in COBOL with the USING clause of the PROCE-DURE DIVISION statement. It requires that an appropriately-formatted 01-level group item be defined in the linkage section, and that the procedure division be coded properly.

The data items necesary to support this in COBOL are:

Figure 14.11   Format of PARM data.

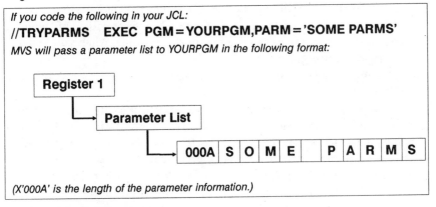

If you code the following in your JCL:
//TRYPARMS   EXEC PGM = YOURPGM,PARM = 'SOME PARMS'
MVS will pass a parameter list to YOURPGM in the following format:

```
Register 1
     └──▶ Parameter List
               └──▶ 000A  S  O  M  E     P  A  R  M  S
```

(X'000A' is the length of the parameter information.)

```
      LINKAGE SECTION.
01    PARM-INFO.
      05    PARM-LENGTH PIC S9(4) COMP SYNC.
      05    PARM-INFO    PIC X  OCCURS 1 TO 100 TIMES
                         DEPENDING ON PARM-LENGTH.
```

The procedure division coding for this is

```
      PROCEDURE DIVISION USING  PARM-INFO.
      MOVE PARM-LENGTH TO PARM-LENGTH.
```

You may then access up to PARM-LENGTH bytes of data in the PARM-INFO array. (Accesses past the number of bytes specified in PARM-LENGTH may cause an 0C4 ABEND.) To access this data in assembler, we code the following after chaining the save areas:

```
      L     R1,0(R1)          PARM FIELD ADDR
      LH    R3,0(R1)          GET PARM LENGTH
      LTR   R3,R3             TEST FOR ZERO
      BZ    NOPARMS           ZERO – NO PARMS
      LA    R2,2(R1)          POINT TO PARM =
```

We could now use MVCL to move the parameters. Register 2 has the address of the bytes passed from the EXEC statement, and R3 has the length. NOPARMS would have to be defined as a label elsewhere to continue processing if no PARM data were present.

14.7.2   Passing Parameters from the START Command (VM)

VM/CMS provides services similar to those just described for the MVS JCL PARM operand. This takes the form of *supervisor assisted linkage* when invoking a program in response to a command entered from a CMS virtual console.

Supervisor assisted linkage also applies when invoking a program via the CMSCALL macro, or by the older CMS SVC 202 and 203 methods.

The function generally works like the LINK macro in MVS which we've previously described. However, it includes parameter list processing which is more complex than that expected by MVS linkage conventions.

The parameter list for a CMS command takes the form of the data entered on the same line as the command. For example, when you key in

X ASMPROG ASSEMBLE

the ASMPROG and ASSEMBLE are the parameters for the execution of XEDIT.

VM provides its parameter list processing to simplify the determination of what parameters have been passed. Since VM commands are normally entered interactively from a terminal, a way of determining exactly what parameters are entered is provided.

The way in which this is provided is by the SCAN macro. SCAN is used by CMS to format the command lines you enter into special VM-format parameter lists. You may also use it yourself, and it may be informative to look up how it works in the application development reference manual.

Using this, VM provides a special format for the input command line, called a *tokenized* parameter list. This is a series of 8-byte entries in storage, each of which contains a parameter from the command line. An 8-byte entry of all X'FF' bytes marks the end of the parameters. If an argument on the command line is shorter than eight bytes, it is padded on the right with blanks. If it is longer than 8 bytes, it is truncated to the leftmost 8 bytes.

The address of the tokenized parameter list is provided to your program in register 1. In addition, the leftmost byte of register 1 (bits 0-7) contain a code byte indicating where the input command came from, and hence how the program was invoked. The application development guide lists the codes. A code value of X'0B' indicates a CMS command, or a simulation thereof (TYPCALL=CMS on the CMSCALL macro).

VM also provides what is termed an *extended parameter list*. Register 0 contains the address of the extended parameter list when your program is invoked. Not all types of calls provide the extended parameter list; TYPCALL=CMS does, so you have access to one when your program is invoked as a CMS command. This is in addition to the tokenized parameter list.

The EPLIST macro provides a DSECT definition of the tokenized parameter list. EPLIST includes a definition of the invocation codes in register 1. The extended parameter list includes two address pointers called EPLARGBG and EPLARGND. These contain the address of the beginning and end of the parameter arguments respectively if you don't want a tokenized parameter list.

VM also defines a second format for the extended parameter list. This is used with the SENDREQ macro.

Figure 14.12 shows a program which accesses the tokenized parameter list provided with a START command.

Note that Fig. 14.12 shows several new VM macros which we haven't explained yet. These will be discussed in later chapters of the book. The notes to the figures indicate where we will be explaining the new macros.

VM also provides two other macros useful in processing a parameter list. These are PARSECMD and PARSERCB. For more information on these, and on accessing the extended parameter lists, refer to the application development guide manual.

Figure 14.12   Accessing START command parameters.

```
(The numbers in brackets (e.g., "[1]") refer to notes after the figure.)

SHOWPARM   TITLE 'SHOW PARM INFO FROM VM'
SHOWPARM   CSECT
           STM    R14,R12,12(R13)            SAVE REGISTERS
           LR     R12,R15                    ESTABLISH
           USING  SHOWPARM,R12               ADDRESSABILITY
           SPACE 3
*          CHAIN  SAVE AREAS
           LA     R2,SAVEAREA
           ST     R2,8(R13)
           ST     R13,4(R2)
           LR     R13,R2
           USING  SAVEAREA,R13               PGM DATA AREAS
           SPACE 1
*          SAVE PARM INFO INTO R2
[1]        LR     R2,R1
           SPACE 1
*          DISPLAY PARM INFO WE GOT FROM VM
[2]        LINEDIT TEXT = 'ADDRESS:......... ',                      X
               DOT = NO,COMP = NO,SUB = (HEX,(2)),RENT = NO
           LINEDIT TEXT = 'DATA:............................         X
               ...............................',                    X
               DOT = NO,COMP = NO,SUB = (HEX4A,(2)),RENT = NO
           SPACE 1
*          SHOW USE OF LINEDIT TO ISSUE CP MESSAGE COMMAND
*          (EQUIVALENT OF WTO MACRO)
[3]        LINEDIT TEXTA = COMMAND,DISP = CPCOMM,                   X
               DOT = NO,COMP = NO,RENT = NO
           SPACE 1
*          SHOW USE OF LINEDIT TO ISSUE CP DUMP COMMAND
*          EQUIVALENT OF SNAP MACRO)
[4]        LA     R2,SHOWPARM               BEGIN DUMP AREA
```

Figure 14.12   (Continued)

```
            LA      R3,PROGEND                      END OF DUMP AREA
[5]         LINEDIT TEXTA = DUMPCMD,DISP = CPCOMM,              X
            DOT = NO,COMP = NO,SUB = (HEX,(2),HEX,(3)),         X
            RENT = NO
            SPACE 1
ENDEXEC EQU     *
            LH      R0,RETCODE                      GET RETURN CODE
            CVD     R0,DOUBLEWD                     CONV TO DECIMAL
            OI      DOUBLEWD + 7,X'0F'              TURN ON SIGN BITS
            UNPK    MSG803RC,DOUBLEWD               UNPACK
*           ISSUE WRTERM TO WRITE TO MY VIRTUAL CONSOLE
*           (EQUIVALENT OF PUT MACRO TO TERMINAL)
[6]         WRTERM MSG803I,80                       CMS CONSOLE  MSG
*           RETURN TO CALLING PROGRAM
RETURN  EQU     *
            LH      R15,RETCODE                     GET RETURN CODE
            L       R13,4(R13)                      OLD SAVE AREA PTR
            RETURN (14,12),T,RC = (15)             RETURN
            EJECT
*           DATA AREAS
DOUBLEWD DC     D'0'
SAVEAREA DC     18F' + 0
'RETCODE DC     H'0'
            SPACE 1
COMMAND DC      AL1(COMMEND-*-1)                    LENGTH
[7]         DC      C'MSG OPERATOR HELLO THERE'
COMMEND EQU     *
            SPACE 1
DUMPCMD         DC   AL1(DUMPEND-*-1)               LENGTH
[8]         DC      C'DUMP T......:...... *DISPLAY STORAGE'
DUMPEND EQU     *
MSG803I DC      CL21'MSG803I END OF JOB - '
MSG803RC DC     CL2' '
            DC      CL57' WAS HIGHEST RETURN CODE'
            SPACE 1
*           REGISTER EQUATES
[9]         REGEQU
            SPACE 1
            LTORG
            SPACE 1
            CNOP 0,4
PROGEND EQU     * ENDING ADDRESS FOR CP DUMP COMMAND
[10]        SPACE 3
            END     SHOWPARM
```

Notes to Fig. 14.12:

1. Register 1 has a pointer to the parameter information provided by the caller or invoker. This saves the address in register 2, since register 1 will be modified by CMS macros we use later in the program.

2. The LINEDIT macro provides some dumping and display services. We will explain these in Chap. 16. The purpose of these two lines are to display the original contents of register 1 (the parameters from our START command) and to display the data at that area. Refer to the virtual console output shown in Fig. 14.13.

3. This LINEDIT macro is used to issue a message to the VM OPERATOR user identification. This will be explained in Chap. 16.

4. This LINEDIT macro is used to dump the storage in the SHOWPARM program. These two LA instructions set up the beginning and ending addresses of the area to dump.

5. This actually requests the dump through the CP DUMP command. This will be explained in Chap. 17.

6. This WRTERM macro writes out the line labeled "MSG803". See the virtual console output in Fig. 14.13. It is equivalent to a PUT macro, but writes a line to the terminal. This will be discussed in App. 4.

7. This is the text of the message sent to the VM operator. It was used by the LINEDIT macro referenced in note [3].

8. This data is referenced by the LINEDIT macro at notes [4] and [5]. The " AL1(DUMPEND-*-1) " is used to generate the length of the dump command text automatically. The periods in the C-type DC directive which follow are filled in by the LINEDIT macro. Finally, the " *DISPLAY STORAGE " in the C-type constant is printed in the VM dump as an identifier. This will be discussed more completely in Chap. 17.

9. The REGEQU macro generates the register equates (R0, R1, and so forth). It also generates equates for the 370 control registers and for the 370 floating point registers. These are called "C0" through "C15" and F0" through "F6".

10. This label (PROGEND) is included to mark the end address of the program for the CP DUMP command issued via LINEDIT.

Fig. 14.13 presents the CMS console output obtained when executing the program shown in Fig. 14.12. (The figures in brackets refer to the lines which follow them.)

Note that Appendix 4 contains additional information regarding CMS linkage services, particularly in Sect. A4.3.

Figure 14.13   Virtual console output from SHOWPARM program.

```
(The numbers in brackets refer to the notes following the figure.)
[1]
LOAD SHOWPARM
Ready; T=0.05/0.14 16:12:33
[2]
START * SOME PARMS
[3]
Execution begins...
[4]
ADDRESS:0B000850
[5]
DATA:5C404040 40404040 E2D6D4C5 40404040 D7C1D9D4 E2404040
[6]                                              FFFFFFFF FFFFFFFF
COMMAND COMPLETE
[7]
MSG803I END OF JOB - 00 WAS HIGHEST RETURN CODE
[8]
Ready; T=0.02/1.55 16:12:38
```

Notes on Figure 14.13:

1. The LOAD SHOWPARM brings in our SHOWPARM TEXT and prepares it for execution.
2. The START command causes VM to begin execution of SHOWPARM. Note that the fields following START (the "* SOME PARMS") will be passed to the program as parameters.
3. CMS issues this message when it passes control to SHOWPARM.
4. This line is the output of the first LINEDIT macro. The " AD-DRESS:0B000850 " indicates that our parameters are at address 000850 and that the type of the parameter list is X'0B'.

5. This line is the output of the second LINEDIT macro. The parameters are passed as 8-byte entries, as shown below:

Parameter:	Data passed (in hex):
*	5C404040 40404040
SOME	E2D6D4C5 40404040
PARMS	D7C1D9D4 E2404040
	FFFFFFFF FFFFFFFF (marks end of list.)

6. CP issues the " COMMAND COMPLETE " after it completes the DUMP command.
7. This is the output from the WRTERM macro (MSG803I).
8. CMS issues the *Ready* message after SHOWPARM completes execution.

14.7.3   Defining Entry Points

COBOL provides an ENTRY statement in addition to the PROCEDURE DIVISION USING described earlier. This allows programmers to define multiple entry points in a COBOL program.

Assembler provides a similar function with the assembler ENTRY directive. ENTRY is coded similarly to EXTRN. For example,

```
        ENTRY OPENERR
```

defines the symbol OPENERR as an entry point to your program. This allows other programs to code CALL OPENERR and branch to that point in your program. OPENERR must, of course, be defined somewhere in your program.

When using multiple entry points, you must still perform all the program initialization done with a normal subprogram. However, you must make sure that each entry point does this processing. (i.e., each entry point must save registers, establish a base register, et cetera.) The linkage editor keeps track of names you define with an ENTRY and makes them available as subroutines to other programs.

14.7.4   "Weak" External (WXTRN) References

While not common in COBOL, occasionally a situation arises where a subroutine is not always present. In these situations, assembler and the linkage editor provide a way to refer to the subroutine name. However, no error is presented if the subroutine is not present.

This is the WXTRN - "weak EXTRN". It defines a symbol which is not in your program. WXTRN is coded like, and acts like EXTRN. However, the difference is that if a symbol defined in an EXTRN statement can't be found, the linkage editor treats this as a severe error. If a WXTRN symbol can't be found, the linkage editor treats it as a minor error.

14.7.5   Register Operands with the CALL MACRO

The CALL macro examples we have shown so far have all used the names of fields in the program issuing the CALL as parameters. This may hamper construction of a parameter list when the parameter names of addresses are not known.

The Call macro provides a way of providing parameter addresses in registers. This allows the location of the parameter to be unknown up to the point of the CALL itself. This is specified by coding " ...,(register),... " in the parameter list. For example:

```
        CALL SUBPROG,(PARM1,(4),PARM3),VL
```

This tells the CALL macro that the second parameter address will be in register 4 when the CALL macro executes. The CALL macro will then store the contents of register 4 into the parameter list before transferring control to the subprogram. The LINK macro provides a similar service.

14.7.6   The VM COMPSWT Macro

VM provides a macro, COMPSWT, which affects the operation of VM simulation of the LINK macro, and of VM's native CMSCALL macro service. This is the COMPSWT macro, which sets the *compiler switch* on or off in the CMS nucleus. COMPSWT is coded as

COMPSWT   ON *or* OFF

If COMPSWT is set on, CMS will load files with type MODULE in response to LINK and related macros. It does this with the equivalent of the CMS LOADMOD command.

If COMPSWT is set OFF (the default), CMS will load files with type TEXT, or members of a TXTLIB or a LOADLIB. If you experience CMS ABEND codes of 155 or 15A, this may be the reason.

14.7.7   Other Subprogram Esoterica

MVS provides a facility called cross memory services. This allows a program in one address space (job) to pass control to a routine in another address space. This requires special authorization and won't be covered further in this book.

There are two instructions associated with this. The Program Call (PC) instruction is used to pass control to another address space. The Program Transfer (PT) instruction is used to return control from one address space back to another which issued a PC instruction.

14.8   SUMMARY

This chapter has covered many functions and conventions associated with using subroutines in MVS and VM. At this point, you should have a good understanding of the roles of the general purpose registers when calling a subroutine or transferring control back.

Mastering the concepts presented in this chapter are key elements in one's ability to write in assembler language. In current data processing practice, assembler language is probably used in subroutines for other language programs more frequently than it is for main programs. Most importantly, this is often the best way of justifying use of assembler to your management.

Things to Do

1. Key in the GETDSN program and try to use it from one of your COBOL programs. Find the IEFJFCBN DSECT to find out the other information available to you.

2. If your installation has assembler language subroutines, locate them and compare them to the coding techniques listed in this chapter. Do they:

   - Save all the registers?

   - Use complete save area chaining (both forward and backward) or do they just save the address of the old calling program's) save area?

   - Provide valid return codes? Is anything placed in register 15?

   - Use the RETURN macro? With save area tagging (the 'T' operand)?

   - Use DSECTs to describe the calling program's data areas?

3. Can you think of any subroutines which would be useful at your installation? Can you write them?

4. If you want to write a program to execute as a CMS command, read the VM application development guide for information on VM parameter lists and related information. You may then wish to look at the discussion of the SUBCOM, NUCEXT, and IMMCMD services.

Loops and Table Handling

Table handling and loops are closely related subjects. In this chapter, some types of loops in COBOL and in other languages will be covered. From that, we'll generalize the concepts in loop handling. To create the data processed in a loop, some ways to create tables in assembler will be shown. Finally, we'll complete this discussion by showing the assembler instructions which process loops sequentially and we'll show how to do a binary table search in assembler.

Table handling and loops may not be as closely related in other languages as they are in COBOL and assembler. In other languages, you may have more reasons to execute a loop for computation without referencing a table. Calculating square roots or factorials provide examples of this. In COBOL and assembler, however, loops invariably involve access to a table.

High-level languages have several unique loop types. In FORTRAN, the DO loop represents the basic sequential loop provided by most high-level languages ever since the late 1950s. COBOL's PERFORM is unique in providing a loop option (VARYING) which executes code out-of-line rather than in-line as in the DO loop. PASCAL adds the WHILE *condition* DO *loop* and the REPEAT *loop* UNTIL *condition* forms of loops. Other languages provide additional loop options.

In assembler, three instructions provide looping facilities. These are the Branch on Count, Branch Index Low or Equal, and the Branch Index High instructions. Other loop forms must be programmed with a combination of other assembler instructions.

15.1 TABLE HANDLING OVERVIEW
All loops in all languages share certain common elements. These are listed in Fig. 15.1. The COBOL PERFORM with the VARYING option has all of these:

Figure 15.1   Common elements of loops.

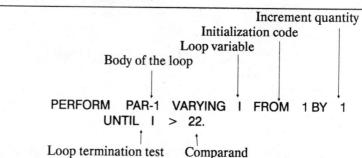

Increment quantity
Initialization code
Loop variable
Body of the loop

PERFORM   PAR-1   VARYING   I   FROM   1 BY   1
UNTIL   I   >   22.

Loop termination test   Comparand

1. A *loop variable* or loop index counter which is incremented during the loop
2. An *increment quantity* which is added to (or subtracted from) the loop variable
3. A *comparand* which defines the ending quantity for the loop variable (loop limit)
4. *Initialization code* which sets up the preceding variable's starting values
5. The *body of the loop* (the code we wish to execute repeatedly)
6. The *loop termination test* code, which compares the loop variable to the comparand and ends if necesary

Assembler language implements fewer loop types. For our purposes, these types (and the instructions for them) are as follows:

1. Iterative loops (BCT, BCTR) — execute a loop a given number of times
2. Address manipulation loops (BXLE, BXH) — execute a loop automatically varying an address
3. Programmatic test loops — where all the loop handling processing is done by the programmer

Before giving examples of each of these and explaining the loop instructions, let's look at how we define a table for a loop.

15.2   DEFINING TABLES IN COBOL AND ASSEMBLER

In COBOL, we use the OCCURS clause to define a table. As discussed in Sec. 8.1, the most direct equivalent to this in assembler is the duplication factor of the DS or DC directive. For example,

05 MONTH-TAB PIC X(3) OCCURS 12 TIMES.

could be considered equivalent to

MONTHTAB DS   12CL3

Other COBOL table options are less straightforward. For example, the DEPENDING ON option of the OCCURS clause may require special processing at execution time to properly size the table. The GETMAIN macro provides one way of creating a variably sized table in both MVS and VM. The esoterica section will show an example of how to use this.

Another problem arises when each table entry contains several fields. For example, the following table has three fields per entry:

```
05 MONTH-TAB      OCCURS 12 TIMES.
   10   MONTH-SHORT      PIC X(3).
   10   MONTH-LONG-NAMEPIC X(9).
   10   DAYS-IN-MONTH      PIC S9(2) COMP-3.
```

Assume that we want to set the first MONTH-LONG-NAME to January if the language in use is English, and to 'ENERO' if the language is Spanish. The code to do this might look like:

```
MOVE 31 TO DAYS-IN-MONTH(1).
IF LANG-TYPE = 'E'
   THEN MOVE 'JANUARY' TO MONTH-LONG-NAME(1)
   ELSE IF LANG-TYPE = 'S'
      THEN MOVE 'ENERO' TO DAYS-IN-MONTH(1).
```

This introduces problems both in defining and referencing the table in assembler. We can now no longer simply define the whole table with one duplication factor, since we have three different subfields. If we define the data as

```
DS      12CL3,12CL9,12PL2
```

we will get three separate tables. The simplest method of handling this is to add up the lengths of the individual fields and define sufficient entries of that length. For our example, the fields (3+9+2) add up to 14 bytes and could be defined as

```
MONTHTAB DS      12CL14
```

The second area where this introduces some problems is in references to the subfields. We will have to have the address of the entry in a register to access the subfields. If we just use the register address to access the data, our corresponding assembler coding would look like this (assuming that register 4 had the table entry address for January):

```
*            COBOL CODE EQUIVALENT SHOWN IN PARENTHESES
         ZAP    12(2,R4), = P'31'  (MOVE 31 TO DAYS-IN-MONTH(1).)
         CLI    LANGTYPE,C'E'  (IF LANG-TYPE = 'E')
         BNE    TESTSPAN
         MVC    3(9,R4), = CL9'JANUARY'   (THEN MOVE 'JANUARY'
*                                          TO MONTH-LONG-NAME(1))
         B      TESTDONE
TESTSPAN EQU    *                          (ELSE)
         CLI    LANGTYPE,C'S'              (IF LANG-TYPE = 'S')
         BNE    TESTDONE
         MVC    3(9,R4), = CL9'ENERO'     (THEN MOVE 'ENERO' TO
TESTDONE EQU    *                          DAYS-IN-MONTH(1).)
```

The address references using explicit register addresses (e.g., " ZAP 12(2,R4),=P'31' ") are not as readable or maintainable as references to labels. Use of a DSECT to define the table entry produces cleaner code.

Let's define a DSECT for the table. (This would normally be placed right before the END statement in your program.)

```
MONTHENT DSECT
SHORTNAM DS    CL3
LONGNAME DS    CL9
DAYSINMO  DS   PL2
```

With this DSECT, our example code becomes

```
          USING  MONTHENT,R4                 ADDRESSABILITY
          ZAP    DAYSINMO, = P'31'
*                                            (MOVE 31 TO DAYS-IN-MONTH(1).)
          CLI    LANGTYPE,C'E'   (IF LANG-TYPE = 'E')
          BNE    TESTSPAN
          MVC    LONGNAME, = CL9'JANUARY'
*                                            (THEN MOVE 'JANUARY'
*                                            TO MONTH-LONG-NAME(1))
          B      TESTDONE
TESTSPAN  EQU    *                           (ELSE)
          CLI    LANGTYPE,C'S'   (IF LANG-TYPE = 'S')
          BNE    TESTDONE
          MVC    LONGNAME, = CL9'ENERO'
TESTDONE  EQU    *
```

The use of labels makes the intent a little clearer.

Another way to provide labels is to move each entry to a predefined set of fields in storage when processing that entry. This is not as efficient, and leads to errors if the fields are referenced after the table entry has been updated and moved back.

15.2.1   Calculating Table Entry Addresses

To use a specific entry, we must compute the address of that entry in the table. We accomplish this by multiplying the table entry number, minus one, by the size of the table entries. This calculation must be done in binary.

The following code shows how we might do this for the MONTHTAB table we have just defined. Assume that we have a field named MO containing the entry number and defined as DS PL2, and a field called DOUBLEWD defined as DS D.

```
          ZAP    DOUBLEWD,MO           MOVE TO CONVERT
          CVB    R4,DOUBLEWD           GET MO IN BINARY
          SH     R4, = H'1'            SUBTRACT ONE
          MH     R4, = H'14'           MO * ENTRY LEN
*                                      = OFFSET IN TABLE
          LA     R4,MONTHTAB(R4)       ADD TO TBL START
*                                      = ENTRY ADDRESS
```

A few notes are probably appropriate here. We must eventually wind up with a binary number to use with the Load Address (LA) instruction. Thus, while we could have done the earlier calculations in packed decimal (with MP, for example), usually it's more straightforward to do all the calculations in binary.

We must subtract one from the entry number to calculate a correct offset. The reason for this is that the first entry has an offset of 0 bytes. (There is no storage before it in the table.) Thus, entry 1 should have an offset of 0. For our MONTHTAB example, entry 2 should have an offset of 14 (2 minus 1 times 14). Entry 3 should have an offset of 28, and so forth.

You may also subtract the entry length from the calculated offset instead, but decrementing the desired entry number is more prevalent.

15.3 LINEAR TABLE PROCESSING

Linear processing, for our purposes, means processing a table one entry after another. This is in contrast to binary searching of a table, which we'll discuss later. The assembler instructions usually employed for table processing follow this form.

The three instructions have indistinct equivalents in COBOL. Branch on Count most closely resembles PERFORM with the TIMES option. Branch Index Low or Equal and Branch Index High sort of correlate to a PERFORM with the VARYING OPTION and/or a SET verb in the PERFORMed code.

To illustrate these instructions, we'll show how they both implement the following COBOL code, which clears the contents of each field in the MONTH-TAB array defined earlier. Assume that we have an index defined as

            77 I PIC S9(8) COMP.

and wrote code to clear the table as follows:

            PERFORM CLEAR-TAB VARYING I FROM 1 BY 1
                UNTIL I > 12.

            ... ...

            CLEAR-TAB.
            MOVE SPACES TO MONTH-SHORT(I).
            MOVE SPACES TO MONTH-LONG-NAME(I).
            MOVE ZEROES TO DAYS-IN-MONTH(I).

15.3.1 Branch on Count

Branch on Count has both an RX-format (opcode BCT) and an RR-format (opcode BCTR) implementation. Both BCT and BCTR are similar to the FORTRAN DO loop with a negative increment. A register is initialized to the loop count, then is decremented by the BCT or BCTR instruction, which must be at the end of the loop code.

BCT and BCTR loop through a section of code "n" times. The instruction subtracts one from the loop counter register, then tests its value. If the value is not 0, BCT and BCTR branch to the label provided as the second operand, which is normally the start of the loop. BCT and BCTR stop if and only if the loop counter register becomes 0.

These two instructions are normally used in conjunction with the LA instruction to point to the next table entry.

An example of the BCT instruction follows. This code clears each set of fields in MONTHTAB to blanks or zero as appropriate.

```
[1]        LA    R4,MONTHTAB          GET TABLE ADDR
           USING MONTHENT,R4          ADDRESSABILITY
[2]        LH    R5, = H'12'           NBR OF ENTRIES
LOOP1      EQU   *
[3]        ZAP   DAYSINMO, = P'0'      SET TO ZERO
           MVC   LONGNAME, = CL9' '    SET TO BLANKS
           MVC   SHORTNAM, = CL3' '    SET TO BLANKS
[4]        LA    R4,14(R4)            POINT TO NEXT ENT
[5]        BCT   R5,LOOP1             REPEAT 12 TIMES
```
Notes:
1. The first LA instruction sets the address of the first entry in MONTHTAB into register 4.
2. The LH instruction sets the number of entries (12) into register 5.
3. Within the loop, the ZAP and MVC instructions initialize an entry in the table.
4. The last LA instruction puts the address of the next table entry (14 bytes past the current entry) into register 4.
5. Finally, the BCT instruction subtracts 1 from register 5. As long as register 5 is not 0, the BCT instruction will branch to LOOP1 and continue the loop.

One problem sometimes arises with BCT. If the number of entries is not set into the loop counter register before the loop, you will have a loop which probably does not execute the proper number of times. If the loop counter value is too large, you normally get an 0C4 ABEND by exceeding the end of the table. If the loop counter value is too small, you will not properly initialize the table, which leads to subtler errors.

If you alter the loop counter register within a BCT loop, you may create an endless loop, or you may not process the entire table. The same situation arises if the table address register (R4 in our example) is improperly initialized or is modified during the loop. Both the loop counter register and the table address register must be set up before the loop starts, or you will have one of the errors discussed here.

The BCTR instruction is similar, but the second operand is a register which must contain the address of the start of the loop. This form of BCTR is not frequently used.

BCTR has a side effect, however, which is widely used. If the second operand is 0, no branch occurs under any circumstances. However, the first operand register is still decremented. This has the effect of subtracting one from the register without requiring a constant in storage. For example, if register 6 contains hex X'00000041' (decimal 65), the instruction

    BCTR   R6,0

would change the value in register 6 to hex X'00000040', or decimal 64.

BCTR does not set the condition code, however, so there is no efficient way to test for a positive, negative, or zero result from the BCTR subtraction. If you need to branch based on the result of the operation, an SH instruction is probably more appropriate. Use of BCTR is probably best restricted to decrementing previously range-checked positive numbers.

Finally, the common use of BCT and LA results in the table entry address register pointing past the end of the table after the loop. You should avoid any use of the table address register (register 4 in our example) after a BCT loop until reinitializing it.

15.3.2   Address Manipulation Loops and BXLE/BXH

The Branch Index Low or Equal (opcode BXLE) and Branch Index High (opcode BXH) instructions are intended for table handling loops exclusively. BXH is very similar to BXLE, so we'll discuss BXLE in detail, then outline the differences with BXH.

BXLE, like BCT, automatically manipulates a register. Unlike BCT, BXLE increments or decrements the table address register. This removes the need for the LA instruction to update the next entry address in each loop iteration. Figure 15.2 summarizes the differences between BCT and BXLE/BXH.

Figure 15.2   Comparison of BCT and BXLE/BXH instructions.

Item	BCT	BXLE/BXH
Increment amount	Always 1	Any 31-bit binary number
Index arithmetic	Decrement only	Either add (BXLE) or subtract (BXH)[1]
Loop limit	Zero only	Any 31-bit binary number (positive or negative)

1   The effect of adding or subtracting is achieved by providing a positive or negative increment amount.

BXLE is considerably more complicated than BCT. It requires three registers instead of one. These are used as the table address (index), the entry length increment, and the loop limit comparand. The index and increment registers must normally be an even-odd pair.

Our table-clearing example shown in the previous section looks like this with BXLE:

```
[1]         LA    R4,MONTHTAB            GET TABLE ADDR
            USING MONTHENT,R4            ADDRESSABILITY
[2]         LH    R5, = H'14'            GET LEN OF ENTRY
[3]         LA    R6,MONTHTAB + 167 POINT TO LAST BYTE OF TBL
LOOP1       EQU   *
            ZAP   DAYSINMO, = P'0'       SET TO ZERO
            MVC   LONGNAME, = CL9' '     SET TO BLANKS
            MVC   SHORTNAM, = CL3' '     SET TO BLANKS
            BXLE  R4,R6,LOOP1            CONTINUE 12 TIMES
```

Notes:

1. The first LA instruction sets up the table address register (R4) just as with the BCT example.
2. The LH instruction initializes the entry length increment.
3. This was not required for the BCT instruction. The last LA instruction, using R6, sets up the comparand value. This determines when the loop ends.

The operation of BXLE is to add the table entry length value (in R5 in our example) to the index register (R4 in our example). (Note that R5 is not explicitly coded in the BXLE instruction. It is implied as being the next odd-numbered register after register 4.) The resulting value is compared to the loop limit comparand (register 6 in our example).

What happens at this point depends on the instruction coded. BXLE will branch back to the beginning of the loop if the value in the index register is less than or equal to the value in the comparand register. BXH branches back if the value is greater (higher) than the comparand register.

This means that BXLE is intended to process a table from first entry to last entry, while BXH is intended to process a table from last entry to first entry.

Another instruction from our example which bears explaining is " LA R6,MONTHTAB+167 ". This sets up the loop limit comparand into register 6. How did we arrive at MONTHTAB+167?

Well, BXLE continues branching until the index register contains a larger value than the loop limit comparand. If the values are equal, the loop continues. Thus, we must set the loop limit comparand to have a value greater than or equal to the address of the last entry in the table, but less than the address of the byte following the last entry in the table. (If we set the loop limit comparand to point to the byte after the end of the table, we would process that as an additional entry. This would make our loop execute one more time than intended.)

It turns out that MONTHTAB is 168 bytes long (12 entries times 14 bytes per entry). So, MONTHTAB+167 is the last byte of the table and will serve correctly as a loop limit comparand.

A simpler way of doing this is to define a label at the last byte of the table, then use Load Address to get that value. For MONTHTAB, we might define it as

```
MONTHTAB DS     12CL14
MOTBEND   EQU    *-1
```

MOTBEND (Month Table End) is defined as being the current location (*) minus one. This defines MOTBEND as being the last byte of MONTHTAB. We could then code

```
          LA     R6,MOTBEND
```

and generate the same code as if we had coded

```
          LA     R6,MONTHTAB+167
```

15.3.3   An Example of BXH

BXH operates like BXLE, but normally adds a negative increment and branches back to the start of the loop only if the index value is higher than the loop limit comparand. This approximates, for the COBOL code we gave earlier in this section

```
          PERFORM CLEAR-TAB VARYING I FROM 12 BY -1
                    UNTIL I < 1.
```

As mentioned earlier, BXH is used when processing a table from last entry to first entry. The equivalent loop using BXH is

```
          LA     R4,MONTHTAB+154      LAST ENTRY ADDR
          USING  MONTHENT,R4          ADDRESSABILITY
          LH     R5,=H'-14'           LENGTH OF 1 ENTRY
          LA     R6,MONTHTAB          POINT TO 1ST BYTE
LOOP1     EQU    *
          ZAP    DAYSINMO,=P'0'       SET TO ZERO
          MVC    LONGNAME,=CL9' '     SET TO BLANKS
          MVC    SHORTNAM,=CL3' '     SET TO BLANKS
          BXH    R4,R6,LOOP1          REPEAT 12 TIMES
```

15.3.4   Selecting a Loop Instruction

Choosing which instruction to use presents both performance and maintainability issues. BXLE and BXH are marginally faster than BCT, since they both update the index address and branch back in the same instruction. This will show up as an important advantage if your program performs simple processing of very large arrays many times. If your program performs extensive processing on each entry, the performance advantage is not worth considering.

BCT may be more maintainable than BXLE or BXH. The most important factor is that most assembler language programmers learn BCT first and see no reason to change. Many assembler programmers actively dislike BXLE and BXH, and this may be a consideration in your use of these two instructions. BXLE and BXH have one important disadvantage — they both require three registers for normal table processing. BCT requires only two.

15.3.5 Programmatic Loop Control

Situations may arise where you must program a loop which doesn't fit the instructions described up to this point. For example, you may need to loop for an unknown number of times, such as when scanning a table.

To do this type of loop, you must code the loop control instructions yourself rather than rely on BCT or BXLE. We'll evaluate one example of this type of loop — PERFORM with the UNTIL option.

Let's first set up a COBOL example of this type of loop. Assume that we wish to compute the number of payments needed to reduce a mortgage balance to a given amount. Assume we have the following data fields:

```
77   PRINCIPAL-AMOUNT PIC S9(7)V99   COMP-3.
77   DESIRED-BALANCE  PIC S9(7)       COMP-3.
77   NO-PAYMENTS PIC S9(4)            COMP-3.
```

as well as fields for the interest rate, payment amount, and so forth. Assume that we have another routine called PAY-CALC that computes the effect of a payment, and that we code the loop as

```
        PERFORM  CALC-PAR
            UNTIL PRINCIPAL-AMOUNT < DESIRED-BALANCE.
... ... ... ... ...

        CALC-PAR.
        PERFORM PAY-CALC.
        ADD 1 TO NO-PAYMENTS.
```

Now let's look at how we might do this in assembler. Assume that we have corresponding data fields like the following:

```
PRINAMT    DS    PL5                    (PRINCIPAL-AMOUNT)
DESDBAL    DS    PL4                    (DESIRED-BALANCE)
NOPAYMTS DS    PL3                      (NO-PAYMENTS)
```

and a separate routine called CALCRTN that computes the effect of a payment, our code might look like

```
PMTLOOP    EQU    *
           BAL    R14,CALCRTN            GO ADD PAYMENT
           AP     NOPAYMTS, = P'1'       ADD TO PMTS MADE
           CP     PRINAMT,DESDBAL        CHECK VS  DESIRED
           BNL    PMTLOOP                NOT LOW - GO ON
```

By itself, this code corresponds to the COBOL example. However, a number of checks are desirable to avoid unintentional endless loops. Unlike BXLE or BCT loops, programmatic loops don't necessarily increment an address as part of their execution. Thus, BCT and BXLE loops have a type of built-in protection — an 0C4 ABEND when the address gets too far out of range. Programmatic loops may have no such failure until they exceed the CPU time for the job, or until the operator cancels the job.

To guard against endless loops when coding this type of loop, you should add some type of *sanity check*. This should take the form of some upper limit to the number of times the loop is executed.

In our example here, this might be the longest repayment period expected. We could assume that any repayment period longer than 100 years represents an error (although this might not be true if housing prices keep increasing!). If we define a limit as

```
MAXPER     DC     P'1200'                    100 YRS @ 12 PMTS/YR
```

We could recode the loop as

```
PMTLOOP    EQU    *
           BAL    R14,CALCRTN                CALC PMT EFFECT
           AP     NOPAYMTS, = P'1'           ADD TO PMTS MADE
           CP     NOPAYMTS,MAXPER            COMPARE TO MAX
           BH     PMTERROR                   HIGH - ERROR
           CP     PRINAMT,DESDBAL            CP TO DESIRED
           BNL    PMTLOOP                    NOT LOW - REPEAT
```

PMTERROR would be a routine to display an error message about the situation, and would also have to be added.

In general, when coding any loop, always have some range check for the loop limit and increment values if you can't code these as constants. And when coding a loop yourself (i.e., without BCT or BXLE), always have some other, separate loop counter limit to prevent unintended endless loops.

15.4 BINARY TABLE SEARCHING

A *binary search* is a method of searching where each comparison eliminates half of the remaining table entries from the search. It operates on tables which are of known length and which are in proper ascending (or descending) order. COBOL implements this form of search with the SEARCH ALL verb.

A COBOL binary search of postal state name abbreviations might be coded as

```
01  STATE-TABLE.
    05  STATE-NAMES OCCURS 50
        ASCENDING KEY STATE-SHORT-NAME
        INDEXED BY STATE-INDEX.
        10  STATE-SHORT-NAME    PIC XX.
        10  STATE-LONG-NAME     PIC X(15).
```

The Procedure Division code for this is as follows:

```
SEARCH ALL STATE-NAMES
    AT END GO TO STATE-ERROR
    WHEN STATE-SHORT-NAME(STATE-INDEX) =
            INPUT-STATE
        MOVE STATE-LONG-NAME(STATE-INDEX)
            TO OUTPUT-STATE.
```

We will assume that INPUT-STATE, OUTPUT-STATE, and STATE-ERROR are defined elsewhere in the program. For a complete table, we would also have to include other possible short postal state names, such as DC for the District of Columbia.

To do a similar search in assembler, our data areas look like

```
STTABLE    DS    50CL17                    ( STATE-TABLE)
STINDEX    DS    F                         ( STATE-INDEX)
STSTEP     DS    F                         (BINARY SRCH VAL)
```

The table entries are described by a DSECT (which normally goes at the end of your program):

```
STATENMS DSECT
STSHORT    DS    CL2                       (STATE-SHORT-NAME)
STLONG     DS    CL15                      (STATE-LONG-NAME)
```

Our search code must do several things that the COBOL SEARCH ALL verb does for us automatically. The binary search routine is shown as Fig. 15.3. First, we must initialize the index pointer to address the middle of the table. We do this by taking the number of entries and dividing by 2. Then we may search the table by comparing the STSHORT field of that entry to the input field (INPUTST).

We will have one of three possibilities after the comparison. If the fields are equal, we should perform the equivalent of the processing in the WHEN clause, then exit the search.

If the current entry is higher than the input field value, we must move to a lower entry in the table. This is done at the routine labeled "BUMPDOWN". To bump down the pointer, we divide the size of the last search step in STSTEP by 2, then subtract that from the current entry pointer. If the division results in a remainder, we add that (always 1) to the new step size.

If the current entry is lower than the input field value, we must move up in the table. The "BUMPUP" routine handles this similarly to the method used in "BUMPDOWN".

You should be able to adapt the logic shown in the figure to other binary searches if necesary. One improvement might be to use a shift instruction rather than a divide.

Figure 15.3   Example of a binary search.

```
            L       R2, = F'50'
            SRDA    R2,32                   SET UP FOR DIVIDE
            D       R2, = F'2'              DIVIDE BY 2
            AR      R3,R2                   ADD REMAINDER
            ST      R3,STSTEP               SAVE STEP VALUE
            ST      R3,STINDEX              SAVE ENTRY NUM
            L       R4,STINDEX              GET  ENTRY NUM
INDXCALC    EQU     *
            SH      R4, = H'1'              SET UP AND
            MH      R4, = H'17'             CALCULATE OFFSET
            LA      R4,STTABLE(R4)          GET ENTRY ADDR
            USING   STATENMS,R4              ADDRESSABILITY
            CLC     STSHORT,INPUTST         COMPARE NAMES
            BL      BUMPUP                  LOW - GO UP
            BH      BUMPDOWN                HIGH - GO DOWN
*                   EQUAL - PROCESS "WHEN" CONDITION AND END LOOP
            MVC     OUTPUTST,STLONG MOVE LONG NAME TO OUTPUT
            B       SRCHDONE                END LOOP
*                   GO UP IN TABLE FOR NEXT COMPARISON
BUMPUP      EQU     *
            L       R2,STSTEP               GET LAST STEP SIZE
            SRDA    R2,32                   SET UP FOR DIVIDE
            D       R2, = F'2'              DIVIDE BY 2
            C       R3, = F'0'              RESULT ZERO?
            BE      STATEERR                YES - END SEARCH
            AR      R3,R2                   ADD REMAINDER
            ST      R3,STSTEP               SAVE STEP SIZE
            L       R4,STINDEX              LAST ENTRY NUM
            AR      R4,R3                   ADD NEXT ENTRY
            C       R4, = F'50'             COMPARE TO MAX
            BNH     BUMPUP02                NOT HIGH - GO ON
            L       R4, = F'50'             HIGH - SET TO MAX
BUMPUP02    EQU     *
            ST      R4,STINDEX              SAVE ENTRY NUM
            B       INDXCALC                GO COMPUTE ADDR
*                   GO DOWN IN TABLE FOR NEXT COMPARISON
BUMPDOWN    EQU     *
            L       R2,STSTEP               SIZE OF LAST STEP
            SRDA    R2,32                   SET UP FOR DIVIDE
            D       R2, = F'2'              DIVIDE BY 2
            C       R3, = F'0'              RESULT ZERO?
            BNH     STATEERR                YES - END SEARCH
            AR      R3,R2                   ADD REMAINDER
            ST      R3,STSTEP               SAVE STEP SIZE
```

Figure 15.3   (Continued)

```
          L      R4,STINDEX          LAST ENTRY NUM
          SR     R4,R3               GET NEXT ENTRY
          C      R4, = F'50'         COMPARE TO MAX
          BNH    BUMPDN02            NOT HIGH - GO ON
          L      R4, = F'50'         HIGH - SET TO MAX
BUMPDN02 EQU     *
          ST     R4,STINDEX          SAVE ENTRY NUM
          B      INDXCALC            GO COMPUTE ADDR
*                SEARCH AND PROCESSING OVER AT THIS POINT.
SRCHDONE  EQU                        *
```

Note that the "STATEERR" error routine is not shown.

15.5   MANIPULATING THE INDEX POINTER

COBOL provides the SET verb for explicit modification of data items defined as USAGE IS INDEX. Assembler's requirements for index addressing make such a specialized function superfluous. However, Fig. 15.4 shows examples of how you may program the equivalent of some common SET verb uses in assembler.

(The examples in Figure 15.4 assume the use of the STATETB used with the binary search example, with a table name of STATETB and an entry length of 17 bytes. Assume that we have a COBOL USAGE IS INDEX variablenamed INDEX-N, and a variable named N which is defined as PIC S9(8) COMP SYNC. Finally, assume that we want or have the entry address in register 4.)

15.6   LOOP AND TABLE HANDLING ESOTERICA

This section discusses two other items which are provided in COBOL: variable-length tables and two-dimensional tables. Additionally, we discuss how to improve the performance of loops, a special use for the BXH instruction, and the absolute limit for BCT loops.

15.6.1   Variable-Length Tables

COBOL provides the DEPENDING ON option of the OCCURS clause to assist in processing of variable-length tables. We will not show a one-to-one correspondence to each COBOL feature used with the DEPENDING ON option, but will discuss the general problem of variable-length tables.

Figure 15.4   Equivalent assembler code for SET verb uses.

COBOL:	Assembler:
SET INDEX-N TO 1	LA R4,STATETB
SET INDEX-N TO N	L R4,N SH R4, = H'1' (DECREMENT) MH R4, = H'17' (ENTRY LEN) LA R4,STATETB(R4)
SET INDEX-N UP BY 1	LA R4,17(R4) (ADD LENGTH)
SET INDEX-N UP BY N	L R5,N MH R5, = H'17' (ENTRY LEN) AR R4,R5 (ADD TO R4)
SET INDEX-N DOWN BY 1	SHR4, = H'17'
SET INDEX-N DOWN BY N	L R5,N MH R5, = H'17' (ENTRY LEN) AR R4,R5 (ADD TO R4)

Generally, we do not know the size of a variable-length table when we assemble a program. We may know the maximum size, in which case we may define that area and treat it as a table of that size. However, if the table size is exceedingly large, we may still have to take special measures to handle it.

One technique for handling such tables is to acquire the storage from MVS or VM rather than coding the table as a DS statement. This has the advantage of making your program smaller, but requires some additional code.

To obtain storage from both MVS and VM, we use the GETMAIN macro. GETMAIN allows us to get storage areas of almost any size. We may specify that the storage may be acquired above the 16-megabyte storage address limit if desired. (VM/CMS also provides the DMSFREE and DMSFRET services to obtain and release storage. We won't be explaining these here, since a subset of GETMAIN is common to both operating systems.)

GETMAIN has several options, but we will introduce only one here: the R-form (register) option. In this case, you make an unconditional request for a single storage area. If the storage is not available, your program ABENDs (usually with an 80A code).

For example, to get 72 bytes of storage, code

```
GETMAIN  R,LV = 72
```

The address of the storage is returned in register 1. As another example, assume that we wish to get an unknown number of bytes. If the number is in a fullword variable called TABSIZE, we could code

```
L      R0,TABSIZE
GETMAIN R,LV = (0)
```

The "(0)" tells MVS or VM that the amount of storage requested is in register 0. Note that coding " LV=0 " instead of " LV=(0) " would request 0 bytes of storage. This would result in an ABEND (804 or 80A, along with message DMS133 in VM). Be careful with the parentheses.

You should always save the address of the storage immediately after the GETMAIN. This is usually done by storing register 1 into a fullword in your program, such as,

```
ST     R1,TABADDR
```

where TABADDR is defined as a fullword.

The storage usually contains binary zeroes, but may not if the storage was previously used and freed by another program. MVCL is the most advisable way of clearing the storage. Alternatively, if you will execute a loop to initialize each entry, you need not do any other clearing. However, do not rely on the gotten area to contain binary zeroes.

Whenever you need to access the table, you must do so by loading the address (stored in TABADDR in our example so far) rather than by using an LA instruction. So, instead of coding

```
LA     R4,STATETAB
```

You should code

```
L      R4,TABADDR
```

wherever any references occur to the table name.

To release the storage after using it, you should use the FREEMAIN macro. A FREEMAIN for our example might be coded as

```
L      R0,TABSIZE           GET STORAGE SIZE
L      R1,TABADDR           GET STORAGE ADDR
FREEMAIN R,A = (1),LV = (0)  RELEASE STORAGE
```

"LV" in the GETMAIN and FREEMAIN macros stands for *length value*. The "A" option of FREEMAIN stands for *address*.

Refer to the MVS Supervisor Services and Macros manual for further details. The list options of GETMAIN (LC=, et al.) are not supported under VM/CMS at the time this was written.

15.6.1.1 GETMAIN In MVS/XA

GETMAIN has an additional operand in MVS/XA and MVS/ESA. This is the LOC= parameter. Specifying LOC=ANY requests storage in any address range, but is normally processed from storage above the 16MB address line. LOC=ANY is only honored when coded with an RC-form GETMAIN. ("RC" stands for Register Conditional.) The RC option will not cause an ABEND (e.g., 80A) if there is not enough storage to fulfill the request. Instead, it places a return code in register 15. The GETMAIN macro example discussed previously would be coded as follows to obtain storage above the 16MB address line:

```
GETMAIN  RC,LV = (0),LOC = ANY
```

The FREEMAIN instruction need not change.

15.6.2 Two-Dimensional Arrays

Processing of two-dimensional and larger arrays involves slight code additions for most cases. As an example, let's assume that we want to count the number of times a player is ejected from a baseball game by an umpire. Assume that we want to have a table of games played by a baseball team, with an entry for each inning.

The team plays 162 games per year. We assume 10 entries to cover the innings per game (9 for the normal innings and 1 for any extra innings). Assume that no more than 32767 players will be ejected from any inning, so that the counter will be a halfword. (Never mind how often your team's players get ejected!) With these assumptions, our table might look like

```
EJECTTAB  DS    CL3240                    (162 x 10 x 2 bytes)
```

Each game would require ten halfwords in the table, or 20 bytes. To indicate that a player was ejected from the 4th inning of the 153rd game, we would need data items like:

```
GAME      DC    H'153'
INNING    DC    H'4'
```

The code to add this in might look like

```
          LA    R4,EJECTTAB              POINT TO TABLE
          LH    R5,GAME                  GET GAME NUMBER
          SH    R5, = H'1'               DECREMENT
          MH    R5, = H'20'              LENGTH OF ENTRY
          AR    R4,R5                    POINT TO GAME
          LH    R5,INNING                GET INNING NUM
          CH    R5, = H'10'              RANGE CHECK
          BNH   CALCINNG                 RANGE 1 TO 10 - OK
          LH    R5, = H'10'              10 IF EXTRA INNINGS
CALCINNG  EQU   *
          SH    R5, = H'1'               DECREMENT
          MH    R5, = H'2'               LENGTH OF ENTRY
          AR    R4,R5                    POINT TO INNING
```

```
*          PROCESS THE INNING EJECTED-PLAYER COUNT.
     LH     R1,0(,R4)                    EJECTIONS COUNT
     AH     R1,=H'1'                     ADD ONE
     STH    R1,0(,R4)                    STORE BACK
```

Note that this code lets us get to a particular inning of a specified game. Should we need to get only to the game to process the ten halfwords as a group item, we would treat EJECTTAB as though it were a single-dimension table with 162 20-byte entries.

15.6.3 Optimizing Loop Performance

For the purposes of this section, *performance* means the CPU time used in processing a loop. There are several general methods for reducing the CPU time required.

First, don't use a loop if possible. When initializing a table, consider MVCL instead of a loop. This will reduce the CPU time used when setting all bytes of each entry in a table to binary zeroes, blanks, high-values, or any other single byte value.

Second, reduce the number of instructions used to manipulate individual fields within a table of group items. Again, if initializing a group item, you might prepare a single entry with the subfields of the group item already initialized. This could then be moved into each entry, rather than initializing each subfield. By reducing the number of instructions used to one MVC (if possible), the loop should run faster.

Third, examine each instruction to determine if it could be done outside of the loop. Alternately, determine if the instruction is necesary for all entries processed, or if it may be moved to a routine only executed when needed for specific entries.

Fourth, consider a binary search. If your algorithm does not require processing every entry in the table, this is a good bet to reduce the CPU time.

Fifth, evaluate BXLE versus BCT. BCT will normally be slightly faster than a programmatic loop, and BXLE will normally be slightly faster than BCT.

Sixth, consider the normal processing of the loop. Does it make sense to process the table in reverse order? Would BXH be more appropriate? Can you reorder the entries in the table to reduce the time spent searching by putting the most frequently referenced entries first?

Finally, evaluate whether the loop is even necesary. Are 99 percent of the searches to the same entry? If so, test for that condition first before starting the loop.

Improving performance in loops is probably the most significant place where the complete control possible with assembler can make a difference in CPU time. The other area where this can be significant is in I/O processing.

15.6.4   Using BXH To Test Return Codes

An obscure side effect (perhaps deservedly so) of the BXH instruction may be used to test the return code from subroutines or operating system services. This side effect is that the same register may be specified for both the loop variable, comparand, and increment amount. (This side effect only works when the register we are testing is an odd-numbered register, such as register 15.)

Code which uses this side effect involves placing the following instruction after a subroutine call or request for MVS services:

```
BXH     R15,R15,ERROR
```

Where the return code is in register 15 and ERROR is a separate routine to process error conditions.

What this does is as follows:

1. Saves the contents of register 15 as the comparand.
2. Adds register 15 (the increment amount) to register 15 (the loop variable register).
3. Compares register 15 to the original comparand value (i.e. the starting contents of register 15).
4. If the ending value in register 15 is greater than the original value, the branch to ERROR is taken.

If register fifteen contains zero when this is executed, no branch is taken, since 0 plus 0 is not greater than zero. However, if register 15 is greater than zero, which indicates an error return code, the code will branch to ERROR in all cases. (For example, if register 15 contained 4, 4 plus 4 is greater than 4, and the branch would be taken to ERROR.)

The value of this coding is that it is smaller and faster than the more common return code test, i.e.,

```
LTR     R15,R15
BNZ     ERROR
```

The disadvantage is that the return code must be divided by two to obtain its original form in the ERROR routine. The more common form using LTR seems to be clearer to most programmers, and hence more maintainable. However, the BXH form is slightly faster, and might be desirable inside a loop which is executed many times.

15.6.5   Absolute Limit For BCT

The longest possible BCT loop occurs when the loop counter has an initial value of zero. In this case, the loop will execute 2^{32} times, or 4294967295 times.

Remember that BCT starts its processing by subtracting 1 from the loop counter register. BCT then compares the result to zero. In this case, BCT will wrap around through values of -1, -2, ..., -2147483648, +2147483647, ..., +2, +1. A range check on the value used for BCT is highly desirable.

15.7 SUMMARY

This section has presented a variety of techniques for handling tables and loops in assembler. You should feel comfortable with converting a table defined with the OCCURS clause into an assembler DS statement. You should be able to write code, following the examples in this chapter, to scan a table using BCT and LA or BXLE. The other information presented will be useful in special situations.

Things to Do

1. Evaluate a loop that uses a table in one of your own COBOL programs. Do any of the performance improvement suggestions in Sec. 15.6.3 seem to apply to it?

2. If you have access to assembler programs — do they include a range check on the loop counter used for BCT?

3. If you are running under VM, review Appendix 4 for further information on the VM-unique CMSSTOR macro. This corresponds to the GETMAIN and FREEMAIN macros.

Special I/O Processing

Up to this point, we've used only the assembler language macros which correspond to normal sequential file COBOL I/O. Many COBOL programmers also make extensive use of two other COBOL I/O features — the DISPLAY and ACCEPT verbs. In this chapter, we'll learn how these can be approximated in assembler, and what functions in these don't exist in assembler.

16.1 THE COBOL DISPLAY VERB

The DISPLAY verb allows a programmer to cause one or more data fields or literals to be displayed on an output file (usually SYSOUT). For example,

DISPLAY FIELD-A.

causes FIELD-A to be converted to EBCDIC if necesary and to be printed on the default COBOL program output device, whose JCL DD name is SYSOUT.

In addition, DISPLAY provides a way for COBOL programmers to write messages to the system operator's console. For example,

DISPLAY 'NUMBER OF INPUT BATCHES IS'
BATCH-COUNT UPON CONSOLE.

causes the following to appear on the system operator's console:

NUMBER OF INPUT BATCHES IS 00004

assuming that BATCH-COUNT had a value of 4.

DISPLAY is frequently used in debugging COBOL programs. If you have TSO TEST available, and your assembler language programs can be tested in that way, the need for an equivalent to DISPLAY in assembler is less pressing.

However, DISPLAY is also sometimes used to write out messages which may be needed by computer operations or data control personnel. In this case, you must probably just define whatever print messages are needed and use the PUT macro to write them out.

Unfortunately, you will also have to include all the conversions to make any needed fields displayable (unpacking, converting from binary, and so on). This means that there is no short cut for displaying printable data in assembler in MVS-like DISPLAY in COBOL.

16.1.1 The VM LINEDIT and APPLMSG Macros

However, VM provides two macros similar in function to the COBOL DISPLAY verb. These are LINEDIT and APPLMSG. They are similar to DISPLAY, in that they combine both editing and display of a data stream. Their syntax is markedly different from that of DISPLAY.

IBM recommends use of APPLMSG for all new applications. We will describe LINEDIT first, then discuss some of the differences when using APPLMSG.

LINEDIT displays text on either the CMS console or on your virtual printer. It has several operands. The ones most appropriate for comparison to DISPLAY are as follows:

TEXT= Specifies the message to be displayed, in single quote marks. It must be one string, unlike DISPLAY. Periods in the text string indicate where the selected variables are displayed.

DISP= Specifies what is to be done with the message after it is edited. The options appropriate here are TYPE (to display it on your virtual console) or PRINT (to print it on your virtual printer)

COMP= Compress the resulting edited data stream by removing blanks. May be YES or NO. We will use NO.

DOT= Add a period (dot) at the end of the edited text message. May be YES or NO; we'll use NO.

RENT= Specifies if the reentrant form of LINEDIT should be generated. May be YES or NO. We will use NO throughout this book.

SUB= Defines the substitutions to be made in the text string. This is how you define the variables to be merged into the text message. It is specified as a series of pairs of operands, with the first item being the type of editing and the second being the source of the data to be edited. The values for type of editing and their source fields are:

HEX,(r)	Hexadecimal conversion
HEXA,label	Hexadecimal conversion
DEC,(r)	Decimal conversion
DECA,label	Decimal conversion
CHARA,(r)	Character data
CHARA,label	Character data
CHAR8A,label	Character data

The source field meanings in the above are

    (r)   (register number)
    label label in your program

CHAR8A formats the data in sequences of 8 bytes, each separated by a single blank.

LINEDIT has many other operands which don't directly apply to a comparison to DISPLAY. We will explain some of these later in the book.

We can best explain how the above parameters work with an example. The steps in converting DISPLAY-form output to a LINEDIT macro are

1. Build the text string, including periods for the locations where the variable data will go.

2. Construct the SUB= series to identify the source for he variable data to be displayed.

3. Code the additional operands to complete the macro.

To illustrate these steps, we'll start with a DISPLAY verb and its related data. Assume that we have the following COBOL data:

```
01 FLAGRANT-DEADBEAT-RECORD.
   05  ACCT-NUM    PIC S9(8) COMP.
   05  LATE-CNT    PIC S9(8) COMP.
   05  CUST-NAME   PIC X(15).
```

and assume that we have

```
DISPLAY 'ACCT # ' ACCT-NUM ' NAME ' CUST-NAME
        ' HAS BEEN LATE ' LATE-CNT ' TIMES'.
```

Let us go through the steps outlined above. First, the text string will be equivalent to the COBOL display characters, with periods added where the displayed fields should go as follows:

```
LINEDIT TEXT = 'ACCT # ........ NAME ................ HAS BEEN X
LATE ........ TIMES',
```

Note that there is one period for each byte of output we want to display. This text string spans two lines and requires a continuation indicator in position 72. (It's not shown to scale above).

Next, we must construct the SUB= sequences to identify the variable data. Assume that we have

```
FLAGRANT  DS    0CL23
ACCTNUM   DS    F
LATECNT   DS    F
CUSTNAME  DS    CL15
```

Our SUB= sequence then looks like:

```
SUB = (DECA,ACCTNUM,CHARA,CUSTNAME,
       DECA,LATECNT)
```

Finally, we add all the other parameters. We want this message to go to the virtual console, so we pick DISP=TYPE. COMP=, DOT=, and RENT= will all be set to NO. This results in

```
LINEDIT TEXT = 'ACCT # ........ NAME ................ HAS BEEN X
LATE ........ TIMES',DOT = NO,                          X
COMP = NO,RENT = NO,SUB = (DECA,ACCTNUM,   X
CHARA,CUSTNAME,DECA,LATECNT)
```

This would result in the following display on the CMS console:

ACCT # 12345678 NAME W.C.FIELDS   HAS BEEN LATE   99 TIMES

One additional thing which we need to cover here is the APPLMSG macro. This is similar to LINEDIT, but adds some additional operands.

APPLMSG is intended to allow an application to call in a message from a standard library, unique to that application. It is normally specified with an application name, application message number, and optional substitutions. It also includes other operands, like COMP and DISP, which are equivalent to those used with LINEDIT.

You may also specify your own message with APPLMSG, and this is the facility which makes it similar to LINEDIT. The following APPLMSG is equivalent to the LINEDIT macro coded above:

```
APPLMSG TEXT = 'ACCT # ........ NAME ...............        X
        . HAS BEEN LATE ........ TIMES',APPLID = CMS,       X
        COMP = NO,RENT = NO,SUB = (DECA,ACCTNUM,   X
        CHARA,CUSTNAME,DECA,LATECNT)
```

The APPLID=CMS specifies the CMS error message library — since we are providing our own message, this has no effect. However, APPLMSG requires it. Also note that DOT=NO is not used with APPLMSG.

16.2 THE WTO MACRO INSTRUCTION

For the other case — DISPLAY UPON CONSOLE — MVS provides the WTO macro (Write To Operator). VM simulates this macro by sending the WTO message to the CMS console. WTO includes several specialized operands which aren't accessible from COBOL. These support special MVS console display and routing functions and will be discussed later. For now, let's look at how we could use WTO to write out the message in the DISPLAY UPON CONSOLE shown earlier:

```
CNTMSG    WTO    'NUMBER OF INPUT BATCHES IS 00004',    X
                 ROUTCDE = (2,11)
```

In this example, CNTMSG is the label for the WTO, the message inside quotes is what we wish to write on the console, and the ROUTCDE=(2,11) is a way of telling MVS which consoles should get this message (more on this later).

Notice, though, that we didn't specify a variable name in the WTO as we did with BATCH-COUNT in the DISPLAY UPON CONSOLE. Once again, we have to perform the conversion and formatting needed to prepare the field for display. Assuming that we have a field defined as

```
BATCHCNT DS    PL3
```

field can be formatted and inserted into the WTO macro data area by the following code:

```
        UNPK   CNTMSG + 35(5),BATCHCNT    UNPACK ACTUAL CT
        OI     CNTMSG + 39,X'F0'          SET SIGN BITS
```

Uh-oh. Where did we get those numbers? The length of 5 on the UNPK is long enough to handle the 5 packed decimal digits in BATCHCNT. (If that doesn't make sense, go back and review the packed decimal conversion discussion in Chap. 13.)

Where did the CNTMSG+35 come from? To answer this, we need to look at what the WTO macro actually generates. To start with, WTO generates 8 bytes before the actual message (4 bytes are in a BAL instruction, and 4 bytes in count and flag bytes). The actual message we specify in quotes is then generated as a C-type DC constant.

We need to put the actual unpacked count of batches in the message. To do this we used UNPK, although MVC would serve just as well. Since we don't have any means of generating a field name automatically for just part of the WTO message, we have to resort to relative addressing and explicit lengths in this example.

If you count the number of characters in the message prior to the place where we want to have the number, you'll find that there are 27 characters preceding that point. If you add the 8 bytes generated at the start of a WTO macro, you come up with 35, hence the use of CNTMSG+35.

This is not a very straightforward or desirable way of converting the number into displayable format and putting it into the message. However, it is typical of the gyrations used to dynamically build the message text.

A slightly more straightforward way of handling this would be to use some combination of the EQU and ORG directives to create a field name at the right place and with the desired length. We can use the EQU instruction to do this, in which case our example coding becomes

```
          UNPK  WTOCOUNT,BATCHCNT        UNPACK ACTUAL CT
          OI    WTOCOUNT+4,X'F0'         SET SIGN BITS
CNTMSG    WTO   'NUMBER OF INPUT BATCHES IS        ',      X
                ROUTCDE=(2,11)
WTOCOUNT  EQU   CNTMSG+35,5,C            DEFINE WTO LABEL
```

The EQU defines WTOCOUNT to have an address equivalent to CNTMSG+35, to have a length of 5 bytes, and to be of type 'C'.

Another way of accomplishing the same thing is to use the following ORG statement:

```
          UNPK  WTOCOUNT,BATCHCNT        UNPACK ACTUAL CT
          OI    WTOCOUNT+4,X'F0'         SET SIGN BITS
CNTMSG    WTO   'NUMBER OF INPUT BATCHES IS  ',            X
                ROUTCDE=(2,11)
          ORG   CNTMSG+35                ORG TO MSG TEXT
WTOCOUNT  DS    CL5                      DEFINE WTO LABEL
          ORG                            ORG BACK
```

(Review the discussion of EQU and ORG if the last two examples don't make sense.)

16.3   WTO ALTERNATIVES UNDER VM

VM supports the WTO macro through OS simulation. However, it does so by sending the data to the CMS virtual console. This is something we can do with the LINEDIT macro as well. However, this simulation doesn't help us with the special case where we really need to send a message to the VM operator. In this case, we need a different approach.

CP provides a service — the MSG command — which allows us to send a data to a specified user identification. How do we invoke this from a program?

VM provides two ways to do this. First is use of the Diagnose instruction to execute a CP command. The second, which we've already shown in Chap. 14, is to send the appropriate CP command with the LINEDIT command.

Here is one of the LINEDIT macros from Fig. 14.12:

```
        LINEDIT  TEXTA = COMMAND,DISP = CPCOMM,       X
                 DOT = NO,COMP = NO,RENT = NO
```

Here is the data associated with the LINEDIT:

```
COMMAND  DC      AL1(COMMEND-*-1)              LENGTH
         DC      C'MSG OPERATOR HELLO THERE'
COMMEND  EQU     *
```

You will notice a few differences in the LINEDIT macro here and the one we created earlier in this chapter. First, the TEXTA parameter specifies a storage address; the TEXT parameter we used earlier specifies a character string.

The text beginning at COMMAND must have a 1-byte binary constant specifying the length of the characters which follow. The AL1 generates a 1-byte binary constant. The "COMMEND-*-1" tells the assembler to subtract the current address (*) from the address of COMMEND, minus one for the AL1 itself.

The character data, " MSG OPERATOR HELLO THERE ", is the same CP command you would enter at your VM terminal. This sends the message "HELLO THERE" to the VM user ID OPERATOR.

The final difference, and one which changes this from a regular LINEDIT macro to one which issues a CP command, is the DISP=CPCOMM (CP Command) operand.

When executed, this causes

```
MSG FROM user_id
: HELLO THERE
```

to appear on the VM operator terminal. Thus, this provides a service closer to the MVS WTO service.

16.4   THE COBOL ACCEPT VERB

The COBOL service that corresponds to DISPLAY for input is the ACCEPT verb. ACCEPT allows you to receive one data field as input. It operates similarly to DISPLAY in that the input is converted from character to whatever other format is appropriate. Input can come from a default file (JCL DD name of SYSIN) or from the system operator's console. For example,

ACCEPT BATCH-CNT.

will read the next card image in the "SYSIN" file and use the first 5 bytes as the value to be placed into BATCH-CNT. Alternatively,

ACCEPT BATCH-CNT FROM CONSOLE.

will ask the system console operator to type in 5 bytes of data. Whatever is keyed in becomes the new value for BATCH-CNT.

As in the case of DISPLAY, there is no real service which corresponds to the use of ACCEPT from the SYSIN file. If you need to obtain parameters from JCL files, you will have to define them with DCBs, and do all the normal processing and conversions needed with any other file.

In the case of ACCEPT FROM CONSOLE, however, MVS provides a macro instruction which corresponds closely to the COBOL service. This is WTOR (Write To Operator with Reply). Example coding is

```
XC     ECB1,ECB1                   CLEAR EVENT CTL
WTOR   'ENTER 5-DIGIT BATCH COUNT',BATCHCNT,5,     X
       ECB1,ROUTCDE = (2,11)
WAIT   1,ECB = ECB1                WAIT FOR REPLY
```

In this example, BATCHCNT is the name of the field we want to get from the console operator, 5 is the length of BATCHCNT, and ECB1 is a field used to wait for the operator's reply. (This would be defined as " ECB1 DS F ".)

This sequence of instructions displays the message ENTER 5-DIGIT BATCH COUNT on the system console. It then waits for the operator to enter a reply. MVS will reject any operator reply longer than 5 bytes. After the operator has replied, MVS will place the response in the field called BATCHCNT. From that standpoint, it works very similarly to the COBOL ACCEPT verb.

There are some differences which must be considered, however. Again, MVS just takes the operator's response and places it into the specified field. Any validation of the operator's response must be done by your program. In addition, the operator may provide a response of less than 5 bytes. Your program must determine this and handle it if necesary.

One other difference is that the COBOL program stops while waiting for the operator to reply. In contrast, the assembler program is free to do other processing while waiting for the reply. In the example shown above, additional instructions could have been placed between the WTOR macro instruction and the WAIT macro. These would have been executed, and then the program would wait for a reply.

Under VM, WTOR waits for a reply from the CMS virtual console.

16.5   GENERAL CAUTIONS ON USE OF WTO/WTOR

The general concept of writing a message to the operator is outdated in most application systems. There is one place where use of this technique may be defensible — printer alignment routines, particularly when printing serially-numbered forms such as checks. It may be appropriate to use WTO or WTOR for other cases where operator intervention is needed, such as resetting a device or dialing a number for a modem.

However, in general, reliance on operator messages and replies is not desirable. You should carefully evaluate the use of this technique before using it.

If you are going to use this technique, be sure you don't go into a loop issuing WTO instructions. This will make you very unpopular with the operators, as well as very visible to your boss. And almost everybody else.

16.6   ADVANCED TOPICS WITH WTO/WTOR

We mentioned the MVS console routing code earlier when describing WTO. Specifically, there is an operand of WTO, named ROUTCDE, which allows assembler programmers to specify which consoles should receive the WTO or WTOR message.

MVS operator consoles are categorized in MVS by two attributes. The first is their authority, which specifies which commands are permitted from that particular console. The second is their routing, which is a series of numbers from 1 to 16. MVS allocates specific meanings to these numbers. (A console may have more than one routing code, and more than one console in a system may receive a copy of specific WTO/WTOR messages.) The routing codes are shown in Figure 16.1.

The idea behind routing codes is to allow messages to go only to the consoles that need to see them. For example, tape mount messages would theoretically specify routing codes of 3 and 5 [ROUTCDE=(3,5)]. This would only cause the message to appear at the tape pool and tape library consoles in a perfect world.

Similarly, messages asking for passwords should theoretically only go to consoles with routing code 9.

Routing code 11 is sometimes referred to as a write-to-programmer routing code. Messages with this routing code will appear in the JES message log at the beginning of your JCL listings.

In practice, almost everything goes to the master console anyway. This writer generally uses ROUTCDE=(2,11). For those situations where you absolutely must use an operator message, however, you should select the appropriate routing code and use it. If writing alignment messages for serially-numbered checks, for example, routing code 7 would probably be appropriate.

Figure 16.1 WTO routing codes.

Code	Meaning
1	Master console action
2	Master console information
3	Tape pool
4	Direct access pool
5	Tape library
6	Disk library
7	Unit record pool
8	Teleprocessing control
9	System security
10	System error/maintenance
11	Programmer information
12	Emulators
13-15	Reserved for customer use
16	Reserved for future use

16.7 SUMMARY

This section has discussed how to execute the equivalent of DISPLAY under VM, DISPLAY UPON CONSOLE in both MVS and VM, and ACCEPT FROM CONSOLE under MVS and VM. You should be able to code a simple WTO and/or LINEDIT macro to display an error message.

Things to Do

1. What installation standards, if any, apply to the use of WTO and WTOR at your MVS shop?
2. Determine what routing codes are in use at your installation. The simplest way to determine this is to ask the operator to do a DISPLAY CONSOLES command. As part of the output of the D CONSOLES, there is a column indicating which routing codes apply to each console.
3. If you can't get access to a console, ask your systems programmer for the routing code information.
4. MVS/ESA expands the number of routing codes to 128. The routing codes listed in Fig. 16.1 are still valid, but new ranges have been added, and routing code 16 is now for customer use. If you are running in an ESA installation, review the WTO macro description in the following manual:

   "MVS/ESA System Programming Library: Application Development Macro Reference", GC28-1857

Other Instructions and Macros

In this chapter we'll clean up some loose ends by describing a few instructions and macros that don't have direct equivalents in COBOL. This will complete our discussion of the basic assembler language instruction set and will prepare us for the remaining chapters, which cover more advanced and less frequently used topics.

The instructions covered in this chapter relate to bit manipulation (setting bits on or off, reversing bits, and testing bit values). Some other specialized instructions, such as those added with MVS/ESA, are also covered briefly.

The directives covered here are TITLE, EJECT, and SPACE. These provide formatting services for assembly listings. The macros covered in this chapter relate primarily to dump and timing services.

17.1 BIT TESTING

The main instruction for testing bit values is the Test Under Mask — TM — instruction. We have already used TM in several examples to determine if DCBs were opened successfully.

TM is a Storage Immediate (SI) format instruction. This format includes a second operand, called the *immediate operand* or *immediate data*, that is stored as part of the instruction. The coding for TM is identical to that for other SI-format instructions, such as CLI, MVI, and so on. A sample is

```
TM      LETTER,X'C0'
```

This tests the bits in the byte at the storage area named LETTER. TM processes the second operand as a mask value, which tells it which bits are to be tested. If a bit in the mask is a 1, the corresponding bit in the first operand — LETTER in this case — is tested. If a bit in the mask is 0, the corresponding bit is ignored.

TM sets the condition code to indicate what it found when testing the bits in the first operand. There are three possible results. The first is that all the tested bits are set to 1. The second possibility is that all the tested bits are 0. The final choice is that there is a mixture, with some tested bits being set to 1 and others being set to 0.

These three possibilities may be acted on with the BO (Branch if Ones), BZ (Branch if Zeroes), and BM (Branch if Mixed) assembler pseudo-operations. TM is coded similarly to CLI and appears at first glance to operate in the same way. TM, however, only tests some of the bits in the byte, depending on the value of the mask. CLI, by contrast, compares the entire byte value. Confusion between TM and CLI is frequent when first learning assembler language, but you should try to avoid this error.

The key to TM is the mask value provided as the second (immediate data) operand. The mask may be coded as a hexadecimal constant (X'..'), a binary constant, (B'........'), a character constant (C'.'), or a self-defining term (0 through 255). The following are all equivalent examples of TM mask coding:

```
TM    LETTER,C' '
TM    LETTER,X'40'
TM    LETTER,B'01000000'
TM    LETTER,64
```

A review of the code table in the 370 reference summary (yellow, pink, or blue card) may show why. Hexadecimal X'40' is the representation of the EBCDIC character blank, which is the same as B'01000000' in binary and the equivalent in decimal of 64.

Bits that are not set on (to 1) in the mask are not examined and cannot affect the condition code.

TM processes the first operand by examining the bits and testing each one in the mask to determine if it is set on. If so, the equivalent bit in the mask is tested. When determining what will happen for a given test, it is usually clearest to show both values as binary values.

Some examples may clarify the foregoing. Assume that we have a byte in storage defined as

```
LETTER    DC    C'B'
```

and that we test it with

```
TM      LETTER,X'C0'
```

The binary value of the mask byte is   1 1 0 0 0 0 0 0
The binary value in the byte at LETTER is   1 1 0 0 0 0 1 0
The mask bits tell TM to   ↑ ↑
test these two bits ──────────────────────────────────┘│

Since both the bits are on, TM will set the condition code to indicate "ones." We can then branch with a BO opcode.

Assume that LETTER was instead defined as

```
LETTER    DC    C'/'                                    (Hexadecimal X'61')
```

Assume also that we test it with the same mask as before

```
TM      LETTER,X'C0'
```

The binary value of the mask byte is   1 1 0 0 0 0 0 0
The binary value in the byte at LETTER is   0 1 1 0 0 0 0 1

The mask bits tell TM to ─────────────────────────────┘
test these two bits

Since one of the tested bits is on and the other is off, TM will set the condition code to indicate "mixed." A BM opcode will branch to a desired routine following this condition.

For another example, assume that we have

BYTE   DC   X'01'

and that we test it with

        TM   BYTE,X'80'

Mask byte: 1 0 0 0 0 0 0 0
Storage byte: 0 0 0 0 0 0 0 1

TM tests: ───────────────────────────────┘

Only one bit is tested, and it is 0, so the resulting condition code reflects "zeroes," and BZ would branch on this condition.

Note that TM ignores the other bits in BYTE. Only the bit set on in the mask is checked. Thus, a condition code of 0 does not indicate that BYTE contains only bits with values of 0 — it only indicates that the bits TM checked were 0.

Also, note that TM only tests one byte. If we had coded BYTE as

BYTE   DC   X'0180'

TM would have produced the same result, even though the tested bit is on in the next byte.

A common bug when using TM is to code an extended branch mnemonic as though testing a CLI instruction. For example,

        TM   BYTE,X'10'
        BE   EQUAL

This is an error. If BYTE had a value of X'10', the condition code would be set to 3 — a result of all ones. BE tests for a condition code of 0 — equal. However, a cursory glance at these two instructions would leave one with the impression that they were acceptable. Remember, TM is not CLI.

17.1.1   TM Esoterica

TM can provide several unique and otherwise difficult tests through imaginative setting of the mask value. The more imaginative the mask, the more difficult the test may be to understand, so use profuse comments when doing this. Some examples of these tests follow.

TM can be used to test for odd or even numbers in storage areas. The logic behind this type of test, as with most of the other indirect uses of TM, is that we can draw certain conclusions if a given bit is on. For this case, an even number will never have the rightmost (1) bit on. All the other bits in a number (either binary or packed decimal) represent powers of 2 (2, 4, 8, 16, and so on).

Assuming that we have the following defined:

```
FULLWORD DC    F'27'
HALFWORD DC    H'78'
PACKDATA DC    PL3'3'
```

we can test each of these for odd or even numbers by the following:

```
TM    FULLWORD+3,X'01'
BO    ODD
```

This tests the rightmost bit (X'01') of the rightmost byte (+3) of FULLWORD. If it is on, the number is odd. Another test is

```
TM    HALFWORD+1,X'01'
BO    ODD
```

This is the corresponding test for HALFWORD. Since a halfword is only 2 bytes long, the rightmost byte has a displacement of +1. Another test is

```
TM    PACKDATA+2,X'10'
BO    ODD
```

This test is logically the same as the other two. However, the rightmost 4 bits of a packed decimal number are the sign bits. As a result, we test the first bit to the left of the sign with the X'10'. Since PACKDATA is 3 bytes long, we use a displacement of one less than that ("+2") to get to the last byte.

TM also can test for positive or negative numbers in storage. For binary numbers, a mask of X'80' tested against the high (leftmost) byte of a binary number will do a negative-positive test without loading the number into a register and using the LTR instruction. A resulting condition code of "ones" indicates that the number is negative.

For packed decimal numbers, a TM with a mask of X'03' against the packed decimal sign does the same. If the condition code is "mixed", this indicates that the number is negative. (This assumes use of the preferred packed decimal sign values of hexadecimal X'C' and X'F' for positive numbers and X'D' for negative numbers.)

For example, assume that we have the following values:

```
NEGFULL    DC    F'-5'
POSHALF    DC    H'0'
DECMINUS   DC    PL2'-99'
```

We can test each of these with

```
TM    NEGFULL,X'80'
BO    NEGATIVE
```

This tests the leftmost bit (X'80') of the leftmost byte of NEGFULL (no offset). If it is on, this is a negative number. Another test is

    TM   POSHALF,X'80'
    BZ   POSITIVE

This is the same test on a halfword value. A result of 0 indicates a positive number. Another test is

    TM   DECMINUS + 1,X'03'
    BM   NEGATIVE

This is less straightforward than the binary number tests. The sign for the packed decimal number is in the rightmost 4 bits of the rightmost byte, so we must include an offset of one less than the length of the packed decimal field ("+1"). The mask value of X'03' tests the leftmost two bits of the sign. If they are both on or both off, the number is positive. If the test result is mixed, the number can be considered to be negative.

If the packed decimal sign test does not make sense, try to imagine three packed decimal numbers with the sign values of X'C', X'D', and X'F' (we use 'x' in the digit bit positions which do not matter for this test):

Positive (X'C')   x x x x 1 1 |0 0|

Negative (X'D')   x x x x 1 1 |0 1|

Unsigned (X'F')   x x x x 1 1 |1 1|

Mask: 0 0 0 0 0 0 |1 1|

    Tested bits   ─────────────────────┘

If the number has a positive sign, the rightmost 2 bits are both zeroes. If the number is unsigned (i.e., just packed, with no arithmetic done yet), the rightmost 2 bits are both ones. These two conditions can be acted on with the BZ and BO opcodes.

If the number has a negative sign, one bit is on and one is off. Hence the BM opcode will branch if the packed decimal number is negative.

Numerous other tests are possible with TM. However, you should comment the nature of the test adequately to avoid confusing future programmers who have to maintain this.

17.2 LOGICAL INSTRUCTIONS

In this context, *logical* means that the instructions are used to perform *Boolean* bit-value manipulations. This comes from the engineering term *Boolean logic*, which refers to two-state binary design. George Boole, an English mathematician, developed this in the 1800s, and it is part of the foundation of modern digital engineering.

A more prosaic description is bit manipulation of data in registers or storage. We have already seen examples of one of these instructions — the OR instruction — when manipulating the sign value of packed decimal numbers.

The general use of logical instructions is to perform bit manipulation. The three logical functions are

Function	Purpose
AND	Used to turn bits off (0)
OR	Used to turn bits on (1)
Exclusive OR	Used to invert (reverse) bits

Each of these three types has four implementations, in the RR, RX, SI, and SS formats. To prevent misinterpretation, we will capitalize AND, OR, and Exclusive OR in this section. This will avoid confusion with the English words of the same name.

For all the logical instructions, the first operand is a register or storage field to be operated on. The second operand is a mask that is applied bit-by-bit to the first operand.

The results of the operations vary with the type. The AND instruction sets a bit on (to 1) in the result if and only if the corresponding bit is on in both the first operand *and* the second operand. OR sets the bit on in the result if it is on in either the first operand *or* the second operand. Exclusive OR sets a bit on in the result if it is on in the first *or* second operand *exclusively*, i.e., is on in one but is off in the other.

Since AND sets a bit to 0 unless it is 1 in both operands, providing a 0 bit in the mask value will force the corresponding bit to be 0 in the result. Setting a bit to 1 in the mask will leave the bit unchanged from the first operand, since the result will be 1 if the first operand had a 1 and 0 if it had a 0 in the corresponding bit position. Since the placement of the 0 bits in the mask forces 0 bits in the result, the AND instruction is used to set bits off.

Since OR sets a bit to 1 if it is a 1 in either operand, setting bits to 1 in the mask forces these to be 1 in the result. Mask bits of 0 will leave the first operand unchanged. As a result, OR is used to set bits on.

Exclusive OR is slightly more complicated. It cannot be used to force 0 or 1 bits in the result, since the value of both the mask and first operand bits must be known to predict the result. However, setting a bit in the mask to 1 has the effect of inverting or reversing the corresponding bit in the first operand. If the first operand bit is a 1, a 1 in the mask bit forces Exclusive OR to set the bit to 0. If the first operand bit is 0, a 1 in the mask bit will force the result bit to 1.

Figure 17.1 shows the processing for all possible bit combinations for these three operations. Table 17.1 shows the specific operation codes for the logical instructions by type and format.

Table 17.1   Logical Instruction Operation Codes

	F o r m a t s			
	RS	RR	SI	SS
	Register	Register	Storage	Storage
	to	to	Immediate	to
	Storage	Register		Storage
Operations				
AND	N	NR	NI	NC
OR	O	OR	OI	OC
Exclusive OR	X	XR	XI	XC

Figure 17.1   Processing for logical instructions.

	I n s t r u c t i o n s		
	AND	OR	Exclusive
Operands			**OR**
1st			
operand	1100	1100	1100
Mask	1010	1010	1010
Result	1000	1110	0110

(All values are in binary.)

17.2.1   Uses of the Logical Instructions

We have already seen examples of the OI instruction to set on packed decimal sign bits. Rather than provide detailed explanations of each of the instructions for each format, let's look at some typical uses for them.

The OC — OR Characters — instruction can be used to set a lowercase EBCDIC value to uppercase. For example, the WTOR instruction receives a reply from an operator console. You must either test the reply in both uppercase and lowercase, since the console may reply in either form, or you must convert the reply to one or the other. One way to do this is to OR the reply with a field of blanks, which will turn all the lowercase letters into uppercase, but will not affect the special characters, uppercase letters, or digits.

The reason for this is that ORing with a mask of blanks will set on the X'40' bit in all the result bytes. This bit is already set on in uppercase letters. (For example, 'A' is binary 11000001, which has the X'40' — binary 01000000 — bit on.) This bit is also set on in the digits (X'F0' through X'F9') and special characters (such as X'61' — slash — or X'4B' — period).

However, lowercase letters do not have this bit set on. For example, "a" is X'81' or binary 10000001. ORing this with blanks —

"a"   10000001
blank   01000000
produces
           11000001

which is uppercase "A" (hexadecimal X'C1').

We will see another way to do this conversion when we discuss the Translate instruction in Chap. 20.

Exclusive OR can clear a field to all binary zeroes (COBOL LOW-VALUES). It does this if the first operand and the mask are the same. The reason for this is that when Exclusive ORed with itself, each 1 bit in an operand will be Exclusive ORed with a 1 bit and each 0 bit will be Exclusive ORed with a 0 bit. This produces a result of all 0 bits. For example,

        XC   FIELDA,FIELDA

will set FIELDA to contain all binary zeroes. (XC is a storage-to-storage instruction that can clear any field up to 256 bytes in length. MVCL is probably preferable for very long fields.)

Another example of this is

        XR   R3,R3

This will set the contents of register 3 to 0. This is sometimes used in preference to SR, but the two usages are equivalent.

A side effect of the XC instruction is that it can be used to interchange the contents of two equal-length storage areas without use of an intermediate field. The sequence of instructions

        XC   A,B
        XC   B,A
        XC   A,B

will swap the contents of the fields A and B in storage. This side effect is too neat to ignore, and every assembler programmer writes a program to take advantage of it. In most situations, however, it is of minor value, with the possible exception of fixed-length table sorts. XR can interchange two registers' contents in the same way.

Other unique uses of the logical instructions include floating-point conversion with O/OR and N/NR, branch mask manipulation (see the discussion of the ALTER verb), and simulation of the *rotate* instructions of other CPUs. In general, these are infrequently seen.

17.3   THE SUPERVISOR CALL INSTRUCTION

Supervisor Call — opcode SVC — is used to request services from MVS or CMS. It is an RR-format instruction, but its only operand is a number from 0 to 255, specifying some service.

The SVC instruction causes an *interrupt*, which will cause the operating system to get control. The 370 CPU will store the current Program Status Word (PSW) in fixed low storage of the CPU at location X'20'. The 370 CPU then loads a new PSW from location X'60', which will cause the MVS SVC Interrupt Handler to receive control and eventually have your service request performed. Figure 17.2 shows this process. (Refer to the reference summary under the heading "Fixed Storage Locations" for information about other PSWs.)

Figure 17.2 Interrupt PSW processing.

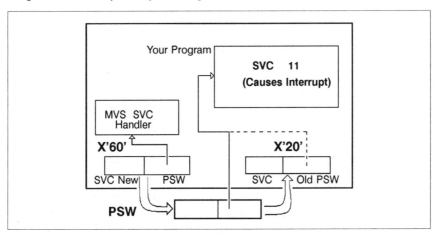

When the service has been completed, MVS will return control to the next instruction in your program.

SVCs work on the same concept as BAS/BASR, but they cause context switching as well, allowing the operating system to get control in supervisor state. Normally, SVC instructions are generated as part of OS macro instructions. For example, the OPEN macro generates SVC 19 to actually have MVS or VM open the requested DCBs. Table 17.2 shows a list of commonly used macros and the SVCs used to perform the services.

An example of coding SVC is

      SVC   3

SVC 3 is the EXIT service, which is close to the COBOL STOP RUN statement. It ends execution of the current program, even if issued from a subprogram.

Too many other macros exist to completely cover here. VM supports the macro services listed in Table 17.2.

Table 17.2 MVS SVCs for Common Services	
SVC number	Macro/service provided
0	EXCP – Used for I/O by GET and PUT
6	LINK – Like COBOL call with DYNAM option
7	XCTL – See Chap. 14
8	LOAD – See Chap. 14
9	DELETE – Like COBOL CANCEL
11	TIME
13	ABEND
19	OPEN
20	CLOSE
31	FEOV – See Chap. 5
35	WTO – See Chap. 16
51	SNAP
55	EOV – End-of-volume – like COBOL CLOSE REEL option
64	RDJFCB – Get file information – see Chap. 14
68	SYNADAF – See Chap. 17
120	GETMAIN/FREEMAIN (Older forms use SVC 4, 5, or 10)
121	VSAM – Various functions

17.4   ASSEMBLY LISTING FORMAT CONTROL

Assembler provides three directives for more attractive listings. These are the EJECT, SPACE, and TITLE directives.

EJECT causes the assembler to skip to top of the next page in the output listing. It is identical in this regard to the COBOL EJECT statement.

SPACE causes the assembler to skip a specified number of lines. It is coded as

        SPACE n

which tells the assembler to skip "n" lines on the output listing. This is similar to the COBOL SKIP1/SKIP2/SKIP3 statements. However, assembler does not restrict the number of lines skipped.

The TITLE directive is used to provide a title at the top of each page of the assembly listing. It is coded as

        TITLE   'TITLE FOR TOP OF LISTING'

The assembler places the title — whatever is in the single quotation marks — at the top of each page of the assembly listing after that. It also causes the assembler to immediately skip to the top of the next page. (However, if the TITLE directive is at the beginning of the program, there is no need to skip to the next page, so TITLE will not produce a blank page in that case.)

17.5   370 AND MVS TIMING FACILITIES

The 370 CPU provides several timing facilities, but only one of these is generally available to applications programmers. MVS uses the 370 timing facilities to provide timing services through various macro instructions. We will discuss each of these in turn. VM provides a subset of these services through OS simulation.

17.5.1   The Store Clock Instruction

Originally, the 360 CPU had only one timer facility, called the *interval timer*. This was at storage location 80 and was updated 300 times per second. The update consisted of subtracting 1 from bit position 23 of the fullword at location 80. Location 80 could be directly accessed by applications programs, but the value there had no intrinsic meaning, since it would be updated frequently by the operating system.

The 370 added three additional timing facilities, but only one of these is directly accessible to applications programs. These are the CPU timer, the Time-Of-Day clock, and the clock comparator.

The Time-Of-Day (TOD) clock can only be set in supervisor state, and it also requires that the computer operator depress a special switch while it is being set. The application program can access the value in the TOD clock through the Store Clock — STCK — instruction.

STCK is coded with only one operand. This specifies a doubleword in storage, which will receive a copy of the TOD clock.

The TOD clock is a doubleword binary number, in which bit position 53 represents 1 microsecond. This scaling gives a total cycle time for the clock of 143 years. IBM's convention is that a value of all 0 bits indicates January 1, 1900, 00:00 A.M. Greenwich Mean Time. IBM calls this the *standard epoch*.

This scaling also means that bit 31 (the low-order bit of the first word) of the doubleword) has a value of 1.048576 seconds. This provides a convenient 4-byte time and date stamp for such purposes as journaling, audit trails, and other types of transaction records.

The condition code following STCK indicates if the time in the clock is valid. It the condition code is other than 0, there is some problem with the clock. The following shows an example of STCK:

```
         STCK    DOUBLEWD
         BNZ     ERROR
         MVC     LOGTIME,DOUBLEWD
         ..............
DOUBLEWD DS      D
LOGTIME  DS      F        (High-order value of timer)
```

17.5.2   Other Timing Facilities

Other 370 CPU timing facilities are normally not used by applications programs. The interval timer and CPU timer are decremented by 1 periodically, and these will give an interrupt when they reach 0. This is best for timing specific periods. The clock comparator is compared periodically to the TOD clock and causes an interrupt when the two are equal. This is best for causing an interrupt at a specific time.

Since you must be in supervisor state to use the instructions that change these timers, you will probably not ever use them.

17.5.3   MVS Timing Services

Using the STCK instruction by itself does not provide all the timing services programmers need. MVS provides several services to determine the time and date, to wait for a specified period, or to have your program notified when a specified period of time passes.

The MVS TIME macro provides a service equivalent to the COBOL TIME-OF-DAY special register or to the ACCEPT . . . FROM DATE in VS COBOL II. It returns the time of day and the system date. You may specify several forms for this, but the normal option is the DEC (packed decimal) option. To get the time and date, code

```
        TIME    DEC
```

and the time and date will be available in registers 0 and 1, respectively. It is supported by VM in this form.

The time will be in the format of "HHMMSSTH", which comprises hours (HH), minutes (MM), seconds (SS), and tenths and hundredths of seconds (TH). This will be in packed decimal digits, but with no sign.

The date will be in the format 00YYDDDS, which comprises two digits of leading packed decimal zeroes (00), the year (YY), the day of the year (DDD), and a packed decimal sign (S). This form is normally termed a *Julian date*.

Both the time and date require some processing before they are displayed. An example of this for the time, assuming that we want the time in a field called RUNTIME, would be

```
        TIME    DEC                             GET TIME OF DAY
        ST      R0,WORK                         STORE
        MVC     RUNTIME, =X'4021207A20207A2020'  MOVE MASK
        ED      RUNTIME,WORK                    EDIT TO HH:MM:SS
```

This assumes that RUNTIME is defined as CL9 to hold the edit mask.

The date also may be edited by

```
        ST      R1,WORK
        MVC     RUNDATE, =X'40212061202020'     MOVE EDIT MASK
        ED      RUNDATE,WORK + 1                EDIT TO YY/DDD
```

You also may wish to convert the DDD portion to month and day. This requires a table and loop and might be coded as follows. The loop will place the month and day into the fields called MOVAL and DAYVAL at the end. Note that the loop uses TM to determine if this is a leap year.

```
          TM    WORK+1,X'01'            IS YEAR ODD?
          BO    NOTLEAP                 NOT A LEAP YEAR
          TM    WORK+1,X'12'            LEAP YEAR PATTERN
          BM    NOTLEAP                 NOT A LEAP YEAR
          ZAP   MOTB+2,=P'29'           SET DAYS FOR FEB
NOTLEAP   EQU   *
          LA    R2,MOTB
          ZAP   MOVAL,=P'1'
          ZAP   DAYVAL,=P'0'
LEAPLOOP  EQU   *
          CP    0(2,R2),WORK+2(2)       COMPARE TO TABLE
          BNL   LOOPDONE                NOT LOW - DONE
          AP    MOVAL,=P'1'             ADD TO MONTH
          SP    WORK+2(2),0(2,R2)       SUBTRACT DAYS
          LA    R2,2(R2)                NEXT ENTRY
          B     LEAPLOOP                CONTINUE LOOP
LOOPDONE  EQU   *
          ZAP   DAYVAL,WORK+2(2)        SET UP DAY
          . . . . . . . . . .
MOTB      DC    PL2'31'                 JANUARY
          DC    PL2'28'                 FEBRUARY
          DC    PL2'31'                 MARCH
          DC    PL2'30'                 APRIL
          DC    PL2'31'                 MAY
          DC    PL2'30'                 JUNE
          DC    PL2'31'                 JULY
          DC    PL2'31'                 AUGUST
          DC    PL2'30'                 SEPTEMBER
          DC    PL2'31'                 OCTOBER
          DC    PL2'30'                 NOVEMBER
          DC    PL2'31'                 DECEMBER
          DC    PL2'999'                JUST IN CASE
MOVAL     DC    PL2'0'                  MONTH CALCD HERE
DAYVAL    DC    PL2'0'                  DAY CALCD HERE
```

The logic behind the calculation should be straightforward with what we have covered so far. However, the leap year test is another esoteric use of TM that requires some explanation.

Leap years are evenly divisible by 4. The year at the beginning of a century is not a leap year (e.g., 1900). Thus the first five leap years of this century were 1904, 1908, 1912, 1916, and 1920. These years have unique bit patterns when compared to other even-numbered years. For example, look at four years in their binary combination, along with the mask bits we tested:

04	00000100
06	00000110
10	00010000
12	00010010
Mask	00010010

The first and last are leap years, while the middle two are not. Note that in the leap years, either both the bits are on or both the bits are off. Thus the first test shows us that the year is even, and the second test tells us that the year is not a leap year if the test result is mixed.

The careful reader may ask the question, "what about the year 2000?" Well, fortunately for this algorithm, the year 2000 is a leap year. The specific rule in the Gregorian calendar is that centennial years are not normally leap years, but that every 400 years they are leap years.[1] Thus this algorithm will work satisfactorily through the year 2099. Conversion after that point will be left as an exercise for the reader. Use this to amaze your friends. This is a fairly esoteric use of TM.

Other timing services include the STIMER and TTIMER macros. These provide several services that we will not discuss further.

17.6　DUMP SERVICES
Both MVS and VM provide several other services useful for program debugging. These have no direct equivalents in COBOL. We will discuss two of these — the ABEND and SNAP services.

17.6.1　MVS Dump Services
The MVS ABEND macro is used to force an abnormal termination of a task. This macro is widely used throughout the operating system to cause ABENDs when MVS detects errors in your task requests. You also can use it to cause ABENDs yourself. ABEND is coded with several options, as shown in Fig. 17.3.

The SNAP macro is useful when debugging programs or when you wish to avoid printing a complete dump. SNAP causes MVS to print a dump, using the same formats as the MVS SYSUDUMP output. However, programmers can specify exactly what fields are displayed and can add their own message headers to the dump. Figure 17.4 shows the format of the SNAP macro.

SNAP has several other options that we won't cover here.

1　Encyclopaedia Brittanica, 15th ed. (1988), *s.v.* "Calendar," by Colin Alistair Ronan. Note that an additional day must be taken away about every 3,323 years — as a result, every fortieth century (i.e., the years 4000, 8000, …) is not a leap year, even though it is divisible by 400.

Figure 17.3   ABEND macro operands.

The ABEND macro operands are coded as follows:

ABEND code,DUMP,STEP,code-type

The operands have the following meanings:

code — This is the abend code. It may either be a decimal number in the range of 0-4095 (for normal user ABENDs) or a hexadecimal number such as X'213'.

DUMP — This tells MVS to print a dump for this task. This will be printed on the SYSUDUMP, SYSABEND, or SYSMDUMP data set.

STEP — This indicates that you wish to ABEND the entire job step. If your program is the only program in the step, this is what happens anyway.

code-type — This is either USER or SYSTEM, with a default of USER.

An example of SNAP is coded below, showing the SNAP macro and the data areas used with it. PROGNAME and ENDPROG are labels at the beginning and end of the program, respectively. In addition, we will dump a buffer area. Register 7 has the beginning address of the buffer, and register 8 has the ending address. This example provides two storage headers to identify the program and buffer areas, respectively.

```
        SNAP    DCB = SNAPDCB,PDATA = (REGS),              X
                STORAGE = (PROGRAM,ENDPROG,(7),(8)),       X
                STRHDR = (HDR1,HDR1)
                .................
HDR1    DC      AL1(100)                   MESSAGE LENGTH
        DC      CL100'PROGRAM STORAGE:'    MESSAGE TEXT
HDR2    DC      AL1(40)                    MESSAG E LENGTH
        DC      CL40'BUFFER AREA:'         MESSAGE TEXT


SNAPDCB DCB     DSORG = PS,RECFM = VBA,MACRF = (W),        X
                LRECL = 125,BLKSIZE = 1632,DDNAME = SNAPDD
```

We would have to include the following in our MVS JCL:

```
//SNAPDD          DD SYSOUT = A
```

Or whatever SYSOUT class is appropriate. For VM, we would need a FILEDEF such as FILEDEF SNAPDD PRINT.

To use the preceding to only dump your program area, code the last two operands on SNAP as

```
                STORAGE = (PROGRAM,ENDPROG),               X
                STRHDR = (HDR1)
```

Figure 17.4   SNAP macro operands.

The SNAP macro operands are coded as follows:

```
SNAP    DCB = DCB name,                 X
        SDATA = (options),              X
        PDATA = (options),              X
        STORAGE = (start,end),          X
        STRHDS = (header label address)
```

The operands have the following meanings:

DCB name — This is the label on a specially coded DCB for use with SNAP. The DCB must have the following options:

```
DCB    DSORG = PS,RECFM = VBA,MACRF = (W),              X
       LRECL = 125,BLKSIZE = 1632,DDNAME =  name
```

The DD name may be anything you choose, but it may not be SYSUDUMP, SYSABEND, or SYSMDUMP. You must also OPEN the DCB before issuing SNAP.

SDATA options — This operand allows several system control blocks to be formatted. These options result in printing the same control blocks that appear at the beginning of a SYSUDUMP dump. For example, specifying CB here prints the control blocks that usually appear in the first two or three pages of a SYSUDUMP. Specifying DM formats the data management control blocks, such as DCBs. Refer to the appropriate supervisor services and macros manual for complete descriptions.

PDATA options   — These specify information which is usually of more interest than the SDATA options, including

PSW — the PSW when the SNAP is issued

REGS — the registers when the SNAP is issued

SA — the save area chain

JPA — the programs in the job pack area (your program)

SPLS — any storage acquired with the GETMAIN macro

STORAGE — This is a list of pairs of addresses. Each pair marks the beginning and ending addresses of an area you want to dump. You may either specify these as labels in your program or provide each address in a register. See example below.

STRHDR — This indicates the storage headers for the areas specified in your STORAGE operand. These are labels (maximum 100 bytes) that SNAP prints before dumping your storage area. You must provide a 1-byte binary length at the beginning of the label.

17.6.2   VM Dump Services

VM also provides abnormal end and dump services. In addition, VM OS simulation will process the ABEND and SNAP macros.

VM issues an abnormal end by means of the DMSABN macro. This is coded as

DMSABN hexcode,TYPCALL = SVC | BALR

"hexcode" indicates the abnormal end code. It is coded as a value between 0 and FFF. It also may be provided in a register. In this case, it must be coded within parentheses, e.g., (2), to specify that register 2 has the abnormal end code. The TYPCALL parameter specifies how DMSABN is invoked. You should code SVC.

Dump services in VM are provided by the CP DUMP command. We used this in the "SHOWPARM" program in Fig. 14.12. The code to do this was

```
        LA    R2,SHOWPARM              GET BEGIN ADDR
        LA    R3,PROGEND               GET ENDING ADDR
        LINEDIT TEXTA = DUMPCMD,DISP = CPCOMM,           X
            DOT = NO,COMP = NO,SUB = (HEX,(2),HEX,(3)),   X
            RENT = NO
```

The data areas this used were

```
DUMPCMD  DC    AL1(DUMPEND-*-1)           LENGTH
         DC    C'DUMP T......:...... *DISPLAY STORAGE'
DUMPEND  EQU   *
```

The AL1 generates a 1-byte binary constant of the length of the DUMP command text. Note that the DUMP command is followed by two variable areas, delimited by six periods each. The LINEDIT macro will edit the addresses in registers 2 and 3 into these areas before passing the command to CP.

The " *DISPLAY STORAGE " will be printed on the dump as an identifier. You could display a counter or other unique information here to identify dumps more easily.

The CP dump is produced on your virtual printer. You will need to issue a SPOOL PRINT CLOSE command to release your print file up to the point of the dump.

The CP dump will include the PSW, all registers, the storage designated by the beginning and ending addresses in registers 2 and 3, and some storage key and location information. This may produce more data than you really wish for a particular problem.

17.7 OTHER INSTRUCTIONS

This section covers three instructions that you may encounter. They have relatively specialized uses.

17.7.1 The Test and Set Instruction

The Test and Set instruction — opcode TS — was designed in the original 360 instruction set. It provided an early form of serialization for multitasking and multiprocessing applications. We have previously covered the Compare and Swap instructions (opcodes CS and CDS), which are intended to replace TS.

TS tests the leftmost bit in a byte, sets the condition code, and sets the tested byte to X'FF", all in one operation. TS is coded with one operand:

```
TS    BYTE
```

where we wish to test the leftmost bit of BYTE. This is equivalent to the two instructions

```
TM    BYTE,X'80'
MVI   BYTE,X'FF'
```

However, TS sets the condition code differently. Refer to the reference summary for further information. TS is used in the VSAM access method for serialization in certain control blocks.

17.7.2   The Program Mask

The 370 PSW includes a 4-bit field called the *program mask*. Two instructions are available to manipulate this — Set Program Mask (SPM) and Insert Program Mask (IPM).

In 370 addressing mode (24-bit), the BAL and BALR instructions place the right half of the PSW into the first operand register. In the leftmost byte, this includes the instruction length code, the condition code, and the program mask.

In XA addressing mode (31-bit), BAL and BALR cannot be used to obtain this information, so a separate instruction is provided to get this. This instruction is Insert Program Mask (IPM), and it also gets the instruction length code, the condition code, and the program mask.

The program mask allows you to cause or avoid program check ABENDs for certain arithmetic errors. These are:

- Fixed-point binary overflow (0C8)

- Packed decimal overflow (0CA)

- Floating-point exponent underflow (0CD)

- Floating-point significance exception (0CE)

You have probably never seen these ABEND codes, for several reasons. MVS and VM normally set the program mask bits off. With the bits off, an overflow results in a condition code setting, which you can test. (This is the ON SIZE ERROR clause processing in COBOL.)

You may obtain the program mask with IPM or BALR and then change it with the NR or OR instruction. SPM would then be used to set the program mask back.

This is not frequently used, since it is usually easier to check for an overflow condition code than to look at a dump. However, SPM also can be used to set the condition code. This allows you to code a comparision, save the result, do some other processing, and then restore the old condition code and branch based on the original comparison. For example, assume that we needed to test for a negative balance, reset the balance to 0, and then branch if the original balance was negative:

```
CP      BALANCE, = P'0'              COMPARE TO ZERO
IPM     R1                           SAVE COND CODE
ZAP     BALANCE, = P'0'              RESET TO ZERO
*       PERFORM ANY OTHER PROCESSING NEEDED HERE
SPM     R1                           GET OLD CONDITION CODE BACK
BM      NEGATIVE_BALANCE             BRANCH IF MINUS
```

For this specific example, it would probably be easier and clearer to save the original balance in another field. However, this example shows how to save and reset the condition code if needed.

If IPM is not available on your CPU, you could code " BALR R1,0 " in its place in this code and produce the same results.

17.7.3 Monitor Call

The Monitor Call instruction — opcode MC — was added in the early 1970s to provide a way of passing information to the operating system for debugging or performance evaluation purposes. It is usable in problem state programs, but it is used for specialized cases in both MVS and VM.

In MVS, Monitor Call is used within the GTRACE macro instruction. GTRACE passes data to the MVS Generalized Trace Facility (GTF) for operating system tracing. GTF requires operator and systems programmer involvement for its use in almost all installations.

In VM, Monitor Call is used to pass information to CP for use by the VMAP or VMMAP program products. The CP operator command MONITOR is used with this. As with GTF, operator and systems programmer involvement is usually required.

Owing to the specialized nature of MC, you should not code it.

17.8   INSTRUCTIONS USED WITH MVS/ESA

The MVS/Enterprise Systems Architecture™ operating system includes a feature that dramatically increases the amount of data that one program can address. This is done by adding a new type of virtual storage called *data spaces*.

We do not have space for a complete treatment of this topic — it could easily take an entire book in itself. However, we'll describe the instructions that you can use in your programs under MVS/ESA. We'll also discuss some of the MVS/ESA services that you need to use to create and access data spaces.

17.8.1   MVS/ESA Data Spaces

A data space is a separate area of virtual storage that is up to 2 gigabytes (2^{31}-1 bytes) in size. It is like other MVS/XA address spaces, but it has three important limitations or features:

1. A data space may only contain data.

2. A data space does not contain any MVS control blocks. You have complete control over the entire area, from location 0 to the end.

3. A data space may be shared between different jobs (if properly created).

IBM has made several extensions to both the 370 hardware design and to MVS services to support this mode of operation. Note, however, that MVS/ESA normally runs programs in the addressing mode for which they were designed (24-bit or 31-bit). The addressing mode does not change to use data spaces unless you tell MVS/ESA to do so in your program. Older programs thus remain compatible and do not have to be changed.

To create a data space, you use a macro instruction called DSPSERV. This macro has several options. The CREATE option asks MVS/ESA to build a data space for you. (You may wish to think of DSPSERV CREATE as a special kind of GETMAIN macro. Note that you must be running in 31-bit addressing mode to use DSPSERV.)

You may then tell MVS/ESA how you intend to use the data space with the DEFINE option of DSPSERV. The most common case of this is if you want to do I/O to the data space.

To get to the data space, you must set up a new hardware feature. This is a set of 16 additional registers called *access registers*. Access registers are like general purpose registers — they are 32 bits long and are numbered 0 through 15.

Access registers, however, may only contain addresses. It may be more appropriate to consider access registers as containing address modifiers. Specifically, access registers are used to identify a data space where you have stored data. This is done by matching each access register with its corresponding general purpose register.

How does this work? When you are in the right addressing mode to use data spaces, the CPU automatically appends the value in the access register to your base register values. This causes the CPU to use the data in the data space instead of what is in your normal address space. (The normal address space, where your programs and all the MVS control block information reside, is called the *home address space*.)

The addressing mode that uses the addess registers is called *access register mode* or *AR-mode*. When switching to or from AR-mode addressing, MVS/ESA provides a new macro called SYSSTATE . Additionally, the operation of an instruction called Set Address Space Control (opcode SAC) is modified to allow you to start or stop AR-mode addressing.

When your program is in AR-mode, each base register value is automatically changed by the corresponding access register. Thus, if you are using register 2 as a base register for a DSECT, the CPU will automatically add (append) the data space identifier. Your references to storage using base register 2 will automatically — and always — be changed to references to storage in the data space.

This means that you may have up to 15 separate data spaces in addition to your home address space. You thus have access to up to 32 gigabytes of storage from your program in AR-mode. In fact, you may have more than 15 data spaces and may switch between them by changing the access registers.

It is important to note that the access register does not actually change the base register value. The contents of register 2 in our earlier example wouldn't be changed. What does change is how the CPU uses the base address in register 2.

Also, the access register contains several fields. The important one for our purposes is the Access List Entry Token (ALET) which is stored in the rightmost 16 bits of the access register. This is appended to the front of your base register value to form a 48-bit unique address.

The ALET is provided to you by the DSPSERV macro in a parameter called an STOKEN. You should not change this value or you may experience program checks or other problems.

Figure 17.5 provides an overview of the relationship between your home address space, data spaces, and access registers.

Figure 17.5 Relationship of address and data spaces and access registers.

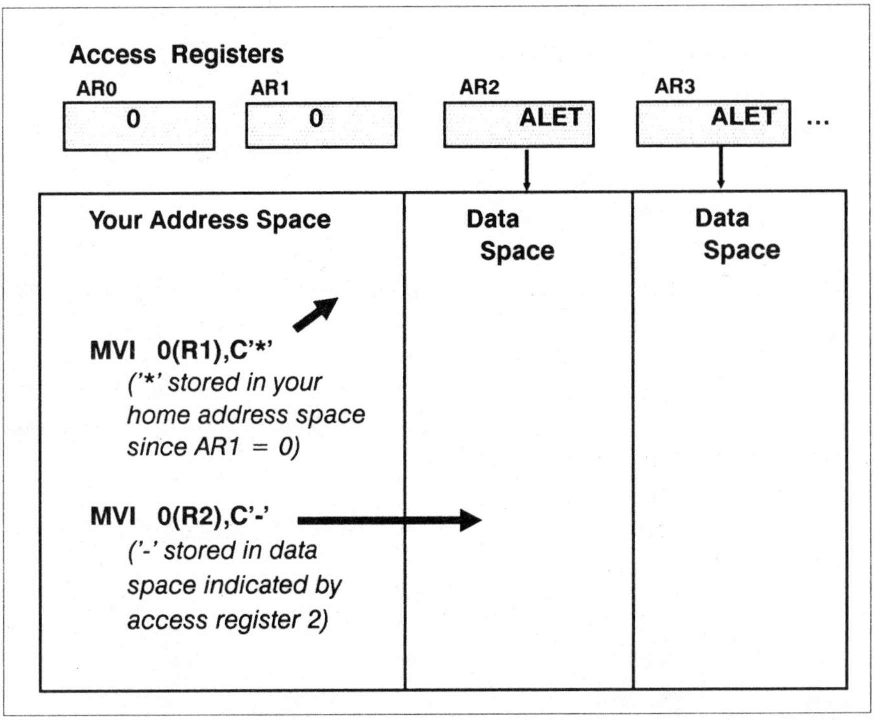

The CPU also places special meanings on three values in access registers. If an access register contains 0, it tells the CPU that there is no separate data space for this base register. You can use this feature to turn on or turn off AR-mode access for individual data spaces if you wish. (A value of 0 refers to a *primary* address space, which we will consider to be the home address space for our purposes.)

If an access register contains a value of 1, it tells the CPU that you are addressing another address space used with the dual-address-space feature. (We referred to this earlier when we talked about the PC and PT instructions in Chap. 14. You must be specially authorized to use this feature. We won't discuss it further.)

If an access register contains a value of 2, it tells the CPU that you are addressing your home address space. For our purposes, values of 0 and 2 are interchangeable.

You tell MVS/ESA that you want to start using a particular data space by coding the ALESERV macro. ALESERV requires the STOKEN, which we got from the DSPSERV CREATE macro. Finally, you may use the DSPSERV macro with the DELETE parameter to get rid of a data space when you are through with it.

17.8.2 ESA/370 Access Register Instructions

IBM provides six instructions we can use in our programs to manipulate access registers. These are

- CPYA — Copy Access Register
- EAR — Extract Access Register
- LAE — Load Address Extended
- LAM — Load Access Multiple
- SAR — Set Access Register
- STAM — Store Access Multiple

These are generally equivalent to the LR, LM, STM, and LA instructions but use access registers in their execution. Figure 17.6 shows the general flow of data for some of these instructions.

CPYA works like the LR — Load Register — instruction. However, the sending and receiving registers are access registers rather than general purpose registers. For example,

        CPYA   9,10

copies access register 10 into access register 9. Access register 10 is not changed.

EAR is used to get a copy of an access register into a general purpose register. It operates like LR, but the second operand is an access register. For example, if we code

        EAR   9,10

the value in access register 10 is copied into general purpose register 9. Note that we cannot directly use the ALET for addressing when it is in a general purpose register. EAR is probably best for temporarily saving an ALET value for a short time.

SAR is the logical opposite of EAR. It also works like LR, but the first operand specifies an access register rather than a general purpose register. For example,

SAR   8,9

copies the ALET value we put in register 9 with the EAR example into access register 8.

LAM operates like the LM — Load Multiple — instruction but specifies access registers only. It is coded like LM, with two register values and a storage location. For example,

LAM   8,10,LOC1

loads access registers 8, 9, and 10 from the three fullwords at LOC1. The contents of LOC1 are not changed.

STAM, conversely, operates like Store Multiple, but specifies access registers only. It is coded like STM. For example,

STAM   0,15,LOC1

will save all the access registers in storage location LOC1. LOC1 must be 16 fullwords long. STAM will only store one register if the starting and ending registers are coded as the same value; that is,

STAM   9,9,LOC2

will only store access register 9 at LOC2. With this coding, STAM is operating like the ST — Store — instruction for general purpose registers.

Figure 17.6   Data flow for ESA instructions.

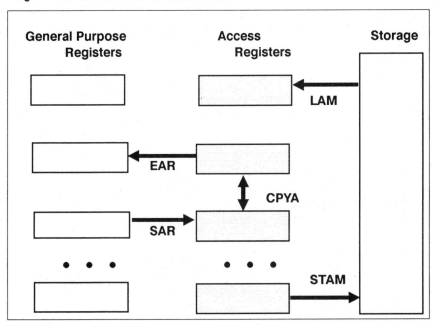

Note that STAM and LAM must use storage locations on fullword boundaries. LM and STM do not require this, but it is recommended. You will receive a specification exception (0C6) if you neglect this.

The LAE — Load Address Extended — instruction operates something like the LA — Load Address — instruction. However, LAE changes both a general purpose register and its associated access register. LAE is coded like LA. The difference in operation is that the first operand register and base register specify both a general purpose register and the associated access register. Thus, if we code

LAE   9,7(,10)

the contents of general purpose register 10 plus the displacement — 7 — are added together and placed into general purpose register 9. This is what the LA instruction does. LAE then also copies the contents of access register 10 (the base register used in the second operand) into access register 9 (the first operand register). Note that the displacement is *not* added to the access register contents.

LAE should be used whenever you are dealing with data spaces. If the access register corresponding to the second operand base register

Figure 17.7 Comparison of LA and LAE instructions.

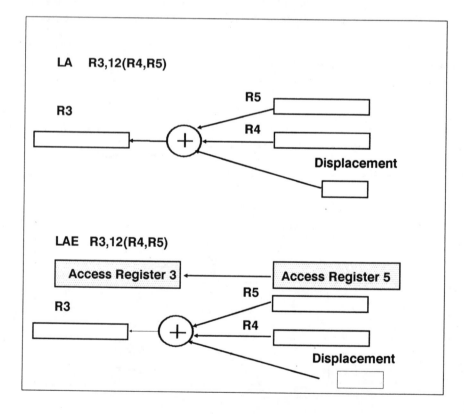

contains 0, LAE operates much like LA. It will have the side effect of loading 0 into the first operand access register. However, this is probably what is desired in this case. Figure 17.7 contains a diagram comparing the LA and LAE instructions.

Another instruction which you must use for AR-mode processing is SAC — Set Address Space Control. This is the only example we will discuss of a class of instructions which IBM calls *semiprivileged instructions*.

A semiprivileged instruction is one which may or may not be permitted, depending on the mode or status of the program using it. SAC is not usable unless your program is running in 31-bit mode, for example. You should use SAC to switch between regular 31-bit addressing mode and AR-mode addressing.

To switch into AR-mode, code:

```
SAC     512
```

To switch back to 31-bit addressing mode, code:

```
SAC     0
```

For a full discussion of the SAC instruction, refer to the principles of operation manual.

IBM also has made significant other instruction changes to support AR-mode processing.

17.8.3   Index Registers and Access Registers

Access registers are used to extend the address provided in a base register. They are not used to extend the address value provided in index registers.

Because of this, there is one thing that we must do to prepare for future use of data spaces. This is to take extreme care in the coding of RX-format instructions. If you remember from our short discussion of this in Chap. 7, RX-format instructions include both a base register and an index register for the second operand.

The assembler's syntax for RX instructions, using Load as an example, is

```
L       target,displacement(index_reg,base_reg)
```

where "target" is the first operand register. For example,

```
L       R3,0(R4,R5)
```

tells the CPU to add the addresses in registers 4 and 5 together and then copy the fullword at the resulting address into register 3.

Where we get into trouble is in coding an RX-format instruction without an index register. To load register 3 from the address contained in register 5, we should code

```
L       R3,0(,R5)
```

with the comma inside the parentheses indicating that the index register is omitted. However, many assembler programmers would code the preceding as

```
L       R3,0(R5)
```

The assembler would take this to mean that we have coded an index register (R5) and no base register.

In older addressing modes, this makes absolutely no difference. Since the base and index registers are added together by the CPU to determine the storage location, we get the same address in all cases.

For MVS/ESA, however, we have big problems. The CPU does not apply an access register prefix to index registers. (Since the access registers contain data space IDs rather than address values, it would not be logical to do so.)

Assuming that access register 5 contains an ALET and is being used with a data space, then

            L   R3,0(,R5)
will load register 3 from the data space, and

            L   R3,0(R5)
will load register 3 from our home address space.

Note, however, that if access register 5 contained 0 or 2 (i.e., was pointing to our home address space), the two instructions would be equivalent.

This is especially confusing because other instruction formats have equivalent coding that works properly in AR-mode. For example,

            MVI   0(R5),C'*'
properly stores a byte into a data space identified by access register 5. However,

            STC   R3,0(R5)
does not. (MVI is an SI-format instruction; STC is an RX- format instruction.) If you access values with a DSECT, the assembler places the base register properly, and this problem does not arise.

If your brain is now completely puréed, the problem identified by this subsection can be distilled into one simple rule: *Always code a comma inside the parentheses when coding an RX-format instruction if you do not use a DSECT*. You will avoid many problems in an MVS/ESA environment if you always follow this rule.

17.8.4   Summary of AR-Mode Processing

If you haven't gotten the idea by now, AR-mode processing is more complicated than normal assembler programming. You should have a significant degree of experience in assembler before tackling it.

To use AR-mode processing, you must have three things:

1. An understanding of AR-mode addressing. We have covered some parts of this, but this is not a complete explanation.

2. An understanding of the hardware instructions (CPYA and so forth) and the MVS/ESA macro instructions (DSPSERV and so forth) that process data spaces.

3. A real need to access huge amounts of storage. This may be in the form of tables that you can't load into storage with your current programs, for example. However, don't use AR-mode addressing just because it seems like a neat idea.

To start using AR-mode addressing in your programs, you should have the ESA/370™ "Principles of Operation," reference summary, and other MVS/ESA manuals we listed in Chap. 1. In addition, you also will need some manuals that we didn't list in Chap. 1. These include

- "MVS/ESA System Programming Library: Application Development — Extended Addressability," GC28-1854

- "MVS/ESA System Programming Library: Application Development Guide," GC28-1852

- "MVS/ESA System Programming Library: Application Development Macro Reference," GC28-1857

These titles and order numbers are current as of November 1989. You may find that other manuals supersede these as the 1990s progress.

Note that many of the other MVS macros we have discussed in this book have new versions for use in AR-mode addressing. These are usually identified by an "X" following the macro name. For example, "LINKX" is an AR-mode version of the LINK macro, and "SNAPX" provides a method for dumping data spaces. Additionally, see the "Things To Do" section for a related macro change.

17.9 SUMMARY

This chapter completed our coverage of the IBM 370 instructions that do not have direct COBOL equivalents. In addition, we also covered special time and dump services and introduced the functions used with MVS/ESA data spaces.

The next four chapters will examine some specialized aspect of COBOL and show corresponding assembler facilities. These include the COBOL declaratives and assembler exits, internal sorts, character string processing, and VSAM file processing. The last chapter will cover the assembler macro facility, which has no direct COBOL equivalent.

At this point in the book, you have been exposed to every major assembler instruction, with the exception of EX, TR, and TRT, which we will discuss in Chap. 20.

Things to Do

1. Code a subroutine for use by a COBOL program to dump storage areas using the SNAP macro. Remember to test for error conditions in the parameters, such as invalid addresses, incorrect lengths, and related items. Also provide error return codes if the OPEN or SNAP macros have errors. (For VM, use the CP DUMP command.)

2. Investigate the usefulness of a similar subroutine for the ABEND service. (For VM, use the DMSABN macro.)

3. If you are interested in using the MVS/ESA data spaces, obtain the manuals listed in Sec. 17.8. Write a program to dump the access register contents using the SNAP (or SNAPX) macro. How do the contents compare to Fig. 17.5?

4. IBM has introduced several new macros for MVS/ESA. One is called SWAREQ. This is intended as a replacement for RDJFCB, among other older macros and services. Obtain the MVS/ESA manuals listed in Sec. 17.8 and review this macro. After completing this, rewrite the GETDSN subroutine (from Chap. 14) to use SWAREQ in place of RDJFCB. (Be sure to use the UNAUTH=YES keyword to avoid 0B0 ABENDs.)

5. Another new macro added for MVS/ESA is the STORAGE macro. This provides storage acquisition and release services like the GETMAIN and FREEMAIN macros. If your installation has programs which use GET-MAIN, obtain the MVS/ESA manuals and investigate conversion of existing uses of GETMAIN to the STORAGE macro.

Assembler Language Exits

Assembler language provides access to a wide variety of MVS and VM services that are not accessible from COBOL. One example of these is the MVS services available through exit programs. COBOL does provide access to a few of the exits allowed by MVS. In this chapter we'll learn how exits generally work. We'll then show how one MVS exit — the SYNAD exit to handle I/O errors — works in both COBOL and assembler. Finally, we'll review some of the other MVS exits that you may want to use. We'll also show an example of a VM-only exit — the ABNEXIT — used to recover from CMS ABEND codes.

18.1 WHAT'S AN EXIT?

An *exit*, in IBM MVS terminology, may be thought of as a subroutine of your program. Like a subroutine, it only receives control part of the time. Unlike a subroutine, exits receive control only when certain previously specified conditions arise. Also unlike subroutines, exits receive control from the MVS or VM operating system rather than directly from your program.

Exits are most commonly used for error recovery of some type. We will discuss how you may use an exit for I/O error recovery in this book. The last section of this chapter also describes some other MVS exits that you may find useful.

In order for exits to operate properly, you have to treat them differently than your main program code or subroutines. To correctly use an exit, you must normally provide three separate segments of code. These are:

1. Instructions to establish the exit
2. The exit routine itself
3. For certain types of exit, a retry routine

Establishing the exit refers to the processing you must do to let MVS or VM know about the exit. Exits are normally optional. You must issue special macro instructions or code macro instructions differently to identify the exit to the operating system.

The *exit routine* itself is a section of code, similar to a subroutine, that gets control whenever the specified condition arises. The operating system will detect an error and will normally call the subroutine following that. MVS and VM provide certain predefined information to the exit, which can then determine what to do next to recover from the problem.

If recovery is possible, or if you wish for a cleanup routine to get control before ending the program, you usually supply a *retry routine*. A retry routine can start the program processing again, can perform error handling, or can just close files and end the program.

Figure 18.1 shows how these steps interact for the I/O error SYNAD routine in MVS. (VM operation is similar.) You specify the exit name as a parameter on the DCB macro. The exit receives control after I/O errors.

Figure 18.1   General flow of control for exits.

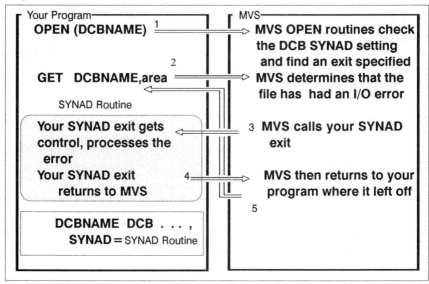

18.2   EXITS IN COBOL: DECLARATIVES

COBOL provides access to some of the exits allowed in MVS through the Declaratives Section of the Procedure Division. Many COBOL programmers have not coded these before, so a short description may help here.

You specify a declaratives procedure in a special section immediately following the Procedure Division statement. You identify declarative procedures by coding them following a DECLARATIVES statement.

Each individual declarative procedure is executed when a specified condition arises. In COBOL, the declarative we'll examine is for processing you wish to perform following an I/O error. To identify the purpose of an individual declarative, you code a USE statement.

The declarative procedure itself is a normal COBOL paragraph or section. You terminate a declarative by either another USE statement or by an END DECLARATIVES statement.

An example might be coded as follows. Assume that we have an FD called FILE1:

```
PROCEDURE DIVISION.
DECLARATIVES.
    USE AFTER STANDARD ERROR REPORTING ON FILE1.
HANDLE-FILE1-ERROR.
    DISPLAY         'I/O ERROR ON FILE1' UPON CONSOLE.
    MOVE 1 TO TOTALS-SWITCH.
END DECLARATIVES.
OPEN-FILES.
```
(normal program Procedure Division follows)

You have the option of coding one declarative routine for all files with a given type of I/O processing. In the preceding processing, this would be indicated by coding

USE AFTER STANDARD ERROR REPORTING ON INPUT.

This identifies a declarative to handle errors on all FDs opened as input.

The way that the declarative works is that your program issues a normal I/O verb, such as READ. If MVS or VM detect an error on the I/O operation, they then cause the declarative routine to receive control. When the declarative routine ends, control goes to the statement following the READ verb, just as if nothing had happened.

You should refer to the COBOL language manual for a fuller discussion of declaratives if needed. Note, however, that the COBOL declaratives follow the pattern of processing needed for an exit. The declarative routine was established by the USE statement. The exit itself was coded following the USE statement. Finally, the retry routine consists of having the program proceed normally.

From this general description of declaratives, let's see how this would have been done in assembler.

18.3   AN EXAMPLE: THE SYNAD DCB EXIT ROUTINE

MVS provides multiple exits for handling various errors in I/O processing. We'll look at the one most directly associated with I/O errors — the SYNAD routine (pronounced "sin-add"). This exit is supported under VM. SYNAD routines are only invoked for true I/O errors, which normally produce an 001 ABEND. VM produces messages DMS120, DMS128, or DMS129 in this case; MVS produces messages IEA000 or IEC020.

You establish a SYNAD routine by specifying an option on the DCB macro. The SYNAD= operand specifies a label in your program that processes the error. Assuming that we have a routine called IOERROR, we would code

```
INPUT      DCB    DDNAME = INFILE,DEVD = DA,MACRF = (GM),        X
                  RECFM = FB,LRECL = 80,BLKSIZE = 0,             X
                  EODAD = ENDDATA,SYNAD = IOERROR
```

The routine itself is normally placed outside the mainline of your program. The processing for a SYNAD routine differs from that for normal subroutines. First, no save area is provided in register 13. The SYNAD routine must provide both a save area for the operating system register contents and its own save area.

When your SYNAD routine receives control, it should perform any processing needed when you can't read or write data effectively. Your routine should not attempt to retry the I/O operation — the operating system has already tried this several times. By the time your SYNAD routine gets control, the data block in question should be considered unusable. It is *B-A-D*.

The type of processing depends on what your program does. If there were any batch balances up to the point of the error, you might print these. You might display the last good record. You also might wish to display the block you actually received in some cases. There is no set rule for what to do when I/O errors arise. You should decide what to do when designing the system that creates and uses the file in question.

To simplify the process and to provide more information, however, two macro instructions should be used. These are SYNADAF and SYNADRLS. SYNADAF provides a save area and evaluates the error information to produce an error message. The text of the error message is similar to that of IBM error messages, such as MVS IEA000I or IEC020 or VM DMS120. For input processing, SYNADAF also provides your routine with the address and length of the block read in.

An example of a SYNAD routine is shown in Fig. 18.2. The output from this routine is shown in Fig. 18.3. (To create this error, we used an input data set with a longer BLKSIZE than that used in the DCB macro itself.) You should refer to the Data Management Services Guide for more information about the SYNAD routine and the data it provides. Note that the HEXCONV routine will be explained in Chap. 20.

Figure 18.2   Example of a program with a SYNAD routine.

```
PROGNAME  CSECT
          STM    14,12,12(13)              SAVE REGISTERS
          LR     R12,R15                   GET PGM ADDRESS
          USING PROGNAME,R12               SET UP BASE REG
```

Figure 18.2   (Continued)

```
*         CHAIN SAVE AREAS
          ST    R13,SAVEAREA+4        CHAIN
          LA    R2,SAVEAREA           SAVE
          ST    R2,8(R13)             AREAS
          LR    R13,R2                UPDATE REG 13
*         OPEN FILES
          OPEN  (INFILE,INPUT)
          LA    R1,INFILE             GET ADDR OF DCB
          USING IHADCB,R1             SET UP  BASE REG
          TM    DCBOFLGS,X'10'        TEST GOOD OPEN
          BNO   OPENERR               NO - OPEN FAILED
          OPEN  (PRINTER,OUTPUT)
          LA    R1,PRINTER            GET ADDR OF DCB
          USING IHADCB,R1             SET UP BASE REG
          TM    DCBOFLGS,X'10'        TEST GOOD OPEN
          BNO   OPENERR               NO - OPEN FAILED
          PUT   PRINTER,HEADLINE      WRITE  HEADING
          SPACE 1
*               MAIN LINE PROCESSING
MAINLINE  EQU   *
          GET   INFILE,INAREA         READ A RECORD
          MVC   DATA,INAREA           MOVE TO PRINT
          AP    RECNUM,ONE            ADD TO REC COUNT
          OI    RECNUM+3,X'0F'        SET SIGN BITS
          UNPK  NUMBER,RECNUM         MOVE TO PRINT
          PUT   PRINTER,LINE          WRITE PRINT LINE
          AP    LINECT,ONE            ADD TO LINE CT
          CP    LINECT,P50            AT PAGE END?
          BL    MAINLINE              NO - CONTINUE
          ZAP   LINECT,ZERO           RESET LINE COUNT
          PUT   PRINTER,HEADLINE      WRITE  HEADING
          B     MAINLINE              PROCESS NEXT REC
          SPACE 1
*         END-OF-FILE ROUTINE.
ENDDATA   EQU   *
          PUT   PRINTER,ENDLINE       WRITE ENDING LINE
          CLOSE (INFILE,,PRINTER)     CLOSE FILES
          L     R13,4(R13)            OLD SAVE AREA
          RETURN (14,12),RC=0         RETURN TO MVS
*         ERROR OPENING A FILE. END WITH RETURN CODE = 16.
OPENERR   EQU   *
          MVC   OPENWTO+13(8),DCBDDNAM MOVE BAD DDNAME
OPENWTO   WTO   'DD =        COULD NOT BE OPENED'
          L     R13,4(R13)                GET OLD SAVE AREA
```

Figure 18.2   (Continued)

```
          RETURN  (14,12),RC = 16              RETURN TO MVS
          SPACE 3
          CONVERT FROM HEXADECIMAL TO DISPLAYABLE EBCDIC
HEXCONV   EQU     *
          MVC     HEXWORK(4),0(R1)
          UNPK    EBCDICEQ(9),HEXWORK(5)       UNPACK
          TR      EBCDICEQ(8),HEXTAB-240       CONV TO EBCDIC
          BR      R14                          RETURN TO CALLER
EBCDICEQ  DC      CL8' ',C' '
HEXTAB    DC      C'0123456789ABCDEF'
HEXWORK   DC      XL4'00',X'00'
          CNOP    0,4                          ALIGNMENT
          SPACE 3
*         SYNAD EXIT ROUTINE FOR ERRORS ON INPUT TAPE
INSYNAD   EQU     *
          SYNADAF ACSMETH = QSAM GET ERROR INFORMATION
          ST      R14,SAVE14                   SAVE RET ADDR
*         DISPLAY ERROR INFORMATION
          LR      R4,R1                        SAVE MSG ADDR
          LA      R1,8(R4)                     ADDR OF BUFFER
          BAL     R14,HEXCONV                  CONVERT TO HEX
          MVC     SYNBUFAD,EBCDICEQ            MOVE TO PRINT
          LA      R1,12(R4)                    LENGTH OF DATA
          BAL     R14,HEXCONV                  CONVERT TO HEX
          MVC     SYNLEN,EBCDICEQ              MOVE TO PRINT
          MVC     SYNMSG(114),14(R4)           SYNADAF MSG
          PUT     PRINTER,SYNLINE1
          PUT     PRINTER,SYNLINE2
          LR      R1,R4                        RESTORE ADDRESS
          AP      ERRBLKS, = P'1'              BAD BLOCK CTR
          SPACE 1
*         PRINT BUFFER CONTENTS
          ZAP     SYNPRINT, = P'25'            LIMIT TO  25 LINES
          L       R8,8(R4)                     GET BUFFER ADDR
          LA      R6,80                        REC LEN IN REG 6
          LH      R7,12(R4)                    LEN OF DATA READ
          AR      R7,R8                        ADD,GET END ADDR
          SH      R7, = H'1'                   MINUS 1 FOR BXLE
          BNP     SYNDONE                      NOT PLUS - END
INSLOOP1  EQU     *
          MVC     SYNDATA,0(R8)                MOVE  FROM BUFF
          PUT     PRINTER,SYNLINE3             WRITE LINE
          SP      SYNPRINT, = P'1'             DECREMENT  CTR
          BNP     SYNDONE                      NOT POSITIVE, STOP
```

Figure 18.2   (Continued)

```
          BXLE   R6,R8,INSLOOP1              ELSE CONTINUE
SYNDONE   EQU    *
          SPACE  1
          SYNADRLS                          RELEASE WK AREA
          L      R14,SAVE14                 GET RET ADDRESS
          BR     R14                        RETURN TO MVS
          SPACE  1
*         DATA AREAS FOR SYNAD EXIT
SAVE14    DS     F                          SAVE REGISTER 14
          SPACE  1
*         PACKED DECIMAL FIELDS
BLOCKCTR DC      PL4'0'
ERRBLKS   DC     PL4'0'
SYNPRINT  DC     P'025'
          SPACE  3
*         PRINT LINES FOR SYNAD ERROR EXIT
SYNLINE1  DC     C'-'
SYNMSG    DC     CL120' '
          DC     CL12' '
SYNLINE2  DC     C' '
          DC     C' INPUT BUFFER ADDRESS = '
SYNBUFAD DC      CL8' ',C' LENGTH READ = '
SYNLEN    DC     CL4' '
          DC     CL84' '
          SPACE  1
SYNLINE3  DC     C' DATA = '
SYNDATA   DC     CL80' '
          DC     CL47' '
          EJECT
*         DATA AREAS
SAVEAREA DC      18F'0'                      SAVE AREA
INAREA    DS     CL80                        INPUT DATA AREA
LINE      DC     C' '                        CARRIAGE CONTROL
          DC     C' RECORD '
NUMBER    DS     CL7                         RECORD NUMBER
          DC     C':'
DATA      DS     CL80                        DATA RECORD
          DC     CL36' '                     FILLER
HEADLINE DC      CL133'1 * * * RECORD LISTING * * *'
ENDLINE   DC     CL133'0 * * * END OF REPORT * * *'
LINECT    DC     PL2'0'                      LINE COUNT
RECNUM    DC     PL4'0'                      RECORD NUMBER
ZERO      DC     P'0'                        CONSTANT 0
ONE       DC     P'1'                        CONSTANT 1
```

Figure 18.2   (Continued)

P50	DC	P'50'	CONSTANT 50	
*		DATA CONTROL	BLOCKS	
PRINTER	DCB	DDNAME = PRINTER,DEVD = DA,MACRF = (PM),		X
		DSORG = PS,RECFM = FBA,LRECL = 133,		
		BLKSIZE = 0		
INFILE	DCB	DDNAME = INFILE,DEVD = DA,MACRF = (GM),		X
		DSORG = PS,RECFM = FB,LRECL = 80,		X
		BLKSIZE = 80,SYNAD = INSYNAD,EROPT = ACC,		X
		EODAD = ENDDATA		
*		DATA CONTROL BLOCK DUMMY SECTION (IHADCB),		
*		REGISTER EQUATES, AND END OF PGM NOT SHOWN		

Figure 18.3   Output from the sample SYNAD routine.

(The following text is set in small type to get a 132-column listing to fit within this page size. The numbers in brackets refer to notes which follow.)

```
* * * RECORD LISTING * * *

[1]        [2]         [3]          [4]                    [5]                  [6]              [7]
                       ,AFCASM3 ,GO  ,141,DA,INFILE ,GET  ,WRNG.LEN.RECORD,0000015A001900,QSAM

INPUT BUFFER ADDRESS = 06114E70 LENGTH READ = 0050

DATA = //AFCASM3 JOB  (6510,,,),MURPHY,MSGCLASS = X,NOTIFY = TS00024

RECORD 0000001://AFCASM3 JOB  (6510,,,),MURPHY,MSGCLASS = X,NOTIFY = TS00024

                       ,AFCASM3 ,GO   ,141,DA,INFILE ,GET   ,WRNG.LEN.RECORD,0000015A001901,QSAM

INPUT BUFFER ADDRESS = 06114EC0 LENGTH READ = 0050

DATA =      PUT   PRINTER,ENDLINE    WRITE ENDING LINE

RECORD 0000002:     PUT   PRINTER,ENDLINE    WRITE ENDING LINE

                       ,AFCASM3 ,GO   ,141,DA,INFILE ,GET   ,WRNG.LEN.RECORD,0000015A001902,QSAM

INPUT BUFFER ADDRESS = 06114F10 LENGTH READ = 0050

DATA =      PUT   PRINTER,SYNLINE3 WRITE LINE

RECORD 0000003:     PUT   PRINTER,SYNLINE3 WRITE LINE
                       ,AFCASM3 ,GO   ,141,DA,/   INFILE ,GET ,WRNG.LEN.RECORD,0000015A001903, QSAM

INPUT BUFFER ADDRESS = 06114F60 LENGTH READ = 0050

DATA =      SPACE 3

RECORD 0000004:     SPACE 3

* * * END OF REPORT * * *
```

Notes to Fig. 18.3:

1. The first 8 bytes of the message provided by SYNADAF contain a block and message length and are not needed by most routines.
2. The first 36 bytes of the SYNADAF message are blank — this allows you to provide your own message number if desired.
3. The job name was AFCASM3 and the step name was GO.
4. The data set with the error was on a direct access (DA), device and the unit address was 141.
5. The block read was too long. SYNADAF reported this as a wrong length record.
6. The long string of hexadecimal characters in the message is the disk cylinder, track, and block number. You might need this information if you wanted to display the failing block, e.g., using the ADRDSSU or IEHDASDR programs.
7. The access method used was QSAM.

These notes apply to all the error messages. Errors on other device types provide different messages — for example, errors on tape receive the block number that caused the error.

18.4   OTHER EXIT TYPES

There are numerous other exit routines that you can include in your assembler programs. MVS also provides for many others that your installation may include as part of MVS for specified functions.

The most common exit types that you may see in other assembler programs are the SPIE, STAE, and certain other data management exits besides SYNAD. (MVS also provides *sort exits*, which correspond to the input and output procedures in COBOL. We will discuss these in the next chapter.)

18.4.1   SPIE: Recovering from Program Checks

SPIE stands for Specify Program Interrupt Exit. SPIE is used to recover from program checks in your program. These normally cause an 0Cx type of ABEND. Many installations provide a SPIE as a subroutine that your COBOL programs may call. The most frequent processing for a SPIE routine is to fix up blank data areas when they cause 0C7 ABENDs.

SPIE, following the description of exits given earlier in this chapter, requires that you establish the exit, provide the exit routine, and optionally provide a retry routine. The SPIE macro is used to establish the exit address, and it also specifies what interruption types (0C4, 0C7, etc.) should be handled.

SPIE provides a control block called a PIE — Program Interrupt Element. MVS provides a macro, IHAPIE — that includes a DSECT describing the PIE.

A SPIE routine receives the failing PSW, along with the registers at the time of the program check. [Part of the registers (14-2) are in the PIE, and part are passed in the registers themselves.] Another control block, called the PICA — Program Interrupt Control Area — holds information about the exit routine and the interrupt types from which it will recover.

A complete description of SPIE processing is included in the Supervisor Services and Macros Manual. Note that there are two macros that provide this service. The SPIE macro has traditionally been used throughout all OS/VS operating systems. MVS/XA adds a macro called ESPIE — Extended SPIE — that handles ABENDs in both 24-bit and 31-bit addressing modes. VM supports both SPIE and ESPIE.

SPIE only recovers from 0Cx types of ABENDs. For other types, such as 80A (inadequate storage) and 806 (can't find program), MVS provides a different type of exit. This is the STAE (or ESTAE).

18.4.2   STAE/ESTAE Recovering from MVS ABENDs

STAE — Specify Task ABEND Exit — provides similar services to SPIE. It may be specified by either the older STAE macro or the ESTAE — Extended STAE — macro. We'll use ESTAE to refer to both types, since they are quite similar. VM supports both STAE and ESTAE.

You establish ESTAE by means of the ESTAE macro instruction. ESTAE requires several parameters, including the exit routine address. ESTAE provides a return code that allows you to verify that it worked successfully.

The ESTAE routine receives control after an ABEND condition is detected but before a dump is processed. A control block called the System Diagnostic Work Area (SDWA) contains extensive information about the ABEND.

The exit routine specifies whether to continue with the ABEND or give control to a retry routine, based on a return code the exit places in register 15. Many other options (e.g., provide a dump even though a recovery routine handles the error) may be specified in the SDWA.

MVS provides a macro for use in ESTAE routines that simplifies the setting of these options. This is the SETRP macro. It provides return parameters for the MVS Recovery/Termination Manager (RTM). SETRP — Set Recovery Parameters — allows you to update registers, cause a dump to be printed, and keep or release the SDWA, and it also provides many other functions.

18.4.3   ABNEXIT: Recovery Under VM

VM supplies the ABNEXIT macro to provide similar services to those allowed by SPIE and STAE under MVS. ABNEXIT lets your program handle any CMS ABENDs that may come up during its execution.

ABNEXIT has three modes of operation. These are:

SET — Identify the exit to VM.

RESET — Tell VM your routine is going to recover (issued from within the exit itself).

CLR— Indicate that your exit is no longer to be used.

In addition, VM provides a DSECT — DMSABW — that maps the data provided to your ABNEXIT.

The ABNEXIT receives information regarding the failure in the ABWSECT work area mapped by the DMSABW DSECT macro. This includes the register contents and PSW at the time of the failure, as well as the CMS ABEND code.

If the exit wishes to recover from the error, it must issue ABNEXIT with the RESET option to terminate VM's processing of the ABEND. It must activate the branch to the retry routine. The retry routine also may be entered by means of the Load PSW — opcode LPSW — instruction. Our example does this. (VM allows use of this instruction — MVS does not.)

Prior to ending execution, a program using ABNEXIT should issue ABNEXIT with the CLR option. This removes the exit, as far as VM is concerned. Any errors occurring after the ABNEXIT CLR are processed normally by VM. You should thus not do this until late in your program's execution.

Figure 18.4 shows an example of an ABNEXIT program. The accompanying notes explain its execution. Figure 18.5 shows the VM console output when the sample program was run.

Figure 18.4   Sample ABNEXIT program.

```
(The numbers in brackets refer to notes at the end of the figure.)

ABNPROG  TITLE  'EXAMPLE OF A VM ABNEXIT'
ABNPROG  CSECT
         STM    R14,R12,12(R13)        SAVE REGISTERS
         LR     R12,R15                ESTABLISH
         USING  ABNPROG,R12            ADDRESSABILITY
[1]      ST     R12,MYPARM1            SAVE PROG ADDR
*        CHAIN  SAVE AREAS
         LA     R2,SAVEAREA
         ST     R2,8(R13)
         ST     R13,4(R2)
         LR     R13,R2
         USING  SAVEAREA,R13           DATA AREAS BASE
[2]      ST     R13,MYPARM2            SAVE AREA ADDR
*        TELL VM WE WANT TO SET UP AN ABNEXIT
[3]      ABNEXIT SET,EXIT = SAMPEXIT,UWORD = MYPARM,       X
                 ERROR = BADABN
```

Figure 18.4   (Continued)

```
            SPACE 1
*           FORCE A PROGRAM CHECK (0C3 - EXECUTE EXCEPTION)
[4]         EX    0,*                           (SEE CHAP. 20)
            SPACE 1
*           THIS IS THE RETRY ROUTINE STARTED BY THE ABNEXIT.
*           IT WILL TERMINATE THE PROGRAM NORMALLY.
RETRYRTN EQU     *
[5]         WRTERM RETRYMSG,80
            B     ENDEXEC                       END EXECUTION
            SPACE 1
ENDEXEC  EQU     *
*           DO ABNEXIT CLEAR TO END THE ABNEXIT'S COVERAGE
[6]         MVC   BADACT,=CL5'CLEAR'            SHOW ACTION
[7]         ABNEXIT  CLR,EXIT=SAMPEXIT
            SPACE 1
            LH    R0,RETCODE                    GET RETURN CODE
            CVD   R0,DOUBLEWD                   CONV TO DECIMAL
            OI    DOUBLEWD+7,X'0F'              TURN ON SIGN BITS
            UNPK  MSG803RC,DOUBLEWD             UNPACK
*           ISSUE WRTERM TO WRITE TO MY VIRTUAL CONSOLE
[8]         WRTERM MSG803I,80                   MSG TO TERMINAL
            SPACE 1
*           RETURN TO CALLING PROGRAM
RETURN      EQU     *
            LH    R15,RETCODE                   GET RETURN CODE
            L     R13,4(R13)                    OLD SAVE AREA
            RETURN  (14,12),T,RC=(15)           RETURN
            EJECT
*           THIS IS THE ABNEXIT EXIT ITSELF. IT WILL RECEIVE
*           CONTROL AFTER ANY PROGRAM CHECKS OR ABENDS.
*           THIS ROUTINE JUST DISPLAYS THE ERROR INFORMATION
*           IN THE ABWSECT AREA VIA LINEDIT, THEN ENDS.
SAMPEXIT EQU     *
[9]         USING *,R15                         TEMPORARY  USING
*           SAVE VM'S REGISTERS
            STM   R14,R12,12(R13)               SAVE VM'S REGS
            LA    R2,EXITSAVE                   EXIT SAVE AREA
            ST    R2,8(R13)                     CHAIN
            ST    R13,4(R2)                     SAVE
            LR    R13,R2                         AREAS
[10]        LR    R2,R1                         WORKAREA ADDR
            USING ABWSECT,R2                    SET UPBASE REG
[11]        L     R12,ABNUWRD                   ADDR OF ABNPARM
[12]        LM    R12,R13,0(R12)                GET  BASE REGS
```

Figure 18.4   (Continued)

```
[13]       DROP  R15                            END TEMP USING
*          USE LINEDIT TO ISSUE CP DUMP COMMAND
[14]       LA    R2,ABNREGS                     AREA BEGIN ADDR
           LA    R3,ABNCODE+4                   GET ENDING ADDR
           LINEDIT  TEXTA=DUMPCMD,DISP=CPCOMM,RENT=NO,  X
                 DOT=NO,COMP=NO,SUB=(HEX,(2),HEX,(3))
*          DO ABNEXIT RESET TO TELL VM WE ARE RETRYING
[15]       MVC   BADACT,=CL5'RESET'             SHOW ACTION
           ABNEXIT  RESET,ERROR=BADABN
[16]       LA    R15,RETRYRTN                   ADDR OF RETRY RTN
           STCM  R15,7,ABNPSW+5                 PUT IN 24-BIT PSW
           LR    R1,R2                          R1=ABNSECT ADDR
[17]       LM    R2,R11,ABNREGS+8               RESTORE OUR REGS
           DROP  R2                             END ABWSECT BASE
           USING ABWSECT,R1                     SET UP BASE REG
[18]       LPSW  ABNPSW                         LOAD RETRY
*                                               ROUTINE PSW
           SPACE 1
*          THE FOLLOWING WOULD BE USED IF WE COULD NOT
*          RETRY: RETURN TO VM AND LET IT HANDLE THE ABEND
[19]       L     R13,4(R13)                     VM SAVE AREA
           LM    R14,R12,12(R13)                RESTORE VM'S REGS
           BR    R14                            RETURN TO VM
           SPACE 1
*          ERROR IN AN ABNEXIT MACRO - GIVE UP
BADABN     EQU   *
[20]       STH   R15,RETCODE                    SAVE RETURN CODE
           WRTERM  BADMSG,80                    WRITE ERROR MSG
           B     ENDEXEC
           EJECT
*          DATA AREAS
DOUBLEWD        DC                              D'0'
SAVEAREA DC     18F'+0'
EXITSAVE  DC    18F'+0'
MYPARM    EQU   *
MYPARM1 DC      F'+0'
MYPARM2 DC      F'+0'
RETCODE DC      H'0'
COMMAND DC      AL1(COMMEND-*-1)                LENGTH
          DC    C'MSG OPERATOR HELLO THERE'
COMMEND EQU     *
DUMPCMD DC      AL1(DUMPEND-*-1)                LENGTH
          DC    C'DUMP T......:...... *DISPLAY STORAGE'
DUMPEND EQU     *
```

Figure 18.4   (Continued)

```
BADMSG    DC      CL24'ERROR IN ABNEXIT MACRO ('
BADACT    DC      CL5'SET      ',CL51')'
          SPACE 1
RETRYMSGDC        CL80' * * * RETRY ROUTINE ENTERED'
MSG803I   DC      CL21'MSG803I END OF JOB - '
MSG803RC DC       CL2'    '
          DC      CL57' WAS HIGHEST RETURN CODE'
*         REGISTER EQUATES
          REGEQU
          LTORG
          CNOP  0,4
PROGEND   EQU   *                    END ADDRESS FOR CP DUMP
          PRINT  ON,GEN
*         ABEND WORK AREA DSECT
[21]      DMSABW
          PRINT  ON,NOGEN
*         VM NUCLEUS DSECT
[22]      NUCON
          END   ABNPROG
```

Notes to Fig. 18.4:

1. This saves the beginning address of the program in MYPARM1. This is necesary, since we don't know if some future error will destroy the base register contents.
2. This saves the save area address in MYPARM2.
3. Establish the exit. VM will branch to SAMPEXIT when an error occurs. The address of MYPARM will be passed in the ABWSECT work area. If an error arises trying to establish the exit, control will go to BADABN.
4. This instruction forces a unique program that which is reported as an 0C3. We will explain the EX — Execute — instruction in Chap. 20.
5. This is the retry routine. It will receive control when the exit SAMPEXIT processes an ABEND. This routine just prints out a message with WRTERM and ends execution.
6. We should do an ABNEXIT CLR to end the ABNEXIT's coverage of our routine. This statement sets up an indicator if the ABNEXIT CLR has an error.
7. Issue ABNEXIT CLR to end SAMPEXIT's validity.
8. This writes out a line indicating the highest return code we encountered.
9. This starts the ABNEXIT named SAMPEXIT. The code here saves the registers and uses register 15 as a base register temporarily. Note that we also use a separate save area.

10. This gets the address of the ABWSECT ABEND work area.

11. This gets the address of our parameter word (MYPARM).

12. This restores R12 and R13 from the parameter area.

13. Since we have our original base registers back, we no longer need the temporary addressability we had with register 15. This ends it.

14. This sequence of code dumps the ABEND work area. Note that register 2 is used in the LINEDIT but still points to the beginning of ABWSECT. We would dump any additional areas desired at this point but would have to preserve register 2.

15. At this point we want to invoke the retry routine. This tells VM we will recover from the error ourselves.

16. This code sets up the address of RETRYRTN into the PSW inside ABNPSW. It assumes that we are in 24-bit mode.

17. This restores the contents of registers 2 through 11 at the time of the error. Note that we saved the ABWSECT address in register 1 before doing this and changed the ABWSECT base register to R1.

18. The LPSW instruction loads the program status word at ABNPSW that we modified back at note [16]. This acts as a branch to RETRYRTN, among other things.

19. This code is not used in this example, but it shows how we would return to VM if we decided we could not recover from the error.

20. This routine gets control if VM detects an error in one of our ABNEXIT macros. We really ought to have a separate one for the ABNEXIT RESET in SAMPEXIT.

21. This generates the ABEND work area DSECT.

22. This generates the CMS nucleus DSECT. ABNEXIT requires this, even though we don't use it.

(Figure 18.5 shows the output from the program shown in Fig. 18.4. CMS commands entered from the virtual console are shown in bold type; the remainder are responses and program output from the program in Fig. 18.4.)

Figure 18.5 CMS console output from ABNPROG

(The numbers in brackets refer to notes following Figure 18.5).
load abnprog
Ready; T = 0.05/0.12 17:25:51
start *
Execution begins...
DMSITP141T Execute exception occurred at 020056 in routine *   [1]
COMMAND COMPLETE   [2]
  * * * RETRY ROUTINE ENTERED   [3]
MSG803I END OF JOB - 00 WAS HIGHEST RETURN CODE   [4]
Ready; T = 0.02/1.54 17:25:54

Notes to Fig. 18.5:

1. This message appears even though we have an exit routine to handle it.
2. COMMAND COMPLETE is issued by CP after it completes the DUMP command.
3. This message is written out by RETRYRTN.
4. This message is written out by the ENDEXEC routine.

18.4.4 DCB-Related Exits

Another frequently encountered set of exits consists of those for data management other than the SYNAD routine. These can receive control under specified conditions. For example, MVS provides an end-of-volume exit, which receives control at the end of each tape volume or disk extent. COBOL uses this facility to control checkpoint processing. (See the RERUN clause of the I/O CONTROL paragraph in the Environment Division.)

These other exits require a special data area called an *exit list*. To indicate that you have an exit list, you code

...,EXLST = name

as part of your DCB options. EXLST refers to a label elsewhere in your program, which heads an exit list.

The exit list itself is coded much like a parameter list for a subroutine. It consists of a series of addresses, with the last address flagged with the high-order bit.

Unlike the parameter lists discussed earlier, the DCB exit list also includes an exit type identification as part of the list entry. This is done by coding a specified value as the first byte of each fullword in the exit list, followed by the 3-byte address of the routine or data area.

(We have already looked at one example of an exit list in the discussions on subroutines. The GETDSN example used an exit list. Note that since the address is only 24 bits long, you can't provide an exit routine above the 16-megabyte address limit. This is a limitation of the DCB macro.)

We will examine the DCB ABEND exit as an example of a data management exit. This is used for I/O-related ABEND recovery. It differs from the SYNAD routine in handling all possible I/O-related ABENDs for a specified DCB — SYNAD only handled 001 ABENDs. Thus the DCB ABEND exit may process 213, B37, and many other ABEND types.

The DCB ABEND exit is coded as part of the DCB exit list (like the JFCB). It requires a flag byte of X'11' in the exit list. You provide the address of the DCB ABEND exit as the address part of the exit list entry.

When the DCB ABEND exit gets control, register 1 points to a parameter control block that describes the ABEND. Figure 18.6 shows the format of this control block. (Note that this does not follow the standard MVS parameter list convention.)

Figure 18.6 Format of DCB ABEND exit control block.

ABEND Code	Return Code	Option Flags
DCB Address		
OPEN/CLOSE/EOV Work Area		
Recovery Work Area Address		

In Fig. 18.6, the ABEND code is in the first 12 bits of the first 2 bytes shown (ABEND code), and the return code and options flag fields are both 1 byte long. The other fields are all 4 bytes long. The "Open/Close/EOV Work Area" and the "Recovery Work Area" are discussed in the Data Management Services Guide. (EOV stands for END Of Volume.)

When the DCB ABEND exit receives control, the options flag byte indicates what can be done (contents in hex):

- X'08' = OK to recover
- X'04' = OK to ignore
- X'02' = OK to delay

Note that any combination of these three may be set. The exit then sets the options flag byte to indicate what MVS should do:

- X'00' = ABEND
- X'04' = ignore
- X'08' = delay until other DCBs are opened/closed
- X'0C' = attempt to recover

The "attempt to recover" option is only valid for certain ABEND codes. These include 213-04, 237-04, 413-18, 613-04, and several others.

Recovery is by specifying a new volume serial (e.g., for 213-04) or by ignoring tape block count errors (e.g., for 237-04 or 717-10). You should refer to the Data Management Services Guide for a full description of the recovery options. Note that the ABEND message still appears in your JCL listing, even if you recover or ignore the error.

Figure 18.7 shows a simple program that includes a DCB ABEND exit. To cause an error, the program was executed intentionally with conflicting DCB parameters. Figure 18.8 shows the output from that program. Note that the IEC141 message still appears in the JCL, even though the ABEND was ignored.

Figure 18.7   Sample program using DCB ABEND exit.

```
              TITLE   'DCB ABEND EXIT EXAMPLE PROGRAM'
              PRINT   ON,NOGEN                 SHORTEN LISTING
DCBABEND  CSECT
              STM     R14,R12,12(R13)          SAVE REGISTERS
              BALR    R12,0                    ESTABLISH
              USING   *,R12                    ADDRESSABILITY
*             CHAIN SAVE AREAS
              LA      R2,SAVEAREA
              ST      R2,8(R13)
              ST      R13,4(R2)
              LR      R13,R2
              USING   SAVEAREA,R13             DATA AREAS BASE
*             OPEN SYSPRINT DATA SET
              OPEN    (SYSPRINT,OUTPUT)
              USING   IHADCB,R1       SET UP DCB ADDRESSABILITY
              LA      R1,SYSPRINT              GET ADDR OF DCB
              TM      DCBOFLGS,X'10'           TEST GOOD OPEN
              BO      OPENDONE                 OKAY - CONTINUE
              DROP    R1                       END BASE REG
              ABEND   1,DUMP                   BAD MISSING JCL
*             FORCE 013-14 ABEND BY OPENING A DCB WITH
*             DSORG = DA AGAINST A DATA SET WITH DSORG = PO
OPENDONE  EQU  *
              OPEN    (SYSUT1,INPUT)           OPEN DCB
*             END EXECUTION. CLOSE FILES.
ENDEXEC   EQU     *
              CLOSE   (SYSPRINT)
*             RETURN TO O.S.
RETURN    EQU     *
              L       R13,4(R13)               OLD SAVE AREA
              RETURN  (14,12),T,RC = 0         RETURN TO OS
* Note: This listing does not show all the data areas, including
* SAVEAREA, SAVER14, the SYSPRINT DCB, register equates, and the
* DCBD macro. The "HEXCONV" routine is also not reproduced.
*             DATA AREAS
DOUBLEWD          DC                      D'0'
SAVER1    DC      F'+0'    SAVE DCB ABEND PARM LIST ADDR
SAVE14    DC      F'+0'    SAVE RETURN ADDRESS IN EXITS, ETC
BLANKS    DC      CL132' '
*             DATA CONTROL BLOCK WITH DCB ABEND EXIT
SYSUT1    DCB     DDNAME = SYSUT1,DSORG = DA,MACRF = (RC),   X
                  BLKSIZE = 24000,RECFM = F,EXLST = SYSUT1EX
```

Figure 18.7   (Continued)

```
          CNOP 0,4                        ALIGNMENT
SYSUT1EX  EQU  *                          SYSUT1 EXIT LIST
          DC   X'11',AL3(SYSUT1AB)        DCB ABEND EXIT
*         DC   X'07',AL3(SYSUT1JF)        JFCB AREA
          DC   X'80',AL3(0)               ENDING ENTRY
*         DCB ABEND EXIT
SYSUT1AB  EQU  *
          ST   R14,SAVER14                SAVE REGISTER 14
          BAL  R14,HEXCONV                CONV ABEND CODE
          MVC  ABENDCD,EBCDICEQ           MOVE ABEND CODE
          MVC  ABENDRC,EBCDICEQ+4         MOVE RET CODE
          MVI  ABENDDS,C'-'               MOVE DASH
          ST   R1,SAVER1                  SAVE R1
          BAL  R14,HEXCONV                GO CONV TO HEX
          MVC  ABENDPL1,EBCDICEQ          MOVE TO PRINT
          LA   R1,4(R1)                   POINT TO NEXT
          BAL  R14,HEXCONV                GO CONV TO HEX
          MVC  ABENDPL2,EBCDICEQ          MOVE TO PRINT
          LA   R1,4(R1)                   POINT TO NEXT
          BAL  R14,HEXCONV                GO CONV TO HEX
          MVC  ABENDPL3,EBCDICEQ          MOVE TO PRINT
          LA   R1,4(R1)                   POINT TO NEXT
          BAL  R14,HEXCONV                GO CONV TO HEX
          MVC  ABENDPL4,EBCDICEQ          MOVE TO PRINT
          LA   R1,PGMADDR                 POINT TO START
          BAL  R14,HEXCONV                GO CONV TO HEX
          MVC  ABENDBEG,EBCDICEQ          MOVE TO PRINT
          PUT  SYSPRINT,ABENDLN           WRITE ABEND LINE
          L    R1,SAVER1                  RESTOREADDR
          L    R14,SAVER14                RESTORE RET ADDR
          TM   3(R1),X'04'                CAN WE IGNORE IT?
          BNO  GOBACK1                    NO - CONTINUE
          MVI  3(R1),X'04'                SET IGNORE CODE
          BR   R14                        RETURN
GOBACK1   EQU  *
          TM   3(R1),X'02'                CAN WE DELAY IT?
          BNO  GOBACK2                    NO - CONTINUE
          MVI  3(R1),X'02'                SET DELAYED CODE
          BR   R14                        RETURN
GOBACK2   EQU  *
          MVI  3(R1),X'00'                O CONTINUEABEND
          BR   R14                        RETURN
PGMADDR   DC   A(DCBABEND)
```

Figure 18.7   (Continued)

```
ABENDLN  DS    0CL133
         DC    C'-***ABEND OCCURRED:'
ABENDCD  DS    CL3
ABENDDS  DS    C
ABENDRC  DS    CL2
         DC    C' PARM LIST:'
ABENDPL1 DC    CL8' ',C' '
ABENDPL2 DC    CL8' ',C' '
ABENDPL3 DC    CL8' ',C' '
ABENDPL4 DC    CL8' ',C' '
         DC    C'       PROGRAM BEGINS AT:'
ABENDBEG       DC                          CL8' '
         DC    CL48' '
         CNOP  0,4
         LTORG
         PRINT ON,NOGEN
*        DEFINE DCB DSECT MACRO
         DCBD  DSORG = (PS),DEVD = (DA)
         END   DCBABEND
```

(The following is the JCL listing and output from the above program.
Note that some of the messages are not shown completely. The numbers in
brackets refer to notes at the of the listing. The JCL listing is set in smaller
type to allow a 120-byte line to print in this page size.)

Figure 18.8   Output from sample DCB ABEND exit.

```
JES2 JOB LOG — SYSTEM IPO1 — NODE N1
18.40.19 JOB 1510 + IEF677I WARNING MESSAGE(S) FOR JOB DCBABEND ISSUED
18.40.19 JOB 1510 $HASP373 DCBABEND STARTED - INIT 2 - CLASS A - SYS IPO1
18.40.36 JOB 1510 --TIMINGS (MINS.)- - -PAGING COUNTS--
18.40.36 JOB 1510 -JOBNAME  STEPNAME PROCSTEP  RC    EXCP
18.40.36 JOB 1510 -DCBABEND ASSEMBLE ASM      00 262
18.40.40 JOB 1510 -DCBABEND ASSEMBLE LKED     00 27
18.40.40 JOB 1510 IEC141I 013-14,IFG0194E,DCBABEND,GO,SYSUT1, 143,TSO004,        [1]
18.40.40 JOB 1510 IEC141I TSO0024.MURPHYVM.PRINT
18.40.41 JOB 1510 -DCBABEND ASSEMBLE GO       00 9
18.40.41 JOB 1510 -DCBABEND ENDED. NAME-MURPHY TOTAL CPU TIME = .07 TOTALELAPSED TIME = .3
18.40.42 JOB 1510 $HASP395 DCBABEND ENDED
- - - JES2 JOB STATISTICS - - -
07 OCT 88 JOB EXECUTION DATE
```

[Remainder of JCL listing not shown — following is the output listing]

```
[2]
***ABEND OCCURRED:013-14 PARM LIST:01301486 80115E60 00959BF8 00000000   PROGRAM BEGINS
AT:00115C90
```

Notes to Fig. 18.8:
1. This message appears on the job JCL listing and the MVS console, even though we are handling the error in our DCB ABEND exit.
2. This line is the output from the DCB ABEND exit.

18.5 SUMMARY

In this chapter we have explained what exits are and how you may be able to use them. We have looked at two exits in some detail — the I/O error SYNAD routine and the DCB ABEND routine.

You may not see either of these exit types used at your installation. However, exits in general provide many advantages and also provide options that do not exist in COBOL. In particular, the ability to avoid errors and unneeded dumps is beneficial. With experience, you can probably find many uses for them.

In the next chapter we'll look at another type of exit that is probably more familiar to you than the declaratives section. This is the sort exit, used in internal sorts, which is our next topic.

Things to Do

1. When was the last time you had to recover from an I/O error? Would use of a SYNAD exit (or declaratives section for COBOL) have simplified your recovery actions?
2. Does your installation have a general purpose SPIE subroutine to fix up program check ABENDs? If so, locate the source program. See if you can find the section of code that establishes the exit. Also, see if you can then find the exit itself. (You will probably need to refer to the Supervisor Services Manual.)
3. When was the last time you had to recover from a simple I/O-related ABEND — for example, a B37? Would your recovery from this have been simpler if you had been able to use a DCB ABEND routine (or ESTAE routine) to handle the problem?
4. How many of the 001 ABENDs at your installation are due to improper block size specification (e.g., bad BLOCK CONTAINS clause)?

Internal Sorting in Assembler

COBOL internal sorting is a mainstay of COBOL batch programming. The SORT verb provides one of COBOL's most powerful capabilities for data processing. You have probably used this several times in your own programs.

Occasionally, however, a need arises for sort functions that aren't easily usable or aren't available in COBOL. Or your installation may periodically need to run very large sorts for which maximum performance is essential. Or you may need to do something in an internal sort that can't be done easily in COBOL but which is possible in assembler.

For whatever reason, internal sorting in assembler has certain advantages over COBOL internal sorts. For one, all facilities of the sort program are available in assembler. This includes many programming facilities besides the input and output procedures you know from COBOL.

(More control is possible with the VS COBOL II compiler. You can override certain sort parameters with the IGZSRTCD DD statement in JCL. Refer to the IBM manuals listed at the end of Chap. 1. VS COBOL II also provides the SORT-CONTROL special register to change the IGZSRTCD DD name if desired.)

Additionally, it is usually slightly more efficient in terms of main storage to use an assembler program rather than a COBOL program. I/O processing also may be faster, particularly if dealing with a non-IBM database system that has more performance options available in assembler.

This chapter will cover the basic elements of running sorts from an assembler program. This will involve a comparison of the sort options available in COBOL and assembler. To complete the explanation, a simple COBOL program with an internal sort will be converted to assembler.

The sort program used to develop these examples was IBM's DFSORT program product, program number 5740-SM1, at release 9. The sort options covered in this chapter also should be equally available in non-IBM sort programs. If your installation uses another product, you should consult the appropriate manuals for that sort program.

You also may wish to obtain information about what sort options were selected at the time of product installation. For example, the SIZE (or

MAINSIZE) parameter will decide the amount of memory the sort uses. SIZE=MAX or MAINSIZE=MAX tells DFSORT to use all available main storage in a region, which improves sort performance. If your installation has not selected this, you can improve performance by specifying this choice in the OPTIONS control statement for the sort.

You also may want to look at your installation's sort options. These may be found in a data set called DFSORT.V1R9M0.ICEMAC. (Note that the middle qualifier will vary with the release of the DFSORT program. You may need to consult your installation's systems programmer to determine which options your installation has chosen. The names for the sort libraries also may have been changed.)

Before starting with this comparision and explanation of sort options, let's review the basic elements of the COBOL sort feature.

19.1   THE COBOL SORT FEATURE

The COBOL language provides sufficient features to allow general-purpose sorting of files on command from a COBOL program. The object of the sort either may be a separate file or the program may supply an input procedure to pass records to the sort process instead. A similar facility exists for the result of the sort, which may be either a file or records passed to an output procedure in the COBOL program.

To optimize the sort process, the COBOL language defines several special registers to pass information between COBOL programs and the sort program. These allow the programmer to specify parameters to improve the performance of the sort. The information that may be passed to the sort includes the amount of main storage for the sort program to use, the size of the sort input (in records), the most frequent record size (for sorts of variable-length records), and the name of a file for the sort program to use to produce messages. The information returned by the sort to the COBOL program is a return code indicating if the sort was successful.

COBOL support for sorting requires that programmers define the records to be sorted. The method supplied for this is the SD entry in the data division file section. The format for an SD entry is

```
SD   sort-file-name
RECORD CONTAINS #-1 TO #-2 CHARACTERS
DATA RECORD IS 01-level name.
```

The 01 levels describing the sort records would then follow the SD. There may be multiple data record descriptions. If you are sorting fixed-length records, the TO #-2 portion of the RECORD CONTAINS clause is omitted.

The program invokes the sort by using the SORT verb. Oversimplifying slightly, this has the following format:

SORT SD-name
ON ASCENDING KEY field-name-1, field-name-2, ...
INPUT PROCEDURE section-name-1
OUTPUT PROCEDURE section-name-2.

You may specify DESCENDING KEY instead of ASCENDING KEY for sorts in reverse sequence, and you may code more than one ASCENDING and/or DESCENDING KEY clause. The fields defined by "field-name-1" and so on, must be defined in one of the 01 levels following the SD entry in the data division.

You may specify that a particular file should be sorted. In this case, the INPUT PROCEDURE clause should be replaced by

USING file-name-1

where "file-name-1" is an FD defined in your program. Similarly, the OUTPUT PROCEDURE clause may be replaced by

GIVING file-name-2

to produce another file as output rather than passing records to your output procedure.

You also may specify that an alternative character set (such as ASCII) is being sorted by including the following clause:

COLLATING SEQUENCE IS alphabet-name.

Refer to the COBOL programmers' manuals for further information about this option.

You may specify certain information for sort program optimization through the special registers SORT-CORE-SIZE, SORT-FILE-SIZE, and SORT-MODE-SIZE. SORT-CORE-SIZE allows you to specify how much main memory is available to the sort program. A value of +999999 tells the sort program to use all available memory in the address space. A negative value tells the sort program to use the amount of storage selected when the sort program was installed minus the absolute value of the amount specified in SORT-CORE-SIZE.

SORT-FILE-SIZE allows you to specify the estimated number of records to be sorted. This allows the sort to set up to handle this number of records most efficiently. SORT-MODE-SIZE only applies when sorting variable-length records. In this case, the size of records may vary within a low to high size range. SORT-MODE-SIZE allows you to specify the most frequently occurring record size in the sort input. This allows the sort to handle this size record most efficiently. For example, if you have a file with 200-byte header records, 100-byte detail records, and 300-byte trailer records for each department and there were multiple detail records for each department, the mode size would be 100.

SORT-MESSAGE is a special register used to route messages from the sort program. DFSORT will print messages using a DD name of

SYSOUT, which is also used for things such as the COBOL DISPLAY verb output. To avoid this conflict, you may specify an 8-byte DD name for the sort to use in SORT-MESSAGE.

As alluded to previously, VS COBOL II also includes a DD statement — IGZSRTCD — that may be used to provide sort control statements to invoke other sort options. This DD name also may be changed by moving the desired DD name to the special register SORT-CONTROL.

You use each of these special registers by moving a value to them before issuing the SORT verb. After the sort completes, you receive an indication of its success or failure in the special register SORT-RETURN-CODE. This will contain zero if the sort was successful. A nonzero value indicates some problem during the sort.

(The nonzero values are the same as the condition code produced by the sort program when it is run by itself, i.e., through JCL. A value of 0 indicates a successful sort. A value of 16 indicates some failure in or an early end to the sort. A value of 20 indicates that the sort program could not open its message output DD name, in which case you should look for MVS message IEC141 to find out what DD name is missing. Refer to the sort programmers' guide for the meanings of other specific return codes.)

After setting up any desired special registers and invoking the sort program with the SORT verb, you must provide coding to pass records to and receive records from the sort if you are using input and output procedures. To pass records to the sort program, COBOL provides the RELEASE verb. This is coded as

RELEASE sort-record-name FROM data-name.

The "sort-record-name" is an 01-level name following the SD. The FROM clause need not be coded if the sort record is moved into the 01 level before the RELEASE verb is executed.

COBOL also includes the RETURN verb to retrieve records back from the sort in the output procedure. This is coded as

RETURN SD-name RECORD INTO data-name
AT END imperative-statement.

The INTO clause is not necessary if you will refer to the sorted record's fields by their names as defined in the sort record 01 level.

Finally, to end an input or output procedure, simply pass control to the end of that section.

Figure 19.1 shows a simple COBOL program that uses the sort feature. We will be showing the same program in assembler later in this chapter.

This has been a brief (and oversimplified) overview of the COBOL sort facility. To get complete information on how the respective COBOL and sort facilities operate, refer to the appropriate COBOL and DFSORT manuals.

Figure 19.1   A sample COBOL program using the SORT verb.

```
IDENTIFICATION DIVISION.
PROGRAM-ID. PROGNAME.
REMARKS. SAMPLE PROGRAM IN COBOL WITH SORT VERB.
ENVIRONMENT DIVISION.
CONFIGURATION SECTION.
INPUT-OUTPUT SECTION.
FILE-CONTROL.
      SELECT INFILE   ASSIGN TO UT-S-INFILE.
      SELECT PRINTER   ASSIGN TO UT-S-PRINTER.
      SELECT SORT-WORK-FILE   ASSIGN TO COMMENT.
DATA DIVISION.
FILE SECTION.
FD   INFILE
      BLOCK CONTAINS 0
      RECORD CONTAINS 80 CHARACTERS
      RECORDING MODE IS F
      LABEL RECORDS ARE OMITTED
      DATA RECORD IS A-RECORD.
01   A-RECORD.
      05   FILLER         PIC X(80).
FD   PRINTER
      BLOCK CONTAINS 0
      RECORD CONTAINS 133 CHARACTERS
      RECORDING MODE IS F
      LABEL RECORDS ARE OMITTED
      DATA RECORD IS A-LINE.
01   A-LINE.
      05   FILLER   PIC X(133).
SD   SORT-WORK-FILE
      RECORD CONTAINS 80 CHARACTERS
      DATA RECORD IS SORT-REC.
01   SORT-REC.
      05   SW-MANUAL-NUMBER   PIC X(8).
      05   SW-MANUAL-BREAKDOWN
           REDEFINES SW-MANUAL-NUMBER.
           10   SW-TYPE-BYTE      PIC X.
           88   MANUAL-IS-LICENSED   VALUE 'L'.
           88   MANUAL-SALE-ITEM VALUE 'S'.
           10   FILLER         PIC   X(7).
      05   SW-MANUAL-TITLE  PIC   X(60).
      05   FILLER                PIC   X(12).
WORKING-STORAGE SECTION.
77   LINECT    PIC S999 COMP-3   VALUE ZERO.
```

Figure 19.1 (Continued)

```
77   RECNUM  PIC S9(7) COMP-3    VALUE ZERO.
77   INT-CODE PIC S9(8) COMP     VALUE ZERO.
77   ONE  PIC S999 COMP-3 VALUE +1.
77   P50  PIC S999 COMP-3 VALUE +50.
77   INPUT-SWITCH PIC X      VALUE '0'.
     88   MORE-INPUT  VALUE '0'.
     88   INPUT-FINISHED    VALUE '1'.
77   SORT-DONE-SWITCH     PIC X VALUE '0'.
     88   SORT-NOT-DONE     VALUE '0'.
     88   SORT-FINISHED     VALUE '1'.
01   INAREA.
     05   MAN-NUM-HALF1   PIC X(4).
     05   MAN-NUM-HALF2   PIC X(4).
     05   MAN-TITLE    PIC X(60).
     05   FILLER   PIC X(12).
01   PLINE.
     05   PLINE-CCPIC X     VALUE SPACES.
     05   FILLER   PIC X(8)  VALUE ' RECORD '.
     05   PNUMBER    PIC X(7).
     05   FILLER   PIC X     VALUE ':'.
     05   PMAN-NUM1  PIC X(4).
     05   FILLER   PIC X     VALUE '-'.
     05   PMAN-NUM2  PIC X(4).
     05   FILLER   PIC X     VALUE SPACES.
     05   PMAN-NAME  PIC X(60).
     05   FILLER   PIC X(45) VALUE SPACES.
01 HEADLINE.
     05   HEADLINE-CC PIC X     VALUE '1'.
     05   FILLER   PIC X(133)
          VALUE ' * * * LISTING OF IBM MANUALS  * * *'.
01   ENDLINE.
     05   ENDLINE-CC  PIC X     VALUE '1'.
     05   FILLER   PIC X(132)
          VALUE ' * * * END OF REPORT * * *'.
PROCEDURE DIVISION.
A-SECTION SECTION.
0100-OPEN-FILES.
     OPEN INPUT INFILE.
     OPEN OUTPUT PRINTER.
     WRITE A-LINE FROM HEADLINE.
0200-MAIN-LINE-PROCESSING.
     SORT SORT-WORK-FILE
          ASCENDING KEY SW-MANUAL-NUMBER
          INPUT PROCEDURE 1000-SORT-INPUT
          OUTPUT PROCEDURE 2000-SORT-OUTPUT.
```

Figure 19.1   (Continued)

```
                  IF SORT-RETURN NOT = 0
                     THEN MOVE SORT-RETURN TO INT-CODE
                          DISPLAY '*** SORT ERROR - RETURN CODE ',
                          INT-CODE, '***'.
              0900-END-DATA.
                  WRITE A-LINE FROM ENDLINE.
                  CLOSE INFILE  PRINTER.
                  GOBACK.
              1000-SORT-INPUT SECTION.
              1001-SORT-INPUT-START.
                  PERFORM 1100-SORT-RELEASE
                     UNTIL INPUT-FINISHED.
                  GO TO 1999-SORT-INPUT-EXIT.
              1100-SORT-RELEASE.
                  READ INFILE INTO INAREA
                     AT END MOVE 1 TO INPUT-SWITCH.
                  IF MORE-INPUT
                     THEN RELEASE SORT-REC FROM INAREA.
              1999-SORT-INPUT-EXIT.
                  EXIT.
              2000-SORT-OUTPUT SECTION.
              2001-SORT-OUTPUT-START.
                  PERFORM 2100-SORT-RETURN
                  UNTIL SORT-FINISHED.
                  GO TO 2999-SORT-OUTPUT-EXIT.
              2100-SORT-RETURN.
                  RETURN SORT-WORK-FILE
                     INTO INAREA
                     AT END MOVE 1 TO SORT-DONE-SWITCH.
                  IF SORT-NOT-DONE
                     THEN PERFORM 2200-PROCESS-OUTPUT.
              2200-PROCESS-OUTPUT.
                  ADD ONE TO RECNUM.
                  MOVE RECNUM TO PNUMBER.
                  MOVE MAN-NUM-HALF1 TO PMAN-NUM1.
                  MOVE MAN-NUM-HALF2 TO PMAN-NUM2.
                  MOVE MAN-TITLE TO PMAN-NAME.
                  WRITE A-LINE FROM PLINE.
                  ADD ONE TO LINECT.
                  IF LINECT  > P50
                     THEN MOVE ZERO TO LINECT
                          WRITE A-LINE FROM HEADLINE.
              2999-SORT-OUTPUT-EXIT.
                  EXIT.
```

19.2   SORT FACILITIES FOR ASSEMBLER PROGRAMS

Assembler programs have all the COBOL facilities available to them, as well as many other less frequently used sort options. Assembler programs use these options differently, however. Table 19.1 shows the sort functions and how they are implemented in COBOL and in assembler.

Sort facilities for assembler programs are provided in the parameter list format available to assembler programs and in the types of routines that the sort will invoke if requested by the programmer. These routines are called *sort exits* and you have to write them. The COBOL input and output procedures make use of the sort exit facility; assembler language provides access to several more exit types.

There is one fundamental difference between the logic of a COBOL sort procedure and a sort exit. In COBOL, you process records for the sort by a RELEASE or RETURN statement. Thus, your sort procedure is executed one time, and it will execute multiple RELEASE or RETURN verbs — one for each sort record.

An assembler sort exit is different. A sort exit is a type of subroutine to the sort. It is called by the sort program once for each record. You control the sort input and output by return codes you pass back to the sort when your exit routine ends.

You can do the same processing in a sort exit that you can do in a COBOL sort procedure. However, your exit will be executed many times — not once.

Running internal sorts in assembler requires a good understanding of some of DFSORT's options. You should spend some time reading the appropriate sort application programmers' guide before attempting to implement a production sort exit.

With this caveat in mind, let's look at the steps in running an internal sort in assembler. For our purposes, we will break this into four parts:

- Invoking the sort from the main assembler program
- Providing an E15 exit for input processing
- Providing an E35 exit for output processing
- JCL modifications

Table 19.1 Sort Facilities in COBOL and Assembler		
Sort Function	**Assembler Implementation**	**COBOL Implementation**
Starting sort	LINK macro	SORT verb
Input editing	E15 exit	INPUT PROCEDURE
Output editing	E35 exit	OUTPUT PROCEDURE
Key fields	Sort control statements passed as parameters when LINK is issued	ON ASCENDING/ DESCENDING KEY clauses
Input file	SORTIN DD statement (or parameter DD name)	USING clause
Output file	SORTOUT DD statement (or parameter DD name)	GIVING clause
Alternate collating sequence	Sort control statements passed as parameters when LINK is issued	SEQUENCE clause
Sort record description	Sort control statements passed as parameters when LINK is issued, or SORTIN file information	SD entry
Passing records to the sort	E15 exit return code, address in register 1	RELEASE clause in input procedure
Getting sorted records	E35 exit parameter list	RETURN clause in output procedure
Sort success indication	Return code in register 15 after LINK macro	SORT-RETURN- CODE special register
Number of records to sort	FILSZ parameter of OPTIONS data passed to sort	SORT-FILE-SIZE special register
Average record size	LENGTH parameter of RECORD data passed to sort	SORT-MODE-SIZE special register
Main storage available to sort	MAINSIZE parameter of OPTIONS data passed to sort	SORT-CORE-SIZE special register

(Table 19.1 continued on following page)

Table 19.1   (Continued)

Sort Function	Assembler Implementation	COBOL Implementation
Sort program messages DD name	MSGDDN parameter of OPTIONS data passed to sort	SORT-DISPLAY special register

This approach is designed to most closely match the processes you go through when writing an internal sort in COBOL. Assembler also has access to many other sort facilities in the form of sort exits. We will not be covering these in detail, but Table 19.2 shows the sort exit points available to assembler language programs.

Table 19.2 Sort Exits Available in Assembler Language

Exit ID	Purpose
E11	Input phase initialization
E15	Equivalent of COBOL input procedure
E16	Recover when insufficient tape work space is available to sort all the input (does not apply to sorts with disk SORTWKnn work areas)
E17	Input phase termination
E18	Special input processing (set up SYNAD, EXLST, EROPT, and EODAD for SORTIN data set; supply VSAM passwords)
E19	Special input processing (establish SYNAD routine for tape work files; not for disk sorts)
E61	Modify control fields (change length or contents of fields that are sort keys)
E31	Output phase initialization
E32	Supply input for merge operations (not used for sorts)
E35	Equivalent of COBOL output procedure
E37	Output phase termination
E38	Special output processing (similar to exit E18, but affects SORTOUT data set)
E39	Special output processing (similar to exit E19 for output)

Notes: The functions of exits E11 and E17 may be handled in exit E15. The functions of exits E31 and E37 may be handled in exit E35.

19.2.1   Invoking the Sort Program

You must provide some method of starting the sort program. (In COBOL, you do this with the SORT verb.) This may involve a macro and parameter list in your main assembler program, or you may start the sort by means of JCL with no main program. We will describe the first method, since this is conceptually identical to the COBOL approach.

To invoke the sort, you must code an MVS macro that loads in the sort program and transfers control to it. There are several choices: the LINK macro, the ATTACH macro, the XCTL macro, or a combination of the LOAD and CALL macros. We will use the LINK macro in our examples.

To link to the sort program, code

```
LINK    EP = SORT
```

SORT is the name (entry point) of the sort program. You also could use ICEMAN or other sort program names or aliases. The LINK macro will load in the sort program and give it control just as though it had been executed by itself. LINK then gives control to the sort program.

To take advantage of the assembler sort interface, you must provide information to the sort program in the form of a parameter list. You must load the address of this parameter list into register 1 before issuing the LINK macro. The parameter list is similar to the parameter list used when calling a subroutine, which is essentially what we are doing with the sort in this instance.

DFSORT allows two parameter list formats. The older version is optimized for 24-bit (pre-XA) addressing and includes coded parameter type identifications placed in the leftmost byte of the parameter list. This makes it unsuitable for use with 31-bit addressing.

The 31-bit version of the parameter list is streamlined and has fewer parameters (a maximum of 8 versus 21 for the 24-bit version). We will be using this in our example.

The parameter list contains addresses for the following possible entries:

1. Sort control statements (this is almost identical to what you provide the sort when executing it through JCL)

2. E15 input exit

3. E35 output exit

4. A user parameter, which is supplied to the exits

5. Alternate collating sequence table

6. Task ABEND recovery data area (used with ESTAE macro)

7. E18 user exit

8. E39 user exit

The end of the list is marked by a fullword with a value of -1 (hexadecimal X'FFFFFFFF'). The first entry — sort control statements — is mandatory. All the other entries are optional.

Since you probably will not use all the possible options in an exit, DFSORT provides two ways to bypass providing an option. The first is to code the fullword marking the end of the list right after the last parameter you supply. In this case, you have fewer than eight entries.

The second way is to code a value of zero for the address of options that are not provided. Both these techniques may be used in the same parameter list.

Some examples of parameter list coding may clarify this. First, let's code a list where both E15 and E35 exits are provided but no other options are used:

PARMLIST	DC	A(SORTCNTL)	SORT CTL STMTS
	DC	A(SAMPE15)	E15 EXIT PROG
	DC	A(SAMPE35)	E35 EXIT PROG
	DC	F'-1'	MARK END OF LIST

Note that SORTCNTL, SAMPE15, and SAMPE35 are all labels inside the program containing this parameter list. The fullword with a value of -1 marks the end of the parameter list.

Another example:

LIST2	DC	A(STMTS2)	SORT CTL STMTS
	DC	A(0)	NO E15 EXIT
	DC	A(OTHERE35)	E35 EXIT PGM
	DC	A(MYPARMS)	PARAMETERS
	DC	F'-1'	MARK END OF LIST

This is similar to the first list but has a value of 0 for the second entry. This tells DFSORT that no E15 exit (the second entry) is being provided, in which case DFSORT will read the file defined as SORTIN to obtain the input for the sort. The A(MYPARMS) allows us to pass information to or from the sort exit; this address will be passed to the exit as a parameter. (Had an E15 exit been supplied, it also would have received this information when it executed.)

The value of the user parameter is that it allows easy access to common storage areas. This also simplifies addressability to data in the main program for the exit. Our example will demonstrate one possible use for this — to share access to a pair of files, avoiding duplicate OPEN and CLOSE macros.

The structure of your main assembler program and your exits determines how you should apply the user parameter. Your exits may be a part of your main program or may be separate programs. Which data should be shared between the main program and exits will reflect this structure. In our example, we will include the exits inside the main program.

The last thing to consider about invoking the sort is the format of the control statements. This was supplied as the first (required) operand for the parameter list. It has the format of a halfword length, followed by character fields with sort control statements in them.

For example, to sort a group of 80-byte records on an 8-byte key at the beginning of the record:

```
SORTCNTL  DC   AL2(SORTEND-SORTBEGN)    LENGTH
SORTBEGN  DC   C' SORT FIELDS = (1,8,CH,A),FILSZ = E1000 '
          DC   C' RECORD TYPE = F,LENGTH = 80 '
          DC   C' OPTIONS MAINSIZE = MAX,RESALL = 80K '
SORTEND   EQU  *            END OF CONTROL STATEMENTS
```

The AL2 generates a 2-byte binary value of the difference between the address of SORTEND and SORTBEGN. This provides the 2-byte length of the control statements that DFSORT requires.

The SORT FIELDS specifies that the first sort key field is 8 bytes long, beginning at byte 1 of the input record (the first byte). The field contains character values (CH) and should be sorted in ascending (A) sequence. The FILSZ (file size) parameter specifies that we estimate (E) that the file will contain 1000 records. The RECORD specifies that we are sorting fixed-length records (TYPE=F) and that the records are 80 bytes long.

The OPTIONS information specifies that the sort program should use all available main storage (MAINSIZE=MAX) to accomplish the sort. DFSORT should reserve 80 kilobytes of the total available storage for the calling program's use. We would use this if we were to open a file in an exit, for example. (You will have to estimate this based on what you do that may acquire storage in your own sort exits.)

There are many other options that may be specified here, but a complete explanation of the sort program could easily merit a book in itself. Refer to the appropriate sort application programmers' guide for further information.

Note that the parameters we supply in this way are the same that we would provide to DFSORT if we were running it through JCL. Note, however, that there is no fixed format to the statements in storage that we provide. The statements do not have to be 80 bytes long, as they are when provided through JCL, but no comments are allowed.

At this point, we have set up all the information in our main program that the sort program needs to run. We now will see how the sort interacts with the sort exits.

19.2.2   Input Sort Exit E15

When provided to DFSORT in a parameter list from an assembler program, the E15 exit replaces the function of the SORTIN DD statement. The E15 exit will provide all input to the sort. (The E15 exit also may be included in a sort executed through JCL. In this case, the E15 exit will be called for each input record in the SORTIN data set.)

DFSORT calls the E15 exit repeatedly to get input records (or to allow editing of records in SORTIN when invoked through JCL). DFSORT puts the address of a two-word parameter list into register 1.

The first word of the parameter list points to an input sort record if DFSORT is invoked through JCL. This first word contains a value of 0 if there are no input records. This is the case in our example — all input records are provided by the E15 exit (much like an input procedure is mutually exclusive with the USING option in COBOL). The second word of the parameter list points to the user parameter address if one was provided in the original sort parameter list.

The E15 exit must then come up with a record to pass to the sort. It may do this by reading a file, accessing a database system, or whatever other means are necesary. The address of the new record must then be placed into register 1. Your exit should then return control to the sort with a return code of 12 in register 15. This is equivalent to the RELEASE verb in COBOL. (Note that you will have to restore registers slightly differently to pass back the address in register 1. The example program shows how to do this.)

If you have no more input to the sort, you should return control back with a return code of 8. This tells DFSORT that you have no more input and that it should proceed with the sort. Other return codes are available. A return code of 16 tells DFSORT to abandon the sort immediately. A return code of 4 tells DFSORT to delete the current record. Refer to the sort manuals for more details on this.) The sort program will continue to call your E15 exit until it receives a return code of 8.

19.2.3   Output Sort Exit E35

After the sort program has sorted the input records and is ready to produce the sort output, it will call the E35 exit if one is provided. Your E35 exit routine will receive three parameters from the sort. First is the address of the next record from the sort. This is normally the record you want to process. The second parameter is the address of the previous record from the sort. This is provided to allow you to insert records if desired. The third parameter is the address of the user parameter described earlier.

If you have invoked the sort program through an assembler main program, you must dispose of all the sort output through your E35 exit. (The example does this.) If you have invoked the sort through JCL, it will write the output records to the SORTOUT file. You may add, delete, or change the sorted records in the E35 exit in this case.

After receiving control from the sort, the E35 exit must determine what the sort should do with the record. For our example, we will always tell DFSORT to delete the record. This is in accord with what a COBOL output procedure exit does. To tell the sort to delete the record, we return control with a return code of 4. DFSORT will then call us with the next record from the sort.

If there are no more records from the sort, DFSORT will call us with an address value of 0 for the next record from the sort. This should trigger any end-of-file processing or other termination routines that are appropriate.

After doing any termination processing you desire, you must tell DFSORT that you are through processing. You signal this to DFSORT by returning with a return code of 8 in register 15. (If you return with a return code of 8 before you have received the indication from the sort that there are no more records, you may receive message ICE025. A similar condition can arise in COBOL if you exit your output procedure before you have reached the "at end" condition on the RETURN statement. Refer to the DFSORT application programmers' guide for further information on this message and condition.)

As with the E15 exit, other return code values are possible. You should research these through the sort manuals.

After DFSORT has finished its processing, it will return control to your main assembler language program. Register 15 will contain a return code that indicates the success or failure of the sort. A return code of 0 indicates a successful sort. A return code of 16 indicates an unsuccessful sort. A return code of 20 indicates that DFSORT could not open its output message data set.

19.2.4 JCL Modifications

As with use of the COBOL sort feature, you should modify your JCL to include any DD statements that the sort program requires. This should include

- SORTWKnn sort work file DD statements
- SYSOUT or other DD statements for sort messages
- STEPLIB and/or SORTLIB if needed
- SORTCNTL if needed

These must be included with your program's regular JCL.

19.2.5 Summmary of Assembler Internal Sorts

We have now covered the sort facilities in assembler that correspond to the facilities available to you in COBOL. At this point, let's look at an example in assembler (Fig. 19.2). This is the COBOL sample program from Fig. 19.1, rewritten in assembler.

Figure 19.2 Assembler program to invoke sort.

```
PROGNAME    CSECT
            STM    14,12,12(13)        SAVE REGISTERS
            LR     R12,R15             GET PGM ADDR
            USING  PROGNAME,R12        ADDRESSABILITY
            ST     R12,BASEREG         SAVE FOR EXITS
            SPACE 1
```

Figure 19.2   (Continued)

```
*           CHAIN  SAVE AREAS
            ST     R13,SAVEAREA + 4           OLD SAVE AREA
            LA     R2,SAVEAREA                NEW SAVE AREA
            ST     R2,8(R13)                  NEW SAVE  ADDR
            LR     R13,R2                     UPDATE REG I 3
            SPACE 1
*           OPEN FILES
            OPEN   (INFILE,INPUT)
            LA     R1,INFILE                  ADDR OF INPUT DCB
            USING  IHADCB,R1                  ADDRESSABILITY
            TM     DCBOFLGS,X'10'             TEST  GOOD OPEN
            BNO    OPENERR                      NOT ON - FAILED
            OPEN   (PRINTER,OUTPUT)
            LA     R1,PRINTER                 ADDR OF INPUT DCB
            TM     DCBOFLGS,X'10'             TEST  GOOD OPEN
            BNO    OPENERR                      NOT ON -  FAILED
            DROP   R1                         END  USING
            SPACE 1
            PUT    PRINTER,HEADLINE           WRITE PAGE HDG
            SPACE 1
*           MAIN LINE PROCESSING
            SPACE 1
*_____.*
SET UP PARAMETER LIST & CALL SORT
*_____-
            LA     R1,PARMLST                 LOAD PARM LIST
            LINK   EP = SORT                  CALL  DFSORT
[11]        LTR    R15,R15                    TEST RET CODE
            BZ     SORTFINE                   IF ZERO, END JOB
            CVD    R15,DOUBLEWD               CONV RC TO DEC
            OI     DOUBLEWD + 7,X'0F'         SET SIGN
            UNPK   SORTWTO + 37(3),DOUBLEWD   UNPACK INTO WTO
SORTWTO  WTO       '*** SORT ERROR - RETURN CODE ... ***'
            CVB    R15,DOUBLEWD               GET RC AGAIN
SORTFINE EQU       *
            CLOSE  (INFILE,,PRINTER)          CLOSE FILES
            L      R13,4(,R13)                RESTORE R13
            RETURN (14,12),RC = (15)          SET RC & RET
*_____-
*           CREATE PARAMETER LIST
*_____-
            CNOP   0,4                        FULLWORD  ALIGN
PARMLST  DC        A(CNTLSTMT)                CTL STMTS ADDR
[1]         DC     A(MYEXIT15)                USER EXIT E15
```

Figure 19.2   (Continued)

```
           DC    A(MYEXIT35)                   USER EXIT E35
[4]        DC    A(BASEREG)                    EXITS BASE REG
           DC    A(0)                          ALTSEQ XLATE TBL
           DC    A(0)                          STAE WORK AREA
           DC    A(0)                          USER EXIT E18
           DC    A(0)                          USER EXIT E39
           DC    F'-1'                         END  31-BIT PARM S
CNTLSTMT DS     0H                             USED TO GET LEN
           DC    AL2(CTLEND-CTLSTART)
CTLSTART DC     C' SORT FIELDS = (01,08,CH,A) '          [2]
           DC    C' RECORD TYPE = F,LENGTH = 80      '
           DC    C' OPTION EQUALS,FILSZ = E1000 '         [3]
CTLEND     EQU   *
           SPACE 1
*          ERROR WHEN OPENING A FILE. END WITH RET CODE 16
OPENERR    EQU   *
           L     R13,4(R13)                    OLD SAVE AREA
           RETURN      (14,12),RC = 16         RETURN TO MVS
           SPACE 3
*          DATA AREAS
DOUBLEWD DC     D'0'                           WORK AREA
SAVEAREA DC     18F'0'                         PGM SAVE AREA
BASEREG  DC     F'1'                           PGM BASE REGISTER
INAREA     DS    CL80                          INPUT DATA AREA
LINE       DC    C' '                          CARRIAGE CONTROL
           DC    C' RECORD '
NUMBER     DS    CL7                           RECORD NUMBER
           DC    C':'
DATA       DS    CL80                          DATA RECORD
           DC    CL36' '            .          FILLER
HEADLINE DC     CL133'1 * * * RECORD LISTING * * *'
ENDLINE  DC     CL133'0 * * * END OF REPORT * * *'
LINECT     DC    PL2'0'                        LINE COUNT
RECNUM     DC    PL4'0'                        RECORD NUMBER
ZERO       DC    P'0'                          CONSTANT 0
ONE        DC    P'1'                          CONSTANT 1
P50        DC    P'50'                         CONSTANT 50
*          DATA CONTROL BLOCKS
PRINTER  DCB    DDNAME = PRINTER,DEVD = DA,MACRF = (PM),    X
                DSORG = PS,RECFM = FBA,LRECL = 133,         X
                BLKSIZE = 0
INFILE     DCB   DDNAME = INFILE,DEVD = DA,MACRF = (GM),       X
                DSORG = PS,RECFM = FB,LRECL = 80,BLKSIZE = 0,  X
                EODAD = ENDDATA
```

Figure 19.2   (Continued)

```
*              THIS IS THE EQUIVALENT TO THE COBOL CODE IN THE
*              INPUT  PROCEDURE 1000-SORT-INPUT THROUGH
*              1999-SORT-INPUT-EXIT.
MYEXIT15 CSECT
[5]            STM    14,12,12(13)              SAVE REGISTERS
               LR     R11,R15                   ENTRY POINT ADDR
               USING  MYEXIT15,R11
               SPACE 1
*              CHAIN  SAVE AREAS
               ST     R13,E15SAVE+4             CHAIN
               LA     R2,E15SAVE                 SAVE
               ST     R2,8(R13)                   AREAS
               LR     R13,R2                    UPDATE REG13
               SPACE 1
               L      R12,4(R1)                 SET MAIN PROG
               L      R12,0(R12)                 BASE REGISTER
               L      R3,0(R1)                  ADDR OF SORT REC
[6]            LTR    R3,R3                     IT SHOULD BE ZERO
               BNZ    E15ERR01                  IF NOT 0, ABEND
*              READ NEXT RECORD TO PASS TO THE SORT
               GET    INFILE,INAREA             READ A RECORD
               SPACE 1
*              RELEASE RECORD TO THE SORT
               LA     R1,INAREA                 ADDR OF RECORD
               L      R13,4(R13)                OLD SAVE AREA
               LM     R2,R12,28(R13)            RESTORE  REGS
[7]            RETURN    (14,0),RC=12           RET, INSERT RET CD
               SPACE 1
*              END-OF-FILE ON INPUT. TELL SORT NO MORE INPUT.
ENDDATA  EQU    *
               CLOSE (INFILE)                   CLOSE FILE
               L      R13,4(R13)                GET OLD SAVE AREA
[8]            RETURN    (14,12),RC=8           RET, END EXIT E15
               SPACE 1
E15ERR01 EQU    *
               EX     0,*                       FORCE 0C3 ABEND
               SPACE 1
E15SAVE  DC     18F'0'                          EXIT 15 SAVE AREA
               DROP   R11
*              THIS IS EQUIVALENT TO THE COBOL CODE IN THE OUTPUT
*              PROCEDURE 2000-SORT-OUTPUT SECTION THROUGH
*              2999-SORT-OUTPUT-EXIT.
MYEXIT35 CSECT
               STM    14,12,12(13)              SAVE REGISTERS
```

Figure 19.2   (Continued)

```
[9]            LR      R11,R15                    ENTRY POINT ADDR
               USING   MYEXIT35,R11
               SPACE   1
*              CHAIN   SAVE AREAS
               ST      R13,E35SAVE+4              CHAIN
               LA      R2,E35SAVE                 SAVE
               ST      R2,8(R13)                  AREAS
               LR      R13,R2                     UPDATE REG 13
               SPACE   1
               L       R12,8(R1)                  SET UP MAIN
               L       R12,0(R12)                 PROG BASE REG
               L       R3,0(R1)                   ADDR OF SORT REC
[10]           LTR     R3,R3                      SHOULD NOT BE  0
               BZ      E35END                     IF 0, END OF DATA
               SPACE   1
*              PROCESS RECORD FROM SORT
               MVC     DATA,0(R3)                 MOVE TO PRINT
               AP      RECNUM,ONE                 ADD TO RECORD CT
               OI      RECNUM+3,X'0F'             SET SIGN BITS
               UNPK    NUMBER,RECNUM              MOVE TO PRINT
               PUT     PRINTER,LINE               WRITE PRINT LINE
               AP      LINECT,ONE                 ADD TO LINE COUNT
               CP      LINECT,P50                 AT PAGE END?
               BL      E35NEXT                    NO - CONTINUE
               ZAP     LINECT,ZERO                RESET LINE COUNT
               PUT     PRINTER,HEADLINE           WRITE PAGE HDG
               SPACE   1
*              RELEASE RECORD TO THE SORT
E35NEXT        EQU     *
               L       R13,4(R13)                 GET OLD SAVE AREA
               RETURN  (14,12),RC=4               RET, DELETE REC
               SPACE   1
*              END OF SORT INPUT. TELL SORT NOT TO COME BACK.
E35END         EQU     *
               PUT     PRINTER,ENDLINE            WRITE ENDING LINE
               CLOSE   (PRINTER)                  CLOSE FILE
               L       R13,4(R13)                 GET OLD SAVE AREA
               RETURN  (14,12),RC=8               RETURN, ALL DONE
               SPACE   1
E35SAVE        DC      18F'0'                     EXIT 15 SAVE AREA
               DROP    R11
*_ _ _ _ _ _ _ _ _ _ _ _ _ _ _ _ _ _ _ _ _ _ _ _ _ _ _ _ _ _ _
* (THE DCBD MACRO AND REGISTER EQUATES ARE NOT SHOWN
               END     PROGNAME                   END OF PROGRAM
```

Notes to Fig. 19.2:

1. The parameter list was assembled with A-type address constants pointing to the sort control statements, E15 and E35 exits, and user parameters. There was no special processing to set up the parameter list other than to load its address into register 1 before issuing the LINK macro.

2. The SORT control statement shows use of two sort key fields. The first is sorted on ascending sequence and the second on descending sequence.

3. The file size is estimated. If an exact number is used instead (i.e., the 'E' is omited in the FILSZ operand), the sort will end with an error if this number of records is not received.

4. The user parameter in the parameter list contains the address of a fullword called BASEREG. Since this program includes both the exits inside the main program, some way of addressing the main program's data from the exits must be provided. In this program, we pass the program base address as a parameter and then load the main program base register in each of the exits.

5. The E15 exit, which begins at label MYEXIT15, does normal program initialization. Note that both E15 and E35 use separate save areas.

6. E15 tests the first parameter address to see if a record is being provided. If one is, this implies a SORTIN file and a logic error of some sort. The program issues a WTO to identify the error and then returns to the sort with a return code of 16. This tells the sort to terminate immediately, and the main program also will receive a return code of 16.

7. The exit reads from INFILE and passes the record to the sort with a return code of 12 (insert record).

8. When INFILE has been completely read, the E15 exit returns to the sort with a return code of 8 (do not return). This marks the end of the input phase, and the sort actually starts at this point.

9. The E35 exit initialization is similar to that for E15. However, we are expecting records from the sort in this exit. If the record address is not 0, the exit processes the sorted record normally. Since we are not producing an output SORTOUT file, we will delete each of the records by passing return code 4 (delete this record) back to the sort.

10. If the record address is 0, this tells us that we have retrieved all the sorted records. We then perform normal termination (beginning at label E35END) and return to the sort with a return code of 8 (do not return).

11. The main program will then get control back from the LINK macro. It tests the return code, and prints it by means of a WTO macro if it is not 0. The sort return code is then used as the program return code.

This ends our discussion of the sample program, which is as close as possible to a one-to-one conversion of the original COBOL program. You could take this program and modify it for production use if desired. However, this is not advisable. The sample program in Fig. 19.2 does not deliver optimum performance. To see why, let's look at some sort performance factors in the next section.

19.3 IMPROVING SORT PERFORMANCE

Sorts are historically very frequently used. They have been subject to a great deal of performance improvement and research, both by university computer scientists and by computer hardware and software manufacturers. As a result, sorts are among the most optimized programs in existence. As a by-product of this optimization, there are several design factors that affect selection and programming of a sort exit.

The first of these is: Why are we coding an exit here at all? If the input or output processing is merely to read (or write) an input (or output) file and pass it to (or from) the sort, a sort exit is probably going to result in worse performance. With the present state of the art in sort programs (circa 1990), the sort program can probably read or write a sequential SORTIN or SORTOUT file faster than your program can.

On the other hand, if the input to the sort resides in a database system that can not be directly accessed by the sort, then a sort exit will provide a performance improvement over creating a file and passing it to the sort in a separate step. Also, if the exit performs any complicated exclusion and reduces the number of sorted records, then it should lead to a performance improvement. Additionally — among the most common justifications for a sort exit or COBOL internal sort — if the sole purpose of the sort is to produce a subfile for reporting, then an E35 exit or output procedure will require less processing than a sort followed by a separate report processing program step.

A second major design factor is: Do we need a main program or just one or more exits? You may have run across COBOL programs yourself where the "mainline logic" of the program is only a SORT verb, with all the real processing done in an input or output procedure. In this case, the main program represents unneeded overhead, and a slight performance improvement may result by using only the needed exit.

In this case, a preferable method is to invoke DFSORT through JCL rather than with a LINK program from a main program. To accomplish this, you must modify your control statements slightly to add a MODS control statement to process specify the exit names.

In the case of our sample program, the main program and E15 exit do not really contribute anything. The only real processing is the report formatting done in the E35 exit.

To convert E35 to run by itself, we must move the shared data fields into E35 and add a first-time routine to initialize the program by opening the print file and writing a heading. Figure 19.3 shows the sample program's E35 exit modified to run by itself.

In any event, the selection of a sort exit (or even a COBOL internal sort) should not be taken lightly. The sort manuals have additional tuning information and are a valuable reference.

Figure 19.3   Assembler output exit E35.

```
AFCE35    CSECT
          STM    14,12,12(13)              SAVE REGISTERS
          LR     R12,R15                   ENTRY POINT ADDR
          USING  AFCE35,R12                ADDRESSABILITY
          SPACE  1
*         CHAIN  SAVE AREAS
          ST     R13,E35SAVE + 4           CHAIN
          LA     R2,E35SAVE                SAVE
          ST     R2,8(R13)                 AREAS
          LR     R13,R2                    UPDATE REG 13
          SPACE  1
*         GET ADDRESS OF OUTPUT SORTED RECORD
          L      R3,0(R1)                  ADDR OF SORT REC
          LTR    R3,R3                     SHOULD NOT BE 0
          BZ     E35END                    IF 0, END OF DATA
          SPACE  1
*         DETERMINE IF THIS IS 1ST TIME WE HAVE BEEN ENTERED
          TS     E35SW                     1ST-TIME SW
          BNZ    E35NORM                   IF NOT 0, NOT 1ST
          SPACE  1
*         OPEN FILES AND DO OTHER INITIALIZATION
          OPEN   (PRINTER,OUTPUT)
          USING  IHADCB,R1                 ADDRESSABILITY
          LA     R1,PRINTER                ADDR OF INPUT DCB
          TM     DCBOFLGS,X'10'            TEST  GOOD OPEN
          BNO    OPENERR                   NOT ON -  FAILED
          DROP   R1                        END  USING
          PUT    PRINTER,HEADLINE          WRITE PAGE HDG
          SPACE  1
*         NORMAL PROCESSING
E35NORM   EQU    *
          SPACE  1
```

Figure 19.3   (Continued)

```
*          PROCESS RECORD FROM SORT
           MVC   NUM_1ST,0(R3)                MOVE 1ST AND 2ND
           MVC   NUM_2ND,4(R3)                HALVES OF MANL #
           MVC   MANTITLE,10(R3)              MOVE MANUAL TITLE
           CLC   8(2,R3),=CL2' '  IS THERE A REVISION # SUFFIX
           BE    NOSUFF                       NO - PRINT AS IS
           MVI   SUFFDASH,C'-'                ELSE SET SFX DASH
           MVC   NUM_SUFF,8(R3)               MOVE REV NUMBER
NOSUFF     EQU   *
           AP    RECNUM,ONE                   ADD TO RECORD CT
           OI    RECNUM+3,X'0F'               SET SIGN BITS
           UNPK  NUMBER,RECNUM                MOVE TO PRINT LINE
           PUT   PRINTER,LINE                 WRITE PRINT LINE
           MVI   SUFFDASH,C' '                RESET SUFFIX DASH
VALUE      MVC   NUM_SUFF,=CL2'               AND REVISION NBR
           AP    LINECT,ONE                   ADD TO LINE COUNT
           CP    LINECT,P50                   WE AT PAGE END?
           BL    E35NEXT                      NO - CONTINUE
           ZAP   LINECT,ZERO                  RESET LINE COUNT
           PUT   PRINTER,HEADLINE             WRITE PAGE HDG
*          RELEASE RECORD TO THE SORT
E35NEXT    EQU   *
           L     R13,4(R13)                   GET OLD SAVE AREA
           RETURN     (14,12),RC=4            RET +DELETE REC
           SPACE 1
*          END OF SORT FILE. TELL SORT NOT TO RETURN.
E35END     EQU   *
           PUT   PRINTER,ENDLINE              WRITE ENDING LINE
           CLOSE (PRINTER)                    CLOSE FILE
           L     R13,4(R13)                   GET OLD SAVE AREA
           RETURN  (14,12),RC=8               RET TO SORT,  END
           SPACE 1
*          ERROR OPENING A FILE. END WITH RETURN CODE 16.
OPENERR    EQU   *
           WTO   'ERROR OPENING PRINT FILE - ENDING SORT'
           L     R13,4(R13)                   GET OLD SAVE AREA
           RETURN     (14,12),RC=16   RET TO SORT AND STOP
           SPACE 3
           EJECT
*          DATA AREAS
DOUBLEWD   DC    D'0'                         WORK AREA
E35SAVE    DC    18F'0'                       EXIT 15 SAVE AREA
E35SW      DC    X'00'                        FIRST-TIME SWITCH
```

Figure 19.3   (Continued)

```
LINE      DC    C' '                                    CARRIAGE CONTROL
          DC    C' RECORD '
NUMBER    DS    CL7                                     RECORD NUMBER
          DC    C':'
NUM_1ST   DS    CL4                                     MANUAL # 1ST 1/2
          DC    C'-'
NUM_2ND   DS    CL4                                     MANUAL # 2ND 1/2
SUFFDASH  DC    C' '                                    DASH IF SUFFIX
NUM_SUFF  DS    CL2                                     MANL SUFFIX REV #
DC        C' '
MANTITLE  DS    CL70                                    MANUAL TITLE
          DC    CL36' '                                 FILLER
HEADLINE  DC    CL133'1 * * * RECORD LISTING * * *'
ENDLINE   DC    CL133'0 * * * END OF REPORT * * *'
LINECT    DC    PL2'0'                                  LINE COUNT
RECNUM    DC    PL4'0'                                  RECORD NUMBER
ZERO      DC    P'0'                                    CONSTANT 0
ONE       DC    P'1'                                    CONSTANT 1
P50       DC    P'50'                                   CONSTANT 50
*               DATA CONTROL BLOCKS
PRINTER   DCB   DDNAME = PRINTER,DEVD = DA,MACRF = (PM),     X
                DSORG = PS,RECFM = FBA,LRECL = 133,          X
                BLKSIZE = 0
          EJECT
*               DCB DSECT, REGISTER EQUATES NOT SHOWN
          END   AFCE35                                  END OF PROGRAM
```

Figure 19.4 shows the JCL used to run the sort exit E35 shown in Fig. 19.3. With regard to this figure, The STEPLIB and SORTLIB data sets will most likely be different for your installation. Note that the MODS control statement specifies MYLIB — the DD name for the library that holds the AFCE35 exit program. You would probably change this for your installation.

19.4 SUMMARY

This chapter has presented an overview of the COBOL SORT verb. We have then illustrated how to accomplish similar functions using assembler sort exits. You should be able to review an existing COBOL program with an internal sort and determine the equivalent coding or facilities in assembler. Review of the current sort manuals is strongly encouraged, since new sort facilities appear more frequently than changes to other things covered in this book.

Figure 19.4   JCL used to run exit E35 from Fig. 19.3.

```
//AFCE35           JOB provide parameters as required
//SORTDIR          EXEC PGM = SORT,
//                 REGION = 1024K
//STEPLIB   DD   DSNAME = DFSORT.V1R9M0.LINKLIB,DISP = SHR
//          DD   DSNAME = DFSORT.V1R9M0.LPALIB,DISP = SHR
//          DD   DSNAME = DFSORT.V1R9M0.SORTLIB,DISP = SHR
//SORTLIB   DD   DSNAME = DFSORT.V1R9M0.LINKLIB,DISP = SHR
//          DD    DSNAME = DFSORT.V1R9M0.LPALIB,DISP = SHR
//          DD   DSNAME = DFSORT.V1R9M0.SORTLIB,DISP = SHR
//          DD   DSNAME = TS00024.PDS.LOAD,DISP = SHR
//MYLIB     DD   DSNAME = TS00024.PDS.LOAD,DISP = SHR
//SYSOUT   DD  SYSOUT = *
//SORTWK01        DD   UNIT = 3380,SPACE = (CYL,(1))
//SORTWK02        DD   UNIT = 3380,SPACE = (CYL,(1))
//SORTWK03        DD   UNIT = 3380,SPACE = (CYL,(1))
//SYSIN          DD   *
SORT FIELDS = (1,10,CH,A),FILSZ = E100
RECORD LENGTH = (80,80,),TYPE = F
MODS E35 = (AFCE35,20000,MYLIB)
END
/*
//SYSUDUMP        DD    SYSOUT = *
//PRINTER         DD    SYSOUT = *
//SORTIN          DD    DSN = SORT.INPUT.FILE,DISP = SHR
//
```

Things to Do

You can probably think of several things you may want to look at involving sorts in your own installation. However, here are a few starting points to effectively use sort exits:

1. Research your sort installation options. You will probably have to get assistance from your systems programmer to locate and understand this. Some organizations publish this information in their standards manuals.

2. Determine if there are any assembler sort exits at your shop. If you do not know of any, you may be able to review the sort control statements for JCL-invoked sorts to find one with a MODS statement.

3. Review your installation's *batch processing window*. (If you aren't familiar with the term, this is the amount of time for batch processing between shutdown and startup of your online systems.) If there are any major sorts in the critical path of nightly processing, can you improve their performance? (Try to optimize the sort options for that sort before suggesting a sort exit in assembler.)

4. If you have identified a time-critical sort from the preceding step, could you do it faster with sort exits? Develop a list of things you expect can be done faster. Note that for most installations, you will have to reduce the amount of I/O to produce any meaningful improvements. You might do this by not rereading a file after it has been sorted.

5. Convince your boss to let you try.

6. In most current IBM processors, two instructions have been added to assist in sorting. These are intended for use by DFSORT, but they also could be used in your own programs. The instructions are Compare and Form Codeword — opcode CFC — and Update Tree — UPT. These fall into the category of esoterica, but you may wish to review their descriptions in the Principles of Operations Manual.

Character String Handling

Both COBOL and assembler provide several instructions for manipulation of character data. Character data includes both individual strings (e.g., "J.H.Murphy") and words in text (e.g., "Four score and seven years ago...").

Compared to arithmetic operations, character operations involve several differences. First, the nature of character data is essentially unformatted. The basic element is a sequence of bytes (*string*), usually delimited by blanks, commas, or other punctuation. Strings are divisible into the individual words that comprise them.

Just like arithmetic operations, character operations fall into several categories:

1. *Separation* or *decomposition*—breaking up the character string into smaller pieces (usually words)
2. *Concatenation*—merging or adding two strings to produce another
3. *Transformation*—converting all or part of a character string to other values on a character-by-character basis
4. *Scanning*—locating specified bytes in a string
5. *Filling*—concatenating a predetermined character to the end of string

Table 20.1 shows the COBOL verb and assembler instructions used to implement each of these functions.

20.1 CHARACTER STRING VERBS IN COBOL

COBOL provides several verbs to process character strings. These include the following:

STRING—Merge two or more character strings into a larger character string.

UNSTRING—Separate out specified substrings from a larger character string.

INSPECT—Locate a given byte or set of bytes in a character string (newer implementation of this function).

INSPECT with REPLACING option—Locate a given byte or set of bytes and convert into another character string (newer implementation of this function).

EXAMINE—Locate a given byte or set of bytes in a character string (older implementation of this function—not in VS COBOL II).

TRANSFORM—Convert given bytes into another set of bytes in a character string (older implementation of this function—not in VS COBOL II).

EXAMINE with REPLACING option—Locate a given byte or set of bytes and convert into another character string (older implementation of this function—not in VS COBOL II).

We will be covering all these, although with some overlap in the descriptions. INSPECT is very similar to EXAMINE and TRANSFORM. EXAMINE and TRANSFORM are only available in the earlier VS COBOL compiler and its predecessors.

In addition, the MOVE statement provides filling services. You also may be able to do fixed-length concatenation or decomposition with MOVE and data elements using REDEFINES.

Table 20.1 Character Operations in COBOL and Assembler		
Operation	COBOL Verb	Assembler Instruction
Separation	UNSTRING	MVC/MVCL, MVC with TRT
Concatenation	STRING	MVC/MVCL
Transformation	INSPECT ... REPLACING OR TRANSFORM or EXAMINE ... REPLACING	TR
Scanning	EXAMINE or INSPECT	TRT
Filling	MOVE	MVCL

We will be simplifying each of the COBOL formats slightly in the interest of keeping this section to a reasonable length. You should consult the COBOL manuals for your compiler for further information on these verbs.

INSPECT has several formats and options. We will only discuss a few here. First, the basic TALLYING format:

```
INSPECT data-name-1
        TALLYING data-name-2    FOR {LEADING} literal-3.
```

This format will scan the data field identified by *data-name-1* and look for the character string identified by *literal-3*. The count of occurrences of *literal-3* will be placed in the numeric field *data-name-2*. The LEADING option allows you to scan until the first character that is not equal to *literal-3* is found. *Data-name-1* must be a field or group item with COBOL usage of DISPLAY, and this applies to almost all the fields referenced in this section.

For example, if we have fields defined as

```
77   CHAR-FIELD   PIC X(10) VALUE '  HELLO'.
77   CHAR-COUNT   PIC S9(4) VALUE ZERO.
```

then the INSPECT statement

```
INSPECT CHAR-FIELD
    TALLYING CHAR-COUNT
    FOR LEADING BLANKS.
```

would result in a value of 5 being placed in CHAR-COUNT.

Next, we show the REPLACING option of INSPECT:

```
INSPECT data-name-1
    REPLACING ALL | LEADING | FIRST literal-2
    BY literal-3.
```

In this format, INSPECT still scans for the value specified in *literal-2*. When it finds it, however, it changes the value it found to the value specified in *literal-3*, subject to the following rules:

1. If ALL was specified, all occurrences are changed, no matter where they occur.
2. If LEADING was specified, INSPECT scans until it finds a character or character string not equal to *literal-2*. At this point, INSPECT stops.
3. If FIRST was specified, INSPECT scans until it finds an occurrence of *literal-2*. This is changed to *literal-3*. At this point, the instruction terminates.

You may include the TALLYING option with the REPLACING option to find out how many occurrences were found.

The following examples of INSPECT all assume the starting values of CHAR-FIELD and CHAR-COUNT as shown in the preceding example. The statement

```
INSPECT CHAR-FIELD
    REPLACING ALL SPACES
    BY '-'.
```

would result in a value of '——-HELLO' in CHAR-FIELD. The statement

```
INSPECT CHAR-FIELD
    REPLACING FIRST 'O'
    BY SPACES.
```

Would result in a value of '   HELL ' in CHAR-FIELD. The statement

    INSPECT CHAR-FIELD
      REPLACING LEADING 'H'
        BY 'J'.

would result in no change to CHAR-FIELD, because 'H' is not the first character in CHAR-FIELD.

UNSTRING allows us to separate out substrings of characters based on a delimiter. For text, the substrings are words and the delimiters are blanks, commas, and other punctuation marks. The format of UNSTRING is

    UNSTRING data-name-1
      DELIMITED BY literal-2
      INTO data-name-3
        COUNT in data-name-4
      WITH POINTER data-name-5
      TALLYING IN data-name-6.

The INTO/COUNT clause may be repeated. The WITH POINTER clause is used when repeatedly extracting strings from *data-name-1*.

As an example of UNSTRING, assume that we have the following data fields defined in a COBOL program:

    77 SPEECH-STRING   PIC X(30)
        VALUE 'FOUR SCORE AND SEVEN YEARS AGO'.
    77   WORD-1   PIC X(15) VALUE SPACES.
    77   COUNT-1   PIC S9(4) VALUE ZERO.
    77   WORD-2   PIC X(15) VALUE SPACES.
    77   COUNT-2   PIC S9(4) VALUE ZERO.
    77   WORD-COUNTER   PIC S9(4) VALUE ZERO.
    77   SPEECH-POINTER   PIC S9(4) VALUE + 1.

If we execute

    UNSTRING SPEECH-STRING
      DELIMITED BY SPACES
      INTO WORD-1
        COUNT IN COUNT-1
        WORD-2
        COUNT IN COUNT-2
      WITH POINTER SPEECH-POINTER
      TALLYING IN WORD-COUNTER.

SPEECH-STRING will be unchanged, and the other fields will contain

    WORD-1:"FOUR   "
    COUNT-1: 4
    WORD-2: "SCORE   "
    COUNT-2: 5
    WORD-COUNTER: 2 (number of words found)
    SPEECH-POINTER: 12 (where to start UNSTRING next)

We can repeat the execution of this statement until WORD-COUNTER has a value of 0 or until SPEECH-POINTER is equal to 30. This means that no more words were found in the character string or that all characters have been examined. WORD-COUNTER should be reset to zero before each execution.

The STRING verb allows us to build a longer string from several other fields or literals. The format is

```
STRING identifier-1
       data-name-2 DELIMITED BY literal-3 | SIZE
       identifier-4
INTO data-name-5
WITH POINTER data-name-6
ON OVERFLOW imperative-statement.
```

STRING allows multiple operands, which may be either literals or data names. These are shown as *identifier-1* in the preceding examples. If a data name is supplied, each data name may have a separate DELIMITED BY clause. The SIZE option indicates that you wish to concatenate the entire field to the string. *Data-name-5* specifies the receiving field. The WITH POINTER clause allows you to begin creating the resulting character string at a byte other than the first one in *data-name-5*. If the resulting string is larger than the size of *data-name-5*, the statement(s) in the ON OVER-FLOW clause will be executed.

For example, assume the following fields and starting values:

```
77  SALUTATIONS-LINE       PIC X(60) VALUE SPACES.
77  CUSTOMER-LAST-NAME  PIC X(15)VALUE 'PUBLIC'.
77  CUSTOMER-FIRST-NAME PIC X(15)VALUE 'JOHN'.
77  CUSTOMER-INITIAL  PIC X VALUE 'Q'.
```

When we execute

```
STRING   CUSTOMER-FIRST-NAME
             DELIMITED BY SPACES
         ' ' DELIMITED BY SIZE
         CUSTOMER-INITIAL
         '. ' DELIMITED BY SIZE
         CUSTOMER-LAST-NAME
             DELIMITED BY SPACES
INTO SALUTATIONS-LINE.
```

then SALUTATIONS-LINE would contain "JOHN Q. PUBLIC," and the other fields would be unchanged.

The older verbs, EXAMINE and TRANSFORM, are equivalent to INSPECT. The formats will be shown for those programmers already familiar with these. EXAMINE has the format

```
EXAMINE data-name-1 TALLYING
   UNTIL FIRST | LEADING | ALL literal-1.
```

This format counts the number of *literal-1*, based on the value of the LEADING or ALL options. These operate as described earlier in the discussion on INSPECT. The UNTIL FIRST option resembles the LEADING option but counts all characters not equal to *literal-1* until it detects the value specified by *literal-1*.

EXAMINE with the REPLACING option has the format

EXAMINE *data-name-1* REPLACING
FIRST | UNTIL FIRST | LEADING | ALL *literal-1*
BY *literal-2.*

This will scan the field defined as *data-name-1* for occurrences of *literal-2*, following the rules of the FIRST, LEADING, and ALL options. In this format, the UNTIL FIRST option acts like the LEADING option but replaces all characters not equal to *literal-1* by the value specified by *literal-2*.

TRANSFORM is similar to a form of INSPECT with the REPLACING option. TRANSFORM has the format

TRANSFORM data-name-1 FROM literal-2
TO literal-3.

This is equivalent to

INSPECT *data-name-1*
REPLACING *literal-2*
BY *literal-3.*

The COBOL character string instructions provide many more functions and formats than we have shown here. You should refer to the appropriate COBOL programmers manuals for a complete description of these.

20.2   CHARACTER STRING INSTRUCTIONS IN ASSEMBLER

Assembler, like COBOL, provides many instructions that can be used for character and string manipulation. Many of these, such as MVC and MVCL, were discussed earlier in this book.

Assembler provides three instructions, however, that are key to performing the types of string manipulations we have discussed in this chapter. These are the TR, TRT, and EX instructions.

The TRT—Translate and Test—instruction implements a character-by-character scan of a data field. It is a storage-to-storage format (SS format) instruction and can scan up to 256 bytes in one execution.

TRT is very flexible in the values for which you may scan. TRT also requires that you construct a table, which may become quite complex, to control the scan operation. TRT allows us to implement the INSPECT ... TALLYING and UNSTRING instructions. TRT is also applicable for any of the instructions we have discussed in this chapter that have a DELIMITED BY clause, LEADING, FIRST, or other exclusionary clauses. Finally, TRT provides us with a way to implement numeric checks in assembler.

The TR — Translate —instruction implements a character-by-character conversion of a data field. Like TRT, TR is an SS-format instruction that can convert up to 256 characters at a time. Like TRT, TR is flexible, but depends on a 256-byte table whose construction may become quite complex.

The EX—Execute—instruction is not directly related to character scanning. Execute, instead, is an instruction that allows us to temporarily modify another instruction, perform (execute) that instruction, and then continue on. Execute is one of the more complicated instructions in the 370 repertoire.

At this point, we will describe how these three operate. Then we will proceed on to how you can perform COBOL-like functions with these.

20.2.1 Translate and Test (TRT)

The Translate and Test—TRT—instruction requires a 256-byte table as its second operand. The first operand is the field to be scanned. Coding of the table (which we will call a *scan table* in this text) is different from most other data areas you may have coded in the past.

The scan table is used to define *delimiters*, or characters that cause the scan to stop. Logically, this works like the UNTIL FIRST clause described earlier. TRT compares the value in each byte in the first operand to the corresponding byte in the scan table. If the byte in the scan table is hexadecimal X'00', TRT continues the scan with the next byte. If the byte in the scan table contains any other value, the scan stops.

The key element in this is the phrase *corresponding byte in the table.* TRT uses the values in the first operand bytes as index values into the scan table. Thus, if a byte in the first operand contained COBOL LOW-VALUES (X'00'), TRT would evaluate the byte at offset X'00' into the scan table. If the first operand contained a blank (X'40'), TRT would evaluate the byte at offset X'40' (decimal 64) past the start of the scan table. If the first operand contained the character 'A' (hex X'C1'), TRT would evaluate the byte at offset X'C1' (decimal 193) past the beginning of the scan table. The key point is that TRT looks at a byte in the scan table based on the value of each byte in the area being scanned.

Another way of putting this is that TRT scans the first operand, adds the hexadecimal value in each byte to the beginning address of the scan table, and then inspects the byte it finds in the table. If the scan table byte is hexadecimal X'00', the scan continues with the next byte of the first operand as before.

If the byte in the scan table is not hexadecimal X'00', TRT ends by setting the address of the current position in the first operand in register 1, and the value found in the byte in the scan table is set into register 2. The value goes into bits 24 to 31 of the register (the rightmost byte).

Instruction execution then stops, and the condition code is set to 1 or 2. If all bytes of the first operand are examined without finding a nonzero value in the scan table, TRT execution terminates with condition code 0 and registers 1 and 2 are not changed.

What could be simpler?

20.2.1.1   TRT Examples

Well, almost every other instruction in the 370 repertoire is simpler than TRT. However, some examples may show you how it works.

As our first example, let's show how a numeric check operates in assembler with TRT. Assume that we want to verify that an input character field contains only the characters 0 through 9. To do this, we must first code the scan table.

The logic behind the scan table is that you want a value of X'00' in the table positions that correspond to the valid bytes. You need to place values of other than X'00' in all the other bytes.

Since the character code values in EBCDIC of the digits 0 through 9 are hexadecimal X'F0' through X'F9', you will want to have 10 bytes of X'00' at the scan table positions that correspond to these bytes.

Hexadecimal X'F0' is equivalent to decimal 240. Thus we want bytes 240 through 249 of the table to contain X'00'. The rest of the table must contain any characters besides X'00' in each byte. We have accounted for bytes 240 through 249. Now we must fill in the byte positions before and after this.

The table begins at byte 0. To fill it out, we must code enough nonzero bytes to fill from byte 0 to byte 239. And at the end, we must fill from byte 250 through byte 255. (Remember that there are 256 possible combinations of 8 bits—0 through 255.)

To accomplish this, our table would be coded

```
NUMTABLE  DC      240X'04        (Bytes 0 through 239)
          DC      10X'00'        (Bytes 240 through 249)
          DC      6X'04'         (Bytes 250 through 255)
```

We can then test a field called INPUTAMT by coding

```
          TRT     INPUTAMT,NUMTABLE
          BZ      NUMERIC
```

If INPUTAMT begins at location hexadecimal X'10A240' and contains C'12345', the TRT will end with a condition code of 0. This will cause a branch to the label called NUMERIC.

If INPUTAMT contains C'12E45', the TRT will end with a condition code of 1. Additionally, registers 1 and 2 will contain information about what caused TRT to end. In this case, register 1 would contain hexadecimal X'0010A242'—the 'E' is 2 bytes past the start of the field INPUTAMT. Register 2 would contain X'00000004'—the last byte receives the nonzero byte from the scan table.

If INPUTAMT contains C'1234S', the TRT will end with a condition code of 2. This indicates that the very last character of the first operand field is the one that caused the TRT to end. Register 1 will contain X'0010A244', since the 'S' is 4 bytes past the start of the field. Register 2 will again contain X'00000004'.

We will be showing several other examples of TRT later in this chapter. If TRT doesn't seem to make any sense, try to make it through the examples. It is one of the more complicated instructions.

20.2.2   Translate — TR

The TR—Translate—instruction is used to convert from one character set to another. The need for this arises because not all computers use the same character set coding. The two most popular standard character sets today are EBCDIC and ASCII. Many other character coding schemes exist, primarily for telecommunications and paper tape use. At the time of the System 360 introduction, BCD—a 6-bit code—also was used by most IBM equipment.

The need exists to convert from other codes used by outside peripherals or other computers (e.g., CDC, DEC, IBM PC) to EBCDIC for use inside the 370 mainframe. For examples of some of the differences, refer to the 370 Reference Summary (yellow card) "code tables" section.

TR is an SS-format instruction. The first operand is a character field in storage to be converted to another character set (e.g., ASCII to EBCDIC). The second operand is a translate table. The translate table is a 256-byte table containing the desired output character set. TR proceeds left to right through the first operand much like TRT. It adds the value found in each byte in the first operand to the beginning address of the translate table. TR then places a copy of the byte from the translate table into the original first operand byte. This proceeds through each byte in the first operand.

The translate table is 256 bytes long—one position to correspond to each possible combination of 8 bits. An example of a translate table to convert lowercase to upper-case is shown in Fig. 20.1.

Note that each position in the table contains its own value, except for the bytes beginning at X'81', X'91', and X'A2'. These are the beginning positions of the lowercase characters "a" to "i", "j" to "r", and "s" to "z", respectively.

Figure 20.1 Translate table to convert from lowercase to uppercase.

```
TRANSTAB DC   X'000102030405060708090A0B0C0D0E0F'
         DC   X'101112131415161718191A1B1C1D1E1F'
         DC   X'202122232425262728292A2B2C2D2E2F'
         DC   X'303132333435363738393A3B3C3D3E3F'
         DC   X'404142434445464748494A4B4C4D4E4F'
         DC   X'505152535455565758595A5B5C5D5E5F'
         DC   X'606162636465666768696A6B6C6D6E6F'
         DC   X'707172737475767778797A7B7C7D7E7F'
         DC   X'80C1C2C3C4C5C6C7C8C98A8B8C8D8E8F'
         DC   X'90D1D2D3D4D5D6D7D8D99A9B9C9D9E9F'
         DC   X'A0A1E2E3E4E5E6E7E8E9AAABACADAEAF'
         DC   X'B0B1B2B3B4B5B6B7B8B9BABBBCBDBEBF'
         DC   X'C0C1C2C3C4C5C6C7C8C9CACBCCCDCECF'
         DC   X'D0D1D2D3D4D5D6D7D8D9DADBDCDDDEDF'
         DC   X'E0E1E2E3E4E5E6E7E8E9EAEBECEDEEEF'
         DC   X'F0F1F2F3F4F5F6F7F8F9FAFBFCFDFEFF'
```

If you have studied Fig. 20.1, you may have come to the realization that coding the translate table is the most difficult part of the instruction. There is an easier way to create tables such as that shown in Fig. 20.1, where almost all the characters are not changed. This is to generate the table in a loop and then modify only the characters needed.

The following code will generate a table at TRANSTAB:

```
        XC    TRANSTAB,TRANSTAB      MAKE TABLE X'00'S
        LA    R1,255                 SET UP LOOP CTR
FIXTAB  EQU   *
        LA    R2,TRANSTAB(R1)        ADDR OFTBL BYTE
        STC   R1,0(R2)               STORE BYTE IN TBL
        BCT   R1,FIXTAB              LOOP THROUGH TBL
```

Having created the table, let's fix up the lowercase characters. The following code will reset the three ranges of lowercase characters:

```
        MVC   TRANSTAB+C'a'(9),=C'ABCDEFGHI'
        MVC   TRANSTAB+C'j'(9),=C'JKLMNOPQR'
        MVC   TRANSTAB+C's'(8),=C'STUVWXYZ'
```

You may find this more understandable by looking at where the lowercase letters are in EBCDIC in the Reference Summary (yellow card). (You would set the CAPS OFF option in ISPF to enter the lowercase "a", "j", and "s". SET CASE MIXED would allow the same for XEDIT. Similar commands exist for other program editors.)

COBOL uses TR for any code involving a REPLACING option. In addition, there are several special uses of TR for character rearrangement, simple cryptography, hexadecimal to EBCDIC conversion, and so forth. One of these, hexadecimal to EBCDIC conversion, is useful enough in itself to merit some time.

20.2.2.1 Hexadecimal Conversion with TR

You may have seen a core dump from time to time. (I know, you never get them yourself!) One of the recurring needs for assembler programmers is some way of showing what a field contains in hexadecimal—just like a dump. Unfortunately, using a macro to dump a field usually produces more output than is desirable.

We can't just print hexadecimal data, since not every one of the 256 possible character combinations is printable. To get around this, we frequently need a routine to print data in hexadecimal—just like a dump.

The following is an internal subroutine that takes an unknown 4-byte value and makes it into 8 bytes, suitable for printing or displaying. It expects that register 1 will contain the address of the area we wish to display in hexadecimal.

```
HEXCONV   EQU   *
          UNPK  EBCDICEQ(9),0(5,R1)       UNPACK VALUE
          TR    EBCDICEQ(8),HEXTAB-240    TRANSLATE
          BR    R14                       GO BACK TO CALLER
EBCDICEQ  DC    CL8' '                    OUTPUT FIELD
          DC    C' '                      FILLER
HEXTAB    DC    C'0123456789ABCDEF'       TRANSLATE TABLE
```

This routine is somewhat cryptic when you first look at it. The Unpack— UNPK—instruction at the beginning takes the 4 bytes whose address is in register 1 and unpacks them. Why?

Remember what the Unpack instruction does. It takes each 4 bits from a field and places them in the low-order (right) side of bytes in the output field. It also places the numeric zone bits—hexadecimal 'F' in the left side of each byte in the output field. Thus, if a field contained 'xxyz', its unpacked result would be 'FxFxzy'. (Remember that the zone byte for the rightmost byte is the packed decimal sign bit, hence the 'zy' at the end.) Unpack does not care if the data is valid packed decimal digits or not.

Note that the sending field length is 5 bytes and the receiving field length is 9 bytes. Since UNPK flips the 4-bit quantities in the last byte, we have to make sure that it doesn't do this to the fields we want to convert and print, so we add an extra "garbage" byte that goes through this unwanted manipulation.

The TR instruction will then have a field in EBCDICEQ whose bytes will range from X'F0' to X'FF'. Since nothing will be below X'F0', we don't have to provide that part of the translate table.

You may invoke this routine in your program by coding

```
LA    R1,field
BAS   R14,HEXCONV           GO TO CONVERSION RTN
MVC   display-field,EBCDICEQ   MOVE TO OUTPUT AREA
```

This routine has two bugs, which rarely show up. The first is that, since 5 bytes are accessed for the Unpack, you may receive an 0C4 when you access the very last fullword in a program or buffer. You can easily correct for this by moving the desired bytes to a work area in your program and then using that as the input to HEXCONV.

The second is that the HEXCONV routine cannot be located in the first 240 bytes of your program. This is so because of the HEXTAB-240 in the TR instruction. This is usually not too onerous a restriction.

20.2.3   The Execute Instruction – EX

String handling frequently requires that you deal with data items of unknown length. Also, in many other cases, the instruction operands are not known at assembly time. This leads to a requirement to be able to modify the length used with an instruction. The MVCL and CLCL instructions provide this capability. However, most other instructions do not. To modify the length of operands with other instructions, the IBM 370 architecture provides the Execute instruction— opcode EX.

EX—Execute—is an RX format instruction. The concept of Execute is unique to IBM CPUs. It basically allows execution of a one-instruction subroutine. Logically, it somewhat resembles a PERFORM of a one-instruction paragraph, but it also includes modification of the instruction. The format of EX is

EX   *register,instruction_address*

where *register* is a general purpose register, and *instruction_address* is the address of an instruction elsewhere in your program.

The instruction to be executed (called the *target instruction*) is first copied into an internal work area inside the CPU. The CPU then modifies the instruction using the contents of the first operand register. The low-order byte of the first operand register is then ORed with the second byte of the copied instruction.

This modified copy of the instruction is then executed as though it was in the program where the Execute instruction was. The condition code is set based on the executed instruction. The original copy of the instruction in your storage is not changed. The first operand register is not changed by the EX instruction.

There are three key points to understanding how Execute works. The first is the concept of the logical OR operation. You may wish to review this from Chap. 17. The second is the layout of IBM 370 instructions.

Remember that there are five main formats of 370 instructions. The secret to using EX effectively is to understand what is being changed by it when you execute another instruction. Since EX modifies the second byte of the copied instruction, it will modify different things for different instruction formats. Table 20.2 shows the five instruction formats, their

Table 20.2 Instruction Formats and EX Modifications

Format/Name	Typical Instructions	What EX Modifies
RR/Register-to-Register	LR 1,2	Register specification ('1,2')
RX/Register-to-Indexed-Storage	L 1,WORD1	Register (1) and index register specification (none used in example)
RS/Register-to-Storage	LM 14,12,12(13)	Beginning and ending register specification ('14,12')
SI/Storage Immediate	MVI FLD1,C'*'	Immediate character (*)
	TM FLD1,X'02'	Immediate byte (X'02')
SS/Storage-To-Storage	MVC FLD1,FLD1	Length of Move
	UNPK FLD1,FLD2	Length of First and Second operands
	CLC FLD1,FLD2	Length of Compare
	TRT FLD1,TABLE	Length of Translate and Test
	AP NUM1,NUM2	Length of First and second operands

names, representative instructions in that format, and what EX modifies in the instruction. You may wish to review the instruction formats in the 370 Reference Summary (yellow card).

Note that any instruction may be modified with EX, but it is usually only sensible to modify SS-format instructions like MVC. Occasionally, the immediate byte of SI-format instructions may be a reasonable thing to modify with EX. Other instruction formats are generally not amenable to modification with EX.

20.2.3.1 EX Examples

EX examples are more complicated than most other instructions. Use of EX with TRT is among the most complicated instruction combinations in all assembler language.

We'll start with a simple case—modification of an MVI instruction. Assume that we have the following starting values, contents, and instructions:

```
MOVEBYTE  MVI    FIELDA,X'00'
FIELDA    DC     C' NOTE'
```

Assume that register 3 contains hexadecimal X'0000005C'. [X'5C' is the asterisk ('*') character in EBCDIC.]

When we run the instruction

```
          EX     R3,MOVEBYTE
```

FIELDA will contain C'*NOTE'. Register 3 and the MVI instruction at MOVEBYTE are not changed.

Now let's look at how EX changes a storage-to-storage instruction— in this example, a PACK instruction where the length of the second operand is not known. Assume that we have the following instruction, fields, and values:

```
PACKIT    PACK   WORKFLD,0(0,R3)
```

Note that this PACK instruction is set up assuming that register 3 contains the address of the field to pack. The length is 0 since it will be supplied by the EX instruction.

Register 3: Hexadecimal X'0001A708' (Address of field to pack)

Register 4: Hexadecimal X'00000002' (Length of field to pack)

Location X'0001A708': C'175GARBAGE...' (Field to pack)

Note also that we must have 1 less than the length of the field to pack, since the SS-format instructions store the length that way. (This allows the SS-format instructions to carry lengths from 1 to 256 in a 1-byte field, which can only hold values from 0 to 255.) The BCTR instruction is typically used to decrement the true length to get what's sometimes termed the *execute length*.

When we run the instructions

| BCTR | R4,0 | (Decrement length) |
| EX | R4,PACKIT | (Pack value) |

WORKFLD will have the following value:

WORKFLD   DC   PL4'175'   (Hexadecimal X'0000175C')

The other operands and register contents are unchanged.

We will see some further examples using MVC later in this chapter.

20.3   IMPLEMENTING INSPECT IN ASSEMBLER

INSPECT can be implemented with a TRT instruction. INSPECT with the REPLACING option requires a TR instruction. We will see examples of both in this section.

We will assume that we have the following fields and starting values for each of the examples in this section:

CHARFLD	DC	CL10' HELLO'
CHARCNT	DC	H'0'
SCANTAB	DC	XL256'00'
TRANTAB	DC	XL256'00'

(These correspond to the fields CHAR-FIELD and CHAR-COUNT used in the COBOL INSPECT examples earlier in this chapter. SCANTAB and TRANTAB will be used to set up scan and translate tables.)

Let's now look at what's required to implement each of the COBOL INSPECT examples given earlier. First,

INSPECT CHAR-FIELD
   TALLYING CHAR-COUNT
   FOR LEADING SPACES.

To do this or any test like the LEADING option, we need a translate table that stops on every possible byte value except the one specified in the LEADING clause. Thus, our table might be prepared by filling the whole table with non-zero values and then resetting the one byte we want to count—a space, or X'40', in this case. The following code will set up the table:

MVI	SCANTAB,X'04'	FILL WITH
MVC	SCANTAB + 1(255),SCANTAB	NONZERO BYTES
MVI	SCANTAB + C' ',X'00'	CLEAR X'40' BYTE

We can then count the leading blanks by scanning and then subtracting the address where we began scanning from the address where we stopped.

```
            TRT    CHARFLD,SCANTAB    SCAN FOR NON-BLANKS
            BC     8,ALLBLANK         ALL BLANK - SPECIAL CASE
            LA     R0,CHARFLD         GET SCAN START ADDR
            SR     R1,R0              SUBTRACT FROM STOP ADDR
            STH    R1,CHARCNT         STORE IN RESULT FIELD
            B      SCANDONE           FINISHED
ALLBLANK    EQU    *                  SPECIAL CASE
            LA     R1,L'CHARFLD       GET SCANNED FIELD LEN
            STH    R1,CHARCNT         SET LEADING BLANK CT
SCANDONE EQU       * '
```

The preceding code includes processing for a special case that wasn't mentioned earlier. If the field CHARFLD contains all blanks, the scan won't stop. In this case, register 1 is not changed. The condition code tells us if this happens, so we go to a routine called ALLBLANK that handles this special case. (We'll explain the *L'CHARFLD* in Chap. 22. It is a way of obtaining the assembler's calculated length for a field.)

Otherwise, we set up the address of the beginning of the field in register 0, and then we subtract that from the stop address, which will be in register 1. The difference is thus the number of leading spaces in CHARFLD.

20.4   IMPLEMENTING INSPECT ... REPLACING IN ASSEMBLER

The rest of the INSPECT examples given earlier all involved the REPLAC-ING option. This introduces a requirement for modifying the scanned field, which we will do both with the TR instruction and with MVC.

Our second case from the earlier COBOL INSPECT examples is

```
INSPECT CHAR-FIELD
    REPLACING ALL SPACES BY '-'.
```

Any verb with REPLACING as an option usually requires a Translate instruction when doing the same function in assembler. In this case, we do not want to change anything in the string CHARFLD except all occurrences of the space character. These should be converted to dashes.

We could construct a laborious TRT loop, that scans for spaces, replaces each space with a dash, and continues the scan by means of TRT until we have scanned the entire field. However, a simpler approach is to just translate the entire field using a translate table that only modifies the space character and leaves every other byte with its original value.

Replacing a laborious TRT loop with laborious construction of a translate table wouldn't be much of an improvement. However, we can easily construct this type of translate table with a short loop and a few modifications to the table following the loop.

The code used to build a translate table and set it up for this example is

```
        LA      R2,255              HIGHEST BYTE VALUE
TABLP1  EQU     *
        STC     R2,TRANTAB(R2)      STORE BYTE VALUE
        BCT     R2,TABLP1           LOOP THRU TABLE
        MVI     TRANTAB,X'00'       SET UP LOWEST BYTE
```

This code sets up increasing byte values in TRANTAB (hexadecimal values X'00', X'01', X'02', on up to X'FF'). It does it in such a way that each byte value is translated to its original value.

The Store Character—STC—instruction will store the byte in TRANTAB which is in the rightmost byte of register 2. The TRANTAB(R2) uses register 2 as an index register into the table, so each byte is stored at its own index value into the table.

To modify the table to change blanks to dashes, we need to modify the byte in the translate table that will replace blanks. We can do this by coding

```
        MVI     TRANTAB+C' ',C'-'
```

The $+C'$ ' tells the assembler to use the value of a space (hexadecimal X'40') as an offset past the beginning of TRANTAB. It is perfectly legal to use a character as an offset in this way.

With the table set up as we now have it, all we have to do to complete the INSPECT...REPLACING process is to issue the translate instruction

```
        TR      CHARFLD,TRANTAB
```

The next INSPECT example is

```
        INSPECT CHAR-FIELD
          REPLACING FIRST 'O' BY SPACES.
```

This form of INSPECT raises a new requirement. We now will replace only one byte, so a TR is not necessarily required. However, we must find the first letter 'O' to replace, and to do this, we need a TRT. The processing steps are thus to set up a scan table to help us find the first 'O', to scan for the 'O', and to replace it when found. The code to do this is

```
        XC      SCANTAB,SCANTAB     CLEAR SCAN TABLE
        MVI     SCANTAB+C'O',X'04'  STOP IF 'O' FOUND
        TRT     CHARFLD,SCANTAB     SCAN FOR LETTER 'O'
        BC      8,NOGOTS            IF NONE FOUND, END
        MVC     0(1,R1),=C' '       MOVE IN A BLANK
NOGOTS  EQU     *
```

The BC 8,NOGOTS bypasses any replacement if no hit character ('O') is found. The MVC following this moves in a blank. We also could have used an MVI.

The last example of INSPECT ... REPLACING is

```
INSPECT CHAR-FIELD
    REPLACING LEADING 'H' BY 'J'.
```

In this example, we have to find the leading 'H' characters. To find out how many of them there are, we will use a TRT. To replace them, we will use a TR. The code to do this is

```
        MVI    SCANTAB,X'04'            FILL SCANTAB WITH
        MVC    SCANTAB+1(255),SCANTAB   ALL X'04'S
        MVI    SCANTAB+C'H',X'00'       ALLOW 'H' TO PASS
        LA     R1,CHARFLG               SET UP ADDR IF NO 'H'S
        TRT    CHARFLD,SCANTAB          SCAN FOR FIRST LETTER
*                                       THAT IS NOT AN 'H'
        LA     R0,CHARFLD               GET ADDR OF START
        SR     R1,R0                    STOP ADDR - START
        BZ     NOREPL                   IF 0, NO REPLACE
        BCTR   R1,0                     SET UP LEN FOR EX
*       SET UP TRANSLATE TABLE FOR REPLACEMENT
        LA     R2,255                   BUILD DEFAULT TBL
TABLP2  EQU    *
        STC    R2,TRANTAB(R2)           STORE BYTE VALUE
        BCT    R2,TABLP2                LOOP THRU TBL
        MVI    TRANTAB,X'00'            RESET FIRST BYTE
        MVI    TRANTAB+C'H',C'J'        REPLACE 'H' W/ 'J'
        EX     R1,TRANSLAT              EXECUTE TRANSLATE
NOREPL  EQU    *
```

The following is an executed instruction and would be placed outside the main line of program execution.

```
TRANSLAT   TR  CHARFLD(0),TRANTAB    * EXECUTED INSTRUCTION *
```

This code includes elements of the previous examples, such as the instructions to create the scan and translate tables. The subtraction of start from stop addresses tells us how many leading 'H' characters were found. This value, minus 1, is used in the EX instruction as the length to translate.

The techniques presented up to this point for INSPECT also apply to logic that emulates the EXAMINE and TRANSFORM verbs.

20.5 IMPLEMENTING STRING/UNSTRING IN ASSEMBLER

The COBOL STRING and UNSTRING verbs may be implemented with the assembler MVC or MVCL instructions, except for the cases where the DELIMITED clause appears. In this case, we also must use TRT to scan past or for the delimiting character. Most of the techniques needed for this have already been described.

We will now show how our earlier example of UNSTRING could be written in assembler. Owing to the length of the example, we will only show the unstring operation for one word of the text. The equivalent in COBOL would be

UNSTRING SPEECH-STRING
DELIMITED BY SPACES
INTO WORD-1
COUNT IN COUNT-1
WITH POINTER SPEECH-POINTER
TALLYING IN WORD-COUNTER.

We will use slightly shorter data names in the corresponding assembler language code below. The data names and starting values are

```
SPEECH    DC    C'FOUR SCORE AND SEVEN YEARS AGO'
*               (SPEECH-STRING)
WORD1     DC    CL15' '                    (WORD-1)
WORD2     DC    CL15' '                    (WORD-2)
COUNT1    DC    H'0'                        (COUNT-1)
COUNT2    DC    H'0'                        (COUNT-2)
SPEECHPT  DC    H'0'                        (SPEECH-POINTER)
WORDCT    DC    H'0'                        (WORD-COUNTER)
```

The code is shown in Fig. 20.2. This example is fairly complicated. Scanning text in assembler requires that we keep track of six variables:

1. Where to start scanning. In this example, it is at the beginning of the field SPEECH, plus the offset value in SPEECHPT.

2. Where the scan stopped. This will normally be in register 1, but it should be saved in another register as needed.

3. The true length of the word found. This can be calculated from the difference between the start and stop addresses.

4. The execute length of the word found. This should be 1 less than the true length.

5. The true remaining length to scan. This should be set up at the beginning as the total field length, minus any offset values, as in SPEECHPT.

6. The remaining length for the Execute instruction. This should be 1 less than the true remaining length.

In addition to these, we also must bypass any leading delimiters. This is a requirement of the COBOL UNSTRING. The comments at the beginning of each group of instructions should explain what each is doing.

For the final discussion on how to emulate the COBOL character manipulation verbs in assembler, let's look at our final example — the STRING verb. This can generally be implemented by means of either EX and MVC instructions or MVCL instructions. However, we still have a requirement for scanning if we need to remove any trailing delimiters.

Figure 20.2   UNSTRING example in assembler.

```
*               SET UP SCAN ADDRESSES AND LENGTHS
                LA      R3,L'SPEECH-1       GET LENGTH OF SPEECH - 1
                LA      R4,L'SPEECH         GET TRUE LENGTH OF SPEECH
                LA      R5,SPEECH           POINT TO FIELD TO UNSTRING
                LA      R1,0(R4,R5)         POINT PAST END OF FIELD
                A       R5,SPEECHPT         ADD SPEECH-POINTER OFFSET
                S       R4,SPEECHPT         SUBTRACT FROM LENGTH
*               SCAN PAST ANY LEADING DELIMITERS
                MVI     SCANTAB,X'04'                   FILL SCANTAB WITH
                MVC     SCANTAB+1(255),SCANTAB    ALL X'04'S
                MVI     SCANTAB+C' ',X'00'    DON'T STOP ON DELIMITER
                EX      R3,TRT              EXECUTE SCAN
                LR      R6,R1               GET STOP ADDRESS
                SR      R6,R5               SUBTRACT START ADDRESS
                SR      R4,R6               SUBTRACT FROM LENGTH
                BZ      UNSTDONE            0 = ALL BLANKS
*               SET UP TO SCAN TO END OF FIRST WORD
                LR      R3,R4               SET UP LENGTH
                BCTR    R3,0                FOR EXECUTE
                LA      R5,0(R1)            POINT TO NEXT NONBLANK
                XC      SCANTAB,SCANTAB     CLEAR SCAN TABLE
                MVI     SCANTAB+C' ',X'04'  EXCEPT FOR BLANK
                LA      R1,0(R4,R5)         POINT PAST END OF FIELD
                EX      R3,TRT              SCAN FOR END OF WORD
*               COMPUTE LENGTH OF WORD AND MOVE TO WORD1 FIELD
                LR      R6,R1               GET STOP ADDRESS
                SR      R6,R5               MINUS START ADDR = LENGTH
                STH     R6,COUNT1           STORE IN CT FIELD
                LR      R3,R4               SET UP SCAN
                BCTR    R3,0                EXECUTE LENGTH
                BCTR    R6,0                SET UP EXECUTE LENGTH
                EX      R6,MVC              MOVE TO WORD1
*               TEST TO SEE IF THERE ARE MORE CHARACTERS TO SCAN
                SR      R4,R6               COMPUTE REMAINING LEN
                BNP     UNSTDONE            IF ZERO, UNSTRING IS DONE
*               SET UP TO HANDLE MORE UNSTRING OPERATIONS AT
*                   THIS POINT.
UNSTDONE        EQU                         *
```

The COBOL STRING verb example was

STRING CUSTOMER-FIRST-NAME DELIMITED BY SPACES
  ' ' DELIMITED BY SIZE
  CUSTOMER-INITIAL
  '. ' DELIMITED BY SIZE
  CUSTOMER-LAST-NAME DELIMITED BY SPACES
  INTO SALUTATIONS-LINE.

The assembler fields for this example are

```
SALUTATION DC    CL60' '
CUST_LAST  DC    CL15'PUBLIC'
CUST_INIT  DC    CL1'Q'
CUST_FIRST DC    CL15'JOHN'
BLANK      DC    CL1' '
DOT        DC    CL2'. '
```

The assembler language code to accomplish the same result is shown in Fig. 20.3. Note that we assume that the name fields are left justified, i.e., have no leading blanks. Register 3 is used as the pointer into the output field (SALUTATION), and register 4 holds the starting address of each of the fields that are being stringed together.

The executed instruction MOVENAME is

```
MOVENAME MVC   0(0,R3),0(R4)   * * EXECUTED INSTRUCTION * *
```

This example is not a one-for-one replacement for the COBOL STRING example. It tests each name field to make sure that it is not all blanks, and it doesn't add the punctuation if the field isn't supplied. Also, the code is not entirely general purpose, since it assumes hard-coded lengths of 1 and 2 for BLANK and DOT, respectively. Notwithstanding these amendments, this example should be readily modifiable to handle other string concatenation problems.

20.6 STRING HANDLING ESOTERICA

This entire chapter could justifiably be considered as covering esoteric features of both COBOL and assembler. However, the following are a number of other points that you may find useful occasionally.

20.6.1 Branch Tables and TRT

We have consistently set up our TRT scan tables using a nonzero value of X'04' for all the stop bytes. Any nonzero character may be used, but use of values that are multiples of 4 allows use of a technique called *branch tables*. We discussed this technique in Chap. 12.

Branch tables provide a way of implementing a structured programming "case" statement in assembler. The closest COBOL verbs for this function are GO TO with the DEPENDING ON option and the EVALUATE verb in VS COBOL II.

Figure 20.3   STRING example in assembler.

```
            LA      R3,SALUTATION       POINT TO START OF OUTPUT
            XC      SCANTAB,SCANTAB         CLEAR SCAN TABLE
            MVI     SCANTAB+C' ',X'04'      EXCEPT FOR BLANK
            LA      R4,CUST_FIRST              INPUT FIELD ADDR
            LA      R1,CUST_FIRST+L'CUST_FIRST    POINT TO END
            TRT     0(15,R4),SCANTAB        LOOK FOR BLANK
            LA      R0,CUST_FIRST           SET START ADDR
            SR      R1,R0                   COMPUTE LENGTH
            BZ      NO_FIRST                0 = NO FIRST NAME
            BCTR    R1,0                    SET  EXECUTE LEN
            EX      R1,MOVENAME             EXECUTE MOVE
            LA      R3,1(R1,R3)         POINT TO NEXT OUTPUT BYTE
            LA      R1,L'BLANK-1        EXECUTE LENGTH FOR FILLER
            LA      R4,BLANK                ADDRESS FOR MVC
            EX      R1,MOVENAME             MOVE NEXT FIELD
            LA      R3,1(R1,R3)         POINT TO NEXT OUTPUT BYTE
NO_FIRST    EQU     *
            CLI     CUST_INIT,C' '          IS THERE A MIDDLE INITIAL
            BNH     NO_INIT                 NO - DON'T MOVE
            MVC     0(1,R3),CUST_INIT       YES - MOVE INITIAL
            LA      R3,1(R3)                POINT PAST INITIAL
            MVC     0(2,R3),DOT         MOVE IN DOT AND SPACE
            LA      R3,2(R3)                POINT PAST THAT
NO_INIT     EQU     *
            LA      R4,CUST_LAST
            LA      R1,CUST_LAST+L'CUST_LAST     POINT TO END
            TRT     0(15,R4),SCANTAB        LOOK FOR DELIMITER
            SR      R1,R4               SUBTRACT START ADDRESS
            BZ      NO_LAST                 0 = NO LAST NAME
            BCTR    R1,0                    GET EXECUTE LEN
            EX      R1,MOVENAME             MOVE LAST NAME
            LA      R3,1(R1,R3)         POINT TO NEXT OUTPUT BYTE
NO_LAST     EQU     *
```

TRT provides a good place to use this technique. We can specify the name of the routine to handle special cases by coding values of X'04', X'08', X'0C', X'10', and other hexadecimal values in ascending sequence that are multiples of 4. For example, if we wanted to scan for several different types of punctuation symbols in a field called OBJECT and process each one differently, we would use the following code:

```
*          SET UP TABLE
           XC     SCANTAB,SCANTAB     SET SCANTAB TO ALL X'00'
           MVI    SCANTAB+C' ',X'04'  STOP ON BLANK,
           MVI    SCANTAB+C',',X'08'  COMMA,
           MVI    SCANTAB+C'.',X'0C'  PERIOD,
           MVI    SCANTAB+C'-',X'10'  AND DASH
           SR     R2,R2               CLEAR REGISTER 2
           TRT    OBJECT,SCANTAB      LOOK FOR SPACE, ETC.
           B      BRANCHTB(R2)        JUMP INTO BRANCH TABLE
BRANCHTB   EQU    *
           B      NOHIT               NO HIT CHARACTER
           B      BLANK               STOPPED ON BLANK
           B      COMMA               STOPPED ON COMMA
           B      PERIOD              STOPPED ON PERIOD
           B      DASH                STOPPED ON DASH
```

Note that we don't need a limit check at the beginning, since we set up the tables and controlled the values ourselves. Such a check is essential, however, when dealing with variables created by another program or from input data.

The reason why this works is that since register 2 will receive whatever nonzero value is found in the scan table, what you code in the table will automatically become the branch index.

20.6.2 Reverse Scans Using TR String Reversal

Occasionally we have a need to scan in a right-to-left direction rather than in the left-to-right direction provided by TRT. This can be done in two ways. The first is to code a BCT loop using the CLI instruction, which uses the BCT index register as an index into the field being scanned. (We used a similar technique to set up TRANTAB in some previous examples.)

A second way, and one that may execute faster, is to reverse the field being scanned. For example, COBOL reversed would be LOBOC. (Isn't that a town in Texas?)

Some IBM CPUs have an instruction, called Move Inverse — opcode MVCIN — that will do this. Another way is to use TR to reverse the field. The way to do this is to fill the destination field — the one that we want to hold the reversed string — with descending values. These values should start with the value of the displacement of the last (rightmost) byte of the field to be reversed. They should end with a byte value of 0.

TR can then use the field to be reversed as the second operand. We don't have to provide a full 256-byte table for this esoteric use, since the index values we set up don't exceed the length of the field.

For example, if we wanted to reverse the bytes in OBJECT and place them in a field called TCEJBO (yes, that's OBJECT spelled backwards), we could code

```
         LA    R2,TCEJBO              FIELD TO FILL
         LA    R3,L'OBJECT-1          LENGTH OF FIELD TO REVERSE-1
POOL     EQU   *                      (LOOP SPELT BACKWARDS)
         STC   R3,0(R2)               STORE INDEX BYTE VALUE
         LA    R2,1(R2)               POINT TO NEXT BYTE
         BCT   R3,POOL                LOOP THROUGH TCEJBO
         MVI   0(R2),X'00'            SET 0 IN LAST BYTE
         TR    TCEJBO,OBJECT
```

We can then use all our normal left-to-right routines to scan the fields. Note that OBJECT and TCEJBO must be the same length. Also note that both this technique and the MVCIN instruction have a limit of 256 bytes.

20.6.3   String Processing in Other Languages

Other languages provide character processing capabilities, although few approach COBOL STRING/UNSTRING in complexity or flexibility.

One example of this are the three functions LEFT\$, MID\$, and RIGHT\$ in the BASIC language. The corresponding code for these in assembler follows.

LEFT\$ moves the leftmost n bytes of a field. This is done in assembler by the MVC instruction with a coded length, such as

```
         MVC   RESULT(n),FIELD
```

MID\$ provides a simple UNSTRING capability. It provides n bytes from an offset into the field. An MVC with a coded length and offset provides this:

```
         MVC   RESULT(n),FIELD + offset
```

RIGHT\$ provides the last n bytes of a field. The offset coding is slightly different:

```
         MVC   RESULT(n),FIELD + (L'FIELD-n)
```

Other CPUs also have scanning instructions, such as SCANC (Scan for Char) in the DEC VAX architecture and SCAS (used with the REP instruction) in the Intel 8086 (IBM PC) architecture.

20.7   SUMMARY

We have covered the last three problem-state instructions in this chapter. From the discussion of UNSTRING, EXAMINE, INSPECT, and the other verbs in this chapter, you should have a general understanding of how character string manipulation can be done in COBOL.

In addition, we have covered the EX, TR, and TRT instructions. You should be able to construct a scan using TRT and EX from the examples. You also should be able to construct a translate or scan table for use with TRT or TR.

As this chapter has probably shown you, string processing is relatively complex. If you code programs to do this, use plenty of comments. Otherwise, maintenance is a serious challenge.

Things to Do

1. If you have access to existing assembler programs — do any of them use TR, TRT, or EX? Can you understand what they are doing in these programs?

2. Many installations have written assembler subroutines to scan character data and return individual keywords to a calling COBOL program. In many instances, these predate availability of the STRING and UNSTRING verbs. If your installation has these subroutines, can they be recoded in COBOL?

3. Similarly, many installations have subroutines to convert to displayable hexadecimal. If yours does, is the conversion algorithm longer than HEXCONV? Is the conversion function used often enough to make it worthwhile to convert to a shorter algorithm?

VSAM Processing In Assembler

In this chapter we'll build on the coverage of I/O processing in earlier chapters. This chapter also will introduce some of the concepts involved in random record processing, as compared to the straight sequential techniques used up to this point.

To do this, we'll present a general overview of VSAM processing, with some background history. We'll then discuss some general VSAM data-set organizations and concepts. With this information, we can then compare the assembler language macro facilities provided with VSAM to those used with other access methods, such as QSAM. Sample programs illustrate the techniques used.

COBOL provides many VSAM processing facilities and options. This chapter will generally show how to use similar facilities in assembler. However, this chapter stresses things you can't easily do in COBOL but can do in assembler.

VSAM is a complex access method, providing a wide range of options and features. This chapter is not intended to provide complete coverage of VSAM from the ground up. There are several books available describing VSAM, and you may find one of these to be a useful reference. One is *VSAM Concepts, Programming, and Design,* by Jay Ranade (McGraw-Hill, 1988).

You should know a little about VSAM to get the most from this chapter. Specifically, you should know how to use the VSAM utility program IDCAMS. This should include a general knowledge of the DEFINE and DELETE commands to create and scratch VSAM clusters, as well as the LISTCAT, REPRO, and PRINT commands to list file information, copy records, and print VSAM file contents. Additionally, you should be comfortable with the VSAM terms *cluster* and *control interval*. (Oversimplifying somewhat, a *cluster* may be thought of as a data set. A *control interval* is similar to a block of data in a logical sense.)

21.1 RANDOM-ACCESS METHODS: BACKGROUND INFORMATION

Up to this point, we've only used sequential access to read or write records. *Sequential access* implies that we will read all the records in a file and will write out a complete copy of the file if any records must be changed.

For many applications, sequential access is either desirable or required. For example, all accounts receivable must be checked to produce a complete listing of all overdue payments.

In many cases, however, sequential processing is wasteful or even impossible within the allowable time. For example, when processing a single transaction in an online system, it would be wasteful to read the entire file to find the one affected account. This also would provide for incredibly poor response times. (Do not try it. Trust me.)

For online systems, we must instead only read and rewrite the affected records rather than the complete file. To do this, we must be able to get to any record in a file at random. Hence this type of processing is often called *random access*.

A similar requirement exists for batch processing where only a part of the file is affected, such as producing reports for only selected departments. This is a variation that combines elements of both random and sequential access and is often termed *skip sequential processing*.

Back in the good old days of OS/MVT (circa the late 1960s), IBM provided several random access methods. These included BDAM and ISAM. Both allowed either sequential or direct access to a file.

BDAM—the Basic Direct Access Method — allowed random access to blocks in a data set. Access to individual blocks was by block number. (This was either by a 3-byte binary number or by special forms of disk address called TTR or MBBCCHHR.) A keyed search also was available that allowed limited searching for records by a key rather than by a disk address, but only if the starting point was established by the programmer.

The advantages of BDAM included minimum overhead if random access could be based on a record number. This was not always possible for many applications. BDAM's disadvantages included no easy access by a key (a special routine, called a *randomizing routine*, was required) and no access to individual records. (BDAM could only read physical blocks, not records.)

ISAM — the Indexed Sequential Access Method — has Basic and Queued variations (BISAM and QISAM). Access to records is by key (e.g., employee name) rather than by block number or address as in BDAM. ISAM maintained multiple levels of indexes, called *primary* and *cylinder indexes*. The primary index is a separate disk extent; the cylinder index is kept in the data set.

ISAM has two or three separate disk extent entities — data areas, index areas, and an optional overflow area for added records. The main advantage of ISAM was that access was available by a key that was unrelated to the physical location of data in the data set. This allowed applications with more complex access patterns, such as by name, address, and the like.

ISAM's disadvantages were its complexity and speed (or rather the lack thereof). ISAM uses very long channel command word (CCW) chains. (A CCW is a command to an I/O device, created for your program by access methods.) ISAM could generate up to 20 CCWs for operations such as adding a variable-length record. Additionally, ISAM has a complicated internal data structure. The use of disk-based hardware key searches led to very high channel utilization. This combination led to ISAM's earning the unofficial nickname, "Incredibly Slow Access Method."

21.2 VSAM DEVELOPMENT

Lacking a generally satisfactory random access method, IBM developed VSAM — Virtual Storage Access Method — and introduced it in the early 1970s. VSAM had design goals that included better space utilization, easier use for programmers (no randomizing routines), and improved speed for the types of access most used in online applications.

As part of its design approach, VSAM included replacements or equivalents for all the then-existing OS disk data management elements. These are shown in Table 21.1, which covers the equivalence of older data management functions and entities with those announced with VSAM.

Table 21.1 Comparison of OS and VSAM Elements for Disk Data Sets	
OS element	**VSAM replacement or equivalent**
1. OS catalog	VSAM catalog
2. Disk VTOC	VSAM catalog
3. Disk space (free and allocated)	VSAM dataspace
4. Data set	Cluster
5. Data area (all access methods)	Data part of cluster
6. Index area (ISAM)	Index part of cluster
7. ISAM overflow area	In data part of cluster
8. Cylinder	Control Area
9. Block	Control Interval
10. Record	Record

21.3   VSAM DATA SET ORGANIZATIONS

VSAM allows you to access a data set in four ways. The four data set organizations supported by VSAM are discussed in separate sections below. *Data-set organization* refers to several things, but mostly to how you can read, add, rewrite, or delete records.

21.3.1   Entry-Sequenced Data Sets (ESDS)

ESDS data sets are accessed similarly to BDAM data sets. Access may be either sequential or direct. For direct access, the programmer must supply a relative byte address (RBA) that identifies the location of the record. An RBA is a 4-byte binary number.

ESDS allows you to rewrite any record in the data set, but new records may only be added at the end of the data set.

21.3.2   Key-Sequenced Data Sets (KSDS)

KSDS organization allows the same type of access as ISAM allowed — selection of the desired record by a key field provided by the programmer. KSDS maintains a separate index and allows you to insert records at any place you desire.

The size of the key is defined through the IDCAMS utility program when the cluster is created. You may access records either by providing a complete key — one that is as long as the key defined with IDCAMS — or a generic key — one that is shorter than the complete key.

Generic keys are used for such applications as simple name searches. For example, if you wish to look at all accounts for names that begin with the letters "SMI." you could provide a generic key to position to the first name beginning with "SMI."

KSDS is probably the most frequently used of VSAM's data-set organizations.

21.3.3   Relative-Record Data Sets (RRDS)

RRDS organization was added to VSAM in the late 1970s to provide a variation on the ESDS type of organization. RRDS allows you to access records by record number, much like BDAM allows. Access to an RRDS follows most of the same rules as access to an ESDS. We will not discuss RRDS further in this book.

21.3.4   Linear Data Set (LDS)

IBM added another data set organization to VSAM in 1987 as part of Release 2.3 of the Data Facility Product (DFP). This data-set format has a changed control interval format and allows access to data across record boundaries. LDS organization will probably be used more frequently in future IBM software products. DB2 is a good example of this. We will not cover LDS further in this book.

21.4   VSAM CONTROL INTERVALS

VSAM uses a data structure called a *control interval* in place of the blocks of data in sequential-access methods. A control interval — which we will call a CI for the rest of this chapter — may be thought of as a *logical block*. It contains records in some sequential order but may be written as several physical blocks on disk, depending on the CI size.

CIs also allow different techniques when adding records. If you attempt to add records that don't fit into a CI, VSAM will separate half the records in the CI and place them in a separate free space area. VSAM then adds the record into its correct place in the appropriate CI. This process is called a *CI split*. Fig. 21.1 shows a diagram of a control interval.

Figure 21.1   Format of a VSAM control interval.

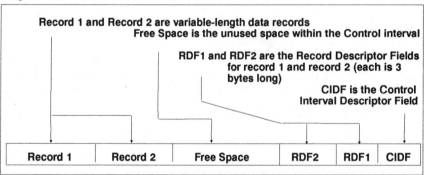

There is generally one RDF (Record Descriptor Field) for each record in a CI, with some exceptions that we'll describe shortly. They are stored at the end of the control interval and are stored in the reverse order of the records in the CI. Thus the RDF for record 1 is at the end of the CI. The RDF for record 2 precedes it, the RDF for record 3 precedes that, and so forth.

RDFs are 3 bytes long. They contain a 1-byte flag that describes the record and the 2-byte length of the record. If that records in a group of records have the same length, however, the RDF layout is different. The flag values include (in hexadecimal):

- X'00' = normal record
- X'40' = length of repeated records
- X'80' = number of repeated records

If all the records in a CI are of a different length, there will be one RDF per record and each RDF will have a flag byte of X'00'.

If, however, all records are the same length in a CI, there will only be two RDFs. One will have a flag byte of X'40' and will contain the length of the records. The other RDF will have a flag byte of X'80' and will contain the number of records in the CI that have the same length.

VSAM creates the RDFs in the same way if only some of the records in a CI have the same length (and are adjacent). In this case, VSAM will create RDFs with flag bytes of X'00' for records with lengths that differ from the records next to them. VSAM also will create the two-RDF series for any records that are adjacent and have the same record length.

The CIDF (Control Interval Descriptor Field) describes the layout of data in the CI rather than describing individual records, as does the RDF. Each 4-byte CIDF contains two values:

1. A 2-byte length of all the records in the CI
2. A 2-byte length of the free space remaining in the CI

The CIDF changes as records are added or deleted. It also changes as records are rewritten with different lengths. VSAM uses the CIDF to determine if a record will fit into a CI.

21.5 VSAM PROGRAMMING

Let's now turn to how VSAM I/O programming differs from the sequential QSAM macros we've used up to this point. VSAM uses different macros in place of some of the ones we've used so far and uses different formats of others. Also, processing for OPEN and CLOSE macros is different in VSAM.

21.5.1 The Access-Method Control Block (ACB)

VSAM uses the ACB as the equivalent of the Data Control Block (DCB) that we've used previously. COBOL generates either an ACB or a DCB depending on the access type of an FD. In our examples up to this point, we've used only a few entries in the DCB macro. Table 21.2 shows what operands of the ACB correspond to these.

You code an ACB similarly to a DCB. The OPTCD (option code) operand allows you to specify how you are going to access records (random or sequential), how you are going to process the data set (input or output), and similar information. A list of some of the values you can code in an ACB is given in Table 21.3.

An example of an ACB macro is

FILEONE   ACB   AM = VSAM,DDNAME = FILEDD1,EXLST = EODLIST, X
            MACRF = (ADR,SEQ,IN)

This ACB specifies sequential input processing for an ESDS. The DD name used is FILEDD1. FILEONE is the ACB name.

The reset option (RST in the ACB MACRF) essentially destroys the current contents of a VSAM cluster and should be used with considerable caution.

21.5.2 The OPEN Macro for VSAM

The OPEN macro is coded in the same way as the OPEN macro for QSAM and other access methods. OPEN processing for VSAM is somewhat different, however. With VSAM The success or failure of the OPEN for all the files involved is indicated by a return code passed in register 15.

Table 21.2   Some DCB Operands and Their ACB Equivalents

Function	DCB operand	ACB equivalent
Define control block name	DCB name field	ACB name field
Define JCL DD name for file	DDNAME =	DDNAME =
Define data: set organization	DSORG =	AM = VSAM
Define device type	DEVD =	Not applicable — VSAM data sets are always on disk)
Define record length	LRECL =	Not applicable — defined by IDCAMS RECSZ
Define block size	BLKSIZE =	Not applicable — defined by IDCAMS CISIZE
Define Macro types used	MACRF =	Combination of MACRF = in ACB and OPTCD in RPL
Define exit at-end-of data	EODAD =	EXLST = operand, plus EXLST macro

As a result, you should always check the contents of register 15 after opening a VSAM file. You should normally use the LTR instruction to do this. If the result is not 0, you should use the BNZ instruction to invoke error recovery or the reporting code in your program.

If you are opening several clusters at the same time, you may wish to be able to test each cluster to determine if it is open. One way to do this is to use the IFGACB DSECT macro. This operates much like the DCBD macro discussed earlier in this book. The following code will test an ACB to determine if it is properly opened:

```
LA     R1,MYACB              GET ACB ADDRESS
USING  IFGACB,R1             ADDRESSABILITY
TM     ACBOFLGS,X'10'        TEST OPEN BIT
BZ     NOTOPEN               0 - ACB NOT OPEN
```

Table 21.3 Some ACB Operands and Their Meanings	
Operand	**Meaning**
AM = VSAM,	Defines VSAM access method
DDNAME =	DD name, Same as other access methods
EXLST = label,	Defines exit list for EODAD/SYNAD/etc.; specifies the address of a VSAM EXLST macro
BUFNI = #,	Number of index buffers
BUFND = #,	Number of data buffers
MACRF = (KEY	Access by key
or ADR	Access by address (RBA)
or CNV	Access by control interval
SEQ	Sequential access
or DIR	Direct (random) access
or SKP	Skip sequential access
IN	Input processing
or OUT	Output processing
NRS	No-reset processing (normal)
or RST	Reset processing — used to scratch all the records in a cluster, but keep the space

You will have to include the IFGACB macro to do this elsewhere in your program. This should preferably be near the end of your program or immediately before your END statement if you have no other DSECTs. To include the IFGACB DSECT, code

IFGACB DSECT = YES

This DSECT allows access to other information about the cluster, and you may wish to review its contents. However, it is often preferable to use the VSAM SHOWCB macro instead, which we will cover in Section 21.5.6. Also, it's usually simpler to just open each ACB separately and test the return code in register 15 instead.

21.5.3   GET and PUT Macros with VSAM

Having successfully opened the ACB, we now may actually do some I/O to the file. To accomplish this, VSAM lets us use the GET and PUT macros with slightly different coding. Rather than coding a DCB name and record area, we instead code the address of a VSAM control block called a Request Parameter List (RPL). We'll go over the contents of the RPL in the next section.

A GET macro is coded as

Name   GET   RPL = RPLname

No other operands are required. *RPLname* is the label on a VSAM RPL macro. A PUT macro is coded as

Name   PUT   RPL = RPLname

with the same operand description.

VSAM includes several other macros that use RPLs to specify the request options. One of these is POINT, which allows us to position within any location (record) in a file that we specify. POINT is coded as

Name   POINT RPL = RPLname

This will be covered in a later example. POINT is used at the beginning of skip sequential processing to position a file at the appropriate place.

VSAM communicates the status of a GET, PUT, or other RPL-based request in several ways. One is in a return code passed back in register 15, in the same way as the OPEN macro. Another is through feedback fields in the RPL itself. The return codes are

- 0   Request completed successfully

- 4   Request not accepted − RPL was busy with another request

- 8   Logical error − see feedback field in RPL (RPL + X'0E') and VSAM manuals

- 12   Physical error − see feedback field as above

IBM provided a macro at one time called IDARMRCD that listed all the RPL error codes, but this may no longer be available or complete.

21.5.4   The VSAM Request Parameter List (RPL) Macro

The RPL control block is similar in function to a control block used in other IBM access methods called a Data Event Control Block (DECB). Basically, an RPL represents a single I/O request to VSAM. The RPL also has the status and any other feedback information from the request after it has completed.

Table 21.4 lists RPL operands and options. Many of the options only apply to specific situations, and coding an RPL is not as difficult as it may

Table 21.4   VSAM RPL Macro Options

Operand and options	Description
AM = VSAM	Specify VSAM access method
ACB = ACB name	Ties RPL back to ACB
AREA = Area name	Where data goes
AREALEN = #	Length of area
ARG = Keyfield	Label of field containing key
KEYLEN = #	Length of key
RECLEN = #	Record length for PUT
OPTCD = (	Options for this RPL:
KEY or ADR or CNV	As in ACB MACRF
SEQ or DIR or SKP	As in ACB MACRF
MVE or LOC	Move mode or locate mode
KEQ or KGE	Key equal or key greater or equal
FKS or GEN	Full key or generic key
FWD or BWD	Forward or backward processing
SYN or ASY	Synchronous or asynchronous
NUP or UPD or NSP	Update, no update, or note position
ECB = label	Event control block address for OPTCD = ASY
MSGAREA = area	Error message area
MSGLEN = #	Error message length

appear. The RPL reflects the numerous options available to VSAM assembler programmers.

A short discussion of each of the operands in Table 21.4 is appropriate here. You will have to refer to the reference books and manuals listed in Chap. 1 to get exhaustive explanations of all the options.

The MVE or LOC options determine where a record is placed after it has been read. MVE indicates that you want VSAM to move the record to a work area that you have provided. LOC means that you only want the address of the record. LOC is slightly more efficient but requires an extra base register and DSECT to access fields with many records.

If you code MVE, you also must provide an area to hold the record. You specify the name of this area with the AREA= operand. You also should specify the size of the record area in the AREALEN= operand. We will use MVE in our examples.

If you are processing a KSDS randomly, you also must provide several pieces of information regarding the type of key access. The options of KEQ or KGE indicate that you are looking for a specific record (the KEQ — key equal — option) or for the first record that matches or exceeds the key value (the KGE — key greater than or equal — option). The name of the field that contains the key must be provided in the ARG= operand.

If you want to find the first record that matches a given pattern at the beginning of the key — say, the first few letters of a last name — you may choose the GEN option. A GEN — generic — key search indicates that you are providing a short key. If this option is used, you also must code the KEYLEN= operand to specify how long the short key is.

The alternative to GEN is FKS. FKS specifies a full key search, which is what was described in the discussion of KGE or KEQ. FKS is the default.

You also may process a VSAM file either forward or backward. The FWD — forward — and BWD — backward — options specify this. There is also an option called LRD — last record — that is used to position at the end of a file with the POINT macro. We will see an example of backward file processing later in this chapter. As you would expect, FWD is the default.

VSAM also allows you to do other processing while waiting for an I/O operation to complete. This is specified with the ASY — asynchronous — option. When you use this method, VSAM gives control back to your program before the I/O has finished. You then have to use another macro — CHECK — to determine when the I/O operation is done. You also should specify the ECB= operand with the ASY option.

The SYN — synchronous — option operates more like the QSAM GET or PUT macros. It is also the default, is simpler, and will be used in the examples in this book.

Normally, you will either be reading an existing record with the GET macro or adding a new record with the PUT macro. The NUP option — no update — specifies this type of processing.

However, VSAM also provides options to update a record in place. The UPD option specifies this. You should provide a RECLEN= operand to specify the new record length when using this option, as well as with any PUT macro.

A third option, separate from NUP or UPD, is called NSP — note sequential position. This allows you to obtain the current location within the VSAM file for later use with the POINT macro.

The final two options listed in Table 21.4 apply to error reporting by VSAM. VSAM will provide you with an error message under certain conditions. To get this, you must specify the MSGAREA= operand to identify your error message area, along with the MSGLEN= operand for the area length.

If the preceding discussion has reached your cranial limits (i.e., your brain is full), some examples may clarify how the RPL works. We'll show a coded example and then proceed with details of the explanation.

21.5.4.1 Example: Read an ESDS sequentially

```
           GET    RPL = READ1
           ...
READ1      RPL    ACB = MAST,AREA = DETREC,AREALEN = 80,      X
                  OPTCD = (ADR,SEQ),MSGAREA = RPLMSG,         X
                  MSGLEN = 132
```

Notes:

1. READ1 is the name of the RPL and must be specified to read a record with the GET macro.
2. There is an ACB macro with a name of MAST elsewhere in the program.
3. The record is to be read into an area called DETREC, which must be defined somewhere in the program. It is 80 bytes long. We did not specify the MVE option in the OPTCD parameter, but it is the default.
4. The OPTCD of ADR and SEQ tells us that this is an ESDS being read sequentially.
5. If an error arises, VSAM may place an error message into a field called RPLMSG. RPLMSG must be defined elsewhere in the program and should be 132 bytes long.

21.5.4.2   Example: Skip sequential processing for an ESDS

```
        POINT RPL = RRDS
   ...
        GET   RPL = RRDS
   ...
RRDS    RPL   ACB = VSAM,AREA = OUTREC,AREALEN = 80,     X
              OPTCD = (ADR,SEQ),MSGAREA = RPLMSG,        X
              MSGLEN = 132,ARG = POINTARG
```

Notes:
1. The same RPL may be used for different macros. In this example, we are using the same RPL for a POINT macro to position ourselves to a spot in the cluster, and then we are using it later for GET macros. (Note that you can't use an RPL for two operations at the same time, however.)
2. The ACB is named VSAM (remember, no reserved words in assembler).
3. The AREA, AREALEN, MSGAREA, and MSGLEN operands are as in the first example.
4. We are processing by address (this is for an ESDS) and sequentially (SEQ).
5. The ARG=POINTARG defines the record location (RBA) where we want to start processing. This RPL and the GET and POINT macros are examples of skip sequential processing, where you may skip to various records in a file, then process sequentially.

21.5.4.3   Example: Read a KSDS backward

```
        POINT RPL = RRDS
   ...........
        GET   RPL = RRDS
   ...........
RRDS    RPL   ACB = VSAM,AREA = OUTREC,AREALEN = 80,     X
              OPTCD = (KEY,SEQ,LRD,BWD),                 X
              MSGAREA = RPLMSG,MSGLEN = 132
```

Notes:
1. This is a variation on the previous RPL. The ACB, AREA, AREALEN, MSGAREA, and MSGLEN operands are as previously described. The GET and POINT macros are similar to the previous example.
2. The OPTCD operand of KEY indicates that we are processing a KSDS.
3. OPTCD of SEQ and BWD means backward sequential processing, as in the previous examples.
4. LRD is used by the POINT macro to indicate that we wish to position to the end of the cluster. Note that no ARG operand is required for this.

21.5.4.4   Example: Direct processing for a KSDS

```
        GET    RPL = RRDS
...
RRDS        RPL    ACB = VSAM,AREA = OUTREC,AREALEN = 80,        X
                   OPTCD = (KEY,DIR),ARG = KEYFIELD,             X
                   MSGAREA = RPLMSG,MSGLEN = 132
```
Notes:

1. This differs from the previous RPLs by using direct processing (OPTCD=DIR) rather than sequential processing.
2. The ARG= operand identifies a key field elsewhere in the program. It must be as long as the key for the cluster as defined with IDCAMS.
3. The other operands are as described in previous examples.

We could provide many other examples of RPLs. However, the key point to be made from the preceding discussion is that you don't need to use all the RPL operands for a given request.

21.5.5   EXLST and CLOSE Macros with VSAM

When processing sequentially, we need to have some way of knowing when we have read the last record in a file. COBOL provides this with the AT END clause of the READ verb. The QSAM access method in assembler provides the EODAD operand of the DCB to specify a routine that should receive control when we have reached the end of file.

VSAM provides the same service in a slightly different implementation. This is with the EXLST (exit list) macro. EXLST specifies the address or name of several routines that may get control from VSAM under certain conditions. You specify the address of the EXLST macro as an operand of the ACB to tell VSAM which routines apply to which ACBs.

EXLST is coded with the following operands:

```
Name     EXLST AM = VSAM,                     X
               EODAD = (address,opt),         X
               JRNAD = (address,opt),         X
               LERAD = (address,opt),         X
               SYNAD = (address,opt),         X
               UPAD = (address,opt)
```

The *Name* operand is the name of the EXLST being coded. AM=VSAM specifies that this EXLST is for use with VSAM ACBs (as opposed to VTAM ACBs). The other operands specify routine types and have the following meanings:

EODAD =   End-of-data routine address
JRNAD =   Journaling routine address
LERAD =   Logical error routine address
SYNAD =   Physical I/O error exit routine address
UPAD =   User processing routine address

The EODAD routine specifies the address in your program to receive control when VSAM reaches the end of file while processing a data set sequentially. (It will not be invoked for direct processing.) This corresponds directly with the EODAD operand of the QSAM DCB and is the most frequently coded exit type.

The JRNAD routine receives control from VSAM for every request to the cluster. The purpose of this exit is to write a journal data set to assist in error recovery and backout. The journal file should contain any added, changed, or deleted records.

The LERAD and SYNAD routines receive control when an error occurs — either a logical error or a physical error. These are similar to the SYNAD exit in a QSAM DCB.

The UPAD exit allows you to do other processing while VSAM waits for I/O operations to complete. This option is not frequently used.

The *address* operand specifies the name of the exit. The *opt* field determines the status of the exit and possibly the location of the exit. The *opt* field values are

- "A" indicating that the exit is active

- "N" indicating that the exit is not active

- "L" indicating that the name provided is that of a program in STEPLIB or JOBLIB invoked by means of the LINK macro

"A" is the default. It means that the exit is available for use by VSAM if needed (active). "N" indicates to VSAM that the exit should not be used if the specified condition arises. This would normally be used when the exit was to be made available later (perhaps using the MODCB macro).

"L" is a special case of "A"indicates that the exit is available, but that it is not part of the program that holds the EXLST macro. In this case, the "address" field should specify a program name in your JOBLIB or STEPLIB libraries. VSAM will load in the program if it is needed. (This is the type of program access used with the DYNAM option in COBOL.)

The most frequent purpose of EXLST is to provide the address of an end-of-data (EODAD) routine. We will only use it for this purpose in this book.

Once we have established the EODAD exit and it receives control, we normally must close the affected files. VSAM uses the normal MVS CLOSE macro service to do this but adds the return-code function described earlier for the OPEN macro. You should test register 15 with a Load and Test instruction to make sure that it is 0, and write out an error message with the return code from register 15 if it is not. We will see examples of this later in this chapter.

21.5.6   The SHOWCB Macro for VSAM

VSAM provides several functions that are not directly usable by COBOL programs. One frequently useful example is the SHOWCB (show control block) service.

The SHOWCB macro allows programmers to obtain information from VSAM for error recovery, tuning and statistics, information retrieval, and just general foolishness. SHOWCB allows you to extract information from several VSAM control blocks, including the ACB, RPL, and EXLST.

SHOWCB is coded with four operands. These are

1. Control block type and name. You tell SHOWCB what type of control block is being interrogated and its name in your program. (This is the ACB=, RPL=, or EXLST= operands.)
2. The address of a response area where VSAM will put the data you requested. (This is the AREA= operand.)
3. The length of the response area. (This is the LENGTH= operand.)
4. The names of the individual fields you want to inquire upon. (This is the FIELDS= (field names) operand.)

Each of the control block names is mutually exclusive as an operand. This is so because you can only extract information from one control block at a time.

The FIELDS= operand provides many choices. Table 21.5 shows some of the more commonly used ones.

The information available from the ACB contains many of the fields that are displayed by IDCAMS in LISTCAT ALL output for VSAM clusters. SHOWCB returns the information in the area you provide one field after another. Thus you may access successive fields by coding "area+4", "area+8," and so forth as their address. Note that DDNAME is an exception to this, owing to its length, and that it will offset the next field by 8 bytes rather than 4.

The most common use for SHOWCB is to retrieve feedback and function code error information after an error is reported by VSAM. Whenever you receive a nonzero return code in register 15 following an RPL-based macro such as GET, PUT, or POINT, you should branch to a routine that issues SHOWCB to obtain this information. Two examples of SHOWCB are shown and explained below.

Table 21.5 Some Commonly Used SHOWCB FIELDS Operands		
Control Block Field Type: Name	**Contents**	**Length**
RPL:		
FDBK	Feedback code – further information about errors in a request	4
FTNCD	Function code – what was being done	4
MSGAREA	Address of a message area where VSAM provides error information (if available)	4
MSGLEN	Length of MSGAREA	4
EXLST:		
EODAD	Address of end-of-data (EODAD) exit	4
Exit name	Address of exit	4
ACB:		
CINV	CI size for VSAM data set	4
NCIS	Total number of CI splits	4
DDNAME	ACB DD name	8
NLOGR	Total number of records in cluster	4
NDELR	Total number of deleted records	4
NINSR	Total number of inserted records	4
LRECL	Maximum record length in cluster from IDCAMS DEFINE	4
NEXCP	Total number of EXCPs to this cluster	4

21.5.6.1. Example: Following an error in a GET or PUT macro

SHOWCB RPL = RRDS,AREA = SHOWPARM,LENGTH = 16,   X
       FIELDS = (FDBK,FTNCD,MSGLEN,MSGAREA)

Notes:

1. This is for an RPL named RRDS.
2. We have defined an area called SHOWPARM elsewhere in the program. SHOWPARM is 16 bytes long.
3. We want the VSAM feedback field (FDBK), the VSAM function code in which the error arose (FTNCD), and the address and length of a VSAM-supplied error message, if any.
4. The feedback field and function code are only 1 byte long and are right-justified. You may use the L, CVD, and UNPK instructions to print them in decimal.
5. The error message address and length will be 0 if no VSAM-supplied error message is present. (If your RPL specified a message area and length, you should use that message instead of getting it from SHOWCB.)
6. You can code a similar SHOWCB for use following an error in the OPEN or CLOSE macros for an ACB. In this case, the appropriate FIELD option is called ERROR.
7. In this example (assuming register 2 was free), to access the following, use the indicated code.

To access	Code:
Feedback code	L R2,SHOWPARM
Function code	L R2,SHOWPARM+4
Message area address	L R2,SHOWPARM+8
Message area length	L R2,SHOWPARM+12

21.5.6.2   Example: Using SHOWCB to get the record length for a cluster

SHOWCB ACB = VSAM,AREA = SHOWPARM,LENGTH = 4,   X
       FIELDS = (LRECL)

Notes:

1. This is for an ACB named VSAM.
2. The information is to be returned in SHOWAREA, which is 4 bytes long.
3. The value requested is the logical record length for the cluster. This will be the maximum record length for variable-length records.
4. To access the record length of a record after reading it, use SHOWCB with the RPL used to read it and specify option RECLEN.

    SHOWCB as used in the first example should be included in all programs that use VSAM. Note that SHOWCB itself may have an error. If

so, it will report it back to you in the same way as other VSAM macros —
by a return code in register 15. This suggests three recommendations for
coding with SHOWCB.

First, always save and print the original error value from register 15
before using SHOWCB. This will allow you to have some error information,
even though it is incomplete. Second, always test register 15 following a
SHOWCB. This goes for almost any VSAM macro. Third, you should include
a special error routine for SHOWCB only that displays the fact that an error
occurred along with the value from register 15. It also might be appropriate
to create a program dump with the ABEND or SNAP macros, since most
SHOWCB errors are user programming errors. Also, note that the length
of the area used by SHOWCB may be longer than the total of the fields with
no ill effect.

21.5.7   Other Useful VSAM Macro Instructions

VSAM provides many macros for purposes other than the ones we've
covered so far. These are summarized in Table 21.6. CHECK and ERASE
are probably the most important of the macros shown. The other have uses
for very specific or systems programming-oriented purposes.

For example, the BLDVRP macro is used by CICS or IMS/DB to
construct buffer pools when shared resources are used. The information to
execute BLDVRP is kept in the CICS File Control Table (FCT). For IMS/DB,
it may be provided as a separate control statement file. The TESTCB (test
control block) macro is related to SHOWCB. It may be used to test for
specific conditions, such as verifying that an ACB is open.

21.6   SOME SAMPLE PROGRAMS

Three sample programs appear in Figs. 21.2, 21.3, and 21.4, following
the end of the chapter. Figure 21.2 shows a VSAM program to do skip
sequential processing on a KSDS. Figure 21.3 shows a program to read an
ESDS sequentially. Figure 21.4 shows a program to read a VSAM file
backwards. These use the techniques discussed in this chapter.

21.7   SUMMARY

This chapter cannot provide a complete introduction to VSAM. There
are simply too many options to cover adequately in this space. However, the
points and examples in this chapter should give you a good foundation in
VSAM for further learning. Use of the manuals and books listed in Chap. 1
should allow you to understand most uses of VSAM that you may encounter.

Table 21.6   Other VSAM Macros
(Macros are listed by their general area of use)

Macro name	Purpose
General:	
CHECK	Check response to a GET/PUT/ERASE (used with OPTCD = ASY only)
ERASE	Delete a record
Control block manipulation:	
GENCB	Generate control block
MODCB	Modify control block
TESTCB	Test control block fields
Increased buffer control:	
ENDREQ	Terminates a request (like BDAM RELEX macro)
MARKBFR	Mark buffer for output or release control of buffer (like BDAM RELEX)
WRTBFR	Forces writing of buffers
BLDVRP/ DLVRP	Build or delete VSAM buffer pool
Mapping macros:	
IFGACB	Defines ACB DSECT
IFGRPL	Defines RPL DSECT
IFGEXLST	Defines EXLST DSECT
Special index access macros:	
GETIX	Read index
PUTIX	Write index
CNVTAD	Convert address — determines volume that holds a given record — not in all MVS systems

Things to Do

1. Find out if there are any VSAM application programs in assembler at your installation and review them, if possible.
2. If you have used IDCAMS, run and review the IDCAMS LISTCAT output for a cluster that is heavily used. Compare the output of LISTCAT to the fields available with SHOWCB as described in VSAM manuals.
3. Locate the feedback codes, function codes, and register 15 return codes in the VSAM manual available to you. (This information is often useful in decoding VSAM's message IEC161.)
4. Write a subroutine to provide SHOWCAT information for COBOL programs.

[This program reads in a file containing manual numbers. The program positions itself to read the record for the specified manual number. It then reads the five records beginning with the specified record. If an error occurs while locating to the specified record, the program prints an error message. If the program reads to the end of file while processing the five records, it also prints a message. (Comments on points of interest in the program are included in brackets.)]

Figure 21.2   VSAM sequential processing with a KSDS.

```
PROGNAME    CSECT
            STM    14,12,12(13)            SAVE REGISTERS
            LR     R12,R15                 GET PGM ADDR
            USING PROGNAME,R12             ADDRESSABILITY
*           CHAIN SAVE AREAS
            ST     R13,SAVEAREA + 4        OLD SAVE AREA
            LA     R2,SAVEAREA             NEW SAVE ADDR
            ST     R2,8(R13)               SET NEW SAVE AREA
            LR     R13,R2                  UPDATE REG 13
*           OPEN FILES
            OPEN   (INFILE,INPUT)
            LA     R1,INFILE               ADDR OF INPUT DCB
            USING IHADCB,R1                ADDRESSABILITY
            TM     DCBOFLGS,X'10'          TEST GOOD OPEN
            BNO    OPENERR                 NO - OPEN FAILED
            OPEN   (PRINTER,OUTPUT)
            LA     R1,PRINTER              ADDR OF PRINT DCB
            USING IHADCB,R1                ADDRESSABILITY
            TM     DCBOFLGS,X'10'          TEST GOOD OPEN
            BNO    OPENERR                 NO - OPEN FAILED
```

[Note that for each VSAM macro, we set up the macro name in the field called VSAMMAC. This can then be used by error routines to document what we were doing if a problem arises.]

```
            MVC    VSAMMAC, = CL8'OPEN'    MACRO NAME IF ERR
            OPEN   (VSAM,INPUT)
            STH    15,RETCODE              RET CODE IF ERR
            LTR    15,15                   TEST OPEN ERROR
            BNZ    OPENERR1                GIVE UP IF ANY
            SPACE 1
            PUT    PRINTER,HEADLINE        WRITE PAGE HDG
            SPACE 1
*           MAIN LINE PROCESSING
MAINLINE    EQU    *
            ZAP RECNUM, = P'0' SET UP RECORD COUNT
            GET    INFILE,INAREA    READ A RECORD
```

Figure 21.2   (Continued)

```
            SPACE  1
*           POINT TO RECORD WHOSE KEY WE JUST READ
            MVC    MYKEY,INAREA                 MOVE KEY VALUE
```

[The following is included as an example of how to use the MODCB macro to change a VSAM control block — in this case, an RPL. This MODCB macro sets the access type option in the OPTCD parameter to DIR (direct). We will then reset it back to SEQ (sequential) prior to reading the five specified records. Note that this is not necesary for the purposes of this program — a POINT macro also can be issued for an RPL with OPTCD=(SEQ). We are including it here only to provide an example of the MODCB macro.]

```
            MVC    VSAMMAC, = CL8'MODCB '       ERR MACRO NAME
            MODCBRPL = READ,OPTCD = DIR         RESET SEQ ACCESS
            LTR    15,15                        TEST RETURN CODE
            BNZ    CBERROR                      IF NOT 0, GO SHOW
            MVC    VSAMMAC, = CL8'POINT'        ERR MACRO NAME
```

[Position ourselves to the record specified in the input.]

```
            POINT RPL = READ                    POINT TO RECORD
            LTR    15,15                        TEST RET CODE
            BNZ    CHECKEND                     IF NOT 0, TEST EOF
```

[Issue MODCB to get RPL into sequential mode.]

```
            MVC    VSAMMAC, = CL8'MODCB'        ERR MACRO NAME
            MODCB RPL = READ,OPTCD = SEQ
            RESET DIRECT ACCESS TO SEQ
            LTR    15,15                        TEST RETURN CODE
            BNZ    CBERROR                      IF NOT 0, GO SHOW
            LA     R4,5                         SET UP LOOP CTR
            SPACE  1
```

[Read records sequentially from the VSAM file.]

```
GETNEXT     EQU    *
            MVC    VSAMMAC, = CL8'GET '         ERR MACRO NAME
            GET    RPL = READ                   READ A RECORD
            LTR    15,15                        TEST RETURN CODE
            BNZ    CHECKEND                     IF NOT 0, TEST EOF
            MVC    DATA,INAREA                  MOVE TO PRINT
            AP     RECNUM,ONE                   ADD TO RECORD CT
            OI     RECNUM + 3,X'0F'             SET SIGN BITS
            UNPK   NUMBER,RECNUM                MOVE TO PRINT LINE
```

Figure 21.2   (Continued)

```
        PUT    PRINTER,LINE              WRITE PRINT LINE
        AP     LINECT,ONE                ADD TO LINE COUNT
        CP     LINECT,P50                AT PAGE END?
        BL     GETLOOP                   NO - CONTINUE
        ZAP    LINECT,ZERO               RESET LINE COUNT
        PUT    PRINTER,HEADLINE
WRITE PAGE HEADING
GETLOOP EQU    *
        BCT    R4,GETNEXT                DO4 MORE RECS
        B      MAINLINE                  DO NEXT MANUAL  #
```

[The following is the end-of-file routine for the input file — not for the VSAM file.]

```
*              END-OF-FILE ROUTINE.
ENDDATA EQU *
        PUT    PRINTER,ENDVSAM           END-OF-VSAM LINE
ENDEXEC EQU *
        PUT    PRINTER,ENDJOB            WRITE ENDING LINE
```

[As with all the other macros, we set ourselves up to process an error in the CLOSE macro if one should occur.]

```
        MVC    VSAMMAC, = CL8'CLOSE '    ERR MACRO NAME
        CLOSE (VSAM)
        LTR    R15,R15                   TEST  CLOSE ERR
        BNZ    OPENERR1                  YES - ERROR
```

[Note that we are using the same routine for OPEN and CLOSE errors.]

```
ENDEXEC2 EQU   *
        CLOSE (INFILE,,PRINTER)         CLOSE FILES
        L      R13,4(R13)               GET OLD SAVE AREA
        LH     R15,RETCODE              GET RETURN CODE
        RETURN (14,12),RC = (15)        RETURN TO MVS
*              ERROR WHEN OPENING A FILE. END WITH RET CODE 16.
OPENERR EQU    *
        MVC    OPENWTO + 16(8),DCBDDNAM MOVE BAD DD NAME
OPENWTO WTO '     COULD NOT BE OPENED'
        L      R13,4(R13)               GET OLD SAVE AREA
        RETURN (14,12),RC = 16          RETURN TO MVS
```

[This program has four separate error reporting routines for different error conditions. This routine processes OPEN and CLOSE macro errors. The reason for the different routines is to report varying types of error information, depending on what is available.]

Figure 21.2   (Continued)

```
*           FAILURE OPENING OR CLOSING VSAM FILE
OPENERR1 EQU   *
         STH   R15,RETCODE              SET UP RET CODE
         MVC   OPMACRO,VSAMMAC
         CVD   R15,DOUBLEWD             DISPLAY
         OI    DOUBLEWD + 7,X'0F'       RETURN
         UNPK  OPR15,DOUBLEWD           CODE
```

[This SHOWCB macro extracts the ACB ERROR field — which is what we should report if there is an error on an OPEN or CLOSE.]

```
         MVC   VSAMMAC, = CL8'SHOWCB '   ERR MACRO NAME
         SHOWCB ACB = VSAM,FIELDS = (ERROR),          X
               AREA = SHOWPARM,LENGTH = 4
```

[Note that we test for an error in the SHOWCB macro as well. If the ACB has been destroyed by a storage overlay, even the SHOWCB may fail.]

```
         LTR   R15,R15                  GOOD SHOWCB?
         BNZ   CBERROR                  NOT 0, SHOWCB ERR
         LA    R1,SHOWPARM
         BAL   R14,HEXCONV
         MVC   OPERR,EBCDICEQ
         PUT   PRINTER,OPLINE1
         PUT   PRINTER,OPLINE2
         B     ENDEXEC2
```

[This error routine handles the situation where a VSAM macro fails which is not related to an ACB or RPL. In this case, we may be in serious trouble, and an ABEND might be appropriate. However, for programs that are being tested, errors in the macros are not unexpected.]

```
*           FAILURE IN VSAM MODCB/SHOWCB OR
*           OTHER NON-ACB/RPL MACRO
CBERROR  EQU   *
         STH   R15,RETCODE              SET UP RET CODE
         CVD   R15,DOUBLEWD             DISPLAY
         OI    DOUBLEWD + 7,X'0F'       RETURN
         UNPK  CBR15,DOUBLEWD           CODE
         CVD   R0,DOUBLEWD              DISPLAY
         OI    DOUBLEWD + 7,X'0F'       REGISTER ZERO
         UNPK  CBR0,DOUBLEWD            CODE
         MVC   CBMAC,VSAMMAC
         PUT   PRINTER,CBLINE
         B     ENDEXEC2
```

Figure 21.2   (Continued)

[This error routine is used to report errors following a GET or POINT macro. It reports the error information from the RPL.]

```
SHOWERR EQU   *
        STH   R15,RETCODE              SET UP RET CODE
        MVC   ERRMAC,VSAMMAC
        CVD   15,DOUBLEWD
        UNPK  ERR15,DOUBLEWD+6(2)
        OI    ERR15+2,C'0'             TURN ON SIGN BITS
        MVC   VSAMMAC,=CL8'SHOWCB '    ERR MACRO NAME
        SHOWCB RPL=READ,AREA=SHOWPARM,LENGTH=16,    X
            FIELDS=(FDBK,FTNCD,MSGLEN,MSGAREA)
```

[The feedback (FDBK) and function code (FTNCD) fields will identify a specific error for later debugging and should always be displayed.]

```
        LTR   R15,R15                  GOOD SHOWCB?
        BNZ   CBERROR                  NO - SHOWCB ERR
        L     1,SHOWPARM               FEEDBACK CODE
        CVD   1,DOUBLEWD
        UNPK  ERRFDBK,DOUBLEWD+6(2)
        OI    ERRFDBK+2,C'0'           TURN ON SIGN BITS
        L     1,SHOWPARM+4             GET FUNC  CODE
        CVD   1,DOUBLEWD
        UNPK  ERRFUNC,DOUBLEWD+6(2)
        OI    ERRFUNC+2,C'0'           TURN ON SIGN BITS
        PUT   PRINTER,ERRLINE          WRITE OUT ERR MSG
        L     2,SHOWPARM+8             GET ERR MSG LEN
        LTR   R2,R2                    TEST RET CODE
        BZ    ENDEXEC                  0, BYPASS 2ND MSG
        L     3,SHOWPARM+12            GET ERR MSG ADDR
        ICM   3,8,=X'40'               SET MVCL FILL CHAR
        LA    0,RPLMSG                 SET UP DESTINATION
        LA    1,L'RPLMSG               REGS FOR MVCL
        MVCL  0,2                      MOVE MESSAGE
        PUT   PRINTER,MESSAGES         WRITE  ERR MSG
        B     ENDEXEC                  GIVE UP
        SPACE 2
```

[This error routine determines if we have read past the end of the VSAM file or if we have tried to issue a POINT macro specifying a record that does not exist. If either of these happens, this routine prints an error message and continues with the next input request. If any other problem exists, it transfers control to the SHOWERR routine above.]

Figure 21.2 (Continued)

```
*          ROUTINE TO TEST FOR EOF FOR POINT OR GET MACROS
CHECKEND   EQU       *
           MVC       ENDMACRO,VSAMMAC        MOVE MACRO NAME
           MVC       ENDKEY,MYKEY            MOVE KEY VALUE
           CH        R15,=H'8'               RC = 8 (LOGIC ERR)?
           BNE       SHOWERR                 NOT =, SHOW INFO
           MVC       VSAMMAC,=CL8'SHOWCB '   ERR MACRO NAME
           SHOWCB    RPL=READ,AREA=SHOWPARM,LENGTH=4,  X
                     FIELDS=(FDBK)
           LTR       R15,R15                 TEST GOOD SHOWCB
           BNZ       CBERROR                 NO - SHOWCB ERR
           MVC       VSAMMAC,ENDMACRO        RESET MACRO NAME
           MVC       ENDCAUSE,ENDEOF         REASON DESC
```

[Test for the feedback code values that indicate end-of- file or record not found.]

```
           CLC       SHOWPARM,=F'4'          FEEDBACK 4 (EOF)?
           BE        ENDPUT                  YES, WRITE EOF LINE
           CLC       SHOWPARM,=F'16'         REC NOT FOUND?
           BNE       SHOWERR                 IF NOT =, REAL ERR
           MVC       ENDCAUSE,ENDNOREC       NO REC FOUND
ENDPUT     EQU       *
           PUT       PRINTER,ENDLINE         WRITE LINE
           B         MAINLINE                GO DO NEXT REQ
           SPACE 2
*          ROUTINE TO CONVERT FROM HEX TO DISPLAYABLE EBCDIC
HEXCONV    EQU       *
           MVC       HEXWORK(4),0(R1)
           UNPK      EBCDICEQ(9),HEXWORK(5)  UNPACK
           TR        EBCDICEQ(8),HEXTAB-240  CONV TO EBCDIC
           BR        R14                     RETURN TO CALLER
EBCDICEQ   DC        CL8' ',C' '
HEXTAB     DC        C'0123456789ABCDEF'
HEXWORK    DC        XL4'00',X'00'
           CNOP      0,4                     ALIGN FOR NEXT RTN
           EJECT
*          DATA AREAS
DOUBLEWD   DC        D'0'
SHOWPARM   DC        4F'0'                   SHOWCB OUTPUT
SAVEAREA   DC        18F'0'                  PGM SAVE AREA
RETCODE    DC        H'0'                    PGM RETURN CODE
INAREA     DS        CL80                    INPUT DATA AREA
VSAMMAC    DC        CL8'MACRO'              CURRENT MACRO
```

Figure 21.2   (Continued)

```
LINE       DC    C' '                              CARRIAGE CONTROL
           DC    C' RECORD '
NUMBER     DS    CL7                               RECORD NUMBER
           DC    C':'
DATA       DS    CL80                              DATA RECORD
           DC    CL36' '                           FILLER
ERRLINE    DC    C'-'                              CARRIAGE CONTROL
           DC    C' ERROR IN:'
ERRMAC     DC    CL8' '
           DC    C', REG 15 ='
ERR15      DS    CL3                               REG 15 (UNPKED)
           DC    C', FEEDBACK CODE = '
ERRFDBK    DS    CL3                               FEEDBACK (UNPKED)
           DC    C', FUNCTION CODE ='
ERRFUNC    DS    CL3                               ERROR FUNC CODE
           DC    CL(ERRLINE+133-*)' ' FILLER
           SPACE 1
ENDLINE    DC    C'0--'
ENDMACRO   DC    CL8' ',C' MACRO PROCESSING THAT BEGAN WITH '
ENDKEY     DC    CL8' '
ENDCAUSE   DC    C'              '
           DC    CL(ENDLINE+133-*)' '              FILLER
ENDEOF     DC    C' WENT PAST END OF FILE. ENDING REQUEST.'
ENDNOREC   DC    C' DID NOT FIND THAT RECORD.              '
           SPACE 1
OPLINE1    DC    C'0*** ERROR DURING:'
OPMACRO    DC    CL8' ',C'; R15:'
OPR15      DC    CL8' ',C', ACB ERROR:'
OPERR      DC    CL8' '
           DC    CL(OPLINE1+133-*)' '
           SPACE 1
OPLINE2    DC    C'0*** MESSAGE:'
OPMSG      DC    CL120'-- NO MESSAGE PROVIDED --'
           SPACE 1
CBLINE     DC    C'0*** ERROR IN '
CBMAC      DC    CL8' ',C'; R15:'
CBR15      DC    CL8' ',C', R0:'
CBR0       DC    CL8' '
           DC    CL(CBLINE+133-*)' '               FILLER
           SPACE 1
MESSAGES   DC    C'-'                              ERROR MSG LINE
RPLMSG     DC    CL132'-- NO MESSAGE PROVIDED --'
HEADLINE   DC    CL133'1 * * * RECORD LISTING * * *'
ENDVSAM    DC    CL133'0 * * * END OF VSAM DATA SET * * *'
```

Figure 21.2   (Continued)

```
ENDJOB    DC     CL133'0 * * * END OF REPORT * * *'
LINECT    DC     PL2'0'                      LINE COUNT
RECNUM    DC     PL4'0'                      RECORD NUMBER
ZERO      DC     P'0'                        CONSTANT 0
ONE       DC     P'1'                        CONSTANT 1
P50       DC     P'50'                       CONSTANT 50
          SPACE 3
*         DATA CONTROL BLOCKS
PRINTER   DCB    DDNAME = PRINTER,DEVD = DA,MACRF = (PM),      X
                 DSORG = PS,RECFM = FBA,LRECL = 133,           X
                 BLKSIZE = 0
INFILE    DCB    DDNAME = INFILE,DEVD = DA,MACRF = (GM),       X
                 DSORG = PS,RECFM = FB,LRECL = 80,             X
                 EROPT = ACC,EODAD = ENDDATA
          SPACE 3
VSAM      ACB    DDNAME = VSAMKSDS,MACRF = (KEY,IN,SEQ,DIR), X
                 MAREA = OPMSG,MLEN = 120
```

[Note that this RPL is modified by the MODCB macro shown previously.]

```
READ      RPL ACB = VSAM,AREA = INAREA,AREALEN = 80,           X
              OPTCD = (KEY,SEQ,SYN,NUP,KEQ,MVE),               X
              ARG = MYKEY,KEYLEN = 8,                          X
              MSGAREA = RPLMSG,MSGLEN = 132
          SPACE 1
MYKEY     DC     XL8'00'                     MANUAL # HERE
          SPACE 1
*         DCB DSECT AND REGISTER EQUATES NOT SHOWN
          END    PROGNAME                    END OF PROGRAM
```

The following program reads an ESDS sequentially and prints it. In addition to printing the record received, the program also prints the VSAM relative byte address (RBA) for each record. (Comments on the program are included in brackets.)

Figure 21.3 VSAM sequential processing with an ESDS.

```
VSAMESDSCSECT
        STM    R14,R12,12(R13)            SAVE REGISTERS
        BALR   R12,0                      ESTABLISH
        USING  *,R12                      ADDRESSABILITY
        SPACE  1
*       CHAIN  SAVE AREAS
        LA     R2,SAVEAREA
        ST     R2,8(R13)
        ST     R13,4(R2)
        LR     R13,R2
        USING  SAVEAREA,R13               DATA AREAS BASE
        USING  IHADCB,R1                  DCB  DSECT
        PRINT  ON,NOGEN
        SPACE  1
*       OPEN THE OUTPUT PRINT FILE
        OPEN   (SYSPRINT,OUTPUT)
        LA     R1,SYSPRINT                GET ADDR OF DCB
        TM     DCBOFLGS,X'10'             TEST GOOD OPEN
        BNO    BADOPEN                    OPEN FAILED - END
        PUT    SYSPRINT,NEWPAGE           SKIP TO NEW PAGE
        SPACE  1
*       OPEN THE VSAM ESDS
```

[As in preceding programs, test for successful OPEN.]

```
        MVC    ERRMACRO, = CL8'OPEN'      ERR MACRO NAME
        OPEN   (VSAM,)
        LTR    15,15                      CHECK OPEN ERR
        BNZ    GOBACK                     GIVE UP IF ANY
        PUT    SYSPRINT,HEADLINE          WRITE HDG LINE
        SPACE  1
LOOP    EQU    *
        PRINT  ON,GEN
        MVC    ERRMACRO, = CL8'GET'       SET MACRO NAME
```

[The GET macro will read records sequentially. No positioning in needed.]

```
        GET    RPL = RRDS                 READ A RECORD
        LTR    15,15                      TEST RETURN CODE
        BNZ    SHOWERR                    IF NOT 0, GO SHOW
        SPACE  1
```

Figure 21.3   (Continued)

```
*          GET THE RBA INFORMATION
           XC     SHOWPARM(16),SHOWPARM
           MVC    ERRMACRO, = CL8'SHOWCB'   SET MACRO NAME
```

[Use the SHOWCB macro to extract the RBA for the record we just read.]

```
           SHOWCB RPL = RRDS,AREA = SHOWPARM,LENGTH = 16,   X
                  FIELDS = (RBA)
           LTR    15,15                     TEST RETURN CODE
           BNZ    GOBACK                    IF NOT 0, GO SHOW
           LA     1,SHOWPARM                RBA (1ST WORD)
           BAL    R14,HEXCONV               CONVERT TO HEX
           MVC    OUTRBA1,EBCDICEQ          MOVE TO PRINT
           SPACE 1
*          WRITE THE OUTPUT DATA
           PRINT  ON,NOGEN
           PUT    SYSPRINT,OUTLINE
           B      LOOP
           SPACE 1
ENDESDS    EQU    *
           MVC    ERRMACRO, = CL8'CLOSE'    SET MACRO NAME
           CLOSE (VSAM)
           LTR    15,15                     CHECK OPEN ERR
           BNZ    GOBACK                    GIVE UP IF ANY
ENDEXEC    EQU    *
           CLOSE (SYSPRINT)
           B      RETURN                    RETURN
           SPACE 1
*          FAILURE OPENING A FILE - SET RETURN CODE AND QUIT.
BADOPEN    EQU    *
           MVC    RETCODE, = H'16'          SET BAD RET CODE
           B      RETURN                    RETURN WITH CC 16
           EJECT
*          ERROR IN SOME VSAM MACRO. PRINT INFO AND END
GOBACK     EQU    *
           SPACE 1
           CVD    15,DOUBLEWD
           OI     DOUBLEWD + 7,X'0F'        SET SIGN BITS
           UNPK   ERRRETCD,DOUBLEWD
           PUT    SYSPRINT,ERRLINE2
           MVC    RETCODE, = H'20'          SET UP ERR RETCD
           B      RETURN                    END EXECUTION
           SPACE 1
```

Figure 21.3   (Continued)

```
SHOWERR EQU   *
        CVD   15,DOUBLEWD
        UNPK  ERR15,DOUBLEWD+6(2)
        OI    ERR15+2,C'0'                 TURN ON SIGN BITS
        MVC   ERRMACRO,=CL8'SHOWCB'        ERR MACRO NAME
        SHOWCB  RPL=RRDS,AREA=SHOWARM,LENGTH=16,   X
              FIELDS=(FDBK,FTNCD,MSGLEN,MSGAREA)
        LTR   15,15                        TEST RET CODE
        BNZ   GOBACK                       IF NOT 0, GO SHOW
        L     R1,SHOWPARM                   FEEDBACK CODE
        CVD   1,DOUBLEWD
        UNPK  ERRFDBK,DOUBLEWD+6(2)
        OI    ERRFDBK+2,C'0'               TURN ON SIGN BITS
        L     1,SHOWPARM+4                 GET FUNCTION CODE
        CVD   1,DOUBLEWD
        UNPK  ERRFUNC,DOUBLEWD+6(2)
        OI    ERRFUNC+2,C'0'               TURN ON SIGN BITS
        L     2,SHOWPARM+8                 GET ERR MSG LEN
        L     3,SHOWPARM+12                GET ERR MSG ADDR
        ICM   3,8,=X'40'                   SET MVCL FILL CHAR
        LA    0,RPLMSG                     SET UP DESTINATION
        LA    1,L'RPLMSG                   REG FOR MVCL
        MVCL  0,2                          MOVE MESSAGE
        PUT   SYSPRINT,ERRLINE             WRITE OUR ERR MSG
        PUT   SYSPRINT,MESSAGE             AND VSAM ERR MSG
        B     ENDEXEC                      GIVE UP
        TITLE 'DATA AREAS'
DOUBLEWD DC   D'0'
SAVEAREA DC   18F'0'
SHOWPARM DC   4F'0'                        SHOWCB FILLS IN
RETCODE  DC   H'0'
         SPACE 1
OUTLINE  DC   C' '                         CARRIAGE CONTROL
OUTREC   DS   CL80                         REC  GOES HERE
         DC   C' RBA:'
OUTRBA1  DS   CL8                          RBA GOES HERE
         DC   CL(OUTLINE+133-*)' '         FILLER
         SPACE 1
HEADLINE DC   C'1'                         CARRIAGE CTL
         DC   C'-ASSEMBLER FOR COBOL PROGRAMMERS '
         DC   C' VSAM ESDS OUTPUT-'
         DC   CL(HEADLINE+133-*)' ' FILLER
         SPACE 1
```

Figure 21.3   (Continued)

```
ERRLINE   DC      C'-'                              CARRIAGE CONTROL
          DC      C' ERROR - REG 15 ='
ERR15     DS      CL3                               REG 15  UNPACKED)
          DC      C', FEEDBACK CODE = '
ERRFDBK   DS      CL3                               FEEDBACK CODE
          DC      C', FUNCTION CODE ='
ERRFUNC   DS      CL3                               ERROR FUNC CODE
          DC      CL85' '                           FILLER
          SPACE 1
MESSAGESDC        C'-'                              ERROR MSG LINE
RPLMSG    DC      CL132' '                          ERR MSG PUT HERE
          SPACE 1
ERRLINE2  DC      C'-********ERROR AROSE ON:'
ERRMACRO  DC      CL8' ',C' RETURN CODE:'
ERRRETCDDC        CL2' '
          DC      CL(ERRLINE2 + 133-*)' '           FILLER
          SPACE 1
NEWPAGE   DC      CL133'1'                          SKIP TO NEW PAGE
          EJECT
          PRINT   ON,GEN                            MACRO EXPANSIONS
```

[The options of ADR and SEQ are used to read an ESDS sequentially.]

```
VSAM      ACB     DDNAME = RRDS,MACRF = (ADR,SEQ),EXLST = STOP
          SPACE 1
```

[We use the same options in the RPL.]

```
RRDS      RPL     ACB = VSAM,AREA = OUTREC,AREALEN = 80,        X
                  OPTCD = (ADR,SEQ),MSGAREA = RPLMSG,           X
                  MSGLEN = 132
          SPACE 1
STOP      EXLST   EODAD = ENDESDS
```

(The RETURN and HEXCONV routines, SYSPRINT DCB, DCBD DSECT, and register equates are not shown. The are not changed from previous examples.)

In addition to reading a file backwards, this program also provides an example of how to extract statistical information about a VSAM cluster. (Comments on the program are included in brackets.)

Figure 21.4   VSAM backwards processing and SHOWCB example.

```
VSAMKSDS CSECT
         STM    R14,R12,12(R13)               SAVE REGISTERS
         BASR   R12,0                         ESTABLISH
         USING  *,R12                         ADDRESSABILITY
         SPACE  1
*        CHAIN  SAVE AREAS
         LA     R2,SAVEAREA
         ST     R2,8(R13)
         ST     R13,4(R2)
         LR     R13,R2
         USING  SAVEAREA,R13                  DATA AREAS BASE
         USING  IHADCB,R1                     DCB  DSECT
         PRINT  ON,NOGEN
         SPACE  1
*        OPEN THE OUTPUT PRINT FILE
         OPEN   (SYSPRINT,OUTPUT)
         LA     R1,SYSPRINT                   GET ADDR OF DCB
         TM     DCBOFLGS,X'10'                TEST  GOOD OPEN
         BNO    BADOPEN                       OPEN FAILED - END
         SPACE  1
*        OPEN THE VSAM KSDS
         MVC    ERRMACRO,=CL8'OPEN'  SET UP MACRO NAME
         OPEN   (VSAM,)
         LTR    15,15                         CHECK OPEN ERR
         BNZ    GOBACK                        GIVE UP IF ANY
         PUT    SYSPRINT,HEADLINE             WRITE HDG LINE
         SPACE  1
*        POINT TO END OF DATA SET
         MVC    ERRMACRO,=CL8'POINT'          ERR MACRO NAME
```

[For this program, we will generalize the error reporting routine by placing the RPL address into register 3 before each request.]

```
         LA     R3,RRDS                       SET RPL ADDRESS
```

[The POINT macro uses an RPL that has the LRD (last record) option. This causes VSAM to position to read from the end of the cluster.]

```
         POINT  RPL=RRDS                      POINT TO END
         LTR    15,15                         TEST RET CODE
         BNZ    SHOWERR                       IF NOT 0, GO SHOW
         SPACE  1
```

Figure 21.4   (Continued)

```
LOOP     EQU   *
         PRINT ON,GEN
         MVC   ERRMACRO, = CL8'GET'      ERR MACRO NAME
         LA    R3,RRDS                   SET RPL ADDRESS
```

[The RPL also has the BWD option, which causes VSAM to read the file backwards.]

```
         GET   RPL = RRDS                READ A RECORD
         LTR   15,15                     TEST RET CODE
         BNZ   SHOWERR                   IF NOT 0, GO SHOW
         SPACE 1
*        GET THE RBA INFORMATION
         XC    SHOWPARM(16),SHOWPARM
         MVC   ERRMACRO, = CL8'SHOWCB'   ERR MACRO NAME
```

[Extract the RBA just for general information.]

```
         SHOWCB RPL = RRDS,AREA = SHOWPARM,LENGTH = 16,   X
               FIELDS = (RBA)
         LTR   15,15                     TEST RET CODE
         BNZ   GOBACK                    IF NOT 0, GO SHOW
         LA    1,SHOWPARM                RBA (1ST WORD)
         BAL   R14,HEXCONV               CONVERT TO HEX
         MVC   OUTRBA1,EBCDICEQ          MOVE TO PRINT
         SPACE 1
*        WRITE THE OUTPUT DATA
         PRINT ON,NOGEN
         PUT   SYSPRINT,OUTLINE
         B     LOOP
         SPACE 1
ENDKSDS  EQU   *
*        GET AND PRINT SOME STATISTICS JUST FOR FUN
         XC    SHOWPARM(16),SHOWPARM
         MVC   ERRMACRO, = CL8'SHOWCB' SET UP MACRO NAME
```

[At this point, we obtain some statistics about the VSAM cluster and print them. You might want to look at other fields as well.]

```
         SHOWCB ACB = VSAM,AREA = SHOWPARM,LENGTH = 16,   X
               FIELDS = (NEXCP,NLOGR,NCIS,NSSS)
         LTR   15,15                     TEST RETURN CODE
         BNZ   GOBACK                    IF NOT 0, GO SHOW
         PRINT ON,GEN
```

Figure 21.4   (Continued)

```
           L     R1,SHOWPARM              GET # OF EXCPS
           CVD   R1,DOUBLEWD              CONV TO PACKED
           OI    DOUBLEWD+7,X'0F'         SET SIGN BITS
           UNPK  STATEXCP,DOUBLEWD        UNPACK
           L     R1,SHOWPARM+4            # OF  RECS IN KSDS
           CVD   R1,DOUBLEWD              CONV TO PACKED
           OI    DOUBLEWD+7,X'0F'         SET SIGN BITS
           UNPK  STATRCDS,DOUBLEWD        UNPACK
           L     R1,SHOWPARM+8            # OF C. I. SPLITS
           CVD   R1,DOUBLEWD              CONV TO PACKED
           OI    DOUBLEWD+7,X'0F'         SET SIGN BITS
           UNPK  STATCIS,DOUBLEWD         UNPACK
           L     R1,SHOWPARM+12           # OF C.A. SPLITS
           CVD   R1,DOUBLEWD              CONV TO PACKED
           OI    DOUBLEWD+7,X'0F'         SET SIGN BITS
           UNPK  STATCAS,DOUBLEWD         UNPACK
           PUT   SYSPRINT,STATLINE        PRINT LINE
           SPACE 1
           MVC   ERRMACRO,=CL8'CLOSE'     ERR MACRO NAME
           CLOSE (VSAM)
           LTR   15,15                    CHECK  CLOSE ERR
           BNZ   GOBACK                   GIVE UP IF ANY
ENDEXEC    EQU   *
           CLOSE (SYSPRINT)
           B     RETURN                   RETURN
           SPACE 1
*          FAILURE IN FILE OPEN - SET BAD RETURN CODE AND QUIT
BADOPEN    EQU   *
           MVC   RETCODE,=H'16'           SET BAD RET CODE
           B     RETURN                   RET WITH CC = 16
           EJECT
*          ERROR IN SOME VSAM MACRO. PRINT INFO AND END
GOBACK     EQU   *
           SPACE 1
           CVD   15,DOUBLEWD
           OI    DOUBLEWD+7,X'0F'         SET SIGN BITS
           UNPK  ERRRETCD,DOUBLEWD
           PUT   SYSPRINT,ERRLINE2
           MVC   RETCODE,=H'20'           ERROR RET CODE
           B     RETURN                   END EXECUTION
           SPACE 1
SHOWERR    EQU   *
           CVD   15,DOUBLEWD
           UNPK  ERR15,DOUBLEWD+6(2)
```

Figure 21.4   (Continued)

```
            OI      ERR15+2,C'0'                    TURN ON SIGN BITS
            MVC     ERRMAC2,ERRMACRO                COPY ERROMACRO
            MVC     ERRMACRO,=CL8'SHOWCB'           SET MACRO NAME
            SHOWCB  RPL=(3),AREA=SHOWPARM,LENGTH=16,              X
                    FIELDS=(FDBK,FTNCD,MSGLEN,MSGAREA)
            LTR     15,15                           TEST RETURN CODE
            BNZ     GOBACK                          IF NOT 0, GO SHOW
            L       1,SHOWPARM                      FEEDBACK CODE
            CVD     1,DOUBLEWD
            UNPK    ERRFDBK,DOUBLEWD+6(2)
            OI      ERRFDBK+2,C'0'                  TURN ON SIGN BITS
            L       1,SHOWPARM+4                    GET FUNC CODE
            CVD     1,DOUBLEWD
            UNPK    ERRFUNC,DOUBLEWD+6(2)
            OI      ERRFUNC+2,C'0'                  TURN ON SIGN BITS
            L       2,SHOWPARM+8                    ERROR MSG LEN
            L       3,SHOWPARM+12                   ERR MSG ADDR
            ICM     3,8,=X'40'                      SET MVCL FILL CHAR
            LA      0,RPLMSG                        SET DESTINATION
            LA      1,L'RPLMSG                      REGS FOR MVCL
            MVCL    0,2                             MOVE MESSAGE
            PUT     SYSPRINT,ERRLINE                WRITE OUR ERR MSG
            PUT     SYSPRINT,MESSAGES               AND VSAM ERR MSG
            B       ENDEXEC                         GIVE UP
            SPACE   1
PACKPARM    PACK    DOUBLEWD,2(0,R1)                PACK
            TITLE   'DATA AREAS'
DOUBLEWD    DC                                      D'0
SAVEAREA    DC      18F'0'
SHOWPARM    DC      4F'0'                           SHOWCB PROVIDES
RETCODE     DC      H'0'
            SPACE   1
OUTLINE     DC      C' '                            CARRIAGE CTL
OUTREC      DS      CL80                            REC GOES HERE
            DC      C' RBA:'
OUTRBA1     DS      CL8                             RBA GOES HERE
            DC      CL(OUTLINE+133-*)' '            FILLER
            SPACE   1
HEADLINE    DC      C'1'                            CARRIAGE CTL
            DC      C'-ASSEMBLER FOR COBOL PROGRAMMERS '
            DC      C' VSAM KSDS OUTPUT -'
            DC      CL(HEADLINE+133-*)' '           FILLER
```

Figure 21.4   (Continued)

```
          SPACE  1
STATLINE  DC     C'- STATISTICS - TOTAL NUMBER OF EXCPS:'
STATEXCP  DC     CL8' ',C' NUMBER OF RECORDS:'
STATRCDS  DC     CL8' ',C' TOTAL C.I.SPLITS:'
STATCIS   DC     CL8' ',C' C.A.SPLITS:'
STATCAS   DC     CL8' ',CL(STATLINE + 133-*)' '
          SPACE  1
ERRLINE   DC     C'-'                              CARRIAGE CTL
          DC     C' ERROR - REG 15 ='
ERR15     DS     CL3                               REG 15 (UNPKED)
          DC     C', FEEDBACK CODE = '
ERRFDBK   DS     CL3                               FEEDBACK CODE
          DC     C', FUNCTION CODE ='
ERRFUNC   DS     CL3                               ERROR FUNC CODE
          DC     C', ON MACRO ='
ERRMAC2   DS     CL8                               ERROR FUNC CODE
          DC     CL85' '                           FILLER
          SPACE  1
MESSAGES  DC     C'-'                              ERROR MSG LINE
RPLMSG    DC     CL132' '                          ERR MSG PUT HERE
          SPACE  1
ERRLINE2  DC     C'-********ERROR AROSE ON:'
ERRMACRO  DC     CL8' ',C' RETURN CODE:'
ERRRETCD  DC     CL2' '
          DC     CL(ERRLINE2 + 133-*)' '           FILLER
          EJECT
          PRINT  ON,NOGEN                          PRINT MACROS
VSAM      ACB    DDNAME = RRDS,MACRF = (KEY,SEQ),EXLST = STOP
          SPACE  1
```

[Note added values in OPTCD.]

```
RRDS      RPL    ACB = VSAM,AREA = OUTREC,AREALEN = 80,      X
                 OPTCD = (KEY,SEQ,LRD,BWD),                  X
                 MSGAREA = RPLMSG,MSGLEN = 132
          SPACE  1
STOP      EXLST  EODAD = ENDKSDS
. . . . . . . . .
```

(The RETURN and HEXCONV routines, SYSPRINT DCB, DCBD DSECT,
and register equates are not shown. The are not changed from previous
examples.)

Introduction to Macro Instructions

And now for something completely different. Assembler's macro facility is unlike anything in COBOL. It allows you to essentially define your own instruction set, extending the IBM assembler instructions and MVS macros.

COBOL has one facility that has some similarities to assembler macros. This is the REPLACING option of the COPY statement, which allows you to modify the copied code. However, macros provide many more services.

Another MVS service which may provide a better analogy is the JCL cataloged procedures in MVS JCL. Similarly, CMS EXECs are like macros in many ways. We will use the JCL procedure analogy for most of our compare-and-contrast examples. However, macros provide several unique functions beyond those allowed with JCL procedures or CMS EXECs. In MVS, the best analogy to macro instructions may be TSO CLISTs, and if you're familiar with these, you understand many macro concepts already.

In this chapter we'll cover some of the services available with assembler language macros. We will illustrate this by coding a macro and adding features to it to show how different services work. At the end of this chapter you will have a general understanding of macros and should be able to research any further points with the aid of the assembler language manual.

Uses of macros include the easy repetition of frequently used, complex code. This often occurs when creating complex data areas (e.g., MVS system generation, CICS tables and terminal maps, etc.). Macros are applicable anywhere that you need customization of code based of assembly-time parameters.

22.1 OVERVIEW OF THE MACRO PROCESS

Assembler language macros require much of the same preparation as a cataloged procedure in JCL. Like a procedure, macros are specially coded sets of ordinary instructions which are processed differently to produce a changed set of instructions.

To use a macro, you must code it and place it somewhere where the assembler can access it when needed. Like a cataloged procedure, this is usually in a separate macro library that is unique to your installation—this corresponds to a procedure library. Also like a cataloged procedure, you may test the macro by coding it ahead of the rest of your program—just like coding a JCL procedure with PROC and PEND statements.

The analogy with cataloged procedures continues when it comes time to invoke the macro. Just like cataloged procedures, you must code the name of the macro as an instruction, along with any parameters you wish to use to change the macro. The assembler then processes the macro instruction, changing it with the parameters you supplied. The assembler prints the changed statements on the listing with a '+' preceding them to identify them as code generated by the macro instruction. (Similarly, the JCL processor prints 'XX' instead of '//' for procedure statements.)

The analogy with JCL cataloged procedures fails, however, at this point. The code generated by a macro need not be a one-for-one copy of the macro you coded. In JCL, what you code in the cataloged procedure is what you get in the execution JCL. We'll be describing this process further later in this chapter.

To summarize the macro process up to this point, though:

- You must code macro instructions before you can use them.

- You must place them where the assembler can get them when needed — either in a special macro library or at the beginning of your program.

- You code the macro name in your program to invoke (call in) the macro.

- The assembler modifies the macro based on the parameters you provide when you invoke the macro. The assembler treats the code that results from the macro just as though you had coded it in your program at that point.

- The assembler prints the instructions that result from the macro with a '+' sign to identify them.

22.1.1 Sources of Macros

Generally, most MVS macro instructions are placed in the system macro library — SYS1.MACLIB. Your installation may have user-provided libraries in addition to or instead of SYS1.MACLIB. IBM also provides some special system macro libraries, called *distribution libraries*. These include SYS1.AMODGEN, SYS1.MODGEN, and SYS1.ATSOMAC. These usually include DSECTs for many MVS control blocks, similar to the DCBD macro.

VM provides six primary macro libraries. These are

DMSSP	MACLIB	VM/SP macros
CMSLIB	MACLIB	Older CMS macros from VM/370
OSMACRO	MACLIB	OS macros which CMS simulates
OSMACRO1	MACLIB	OS macros which CMS doesn't simulate
OSVSAM	MACLIB	Subset of supported OS VSAM macros
TSOMAC	MACLIB	Subset of supported OS TSO macro

You access these by means of the GLOBAL MACLIB command. To access all of these, you could enter the command

MACLIB DMSSP CMSLIB OSMACRO OSMACRO1 OSVSAM TSOMAC

Alternatively, include it in your PROFILE EXEC.

To look at the macros available in a VM MACLIB library, you may use the MACLIB command with the MAP option. Alternatively, the MACLIST command allows a FILELIST-like view of the macros within a MACLIB.

In MVS, you may use additional macro libraries by means of JCL overrides of the ASM.SYSLIB DD statement for the standard IBM-supplied assembly procedures. ASMFC, ASMFCL, and ASMFCLG also have MAC and MAC1 symbolic parameter overrides. In VM, you just reissue the GLOBAL MACLIB command with the appropriate order for the MACLIBs.

For testing, you also may provide macros at the beginning of your program source. (We will show an example of this later.) In any case, the macro instruction format is identical from any of these sources.

22.1.2   Terms Used with Macro Instructions

We will use several special terms in discussing macros. Some of the more fundamental ones are

Macro definition — the set of statements that define the macro instruction—like a JCL procedure

Macro call or **macro invocation**acro invocation — what you code in your program to bring in a macro instruction— such as the EXEC statement in JCL which specifies a cataloged procedure

Macro expansion — what the assembler does to convert the macro definition into generated (expanded) assembler language statements based on your macro call

Formal parameters — variables identified in the macro definition (symbolic parameters, operands, dummy arguments)—like symbolic parameters in JCL

Actual parameters — what you code in the macro call— like symbolic parameters coded on the EXEC statement in JCL

The assembler processes macros similarly to how JCL processes a cataloged procedure, replacing formal (symbolic) parameters with the actual parameters that you code when you invoke the macro.

22.2 CODING MACROS

When coding macros, you provide four separate types of statements: a header, a prototype statement, model statements, and a trailer statement. The *header statement* identifies the start of the macro. It consists of the directive MACRO by itself. A label is not allowed, and no operands are permitted.

The *prototype statement* provides a similar function to the JCL PROC statement. The opcode field defines the macro name. The operands identify symbolic parameter names for later use in the macro and may be assigned a default value, just as in the PROC statement. The label field also should be a parameter, to allow you to place the label where desired in the macro expansion.

Taken together, the header statement and the prototype statement identify the start of the macro, its name, and any symbolic parameters, and together they provide functions equivalent to the PROC statement by itself.

Symbolic parameters identify variable names or text which the assembler must change when expanding the macro. They must start with an ampersand ('&') character. The next character in the name must be alphabetic. The final characters can be taken from the ranges of 'A' to 'Z' or '0' to '9'. Assembler H allows a maximum length of 61 characters. The older assemblers restricted the length of symbolic parameters to the ampersand plus 7 characters.

The following are some examples of valid and invalid symbolic parameter names:

&OPTION	Valid
&Z999999	Valid
&9999999	Invalid – starts with a numeric
&A	Valid
&LONGEST	Valid
&VERYLONG	Valid (in assembler H)
&NO_UNDR	Invalid – underscore not allowed

(If you remember our discussion of the assembler character set in Chap. 2, you may now know why we must take care when coding an ampersand in our programs. The assembler also will scan for ampersands outside of macros—but more on this later.)

Model statements are basically normal instructions with symbolic parameters coded rather than normal operands. They are comparable to the JCL you code in a cataloged procedure in that they make up the actual assembler instructions you wish to generate. You may use the symbolic parameters defined in the prototype statement in these.

In addition, however, the model statements may include several unique directives to control how the assembler processes the macro. These are called *conditional assembly directives*, and they can be used to direct the assembler to ignore statements or to reprocess some statements. You also may include local variable definitions, which allow you to define data that the assembler uses when processing the macro.

The end of a macro is marked by the macro *trailer statement*. This is MEND coded as the opcode. It is similar in function to the PEND statement in JCL but is always required in a macro. You may use special *sequence symbols* as the label. (Sequence symbols are assembler labels, 1 to 7 bytes long, preceded by a period. They are used when skipping or reprocessing model statements inside the macro.)

22.3   EXAMPLE OF A MACRO

Let's now look at a simple macro. We referred in Chap. 12 to the lack of a Divide Halfword — DH — instruction. What we will provide as our first example of a macro is one to perform this function.

Since there is no real DH instruction, we will use that as the macro name. The parameters for the macro will be similar to those for the regular fullword Divide (D) instruction—a register as the first operand and a storage location as the second operand.

We won't really simulate a divide halfword and put both the quotient and remainder in one register. Instead, the output produced by the macro will be the quotient of the division in the first operand register and the remainder in register 0.

Since we need two registers for a real divide operation, we will use registers 0 and 1 for that. We will use register 15 as the divisor.

The macro itself will be coded as follows: (the numbers in brackets refer to the notes that follow:)

```
[1]                 MACRO
[2]     &NAME       DH      &REG,&DIVISOR
[3]     &NAME       LR      0,&REG
[4]                 SRDA    0,32
[5]                 LH      15,&DIVISOR
[6]                 DR      0,15
[7]                 LR      &REG,1
[8]                 MEND
```

Notes:

1. The header statement (MACRO) identifies the beginning of the macro definition.

2. The prototype statement lists the parameters we will use in the macro. &NAME is the label on the statement that invokes the macro, if one is used. &REG is the symbolic name we are assigning to the first operandregister. &DIVISOR is the symbolic name we are assigning to the second operand.

3. This is the first model statement. Note that we provide &NAME as the label here. The assembler will replace &NAME with whatever is coded when the macro is actually invoked. The &REG parameter will be replaced with the actual value coded for the first operand.

4. This sets up the number to be divided in registers 0 and 1, just like a normal divide.

5. This gets the halfword value to be used as the divisor. The assembler will replace &DIVISOR with the value coded as the second operand when the macro is invoked.

6. Divide the two numbers.

7. Load the quotient from the division into the original register coded as the first operand. &REG will be replaced by the value coded when the macro was invoked.

8. This marks the end of the macro instruction.

We would place this macro definition at the very beginning of our program to test it. It could then be placed into an installation's macro library once tested.

Now let's look at what the assembler does when we invoke the macro. Assume that we want to divide the value in register 7 by a halfword in storage called WEEKS. We would invoke the macro by coding

```
        DH      7,WEEKS
```

The assembler would then process the macro to provide the following generated code (the numbers in brackets refer to the notes that follow)

```
[1]         +           LR      0,7
[2]         +           SRDA    0,32
[3]         +           LH      15,WEEKS
[4]         +           DR      0,15
[5]         +           LR      7,1
```

Notes:

1. No label was provided, so &NAME will be blanks. The first operand was register 7, so every occurrence of &REGS will be changed to 7.

2. There were no symbolic parameters coded for this statement and it was not changed.

3. WEEKS was coded for the second operand, so every occurrence of &DIVISOR will be changed to WEEKS.

4. No symbolic parameters in this statement, so no changes.

5. &REG was changed to 7.

If we had coded

```
CALCWKS    DH      7,WEEKS
```

the first generated statement would have been

```
        +CALCWKS  LR    0,7
```

because the assembler would have replaced each occurrence of &NAME with CALCWKS.

If this doesn't make sense at first reading, try coding the macro and running it with various values for the label, first operand, and second operand.

22.4 ADDING FEATURES TO THE MACRO

For the rest of the chapter we will expand on our discussion of the assembler macro facilities by adding features to the DH macro just described. Each of the features will show how additional features of the assembler language macro facility can enhance the macro.

22.4.1 Saving the Registers

One drawback to the DH macro as coded so far is that it uses registers 15, 0, and 1. These are fair game as far as macros are concerned, but there are situations wherein you may not wish to destroy the contents of these registers. In this case, you need to save the registers somewhere and then restore the old contents back when the division is done.

However, we don't always want to save the registers, since we often don't care what happens to registers 15, 0, and 1. Hence, to handle this requirement, we need to make saving the registers optional.

To accomplish this, we need to have the invoking programmer specify an option on the macro that tells us that we should save the registers. Thus we need to add a third parameter that will specify that we should save these registers.

One difference between symbolic parameters in JCL and in assembler is that assembler allows two types. The first, called *positional parameters*, are processed in the order that they are coded when the macro is invoked. The DH macro example uses positional parameters. The GET and PUT macros are also examples of macros that use positional parameters.

The second type of parameter is called a *keyword parameter*. These parameters are similar to the symbolic parameters used in cataloged procedures. They are coded as "keyword=value." They may be coded in any order. The DCB macro uses only keyword parameters, for example. You may assign default values when coding the prototype statement with keyword parameters.

To accomplish our intent of saving the registers, let's define an optional third operand called SAVE. The rules for using this are that coding SAVE=YES will cause the macro to generate a save area and save and restore the three registers after the divide is complete. Coding SAVE=NO will cause the macro to operate just as it did before. If nothing is coded, SAVE=NO will be the default.

Our prototype statement will have to be changed to reflect the additional parameter. It is now coded

```
&NAME       DH      &REG,&DIVISOR,&SAVE = NO
```

Note that we are providing a default value of NO here.

To invoke the macro and save the registers, we would code something like

```
DH      7,WEEKS,SAVE = YES
```

Now that we've coded the prototype statement and invoked the macro including the SAVE option, let's look at the further coding we need to implement it in the macro.

This case is an example where the macro must test for a condition and modify what is generated based on the results of the test. This is an instance where we need the assembler conditional assembly directives.

Conditional assembly allows the assembler to bypass statements in a macro instruction. This provides a branching capability during the assembly only. It allows the assembler to repeat the assembly of certain statements, which provides a looping capability in the assembler.

To do this, we must use some special assembler directives. These are

- AGO — This allows unconditional branching during the assembly step.

- AIF — This allows testing and branching during the assembly step.

- ANOP — This defines internal labels (sequence symbols) for use with AIF and AGO.

Before covering these, let's explain the term *sequence symbol* in some more detail. Sequence symbols are "internal labels" for a macro expansion. They are used as the target ("branch-to" label) of an AIF or AGO directive. Because they are internal labels, sequence symbols defined inside a macro can't be referenced from outside that macro. They follow the same conventions as symbolic parameter names but begin with period rather than an ampersand. Internal labels don't appear in the generated code.

Now onward to the conditional assembly directives. AGO is the simpler of the two conditional assembly branching directives. It serves as an assembler GO TO statement. It is coded with one operand—the sequence symbol to which we wish to branch.

The sequence symbol may be coded on an assembler language statement or may be coded on an ANOP directive. ANOP — the assembler NOP — serves a function similar to the EQU * directive. It allows us to define a label without generating any code. ANOP has no operands and should have a sequence symbol coded in the label field.

AGO and ANOP should be used together. For example, the following "branches around" the statement in the middle.

```
        AGO     .AROUND
        DC      C'IGNORED DC STATEMENT'
.AROUND ANOP
```

This causes the assembler to skip the DC statement in the middle. It will not appear in the listing and will not generate any code.

At this point, you must understand one concept before proceeding any further. An AGO statement is not a branch statement, and a B instruction is not an AGO statement. Similarly, sequence symbols are not labels. And normal labels cannot be used for the same functions as sequence symbols.

Conditional assembly directives have an effect during the assembly only. Strictly speaking, they do not branch. The function of AGO and AIF is to tell the assembler to restart the assembly as though the "branch-to" sequence symbol was the next statement in the input.

AGO and AIF have no effect whatsoever after the assembly. They are not machine instructions — merely directions for the assembler. AGO, AIF, and the sequence symbols they use must be kept entirely separate in your mind from branch instructions and the labels they use.

The real power of conditional assembly requires the AIF directive — the assembler IF statement. This is coded as

AIF   *(test).sequence_symbol*

The *test* expresses some relationship between two symbolic parameters. If the condition is true, the assembler then does an AGO to the *.sequence symbol* specified following the test. The allowable relations are

- EQ — Equal
- NE — Not Equal
- LT — Less Than
- GT — Greater Than
- LE — Less than or Equal to
- GE — Greater than or Equal to

(These are the same abbreviations used with the COND operand in JCL to test the condition code.)

For example,

AIF   (&PARM EQ 22).SEQSYM

checks to see if the symbolic parameter &PARM has a value of 22. If it does (is equal), the assembler starts assembling at the statement with the sequence symbol .SEQSYM. If &PARM has any other value than 22, the assembler continues on to the next statement.

Before explaining any more nuances of the AIF directive, let's see how we can use it in the DH macro. We need to check the &SAVE parameter. If it is equal to YES, we need to generate the instructions to save and restore the registers, as well as to create an area to hold them. (When testing for character values, we need to specify them inside quotes, as in a DC directive.) The test would be coded as

AIF   ('&SAVE' NE 'YES').NOSAVE

This tells the assembler to compare the value coded when the macro is invoked to a constant value of YES. If it is not equal to YES, the assemble should assemble starting with the statement that has the sequence symbol .NOSAVE. If &SAVE has the value YES, the assembler continues with the next statement in the macro.

With this code added, our macro now looks like this (the numbers in brackets refer to the notes that follow):

```
[1]              MACRO
[2]     &NAME    DH      &REG,&DIVISOR,&SAVE = NO
[3]              AIF     ('&SAVE' NE 'YES').NOSAVE
[4]     &NAME    DS      0H
[5]              STM     15,1,DHSAVE
[6]     .NOSAVE  ANOP
[7]              LR      0,&REG
                 SRDA    0,32
                 LH      15,&DIVISOR
                 DR      0,15
                 LR      &REG,1
[8]              AIF     ('&SAVE' NE 'YES').NOSAVE2
[9]              B       AROUND
[10]    DHSAVE   DS      3F
[11]    AROUND   DS      0H
[12]    .NOSAVE2 MEND
```

Notes:

1. No change.
2. We added the SAVE= operand with a default of NO.
3. This tests if the invocation coded SAVE=YES.
4. The label is moved to a separate statement. Since we don't know which statement will be the first instruction now, it's simpler to generate it on a separate statement.
5. Save the registers if SAVE=YES was specified.
6. This marks the end of the instructions to save the registers, if needed.
7. This begins the DH macro as we previously had it.
8. If we saved the registers, we need to provide a three-word save area. This tests to see if this is necesary.
9. Branch around the three-word save area.
10. Define the save area.
11. This provides a label for the branch instruction in note 9.
12. End of the macro. Note that we have put a sequence symbol (.NOSAVE2) on the MEND statement.

22.4.2   Sharing the Save Area

At this stage of development, the DH macro will save the registers. Unfortunately, it can only be used once in a program. This limitation exists because we have two hard-coded labels in the macro—DHSAVE and AROUND. This probably forces too great a limitation on DH, since we'd probably want to use it more than once.

(There are cases where only being able to use a macro once is a permissible limitation. For example, macros to generate complicated tables may have to create predefined name values. In this type of situation, having a hard-coded label is not necesarily bad. However, it's not a good practice in most cases.)

There are several ways to resolve this problem. One is to have the programmer supply the name of a save area when using DH. However, the reason for using macros is to simplify coding. Thus it's probably better for us to generate the save area automatically as required.

There are several ways to accomplish this, and we'll show one or two here. One commonly used approach to this problem is to define names with a suffix number that increases for each use of the macro.

The assembler provides a special symbolic variable to do this called &SYSNDX. &SYSNDX is a 4-byte character number value that increases by 1 for each macro used in an assembly. You can concatenate it to labels in your macro to provide unique names. For example,

```
LAB&SYSNDX EQU  *
```
produces
```
LAB0001 EQU *
```
if used in the first macro instruction invoked in a program. It would become LAB0002 if used in the second macro invoked in a program, and so forth.

For our particular case, we can change the DH macro to create unique labels for each occurrence of DHSAVE and AROUND. The affected statements of the macro would be changed to

```
            STM   15,1,DHSV&SYSNDX
            . . . . . . . . .
            B     ARND&SYSNDX
DHSV&SYSNDX DS    3F
ARND&SYSNDX DS    0H
```

This would generate values of DHSV0001, DHSV0002, and so on for the save area name and ARND0001, ARND0002, and so on for the label to branch around the save area.

This allows us to generate the save area as many times as necesary. However, it is not an ideal solution, since our simple DH macro now generates up to 34 bytes. The three fullwords used for storing the registers are wasted space, since we can't use them for anything else except saving the registers when executing the DH macro.

A better solution for this case is to generate one save area the first time the DH macro is invoked and then share that save area with all the other DH macro usages in the program. To do this, we need some way of communicating between the DH macros.

Assembler provides this as part of another feature — local and global variables. So far, we have only worked with symbolic parameters passed to us when the macro was invoked. Frequently, however, we need to have additional variables when writing a macro — variables that we can test and modify ourselves.

Local and global variables provide this capability. They are named and coded like a symbolic parameter. They may be tested with AIF, just like a symbolic parameter. Unlike symbolic parameters, however, they also may be changed by the programmer.

Assembler provides three types of variables. These are the arithmetic, boolean, and character types. The arithmetic types may hold any numeric value that fits in a fullword. Boolean variables provide a 1-0, true-false, on-off, and yes-no switch capability. Character values hold up to 255-byte character values.

While you may generally refer to local and global variables in the same way as you refer to symbolic parameters, you must define them differently. Symbolic parameters are defined by six directives:

1. LCLA —Defines local arithmetic variables (31-bit numbers)
2. GBLA —Defines global arithmetic variables (31-bit numbers)
3. LCLB —Defines local boolean variables (0-1)
4. GBLB —Defines global boolean variables (0-1)
5. LCLC —Defines local character variables
6. GBLC —Defines global character variables

Unlike symbolic parameters, local and global variables may be defined anywhere in your macro.

As an example, to define a local arithmetic variable called &VARNAME, we would code

    LCLA &VARNAME

We could then refer to it anywhere in the macro.

Once we have defined a local or global variable, we may assign values to it by the SETx directives. There are three of these — SETA, SETB, and SETC — which are used to assign arithmetic, boolean, or character variables, respectively. The format of the assignment statement has the local or global variable name in the label area and the desired value as the operand. For example,

    &VARNAME SETA 27

sets a value of 27 into the local variable &VARNAME. You may also do arithmetic in SET directives. For example,

    &VARNAME SETA &VARNAME + 1

This adds 1 to the current value of &VARNAME.

For our DH macro, we need to have some way of knowing if we have defined the three-word save area yet. If it has not been defined, we should define it. If it has been defined, we should store our registers in it if necesary. Since all the DH macro invocations should use the same name for the save area, we will use our previously defined names again (DHSAVE and AROUND).

Since we only have to communicate the presence of the save area rather than pass any variable values, we will use a boolean global variable to indicate if the save area is defined or not. We will call our variable &DHSAVEA. (We also could have called it &DHSAVE, since there is no relationship between variable names and true labels in the program. However, it's usually clearer to keep the names distinct.)

Before we can reference the boolean variable, we must define it. We do this with

```
    GBLB &DHSAVEA
```

The first time the assembler encounters this, it reserves a switch in its global data areas. Each subsequent time the assembler sees this definition (i.e., for each successive invocation of the DH macro), the assembler determines that the variable has already been defined, and so all references to &DHSAVEA will be to the same variable.

Having defined the global boolean variable, we must then test it. Boolean variables are switches, and they may be tested for values of 0 or 1. We can test the value of &DHSAVEA by coding:

```
    AIF (&DHSAVEA EQ 1).DEFINED
```

and the assembler will start assembling at the sequence symbol .DEFINED.

Since boolean variables have intrinsic values of true (1) or false (0), we also may code the AIF without a test:

```
    AIF (&DHSAVEA).DEFINED
```

and the assembler will process this AIF in the same way as the previous test.

When we determine that we have to generate the save area, we also must indicate to later invocations of the DH macro that the save area has been defined. To do this, we must set the value of &DHSAVEA to 1. The SETB assignment directive does this:

```
&DHSAVEA    SETB    1
```

Now let's see how our DH macro looks with this code added (the numbers in brackets refer to the notes that follow):

```
[1]                    MACRO
          &NAME   DH    &REG,&DIVISOR,&SAVE = NO
[2]                    GBLB  &DHSAVEA
          &NAME   DS    0H
                   AIF   ('&SAVE' NE 'YES').NOSAVE
                   STM   15,1,DHSAVE
          .NOSAVE ANOP
                   LR    0,&REG
                   SRDA  0,32
                   LH    15,&DIVISOR
                   DR    0,15
                   LR    &REG,1
                   AIF   ('&SAVE' NE 'YES').NOSAVE2
[3]                    AIF   (&DHSAVEA EQ 1).DEFINED
[4]       &DHSAVEA SETB 1
[5]                B     AROUND
          DHSAVE   DS    3F
          AROUND   DS    0H
[6]       .DEFINED ANOP
          .NOSAVE2 MEND
```

Notes:

1. Only the changed parts of the macro will have notes.

2. While you may code global and local variable definitions anywhere, it is customary to define them all following the prototype statement.

3. This tests &DHSAVEA to see if it has been set, i.e., if DHSAVE has been defined.

4. Set &DHSAVEA to 1 (true) so that later invocations of DH don't define DHSAVE again.

5. This code is identical to the previous version.

6. This defines a sequence symbol to allow us to bypass the save-area definition code.

Local and global variables have many other nuances. You should study the assembler language reference manuals to get a complete understanding.

22.4.3 Adding Messages to the DH Macro

The DH macro now saves the registers. Another enhancement that may be desirable is to notify the programmer that registers 15, 0, and 1 are being changed. In a perfect world, programmers would know the details of what registers are changed and other side effects of macros. However, in the real world, this is rarely the case.

For this reason, it's desirable to let the programmer know that the registers are being modified. Assembler provides two ways to do this. One is to code comments inside the macro instruction that are printed as part of the macro's expansion. The second uses the MNOTE — Macro Note — directive to create a warning message.

Macros may have two types of comments. One is the normal assembler comment, identified by '*' in the first position of the statement. These print normally each time the macro is expanded.

The second type of comment is intended to document the macro rather than provide information at the time of macro expansion. These are called *local macro comments* and are identified by ".*" in position 1 of the comment statement. Local macro comments don't print on the assembly listing when the macro is expanded.

Comments, however, are easily missed and won't print if the NOGEN option of the PRINT directive is selected. To provide a message that is flagged as an error, we can use the MNOTE directive instead.

MNOTE provides an assembly message that is written to the assembly listing. It also may cause the statement to be flagged in the assembler's error listing. MNOTE is coded with one or two operands. The first is a severity level, and it is optional. Severity levels are usually taken from the set of 0, 4, 8, 12, or 16. The MNOTE severity level will appear as the condition code for the assembly, unless there are more severe errors in the assembly.

The second operand of MNOTE is the message text. This is enclosed in quotes. It prints on the assembly listing. You may code a local variable, global variable, or symbolic parameter inside the message text. The assembler will replace it with the current value.

There are several typical use patterns for MNOTE, and we will give examples of each. One is the general informational message, with no error implied. For example,

       MNOTE 'WARNING - REGISTERS 15, 0, AND 1 ALTERED'

This causes the following to print on the assembly listing:

       WARNING - REGISTERS 15, 0, AND 1 ALTERED

A second general usage is a warning message. This uses a return code of 0 along with the message text. For example,

       MNOTE 0,'WARNING - SECOND OPERAND NOT A HALFWORD'

In addition to a message on the listing, this causes the statement to be flagged in the error listing. However, the assembler's return code will still be 0, unless there are other errors in the assembly.

The third general usage pattern is to produce an error message that affects the assembler return code. This follows the same format as the previous example but has a nonzero severity level. For example,

       MNOTE 8,'ERROR - REGISTER VALUE NOT ALLOWED'

We will incorporate these error messages later.

22.4.4   Checking the Input Values

For our last set of examples of macro facilities, we'll add some validation of the symbolic parameters. We can't validate the values at execution time, but we can verify the data items provided when the macro is invoked.

We should check two things. The first DH operand must be a valid register number, i.e., 0 through 15. If not, this is a serious error, and the LR and other instructions won't assemble properly. Next, the second operand should be a halfword. If it is not, we should produce a warning, but continue the macro expansion.

To "range check' the first operand, we can code some additional AIF statements such as

```
AIF     (&REG LT 0).BADREG
AIF     (&REG GT 15).BADREG
```

and add an MNOTE later in the macro with a sequence symbol of .BADREG.

To verify that the second operand is a halfword, however, we need an additional service from the assembler. This comes in the assembler's maintenance of information about each operand and symbol in the program. This information is kept as *attributes* and may be evaluated independently of the operand or label itself.

The kinds of attributes kept by the assembler include

1. The type of the parameter (T' attribute)

2. The length of the storage a symbol defines (L' attribute)

3. The number of subparameters in a sublist (N' attribute)

4. The count of the number of characters in a symbol (K attribute)

Attributes are specified by coding the attribute type (T, L, K, or N), followed by a single quotation mark, followed by a label in the program or a symbolic variable. For example, L'SAVEAREA requests the length of SAVEAREA. The assembler returns a one-character value for the type attribute and an arithmetic value for the other attributes.

The type of test we want to make here is to determine the type attribute of the second operand. To do this, we use the following AIF:

```
AIF (T'&DIVISOR EQ 'H').TYPEOK
```

This compares the character returned as the attribute to a value of 'H'. Attributes are normally equivalent to the type in a DC or DS statement. Several type attribute values are shown in Table 22.1.

Some notes are appropriate here on Table 22.1:

• Most labels on a DC or DS directive will return the type of the DC or DS.

• *Self-defining terms* are operands whose values are determinable from the operands themselves, such as 4 in the DH above.

Table 22.1 Some Type Attribute Values	
T' value returned	**Definition**
A	A-type address constant
B	Binary
C	Character
D	Doubleword floating-point
E	Fullword floating-point
F	Fullword binary
G	Fullword binary, explicit length (e.g., FL3)
H	Halfword binary
I	Instruction (e.g., label on an instruction)
J	CSECT
K	Floating-point constant, explicit length
L	Long (16-byte) floating point
M	Macro
N	Self-defining term, SETA or SETB variable
O	Omitted (see below)
P	Packed decimal
Q	Q-type address constant
R	Address constant with explicit length (e.g., AL3 or S/Q/V/Y type addresses with explicit lengths)
S	S-type address constant
T	External symbol (operand of an EXTRN)
U	Undefined or special (see below)
V	V-type address constant
W	CCW assembler directive
X	Hexadecimal
Y	Y-type address constant
Z	Zoned decimal
$	External symbol (operand of a WXTRN)

- *Omitted* operands are those which aren't coded when invoking a macro. For example, with our DH macro example, coding

  DH 4

  results in the symbolic parameter &DIVISOR having a type attribute of O.
- *Undefined* may mean that the label is not defined in the program or that it is one of a number of miscellaneous types. These include labels on a

LTORG directive, doubly defined symbols, EQU symbols, &SYSDATE, and so on.

When we add the type checks described above and the error messages described earlier (we'll also include another directive, MEXIT, which we'll explain shortly), our final version of the DH macro looks like this (the numbers in brackets refer to the notes that follow):

```
[1]                      MACRO
          &NAME      DH    &REG,&DIVISOR,&SAVE = NO
                     GBLB  &DHSAVEA
[2]                  AIF   (&REG LT 0).BADREG
                     AIF   (&REG GT 15).BADREG
[3]                  AIF   (T'&DIVISOR EQ 'H').TYPEOK
[4]                  MNOTE 0,'WARNING - &DIVISOR NOT TYPE H'
[5]       .TYPEOK    ANOP
          &NAME      DS    0H
                     AIF   ('&SAVE' NE 'YES').NOSAVE
                     STM   15,1,DHSAVE
          .NOSAVE    ANOP
                     LR    0,&REG
                     SRDA  0,32
                     LH    15,&DIVISOR
                     DR    0,15
                     LR    &REG,1
                     AIF   ('&SAVE' NE 'YES').NOSAVE2
                     AIF   (&DHSAVEA EQ 1).DEFINED
          &DHSAVEA   SETB  1
                     B     AROUND
          DHSAVE     DS    3F
          AROUND     DS    0H
[6]       .DEFINED   MEXIT
          .NOSAVE2   ANOP
[7]                  MNOTE 'WARNING - REGS 15, 0, 1 ALTERED'
[8]                  AGO   .MACEND
[9]       .BADREG    ANOP
[10]                 MNOTE 8,'ERROR - REGISTER VALUE INVALID'
          .MACEND    MEND
```

Notes:

1. Only the changed parts of the macro will have notes.

2. Tests that the &REG first operand register is valid.

3. Tests the type of &DIVISOR to see if it is defined as a halfword.

4. &DIVISOR is not a halfword. Note that this MNOTE will cause the actual value provided to appear in the message, e.g., 0,WARNING - WEEKS NOT TYPE H.

5. This provides a label to bypass the MNOTE if not needed.

6. This uses the MEXIT directive. This has the same effect as an AGO to the end of the macro definition.

7. This MNOTE appears unless SAVE=YES is coded.

8. This AGO also could be an MEXIT.

9. Provide a sequence symbol if the first operand value is out of range.

10. MNOTE with a severity level of 8. This is a real error.

The MEXIT directive terminates the expansion of the macro instruction. It is like an AGO to the MEND directive. Coding MEXIT is usually preferable, since the intent is clearer (i.e., end the macro expansion).

22.5 MISCELLANEOUS MACRO CODING NOTES

At this point, we've covered most of the macro coding facilities. This section adds a few notes about other macro facilities and about other uses of the ones discussed so far.

22.5.1 Length Attribute

The length attribute is commonly used outside of macro instructions. (The part of a program outside of the macro expansions is called *open code*.) This may be used in several situations.

For one example, you may have a need to get the length of a field for use with the EX instruction. You may use the length attribute with a Load Address — LA — instruction to get this, that is,

    LA R2,L'WORD2

This loads the length of WORD2 into register 2. If you want the length minus one, the assembler will do the arithmetic for you if you code

    LA R2,L'WORD2-1

Another common use of the length attribute is with the MVC instruction. If you remember the overlapping MVC used to clear a print line (see Fig. 13.5), the following code shows how to generally set a field of 256 bytes or less to a constant character:

    MVI   TARGET,C' '
    MVC   TARGET+1(L'TARGET-1),TARGET

This moves a blank (C' ') into the first byte of a field called TARGET. It then copies that byte throughout the rest of TARGET. We use L'TARGET-1 because we have already set the first byte.

You may see many other uses of the length attribute in open code. However, there is one point to consider when using it. The assembler sets the length attribute based on the implied or specified length of a field. It does not take the replication factor into account. Thus

    SAVEAREA DS   18F

will generate 72 bytes (18 x 4), but the assembler length attribute for SAVEAREA is 4. (The type of SAVEAREA is F, which has an implied length of 4 bytes.)

22.5.2   Special Assembler Symbolic Values

The assembler provides access to certain information through special symbolic values. These are

- &SYSECT   The current CSECT name
- &SYSDATE   The assembly date (MM/DD/YY)
- &SYSTIME   The assembly time (HH.MM)
- &SYSPARM   The SYSPARM value provided on the EXEC PARM for the assembly

We have already used &SYSDATE and &SYSTIME. &SYSECT returns an 8-byte character value and cannot be used outside a macro expansion. For details on providing &SYSPARM, refer to the assembler programmers' guide.

22.5.3   Avoiding Endless Loops in Macro Assembly

The AIF and AGO directives provide a way of looping in assembler. Unfortunately, every intentional loop also may become an endless loop.

If this happens, the assembly step will eventually exceed the CPU time allowed or be canceled by the operator. To avoid this problem, assembler provides a directive called ACTR. ACTR provides a limit to the number of AGO and AIF statements processed by the assembler. It is coded as

ACTR *number*

Number is the maximum number of times you wish to allow the macro expansion to assemble an AGO or AIF directive. It may be coded inside a macro, in which case it sets a limit for that macro expansion only. It also may be coded outside a macro (i.e., in open code), in which case it sets a limit for the entire assembly. In addition, you may code multiple ACTR directives, each of which changes the limit.

22.5.4   Macro Parameter Sublists

The example we presented in this chapter used defined names for the symbolic parameters. In addition, DH only expects a fixed number of parameters (two or three).

There are occasions when the number of parameters may not be defined. In this case, the assembler provides a facility to process each parameter in turn without defining it in the prototype statement. This is to access the parameter string by means of a sublist.

Sublists are like arrays or tables. You may access them by providing an index value or values. The assembler provides a special variable — SYSLIST — that is used to access the macro parameters.

You access an individual parameter by coding &SYSLIST followed by a subscript. The subscript indicates which entry in the macro parameters you wish to access. For example, &SYSLIST(1) refers to the first parameter in the macro's operands, &SYSLIST(2) refers to the second operand, and so forth. Thus, if we coded

```
DH      5,LOCAL1,ET_CETERA
```

we could access the parameters by

&SYSLIST(1)   (Would provide a value of 5)
&SYSLIST(2)   (Would provide a value of LOCAL1)
&SYSLIST(3)   (Would provide a value of ET_CETERA)

You also may access sublists within an individual parameter. These are coded by placing the sublist within parentheses and are accessed by coding two subscripts. For example, if we coded

```
DH      (2,7),OOPS
```

we could access the parameters by

&SYSLIST(1)   [Would be *(2,7)*]
&SYSLIST(1,1)   [Would be *2*]
&SYSLIST(1,2)   [Would be *7*]

In general, use of sublists often adds more complexity than it saves in coding time.

22.6   THE COPY DIRECTIVE

Assembler provides a directive—COPY—that is equivalent to the COBOL COPY statement. COPY allows only one operand. This is the name of a member in one of the macro libraries used in the assembly.

As in COBOL, the COPY directive brings in the code included in the specified member and then assembles it as though it had been in the program at the point where it was copied.

22.7   SUMMARY

This chapter has presented an overview of assembler macro processing. You should use the assembler language programmers' guide for further research into how macros work if you use them very much.

The DH macro has taken us through several assembler options. In the last example, it would serve for many situations. Note, however, that there are still many enhancements you might add to it. For example, you might test for a 0 divisor and issue a message rather than accept an 0C9 ABEND.

Using your own macro instructions has both advantages and disadvantages. Macros generally make coding of complicated data elements or of frequently repeated instruction sequences much easier. However, this is offset by the time required to program the macro in the first place, along with the time future maintenance programmers need to learn to use the macro.

In general, though, macros are a powerful assembler programming tool. Properly used, they enhance productivity significantly.

Things to Do

1. Determine if your installation has a separate macro library. Review the macros in it to see what is available to you. (If your installation uses CICS, it probably has a separate library for the DSECTs used with CICS Basic Mapping Support maps.)

2. If you are running under MVS, locate the SYS1.AMODGEN (or SYS1.MODGEN) macro library. Review its contents. You may find some of the DSECTs in that library useful, such as IKJEFTCB for the MVS Task Control Block (TCB). You may need to discuss access to this with your systems programmer.

3. Similarly, if you are running under VM, review the DMSSP MACLIB. Use the MACLIST command to do this.

4. If you want to read further on the subject of macros, try to locate the following article by William Kent: "Assembler-Language Macroprogramming: A Tutorial Oriented Toward the IBM 360," *ACM Computing Surveys*, Vol. 1, No. 4, December 1969. (Try a university library.)

Are You an Assembler Programmer Yet?

To those of you who have waded through the entire book: Thank you. Are you an assembler programmer yet? It depends on your standard of reference. Some assembler programmers write simple applications programs; others write MVS. Your talents probably fall somewhere between these two extremes.

If you think that your abilities fall toward the simpler end of that range, you're probably right. Expertise in assembler grows mainly with experience. Not all programmers will benefit in the same way from the same type of experience, but the more assembler your write, the better you become, just as in other languages.

This is more difficult to accomplish in assembler than in other languages because of the widespread management perceptions about the difficulty of programming in assembler. These perceptions are neither entirely false nor absolutely correct.

If your management is unenlightened in this area, you have a selling job. There are several ways to go about convincing your management to let you use assembler when appropriate tasks come about.

First, try to find tasks where assembler's unique attributes of speed and size will make a difference. Do your homework before relying solely on this approach. Know how many records or transactions are processed, for example, for a typical execution of a program you'd like to write in assembler. Be able to present provable reasons why COBOL is not the language for a given job.

Second, try to find tasks where assembler's ability to use MVS or VM system services makes a difference. Be able to show how these services aren't available in COBOL. (Rely more on functionality—the ability to do something you can't do in COBOL—than on perceived performance differences.)

Third, be willing to write an assembler subroutine to do the MVS-unique or VM-unique part of the job. Your management may have heartburn over the perceived future difficulties of maintaining an assembler program. Making the assembler part of the job smaller and reducing it to one specific function can make the future maintenance a smaller concern. It also allows you to use your work in more programs—which will in turn usually provide more opportunities in the future.

Finally, be a good COBOL programmer first. It's generally true that meeting schedules counts for more than technical excellence in programming. Beware of the trap of trying some new technical nuance and being late because you took too much time exploring it. Assembler language is full of these. (You will have fun exploring them, and you should. However, don't let this get in the way of keeping your management happy and doing the underlying job.)

Following these four guidelines won't guarantee that your management will embrace assembler language programming. You should expect to lose more decisions than you win—at least at first. Productive use of assembler language will be a difficult concept for many managers, and it will take time. However, stick to it, and opportunities to use assembler will come your way eventually.

If you have specific comments about this book, I would appreciate hearing from you. If you or your systems programmer is a member of the National Systems Programmer's Association (NASPA), you may send me messages by means of their bulletin board, user ID MURPJOSV. (I highly recommend membership in NASPA if you are a systems programmer or want to become one.) If you have access to Compuserve™, you may send mail to user ID 70033,1174. You also may write me in care of the publisher—but try the electronic mail first— these are the 1990s!

Finally, if you are a rocket scientist, dabbling in this book to amuse yourself before coding new mods to MVS or VM, this writer hopes that you have found something of interest. And for the rest of you, I hope that you will be able to refer to this book in future years as your experience grows.

Binary and Hexadecimal Numbers

Once upon a time, a fellow named Charlie decided to build a computer. And he had the right idea — he wanted the computer to store numbers in decimal, so that he (or his assistants — Charlie's mind easily tired of the mundane) could read the results of his calculations out directly.

A few years later, Charlie's friend Herman, who taught at MIT, decided to build some simpler machines to count things. Herman, being both a smart and a down-to-earth guy, decided that he, too, would store his numbers in decimal. And he did for years, and all was right with the world.

Unfortunately, between the time of Charlie and Herman, a fellow named George developed this odd way of expressing arithmetic calculations. Since there were a lot of guys named George, people called it "boolean algebra" after George's last name. However, no one actually built any computers using this stuff...

Until the second world war, when the demand for more and faster calculations led to several parallel efforts to develop computers. Many of the projects relied on the same familiar decimal system that Charles Babbage and Herman Hollerith had used in their pioneering calculation and data processing designs. A few, however, used a system that was more complicated in concept yet simpler to design—the binary, two-state arithmetic incorporating George Boole's work..

The reasons for selecting this type of design were compelling in the 1940s and are even more so today. Binary (two-state) circuits are easier to design than decimal (ten-state) circuits. To use an analogy, it's easier to discern the difference between black and white than between black and nine shades of gray. This ease of design was accompanied by another major advantage — cost. Binary circuits required one on-off vacuum tube to store a binary digit. The ENIAC, the first electronic digital computer by most accounts, required ten vacuum tubes to store one digit.

Binary logic—more commonly called *digital logic* — remains faster and cheaper to this day. As a result, every computer in widespread use today stores data using the binary number system. And every assembler programmer has to learn how the binary number system works.

In this appendix we cover some basic elements of the binary and hexadecimal number systems. To make the most effective use of this appendix, you must have a 370 Reference Summary — commonly called the *yellow card* or the *pink card* . (The 360 version was called the *green card.*) You should obtain one of these as soon as possible.

(The term "card" has not been appropriate for many years in describing the 370 Reference Summary. It originated as a multi-panel pocket reference printed on green card stock in the 1960s — hence the original common nickname, *green card*. When IBM announced the 370 series of computers, it changed colors to white (one issue) and then to yellow, but remained printed on card stock — hence the later common nickname, *yellow card*. The 370 reference summary changed to a booklet form with the fourth revision (GX20-1850-4, dated October 1981) and has remained so ever since. The XA version changed the cover color to pink or salmon. The most recent incarnation of the reference summary, the ESA version (GX20-0406-0, February 1989, light blue) contains fifty pages. By contrast, the last version of the green card (GX20-1703-9, undated) comprised 14 panels. In spite of this expansion and proliferation of colors, veteran assembler programmers still refer to it as the green card or the yellow card.)

A1.1   THE BINARY NUMBER SYSTEM
Number systems include a concept called *positional notation*. This is a long way of saying that digits represent different values depending on where they are in a number. For example, 370 represents an entirely different number from 703 or 037. Depending on which of these we examine, we either have three hundreds, three tens, or three ones.

The familiar decimal number system is based on ten digits — 0 through 9 — and positional notation. Binary arithmetic is based on a different range of numbers—0 and 1. (It also may be called *base 2 arithmetic.*)

Binary number representation also uses positional notation to indicate values. However, each position has a different value than the corresponding value in decimal. The first seven digit position values are shown below, starting from the right (ones) position:

Position from right	Decimal value	Binary value
1	1	1
2	10	2
3	100	4
4	1000	8
5	10,000	16

And so forth. Each position in decimal increases by a factor of 10. Each position in binary increases by a factor of 2. Each digit in binary is called a *bit*, for binary digit.

Thus the first ten digits in decimal and binary are

Decimal	Binary	(Value)
1	1	(one 1)
2	10	(one 2 and zero 1s)
3	11	(one 2 and one 1)
4	100	(one 4, zero 2s, and zero 1s)
5	101	(one 4, zero 2s, and one 1)
6	110	(one 4, one 2, and zero 1s)
7	111	(one 4, one 2, and one 1)
8	1000	(one 8, zero 4s, zero 2s, and zero 1s)
9	1001	(one 8, zero 4s, zero 2s, and one 1)
10	1010	(one 8, zero 4s, one 2, and zero 1s)

As you might imagine, it takes more digits in binary to store information than in other number systems. For example, 365 in decimal is 10111101 in binary.

In the IBM 370 design, bits are grouped into more manageable sections of 8 bits, and called *bytes*.

An understanding of binary is essential to sophisticated assembler language programming. This takes two forms — how to convert between binary and decimal and how bits are agglomerated to form characters or other symbols. We will spend some time on conversions first.

If this seems completely foreign, you might consider that you have been using a different number system for a long time. Specifically, if you can tell time, you are already familiar with two number systems that use different bases. In time, minutes and seconds are expressed in a base 60 system and hours are expressed in a base 12 system (A.M. or P.M.).

A1.1.1   Binary and Decimal Conversions

The simplest way to convert between binary and decimal is to break down the number into the powers of 2 that constitute it. When converting from decimal to binary, this involves locating the highest power of 2 that is less than the number you're converting. This is subtracted from the original number. You then repeat this process of determining the closest lower power of 2 and subtracting until you have gone through all the lower powers of 2.

While following this process, you place a binary 1 in the result if you perform the subtraction. If a power of 2 is greater than the number (or remainder), you place a binary 0 in the result.

For example, the following uses this process to convert decimal 100 to binary.

100	Number
-64	Lower power of 2 (2**6)

36	Remainder – so put a binary 1 in the result, since we performed a subtraction:	1
-32	Lower power of 2 (2**5)	

4	Remainder – so put a binary 1 in the result:	1
16	is the next lower power of 2 – no subtraction, so put a binary 0 in the result:	0
8	is the next lower power – no subtraction, so:	0
-4	Lower power of 2 (2**2)	

0	Remainder – so put 1 in the result :	1
2	is the next lower power of 2 – so put a binary 0 in the result:	0
1	is the next lower power of 2 – so put a binary 0 in the result:	0

Working from the top down, our binary equivalent of decimal 100 is 1100100.

This may seem cumbersome — and it is. The difficulty of using binary arithmetic led to a slightly simpler way of expressing binary numbers.

A1.2   HEXADECIMAL ARITHMETIC

Hexadecimal arithmetic is one of a number of schemes to use binary numbers without always dealing with long strings of 1s and 0s. The IBM 360 was among the first CPUs to rely on hexadecimal representation. Now, about 25 years after the introduction of the 360, almost every CPU manufacturer relies on it.

Hexadecimal arithmetic relies on a base of 16 rather than 10 (as in decimal) or 2 (as in binary). Because 16 is a power of 2, we can group four binary digits into one hexadecimal digit. This speeds up arithmetic and conversions to and from decimal. (Another commonly used approach was the *octal number system*, which used base 8.)

(You are probably already familiar with a form of hexadecimal arithmetic, although you don't think of it as such. The Anglo-Saxon weight system is based on 16 ounces per pound.)

Hexadecimal (usually called simply *hex*) requires more digit symbols than the 10 in Arabic numerals. To accomplish this, IBM uses the letters A through F to symbolize the added values of decimal 10 through 15. The equivalence is as follows:

Decimal	Hexadecimal	Corresponding binary value
0	0	0000
1	1	0001
2	2	0010
and so on up to		
9	9	1001
10	A	1010
11	B	1011
12	C	1100
13	D	1101
14	E	1110
15	F	1111
For numbers above 15 in decimal:		
16	10	00010000
17	11	00010001
and so on up to		
25	19	00011001
26	1A	00011010
27	1B	00011011
and so on up to		
31	1F	00011111
32	20	00100000

Conversions between hexadecimal and binary are fairly straightforward. Since each hex digit represents 4 bits, conversion from hex to binary only requires that we replace the hex digit with the corresponding 4 bits. Conversion from binary to hex is also simpler. This involves taking groups of 4 bits and replacing them with the corresponding hex digit. Conversion should be done from right to left.

For example, 100 in decimal is 110100 in binary. To convert this to hex, we form groups of 4 bits:

110 0100

We normally fill with 0 bits on the left when doing this conversion:

0110 0100

The hex digit for 0110 is 6. The hex digit for 0100 is 4. Thus the hexadecimal equivalent of binary 1100100 (or decimal 100) is 64.

Conversion of large hexadecimal numbers to decimal is similar to conversion between binary and decimal. The equivalent powers of 16 are subtracted from the original decimal number. However, the conversion is slightly more complicated, since the each hex digit position can have 16 possible values, not just 2.

There are two sections of the 370 Reference Summary that simplify this conversion greatly. The first is a section headed "Hexadecimal and Decimal Conversion." This contains tables with powers of 2 and 16. Additionally, this section contains a table of decimal equivalents for hex digits by position. The table provides data for numbers up to 6 or 8 hex digits long.

Using this table, you perform conversions to hexadecimal by adding up the decimal equivalents for each hex digit. For example, to convert hex 3C1F to decimal, start by looking up the decimal equivalent to 3 in the fourth hex column from the left. (You should find it to be 12,288 in decimal.) Next, look up the equivalent for hex C in the third hex column. (You should find it to be 3072 in decimal.) Continue this process with 1 in the second hex column from the right. (You should find it to be 16 in decimal.) Finally, look up F in the rightmost hex column, which is decimal 15.

If you were unable to follow this with your copy of the 370 Reference Summary, try scanning the table until you find the decimal numbers we mentioned above (12,288, 3072, 16, and 15). Once you find these, you should see the hex digits 3, C, 1, and F, respectively, to their right.

Having found the decimal equivalents of each of the hex digits needed, we then add them up to find the decimal equivalent:

```
   12288
    3072
      16
      15
  _____

   15391
```

Conversely, to convert a decimal number to hex, we must find the hex digit lower than the decimal value and then subtract the decimal equivalent from the original decimal number. This process repeats until we have a remainder of 0.

For example, to convert 1989 in decimal to hexadecimal, we first find the hex number that is closest in value to 1989. This is hex 700—decimal 1792. (You will find this in the third column from the right of the hex tables.)

Following this, we subtract 1792 from 1989, leaving a remainder of 197. The hex number closest to this is C0 — decimal 192. (We found this in the second column from the right.) Subtracting 192 from 197 leaves a remainder of 5, which is also 5 in hex. Thus our converted value of decimal 1989 is 7C5 in hexadecimal.

If you need to do this — and most programmers eventually do — you should acquire a calculator with hexadecimal arithmetic capabilities. There are usually one or more people with this type of calculator in most installations. Even with a calculator, however, you still will need to know how to convert between binary and hexadecimal.

A1.3   REPRESENTING SYMBOLS

If the foregoing discussion has turned your brain completely to highly refined mush, there is a simpler way of converting small numbers among these three number systems. We will show how to do this as part of introducing how we store values other than numbers. To use this section, you must have access to a 370 Reference Summary. Before proceeding, locate the section headed "Code Assignments," "Code Tables," or "Code Translation Table." (The title has varied with different versions of the reference summary. We will refer to all these as the *code tables*.)

Use of binary storage only allows us to store a series of bits. We have seen how we can use this to represent numbers, by assigning different values to different bits. However, a slightly different approach is needed to handle the representation of nonnumeric data — specifically, letters, special characters, and numbers in printable or displayable form.

In the 370 architecture, this is done by designating each storage location (8 bits, or a byte) as being able to hold one character (letter, special character, etc.). Each symbol that we want to print or display is then assigned a value that can be represented in 8 bits.

The largest number we can store in 8 bits is decimal 255. The smallest number we can store is 0. This gives us 256 possibilities, 0 through 255.

The assignments of 8-bit values to displayable characters are codified in IBM's Extended Binary Coded Decimal Information Code. This is abbreviated EBCDIC and is usually pronounced as "ib-see-dick" or "ib-sih-dick." ("Ib" is pronounced here as in rib.)

At this point, let's look at the 370 Reference Summary to see how some letters are represented. The "Code Tables" section has several column headings, as shown below.

Dec.	Decimal value 0-255
Hex.	Hex value 00-FF
Graphics and Controls	The EBCDIC characters
Card Code	The card punches for these
Binary	The binary value
	00000000 through 11111111

There also may be some other columns, such as 7-Track Tape or Instruction Formats, but we will not discuss these here.

Under the "Graphics and Controls" heading, locate the column headed "EBCDIC" or "EBCDIC(1)." This shows the printable or displayable character for a given hex, decimal, or binary value. The first 64 values are normally only used in teleprocessing applications. These begin with the values NUL, SOH, and STX. We will not be discussing these further.

The next 64 values begin the displayable characters. The first of these is the space or blank character. This has a value of decimal 64 or hex 40. You also will see a value of 01000000 in the binary column. Note that the name for blank in the code tables is SP, for space.

You also will note the special character @ adjacent to the SP in the "Graphics and Controls" column. This is the value of decimal 64 or hex 40 in another symbol coding method called ASCII. You should see this subheading at the top of the column.

ASCII is a substitute for EBCDIC used with other CPU types—for example, the Digital Equipment Corporation VAX™ processor family or the IBM PC family. Unless you are dealing with data that came from another CPU, you will usually not need to use the ASCII column and you should ignore it. You also should ignore the BCDIC column if present, which covers the code used with the IBM 1401, IBM 7090, and other CPUs that preceded the 360 family.

Your 370 Reference Summary also may have two different columns of EBCDIC characters. One of these is used with a special text printing character set. You can normally use these interchangeably, but this depends on the printer types in use at your installation.

If you've followed this so far, try to locate the dollar sign character— $. (You should find this at decimal value 91 or hex value 5B. If you found it at decimal 38 or hex 26, you were looking at the ASCII column. Try again!

Now try to find the corresponding information for the capital letter A. (You should find this at decimal value 193 or hex C1 in the table. It you found it at decimal 65 or hex 41, you were reading the ASCII column again.) Now note the binary value that corresponds to this. (You should find it to be 11000001.)

If you have followed this part of the discussion, you should now be able to see how you can use this part of the 370 Reference Summary to convert between hexadecimal, decimal, and binary. Simply look up the value in the appropriate column and then look across for the corresponding value in one of the other representations.

Also, you should note that the 370 doesn't care what value is in a byte. Thus, while in COBOL we define each storage item to have specific characteristics through the PICTURE and USAGE clauses, the underlying real CPU makes no such distinctions. This means that you can accidentally overlay binary (PIC 9, COMP) values with EBCDIC characters and the CPU will not differentiate between the different data types. For example, if you redefine a binary (PIC 9(8) COMP or PIC 9(4) COMP) field as PIC X, you may see results of 1077952576 or 16448 if you overlay that field with spaces.

Note also that not all of the 256 possible combinations in a byte have a displayable value, so you can move "garbage" characters to a field but have them print as blanks. (This is a function of the spool printer's internal character translation.)

A1.4 SUMMARY

This appendix has presented a brief overview of binary and hexadecimal arithmetic. This included several potentially difficult concepts, so you should not feel concerned if you experience information overload.

Use of binary and hexadecimal arithmetic, however, is required of assembler programmers. You may wish to invest in a hexadecimal calculator if hex arithmetic poses continuing difficulties for you.

Note that we discuss the 370 reference summary in Chap. 6.

Further Reading

From Baker Street To Binary, by H. Ledgard, P. McQuaid, and A. Singer (McGraw-Hill, 1987), presents an amusingly simplified introduction to how computers work. This book discusses the early development of computers, binary arithmetic, and several other topics related to this appendix. The unique approach taken is to have Sherlock Holmes do the explanations.

Commonly Used MVS Macro Instructions

This appendix lists a number of MVS macro instructions. These are mostly supervisor services rather than I/O-related macros. You may encounter many other macro instructions. The manuals listed in Chap. 1 should describe most of the macro instructions you will see in typical assembler programs. Appendix 4 covers some VM macro instructions.

If you cannot find a macro in either this appendix or in the manuals listed in Chap. 1, see the section at the end of this appendix for further steps.

The macro instructions are listed alphabetically.

A2.1 MACRO INSTRUCTION DESCRIPTIONS

ABEND

This macro causes your task or job step to abnormally terminate and may create a dump. See Chap. 17 for a fuller description and examples.

ATTACH

This macro creates a subtask of your program. A *subtask* differs from a normal subroutine in that it executes independently of the creating program (i.e., the program that issued the ATTACH macro). In a normal subroutine, your program waits for the subroutine to finish before it receives control back. Attaching a subtask returns control to your program immediately. This allows you to do processing at the same time as the subtask.

You may wait for the subtask to finish by using the WAIT macro. When finished, you may need to get rid of the subtask with the DETACH macro.

A full description of ATTACH and all its options is outside the scope of this book. However, the following is an example of ATTACH that is logically equivalent to using the LINK macro. (Also read the notes under DETACH later.)

```
        ATTACH  EP = SUBPGM1,PARAM = (DATA1,DATA2),        X
                ECB = MYECB
        LR      R7,R1           SAVE TASK CONTROL BLOCK ADDR
        WAIT    1,ECB = MYECB       WAIT FOR SUBTASK TO END
                ...................
MYECB   DC      F'0'                EVENT CONTROL BLOCK
```

The preceding is logically similar to

LINK EP = SUBPGM1,PARAM = (DATA1,DATA2)

CALL

This macro provides the same service as the COBOL verb of the same name, i.e., invoking a subroutine and passing parameters. Chapter 14 describes the CALL macro and subroutine interfaces in more detail.

CHAP

This macro changes the dispatching priority of your task or of a subtask that you have created. (See the ATTACH macro description for more information on subtasks.) CHAP only affects your task's priority relative to other subtasks in the same job. It does not affect priorities relative to other jobs or TSO users in the MVS system.

DELETE

This macro allows you to remove a program from storage. You should have brought in the program with the LOAD or LINK macro instructions. DELETE does not actually remove the program until its storage is needed for other purposes. See Chap. 14 for a discussion of the LINK, LOAD, and related macro instructions.

DEQ

This macro (pronounced "D-Q") allows you to signal MVS that you are through with a resource or that a condition has ended. DEQ is used following the ENQ macro instruction (pronounced "N-Q"). ENQ and DEQ provide a way of serializing certain operations. To do this, all programs that want to perform some controlled operation must use an ENQ macro instruction before doing it. The programs should then use DEQ to indicate that another program may perform the controlled operation.

The ENQ and DEQ operations make use of what are called *major queue names* and *minor queue names*. The meaning of the major and minor queue names are immaterial, as long as all affected programs use the same names. MVS makes wide use of this facility. It is also often used in subtasking environments with the ATTACH macro.

DETACH

This macro removes a subtask from the system. See the description of the ATTACH macro above. DETACH may or may not be appropriate for a particular application, depending on how the subtask ends. If you receive an ABEND trying to use the DETACH macro, you may only need to remove the macro, since it will fail if the subtask has already ended.

DOM

This macro is used to delete an operator message previously displayed with the WTO macro instruction. It requires a message identification, which is provided by the WTO macro instruction. The following example displays a

message, waits 10 seconds, and then deletes it from the operator console
with the DOM macro:

```
        WTO    'DONT CANCEL THIS AND ILL BUY YOU A BEER'
        LR     R2,R1                      SAVE MSG ID NUM
        STIMER WAIT,BINTVL = TENSECS      WAIT TEN SECONDS
        DOM    MSG = (2)                  DELETE THE MSG
               .........
TENSECS DC     F'1000'                    10.00 SECONDS
```

DXR

This macro is provided to allow extended precision floating-point divide
operations. This book does not cover floating-point operations.

ENQ

This macro (pronounced "N-Q") allows you to signal other programs that
you are performing some controlled operation and that other programs
should wait for your program to complete. See the DEQ (pronounced
"D-Q") macro instruction discussion for further information.

ESPIE

This macro stands for Extended SPIE. ESPIE allows you to process 0Cx
ABENDs yourself and avoid a dump. See Chap. 18 for further details.

ESTAE

This macro is the preferred form of the STAE macro under MVS. ESTAE
allows you to identify an exit program to MVS that will handle all ABENDs.
A complete description of ESTAE is beyond the scope of this book. ESTAE
allows you to retry the failing operation, to change dump parameters if
desired, and generally to have complete control over the program environment. See Chap.18 for more background information regarding the concept
of an exit program.

EVENTS

This macro is basically a special form of the WAIT macro. It allows
faster processing when many separate events can occur to satisfy a
WAIT macro instruction.

EXIT

The MVS EXIT macro invokes SVC 3 — the exit service. EXIT is closest to
the COBOL STOP RUN verb in that it indicates that the current program
has completed. This differs from the normal MVS BR 14 return, which only
gives control back to a calling program.

FREEMAIN

This macro is used to return storage to MVS after you have acquired it with
the GETMAIN macro instruction. Both these macros are described in Chap. 15.

GETMAIN

This macro can be used to acquire main storage at run time. It is described more completely in Chap. 15. Chap. 15 also has a description of how to acquire storage above the 16-Megabyte addressing line in MVS/XA.

IDENTIFY

This macro allows you to tell MVS that you have a program entry point that is not otherwise known to MVS. This is an advantage when you want to have two programs in one load module, for example. Situations requiring IDENTIFY are fairly specialized, often involving the ATTACH macro as well.

IHAPIE

This is a mapping macro, like DCBD. It creates a DSECT (dummy section) allowing you to access fields in the extended program interruption element. This is provided when using the ESPIE macro. See Chap. 18 for further background information.

LINK

This macro is similar to the CALL verb in COBOL when the DYNAM option is specified at compile time. Chapter 15 describes how to use LINK in place of the CALL macro. Chapter 19 also has an example showing how to use LINK to invoke the IBM DFSORT program.

LOAD

This macro, a contents-management instruction, allows you to bring a program into storage. Unlike LINK, LOAD does not transfer control to the program. This makes it useful for loading in tables or other reference data kept in separate programs. Chapter 15 has a brief description of LOAD.

PGLOAD

This macro, along with the PGOUT and PGRLSE macros, allows you to improve performance of your program's virtual storage paging. PGLOAD teels MVS that you need a particular address brought into storage so that you do not have a page fault. This allows you to request the page before you actually use it. Note that the page size in MVS is 4 Kilobytes, and that you should probably not use PGLOAD, et al., for areas smaller than that.

PGOUT

This macro allows you to tell the MVS paging supervisor that you are temporarily finished using a 4 Kilobyte page in virtual storage. See the PGLOAD discussion for more information. (To avoid repetitively paging the area in and out (*page thrashing*, or simply *thrashing*) you should not expect to use the area again for some reasonably long period —at least one second.)

PGRLSE

This macro complements PGOUT and PGLOAD by allowing you to tell MVS that you no longer need a virtual page's data. You might use this when you have finished processing a very large table and the data in it may be discarded. PGRLSE tells MVS that the data in the page(s) may be thrown away — this avoids additional MVS I/O operations. (By contrast, PGOUT tells MVS to write out the data in the page(s). With PGRLSE, it's gone.)

RETURN

This macro corresponds most closely to the COBOL STOP or GOBACK verbs. It also may set up the equivalent of the COBOL RETURN-CODE special register. Chapter 15 describes the RETURN macro and its options in some detail.

SAVE

This macro is used to store registers at the beginning of a program or subroutine. This service uses the STM instruction, which you could equally well code yourself. SAVE also creates an optional "eye-catcher" constant in following the beginning of the SAVE macro, which makes it easier to locate in a dump. An example of SAVE coded to do this is

        SAVE   (14,12),,'PROGRAM NAME &SYSDATE &SYSTIME'

The assembler will automatically replace &SYSDATE and &SYSTIME with the correct assembly time and date. The second operand — not coded in the preceding example — specifies that registers 14 and 15 are stored in their usual locations. This option is only necessary when storing other than the normal sequence of registers. The third operand may be coded as an asterisk ('*'), in which case the SAVE macro generates a constant of the control section (CSECT) name.

SEGLD

This macro is used with overlay programs. These are a holdover from earlier real storage operating systems (e.g., OS/360). In an overlay program, not all the program is in main storage at any given point in time. The SEGLD macro brings in a specified overlay and stores it over part of the program that is already in main storage.

You should thoroughly read the linkage editor programmers' guide before attempting to maintain a program that uses overlays. Serious consideration should be given to making overlay programs into large single-load modules, since this technique is a vestige of older days and smaller CPU memories.

SEGWT

This macro is identical to SEGLD, but it waits for the overlay part of the program to be brought into storage. See SEGLD.

SETRP

This macro sets the recovery parameters in an ESTAE exit. This controls what MVS does next — retry or ABEND.

SNAP

This macro allows you to create a small storage dump. You can explicitly control the areas that are dumped. SNAP requires its own specially coded DCB. SNAP was described in Chap. 17.

SPIE

This macro allows you to process program checks (0Cx ABENDs). See Chap. 18 for further information about SPIE.

STAE

This macro is an older form of ESTAE. See ESTAE for further details.

STATUS

This macro is used to halt (STOP) or restart (START) subtasks. See the discussion of the ATTACH macro for more information about subtasks. You should use STATUS STOP for a subtask before using the DETACH macro to end it, unless you have waited for the subtask to end by itself.

STIMER

This macro is used to delay your program's execution by waiting a specified time period (not to exceed 24 hours). Another form of STIMER allows you to specify a timer exit routine, which gets control from MVS when the time period ends. In this form, your program may run until the time period ends. STIMER allows you to specify the time interval as a binary number (in units of one-hundredth of a second) or as an actual time of day. See the DOM macro description for an example of STIMER.

SYNADAF

This macro is used when I/O errors arise. See Chap. 18 for a discussion of how to use SYNADAF.

SYNADRLS

This macro is a companion macro to SYNADAF. See Chap. 18 for further information.

SYNCH

This macro allows you to give control to an exit routine that you also provide. See Chap. 18 for a discussion of exit routines.

TIME

This macro returns the time and date in one of several formats. See Chap. 17 for more information and an example.

TTIMER

This macro allows you to test the amount of time remaining in a time interval. TTIMER is used with certain forms of the STIMER macro. You also may optionally cancel the time period set up with STIMER.

WAIT

This macro allows you to wait for an event to happen or for some operation to complete. It can be used with a wide variety of other MVS macros. Chapter 16 has an example of how to use the WAIT macro with the WTOR macro instruction. The ATTACH macro discussion earlier in this appendix has another example.

WTL

This macro is a variation of the WTO macro that allows you to place information in the hard-copy system log (SYSLOG). It is coded like WTO but has fewer options. For example,

        WTL   'WRITE THIS IN THE SYSTEM LOG'

puts the message in quotation marks in the system log.

WTO

This macro corresponds most closely to the COBOL DISPLAY verb with the UPON CONSOLE option. Chap. 16 is devoted to this macro and to the WTOR macro.

WTOR

This macro provides a service analogous to the COBOL ACCEPT verb with the FROM CONSOLE option. See Chap. 16 for examples of this macro.

XCTL

This macro stands for Transfer Control. It operates like a combination of the LINK macro and the DELETE macro. XCTL passes control from your program to another program, just like LINK. XCTL also removes your program from storage, like the DELETE macro. For example,

        XCTL   EP = OTHERPGM

passes control to a program called OTHERPGM and simultaneously marks your program as eligible for deletion if main storage is needed.

A2.2   OTHER MACRO INSTRUCTION SOURCES

MVS and its related software provide many other sources of macros. Some of these are listed below. However, you may need to do some other research to locate information about particular macros. There are simply too many to exhaustively document here.

A2.2.1   Systems Programming Macros

Many macros are only documented in various systems programming library (SPL) manuals. We have shown some of these in this book, including RDJFCB, IEFJFCBN, and NUCLKUP — all of which were shown in Chap. 14. Many systems services, such as the Systems Management Facility (SMF), have their own collection of macros documented as part of a manual that also covers other topics. There are also several macros provided for the Resource Access Control Facility (RACF). In general, you should ask your systems programming staff for assistance when you encounter an unknown macro. If you are running under VM, you may wish to have your systems programmer search through the MAINT minidisks for files with a type of MACLIB. The MACLIST command will let you search these for a particular macro.

A2.2.2 IBM Program Products

Many IBM program products have their own macro libraries, such as CICS and IMS. You can usually find out about these through the appropriate applications programmers' reference manual.

A2.2.3 User Macro Libraries

Many installations have their own set of installation macros. Some of these may only apply to an individual application system. Your installation's standards manual should document these.

If you are running under VM, you may wish to search the appropriate minidisks for files of type MACLIB.

A2.2.4 Undocumented Macros

IBM also provides many macros that are not documented anywhere in some cases. These are usually mapping macro instructions used to create dummy sections (DSECTs) defining the layout of MVS control blocks. These are usually found in the SYS1.AMODGEN or SYS1.MODGEN macro library.

A2.2.5 Other Steps in Locating Macros

If you are unable to locate documentation on a macro, you should probably try to determine where the macro came from. This involves reviewing the assembly JCL listing, locating all the macro libraries listed for the assembler SYSLIB DD name, and trying to find the macro in those libraries. If you find it in an IBM-provided library, such as SYS1.MACLIB or SYS1.AMODGEN, it should be documented somewhere — keep looking. (Note the exception in the previous section.)

If you find the macro in your installation's private macro library, you may need to document it yourself. This implies that someone put the macro in the library without documenting it.

Cross-Reference of COBOL Verbs to Assembler

This appendix lists the approximate assembler equivalents for most COBOL verbs. A reference is also included to the appropriate chapter for more detailed information. The COBOL verbs and clauses are grouped by COBOL division. Special registers and other items not exclusively related to one division are shown at the end. For each COBOL verb, the approximate assembler equivalent is shown, along with the place(s) in the book where we discuss these.

Note: This appendix is intended for use *after* you've read the whole book. Don't try to read up on how one verb is implemented out of context.

COBOL Verb	Assembler Equivalent	Chapter or Section
Identification Division:		
PROGRAM-ID.	CSECT	3.2
DATE-COMPILED.	&SYSDATE	3.4
(All other Identification Division components are equivalent to comments in assembler.)		

Environment Division:		
SPECIAL-NAMES.	No direct equivalent; CNTRL macro may serve	4
SELECT ... ASSIGN clause	DDNAME = operand of DCB macro	4.1
RERUN clause	Checkpoint/restart not covered in this book	4.1
ACCESS MODE clause	See VSAM manuals	21

COBOL Verb	Assembler Equivalent	Chapter or Section
Data Division:		
FD and all FD clauses	DCB macro	5
SD and all SD clauses	See Chap. 19	19
RD	No equivalent to report writer in assembler	
01-Levels	DS 0CLnnn	5.5
Any intermediate levels	DS 0CLnnn	6.5
Lowest level field definition	DS or DC	6.3
77-Level field definition	DS or DC	6.3
88-Level condition names	No direct equivalent; EQU directive provides a similar service	8.2
FILLER	DS or DC	6
BLANK WHEN ZERO	ED instruction	13
JUSTIFIED	ED + MVC instructions	13
OCCURS	DS with duplication	15.2
PICTURE	DC or DS	6
REDEFINES	ORG directive	8
66-Level RENAMES	ORG directive	8
SIGN	No direct equivalent	
SYNCHRONIZED	Implied in DS or DC type subfield	6,8
USAGE	Implied in DS or DC type subfield	6,8
VALUE	DC	6
WORKING-STORAGE SECTION	DC or DS statements in your program	6
LINKAGE SECTION	DSECT directive	7
COMMUNICATION SECTION	No direct equivalent	
REPORT SECTION	No assembler equivalent	

COBOL Verb	Assembler Equivalent	Chapter or Section
Procedure Division:		
ACCEPT	WTOR	16
ADD	A, AH, AR, AP	11
ALTER	NOP + OI, if you must	12.7
CALL	CALL macro or BASR/BALR	14
CANCEL	DELETE macro	14
CLOSE	CLOSE macro	10.4
COMPUTE	No direct equivalent; see Chap. 11 for arithmetic verbs	11
CONTINUE	EQU * or NOP	12
DELETE	VSAM ERASE macro	21
DISABLE	No direct equivalent	
DISPLAY	WTO, LINEDIT	16
DIVIDE	D, DR, DP	11
ENABLE	No assembler equivalent	
ENTRY	ENTRY directive	14
EVALUATE	Branch table	20
EXAMINE	TRT, or TRT with TR	20
EXHIBIT	No direct equivalent; provide equivalent service with WTO macro or PUT macro and formatting	16
EXIT	BR	12.5
EXIT PROGRAM	RETURN macro	14
GENERATE	No assembler equivalent	
GOBACK	RETURN macro or BR	14
GO TO	B or BR	12
IF	CLC, CLI, CP, C, CH, CR, CLCL, plus branch mnemonics	12
INITIALIZE	MVC or XC	13,17
INITIATE	No assembler equivalent	
INSPECT	TRT, or TRT with TR	20
MERGE	Not covered in this book; see Chap. 19 on sorting	19
MOVE	MVC, MVI, MVCL, ZAP, PACK, UNPK, CVD, CVB, L,LH, ST, STH, ED	13

COBOL Verb	Assembler Equivalent	Chapter or Section
Procedure Division : (continued)		
MULTIPLY	M, MH, MR, MP	11
NOTE	Assembler comments (* in position one)	3.3
ON	No assembler equivalent	
ON SIZE ERROR clause	Branch if overflow	11,12
OPEN	OPEN Macro	10.1
PERFORM	BAS, BASR, BAL, BALR	12.4
READ	GET macro	10.2
READY TRACE	No assembler equivalent; programmer must code instructions to do this	
RECEIVE	No assembler equivalent	
RELEASE	Sort exit coding	19
RESET TRACE	No assembler equivalent; programmer must code instructions to do this	
RETURN	Sort exit coding	19
REWRITE	PUTX macro; also refer to VSAM macro manual	10.5
SEARCH	Binary search	15
SEEK	VSAM POINT macro	21
SEND	No direct equivalent	
SET	See Fig. 15.4	15
SORT	LINK macro plus other coding	19
START	VSAM POINT macro	21
STOP	RETURN or EXIT macros	14
STRING	See Chap. 20	20
SUBTRACT	S, SR, SH, SP	11
TERMINATE	No assembler equivalent	
TRANSFORM	TR instruction	20
UNSTRING	See Chap. 20	20
USE	Exit routines, such as SYNAD routine	18
WRITE	PUT macro	10.3

COBOL Verb	Assembler Equivalent	Chapter or Section
Special registers:		
ADDRESS	LA instruction	14
DATE/DAY/TIME	TIME macro	17.5
LENGTH	L' attribute	22
RETURN-CODE	Register 15	14
SORT-CONTROL	See Tab. 19.1	19
SORT-CORE-SIZE	See Tab. 19.1	19
SORT-FILE-SIZE	See Tab. 19.1	19
SORT-MESSAGE	See Tab. 19.1	19
SORT-MODE-SIZE	See Tab. 19.1	19
SORT-RETURN	See Tab. 19.1	19
TALLY	No direct equivalent; use a register to hold tally	
TIME-OF-DAY	TIME macro 17.5	
WHEN-COMPILED	&SYSDATE, &SYSTIME	3.4

COBOL elements not related to a single division:		
COPY	COPY directive or macros	22.6
EJECT	EJECT directive	17.4
SKIP1/2/3	SPACE directive	17.4
TITLE	TITLE directive	17.4

Some VM Assembler Facilities

This appendix presents some VM-only macros that may be good alternatives to the MVS macro instructions we've discussed up to now.

Before using these instead of the ones shown in the example, you should determine exactly why you should use them before proceeding. The VM OS simulation allows you to develop the same (or similar) code across both operating systems. OS simulation allows device independence through the CMS FILEDEF command. VM may provide some device independence, but use of the macros discussed herein may force your program to use specific device types rather than allow flexibility in substitution.

At the same time, the VM macros allow you some performance improvement over OS simulation. Additionally, not all desirable VM services are available compatibly under MVS, so you may wish to use these where VM-unique services are needed.

We have been using the term VM to cover all the services used under both CMS and CP. We will differentiate between the two services in this appendix. The macros we will discuss provide CMS services. CP services are available through the Diagnose instruction, and we'll provide an example of this at the end of the appendix.

You should obtain the VM manuals listed in Chap. 1 before doing much VM development. The application development reference manual covers the CMS macros. The system facilities for programming manual discusses the diagnose instruction for CP. This appendix is written based on VM/SP Release 6.

A4.1 EQUIVALENT MACROS FOR I/O OPERATIONS

VM provides a series of macro instructions that accomplish the same services as the MVS OPEN, CLOSE, GET, PUT, and DCB macro instructions. The VM macros differ in that they are created for a specific device type rather than for a general I/O service.

OPEN and CLOSE are implicit in VM for the virtual console, virtual printer, virtual reader, and virtual punch. They are required, however, for access to CMS disk files. The equivalent macros are FSOPEN and FSCLOSE, and we'll discuss them later on.

The macros to actually perform I/O are listed below by device type. For the virtual console, IBM provides the LINERD macro to read input from the terminal and LINEWRT to write output. The format for simple output is

LINEWRT   DATA = (line,length)

In the preceding, "line" defines a data area where you have a line to be displayed on the terminal, and "length" defines the size of the data to display. You also may specify the data-area address and/or the length in a register within parentheses. For example,

LINEWRT   DATA = ((2),(3))

specifies that the address of the data area is in register 2 and the length to be displayed is in register 3.

To read input from a terminal, you use the LINERD macro. This may be coded as

LINERD   DATA = (line,length),PROMPT = 'text'

The "line" and "length" operands have the same meaning as for LINEWRT but describe an input area. The "text" operand specifies a message to be displayed on the console to prompt the user for input. (This is similar to the BASIC language INPUT service.) You also may specify a data area and length for the PROMPT keyword.

IBM also provided two macros called RDTERM and WRTERM for terminal input and output. These are older forms and, while not superseded, are not preferable. The form of these are

RDTERM   area,LENGTH = length

and

WRTERM   area,length

with the same register options as listed above. All these macros have additional options, and you should refer to the Application Development Reference Manual for further information.

For the virtual printer, VM provides the PRINTL macro. This prints a line on the virtual spooled printer. Its format is

PRINTL   line,length,CC = option

where "line" and "length" are used as discussed for the LINEWRT macro. The "option" for the CC (carriage control) parameter is YES or NO; use YES if the first byte of your line has ANSI print control.

PRINTL will return an error or condition code in register 15 after an error — return codes of 2 and 3 represent end-of-page (channel 12 or channel 9 on the virtual forms control buffer). The LOADVFCB and SPOOL commands affect the operation of PRINTL. PRINTL also has several other operands.

For the virtual reader, CMS provides RDCARD. This reads in a record from the virtual reader. RDCARD is coded as

    RDCARD   area,length

and the "length" operand is optional — RDCARD assumes a default of 80 if it is not coded.

For the virtual punch, PUNCHC provides a corollary service. PUNCHC does not allow a "length" operand; a length of 80 bytes is assumed.

All these macros have other operands that we haven't covered here. You should refer to the Application Development Reference Manual for a complete explanation.

Tape processing includes four macros. These are RDTAPE, WRTAPE, TAPECTL, and TAPESL. RDTAPE and WRTAPE read and write blocks on tape. TAPECTL provides tape control services, much like those provided by the TAPE command. TAPESL performs some standard label-tape functions.

RDTAPE is coded as

    RDTAPE   area,length,device

where these operands have the same meanings as discussed before. The "device" operand specifies the symbolic name (e.g., TAP0) or the virtual address (e.g., 180) for the tape drive being used. TAP1 (181) is the default if the "device" parameter is not coded. WRTAPE has the same parameters as RDTAPE.

Both RDTAPE and WRTAPE provide a return code in register 15. Return code 2 means end-of-file or end of tape on input or end-of-tape on output. Return code 6 indicate that an output tape is file-protected (no write ring). Other return codes represent permanent device or programming errors.

All these macros have other operands that we haven't covered here. You should refer to the Application Development Reference Manual for a complete explanation.

Disk I/O is more complex. CMS provides several macros to use the CMS file system. These and their approximate MVS equivalents are listed below:

MVS:	CMS:
OPEN	FSOPEN
CLOSE	FSCLOSE
GET	FSREAD
PUT	FSWRITE
DCB	FSCB
DCBD	FSCBD

A CMS file is represented to your program by coding an FSCB — File System Control Block — macro. An example of FSCB is

```
APP4FILE FSCB  'ASMPROG ASSEMBLEA ',BUFFER=0,FORM=E,      X
               BSIZE=80,RECFM=F,RECNO=0,NOREC=1
```

Unlike MVS or OS simulation, where the DDNAME parameter had to relate to a JCL DD statement or a CMS FILEDEF command, the FSCB allows you to specify the disk file name directly. This is the first operand.

It is coded as an 18-byte string within single quotation marks making up the CMS file name:

- The first 8 bytes are the file name.

- The second 8 bytes are the file type.

- The last 2 bytes are the file mode.

Note that if a file name or file type is less than 8 characters, it must be padded to 8 characters with blanks.

In the preceding example, ASMPROG is the file name. It is only 7 bytes long, so it is followed by a blank. ASSEMBLE is the file type. It is a full 8 bytes long, so no padding is needed. The file mode is A and no file mode number is provided.

The FORM=E parameter specifies an extended FSCB, which allows more and larger records in a file. This is highly recommended and will be used through all our examples.

BSIZE=80 specifies that 80 bytes are to be read or written to this file for each request. RECFM=F specifies that the records are in fixed format. (RECFM=V specifies variable length format.)

The RECNO parameter specifies the beginning or current record number for a read or write operation. Specifying RECNO=0, as we have done here, indicates that we want sequential access to the file.

CMS file services allow more than one record to be read or written at a time. We will stick to one record at a time for our examples, but you might wish to experiment with this for performance improvements.

You also may specify the address where records are to be read into or written from in the FSCB rather than in each read or write request. The BUFFER parameter allows you to specify the I/O area address. We will use BUFFER=0 here and specify it on our requests instead.

You also may specify '*' as a valid file name, file type, or file mode. The first file that matches the criteria will be used.

The file name on the FSCB may be changed during the program's execution. The FSCBD provides a DSECT map of the FSCB. You may include an FSCB DSECT by coding FSCBD among your other DSECTs. I recommend placement of these immediately before the END directive.

The following code uses the FSCBD DSECT to modify an FSCB during execution:

```
        LA      R2,APP4FILE          POINT TO FSCB
        USING   FSCBD,R2             ADDRESSABILITY
        MVC     FSCBFN, = CL8'ABNPROG'   MOVE FILE NAME
        MVC     FSCBFT, = CL8'TEXT'      MOVE FILE TYPE
        MVC     FSCBFM, = CL2'A1'        MOVE FILE MODE
        DROP    R2                   END USING
```

This set up the FSCB to access ABNPROG TEXT A1.

CMS file services will automatically open the FSCB when you first use it. However, you may wish to open an FSCB to specify the file parameters. In the following example, we open the FSCB we described earlier but change the record size from 80 to 400 bytes:

```
        LH      R3, = H'400'              SET UP BLOCK SIZE
        FSOPEN  FSCB = PIXLFILE,FORM = E,BSIZE = (3)
        LTR     R15,R15                   TEST GOOD FSOPEN
        BZ      OPENDONE                  ZERO - CONTINUE
        CH      R15, = H'28'              'FILE DOESNT EXIST'?
        BE      OPENDONE                  OK - MAKING NEW 1
*       OPEN FAILED FOR FSCB - ISSUE ERROR MESSAGE
        APPLMSG  APPLID = CMS,                              X
                TEXT = 'FSCB OPEN ERROR RC &&1',            X
                SUB = (DEC,(15))
        B       GIVEUP
OPENDONE EQU    *                         ALL FILES OPEN
```

Note that FSOPEN returns an error code in register 15. In this case, 0 indicates a successful FSOPEN. A return code of 28 indicates a special case — we are opening a file that does not exist. If we receive any other error return code, we display the FSCB OPEN ERROR message and go to GIVEUP.

You may specify how you intend to use the file as part of the FSOPEN. This is done through the OPENTYP= parameter. Possible values for this include:

- **READ** — indicating that you want to read an existing file
- **WRITE** — used when you want to read, write, or rewrite records in a file
- **NEW** — which tells CMS that you want to create a new file and will be writing it
- **REPLACE** — indicating that you want to rewrite the entire file
- **NONE** — which does nothing; return code 28 is set if the file does not exist

The default is NONE. This means that the first FSREAD or FSWRITE macro will open the FSCB automatically.

To write a record to a file, we can code

```
        FSWRITE FSCB = PIXLFILE,FORM = E,BUFFER = (3),        X
               NOREC = 1,BSIZE = (2),RECFM = V
        LTR    R15,R15                           TEST GOOD FSREAD
        BNZ    MACROERR                          NOT 0 - CHECK ERR
```

The FSCB and FORM=E operands are used as previously discussed. The other operands are

- **BUFFER** — which specifies where the record is written from; (3) indicates that register 3 has the address
- **NOREC** — which tells CMS how many records we want to write (1)
- **BSIZE** — which indicates how long the record is; (2) indicates that register 2 has the length
- **RECFM** — which determines the recording format; 'V' indicates variable, 'F' indicates fixed

FSREAD is coded with similar operands. Both FSWRITE and FSREAD also allow you to specify which record is to be written or read. The RECNO parameter specifies this. You may rewrite selected records or skip to various locations when reading a file by specifying this operand. It is normally coded as a value in a register.

To position to a particular record, VM also provides the FSPOINT macro. FSPOINT requires an FSCB or file name, and I recommend FORM=E. Two operands determine where the next records are processed.

WRPNT specifies where the next record is written. A value of -1 indicates that the next record should be added to the end of the file. RDPNT is the operand to specify where the next record should be read from. A value of 0 for both RDPNT and WRPNT tells CMS not to change the read or write pointers. The values for these two operands may be coded as registers or as absolute values.

You may prefer to use the RECNO operand of FSREAD or FSWRITE instead of FSPOINT. However, FSPOINT may be used to validate record numbers or access to a file without actually reading or writing.

When finished processing a CMS file, we should close it with the FSCLOSE macro. This is coded as

```
        FSCLOSE FSCB = PIXLFILE
        LTR    R15,R15                           TEST GOOD FSCLOSE
        BNZ    MACROERR                          NOT ZERO - ERROR
```

FORM=E is not required, since the FORM was set by earlier macros. FSCLOSE provides a return code in register 15, with 0 indicating a successful close.

CMS will perform automatic file closing for you if you do not do so yourself. However, if your program has been linked to, other uses of the file may change the record pointers in the FSCB. For this reason, you should always close the FSCB yourself.

CMS file services also include a macro that can be used to delete a file. This is FSERASE, coded as

```
FSERASE FSCB = FILENAME
```

Note that FSERASE deletes the entire file. It does not delete just one record like the VSAM ERASE macro. Use this with caution. Possible uses are to delete a work file automatically when your program ends, or to erase a file prior to rewriting it.

A4.2   STORAGE MANAGEMENT FACILITIES UNDER CMS

CMS provides services that are equivalent to the MVS GETMAIN and FREEMAIN macros. These are accessed through the CMSSTOR macro. CMSSTOR usage to acquire a 72-byte area is as follows:

```
CMSSTOR   OBTAIN,BYTES = 72
LR        R2,R1                      SAVE ADDR OF STG
```

The OBTAIN indicates that we want to acquire storage. BYTES=72 asks for 72 bytes of storage. (This is equivalent to coding " GETMAIN R,LV=72" under MVS.)

The length of storage desired may be requested in either bytes or doublewords. (Storage requests in doublewords were supported by an earlier CMS storage service — DMSFREE.) In addition, CMSSTOR allows the requested amount to be placed in a register. The following shows a request for 400 bytes expressed as the equivalent number of doublewords in register 0:

```
LH        R0, = H'400'               GET LEN INTO R0
SRA       R0,3                       LEN/ 8  =  DOUBLEWDS
CMSSTOR   OBTAIN,DWORDS = (0)
LR        R3,R1                      SAVE ADDR OF STG
```

(Remember that a right shift of 3 bits is equivalent to dividing by 8.) This CMSSTOR macro is like a GETMAIN R,LV=(0) in MVS.

CMSSTOR returns the address of the gotten storage in register 1. It should be saved immediately into another register or as a fullword in your working storage. CMSSTOR also has a conditional mode of operation. This allows you to determine if a request for storage was successful. The following shows an example of this:

```
L         R0, = F'8000000'           MAKE  SIZE TOO BIG
CMSSTOR   OBTAIN,BYTES = (0),ERROR = *
LR        R4,R1                      SAVE ADDR OF STG
LTR       R15,R15                    TEST RETURN CODE
BNZ       BADSTOR                    NOT ZERO - ERROR
```

The ERROR=* tells CMS that it should let our program know about the error rather than forcing the program to end. Note that CMS will display message DMSFR0159E ("Insufficient storage available...") on your CMS console. (Also note that if your virtual machine is large enough, this example will not automatically fail.)

When it is time to release the storage we have gotten, we still use the CMSSTOR macro, but we specify RELEASE rather than OBTAIN. The operands for the RELEASE are the same as for OBTAIN, but we also must tell CMS where the storage is. We do so by providing the ADDR operand. For example, to release the 72 bytes of storage we acquired in the earlier example, we code

CMSSTOR   RELEASE,BYTES = 72,ADDR = (2)

Remember that we saved the address of the storage immediately into register 2. ADDR=(2) tells CMS that register 2 holds the address of the area we wish to free. (This is equivalent to coding FREEMAIN R,LV=72,A=(2) in MVS.)

We also may free storage by providing the length in a register as well as the address. To free the storage we got in the second example above, we code

```
LH      R0, = H'400'              AMT WE GOT THE 2ND TIME
CMSSTOR    RELEASE,BYTES = (0),ADDR = (3)
```

Note that we acquired the storage earlier as doublewords (DWORDS), but that we can still free it as bytes as long as the lengths are equivalent. (This example is like coding FREEMAIN   R,LV=(0),A=(3) in MVS.)

CMS provided two earlier services for storage management. These were the DMSFREE and DMSFRET macros. These are still supported under VM/SP Release 6, but they should be converted to use CMSSTOR as time permits.

A4.3   PROGRAM LINKAGE UNDER CMS

CMS provides several services that are broadly equivalent to those in MVS. The CMSCALL and CMSRET macros are functionally the same as the MVS LINK and RETURN macros.

CMSCALL uses CMS supervisor-assisted linkage, which affects the layout of the parameter list passed to the called program. The parameter list passed is a *tokenized* parameter list, which is what a program invoked as a CMS command receives. In addition, you may provide an extended parameter list, termed an EPLIST.

The format of the tokenized parameter list is successive 8-byte entries, each containing a parameter. The end of the entries is marked by 8 bytes containing X'FF's (COBOL HIGH-VALUES).

The extended parameter list has a different format that passes the beginning and ending address of the parameter string. (This is the equivalent of the CMS command line.) The extended parameter list does not parse each item into 8-byte entries. Thus, if you want to pass command parameters longer than 8 bytes, you would need to use the extended parameter list.

The extended parameter list has several other pieces of information that we won't cover here. There is a macro to create a DSECT that maps the extended parameter list. This is called EPLIST and is worth reviewing. CMS provides a service to parse a command line or equivalent and construct tokenized and extended parameter lists. This is the SCAN macro. SCAN takes as input an unformatted character string, identified as the TEXT operand. It then produces the output as both extended and tokenized parameter lists. The addresses of the parameter lists are provided in registers 0 and 1.

The TEXT operand may specify a character string in quotes or the address and length of a character string to use in constructing the extended and tokenized parameter lists. The address and length may be coded in registers by specifying the register number within parentheses, as shown in examples of other macros.

The output of the SCAN macro is placed in a work area that you provide. This must be at least 48 bytes long — add 8 bytes for each additional item in the tokenized parameter list. You specify this through the BUFFER parameter and must provide the address and length. These may be in registers if desired.

Once you have built tokenized and extended parameter lists, you may call another program (or CMS command) with the CMSCALL macro. CMSCALL has several operands, including the following

- **PLIST** – which specifies the address of the tokenized parameter list and it may be in a register.

- **EPLIST** – which specifies the address of the extended parameter list and also may be in a register.

- **CALLTYP** – which allows you to simulate various types of command invocation. EPLIST specifies that both types of parameter lists are passed. Other values are listed in the CMS Application Development Reference Manual.

- **FENCE** – which indicates if you have provided the standard 8-byte X'FF' indicator for the end of the tokenized parameter list (YES) or not (NO).

- **ERROR** – which allows you to receive back an error code in register 15 ('*'), pass control to a specified routine (coded as the label of the routine), or ABEND if an error occurs.

Other parameters for CMSCALL are used when a 31-bit caller passes control to a 24-bit routine (the COPY operand) or when the called routine changes the tokenized parameter list (MODIFY).

The following example shows how to use the SCAN and CMSCALL macros to invoke the CMS PUNCH command (the numbers in brackets refer to the notes that follow):

```
[1]              LA    R2,PLISTS                  ADDR FOR PARMS
                 LA    R3,L'PLISTS                LEN OF PARM LIST
*                SCAN DESIRED MESSAGE TO CREATE PARAMETER LIST
[2]              SCAN  TEXT = 'PUNCH SHOWCMSC ASSEMBLE',        X
                       BUFFER = ((2),(3)),                      X
                       ERROR = *
[3]              STM   R0,R1,SAVER0R1             SAVE SCAN MACRO O/P
                       .........
*                CALL 'PUNCH' MODULE
[4]              LM    R0,R1,SAVER0R1             GET PARM INFO AGAIN
[5]              CMSCALL  PLIST = (1),..IST = (0),CALLTYP = EPLIST,
                       FENCE = YES,ERROR = *
                       .........
PLISTS           DS    CL200                      PARAMS GO HERE
```

NOTES:

1. We will be providing the address of the parameter list in registers 2 and 3. These two LA instructions set up for that.
2. The SCAN macro specifies a TEXT operand in quotes and a buffer in registers. The text value 'PUNCH SHOWCMSC ASSEMBLE' is the same as what we would enter on the CMS command line. The buffer operand specifies that the buffer address is in register 2 and its length is in register 3.
3. This saves the addresses of the extended (R0) and tokenized (R1) parameter lists in SAVER0R1. This is needed if we do any other processing between the SCAN and CMSCALL macros.
4. Restore the parameter list addresses. R0 and R1 are the preferred registers.
5. Call the PUNCH module. We specify FENCE=YES, since the SCAN macro set this up for us.

The CMSRET macro is used to return after we have been invoked by CMSCALL. It has an operand called RC to specify a return code. Alternatively, you may load a return code into register 15 and CMS will pass it back unchanged.

When you receive control back in a calling module following issuance of CMSCALL, register 15 will have the return code provided by CMSRET. Alternatively, if there were errors in the CMSCALL macro itself, you will receive negative values in register 15 to indicate this. Refer to the CMS Application Development Reference Manual for specific values.

CMS linkage includes another macro called COMPSWT. This changes the setting of the OSSFLAGS indicator in the CMS nucleus area (NUCON). This affects how CMS processes OS linkage macros.

VM processes the OS LINK and related macros differently depending on this switch setting. If the COMPSWT flag is on, CMS will look for file types of MODULE to satisfy MVS LINK macro requests in OS simulation. If it is off, CMS searches for file types of TEXT or in a LOADLIB or TXTLIB to find the requested program.

To set it on, code

COMPSWT ON

To turn this switch off, code

COMPSWT OFF

Note that the topics in this section are supplemented by the information in Sects. 14.7.2 and 14.7.6. Section 14.7.2 included an example which showed a VM tokenized parameter list. Section 14.7.6 referred to the COMPSWT command.

A4.4   OTHER CMS MACROS

VM provides a standard macro to generate register equates. This is called REGEQU and is coded with no operands. (Many MVS shops have copied this or have coded their own macro with the same name.)

The USERSAVE macro maps the save area provided by CMS when a program is invoked by means of CMSCALL. There are several additional flags at the end of the save area mapped by this DSECT macro. One of these is the USEUFLG byte — this contains a *user byte* of information that can be passed from the CMSCALL macro. The parameter to do this is called UFLAGS on CMSCALL, and it was not described earlier.

You may wish to review the USERSAVE DSECT, as well as the others mentioned here.

IBM has also released a macro called APPLMSG. This is an alternative to the LINEDIT macro, and includes support for multiple message dictionaries, foreign language messages, and so forth. You should refer to the application development manuals for complete details. However, we will show an example of APPLMSG in Fig. A4.1.

Another macro not covered in our earlier discussion of CMS file services is FSSTATE. This macro allows us to determine if a file exists. It is coded with an FSCB, as shown previously.

FSSTATE returns the address of the CMS File Status Table (FST) in register 1. The FST contains key information about a CMS file and is described by the FSTD DSECT generated by the macro of the same name.

The SHOWFILE program, shown in Fig. A4.1 which follows, provides an example of using FSSTATE, along with several other CMS macros. SHOWFILE asks for a CMS file name, then locates that and displays the FST information. It ends when it receives input of 'END'. For debugging, it will abnormally end if it gets input of 'ABEND'. (The numbers in brackets refer to the notes that follow the program.)

Figure A4.1 Sample program using CMS macros.

```
SHOWFILE TITLE 'SHOW STATUS OF A VM FILE'
SHOWFILE CSECT
         STM    R14,R12,12(R13)                 SAVE REGISTERS
         LR     R12,R15                         ESTABLISH
         USING SHOWFILE,R12                     ADDRESSABILITY

*        CHAIN SAVE AREAS
         LA     R2,SAVEAREA
         ST     R2,8(R13)
         ST     R13,4(R2)
         LR     R13,R2
         USING SAVEAREA,R13                     PGM DATA AREAS BASE

*        DISPLAY VERSION OF PROGRAM
[1]      APPLMSG APPLID = CMS,                                       X
         TEXT = 'SHOWFILE PROGRAM &SYSDATE &SYSTIME',                X
              DISP = TYPE

*        READ IN A FILE NAME
GETFILE EQU  *
         MVC    ERRMACRO, = CL8'LINERD'  MACRO NAME IF ERR
         LINERD  DATA = FILEIN,                                      X
[2]             PROMPT = 'ENTER FILE NAME OR "END"',                 X
                PAD = BLANK,ERROR = *
         LTR    R15,R15                         CHECK FOR ERROR
         BNZ    MACROERR                        YES - GO DISPLAY

*        CHECK FOR 'END' OR 'ABEND'
[3]      CLC    = C'END',FILEIN                 TEST INPUT VALUE
         BE     ENDEXEC                         EQUAL - DONE
         CLC    = C'ABEND',FILEIN               TEST ABEND REQ
         BE     ABENDUS                         EQUAL - DO IT

*        USE SCAN MACRO TO REFORMAT INPUT
         MVC    ERRMACRO, = CL8'SCAN'    ERR MACRO NAME
         LA     R2,FILEIN                       GET PARM INFO AGAIN
         LA     R3,L'FILEIN                     GET LENGTH
[4]      SCAN   TEXT = ((2),(3)),                                    X
                BUFFER = (FMTFILE,200),                              X
                ERROR = *
         LTR    R15,R15                         CHECK FOR ERROR
         BNZ    MACROERR                        YES - GO DISPLAY
         LR     R3,R1                    ADDR OF TOKENIZED LIST
```

Figure A4.1 (Continued)

```
[5]          CLI    0(R3),X'FF'              END OF LIST?
             BE     NODATA                   Y - WRITE ERR MSG
             CLI    8(R3),X'FF'              FILE TYPE PROVIDED?
             BE     MOVE10          NO - BLANK OUT TYPE, MODE
             CLI    16(R3),X'FF'             FILE MODE PROVIDED?
             BE     MOVE2                    NO - BLANK OUT
             B      CHKSTATE        OK - CHECK FILE STATUS
MOVE10       EQU    *
             MVC    8(8,R3),WILDCARD         MOVE IN '*       '
MOVE2        EQU    *
             MVC    16(2,R3),WILDCARD        MOVE IN '* '
CHKSTATE     EQU    *

*                   CHECK TO SEE IF FILE EXISTS
[6]          FSSTATE  (3),FSCB=FILEFSCB,FORM=E,ERROR=*
             STH    R15,RETCODE             SAVE RETURN CODE

*                   TEST RESPONSE IN R15
             LTR    R15,R15                 TEST RESPONSE
             BZ     FOUNDIT                 IF 0, GO SHOW DATA

*                   DISPLAY RETURN CODE IN REGISTER 15
             CVD    R15,DOUBLEWD            CONV TO DECIMAL
             OI     DOUBLEWD+7,X'0F'        TURN ON SIGN BITS
             UNPK   FSSTCODE,DOUBLEWD       UNPACK
[7]          LINEWRT  DATA=(FSSTERR,40),                        X
                    HILITE=HIGH,ERROR=*,ALARM=YES
             B      GETFILE                 GET NEXT FILE

*                   DISPLAY FILE INFORMATION
FOUNDIT      EQU    *
[8]          LR     R4,R1           GET FILE STATUS TBL ADDR
             USING  FSTD,R4                 ADDRESSABILITY
             MVC    MNAME,FSTFNAME          MOVE FILE NAME
             MVC    MTYPE,FSTFTYPE          FILE TYPE
             MVC    MMODE,FSTFMODE          FILE MODE
             MVC    MMMDD,=X'402020612020'  DATE EDIT MASK
             ED     MMMDD,FSTADATI+1        EDIT IN VALUE
             MVC    MYEAR,=X'402020'        YEAR EDIT MASK
             ED     MYEAR,FSTADATI          EDIT IN VALUE
             MVI    MYEAR,C'/'              YEAR SEPARATOR
             MVC    MHHMM,=X'4020204B2020'  TIME EDIT MASK
             ED     MHHMM,FSTADATI+3        EDIT IN VALUE
```

Figure A4.1 (Continued)

```
            MVC    MRECFM,FSTRECFM              RECORDING FMT
            L      R0,FSTAIC                    GET RECORD CT
            CVD    R0,DOUBLEWD                  CONV TO DECIMAL
            MVC    MRECCT, = X'402020202020'    MOVE EDIT MASK
            ED     MRECCT,DOUBLEWD + 5          EDIT IN VALUE
            L      R0,FSTLRECL                  GET REC LEN
            CVD    R0,DOUBLEWD                  CONVTO DECIMAL
            MVC    MLRECL, = X'402020202020'    MOVE EDIT MASK
            ED     MLRECL,DOUBLEWD + 5          EDIT IN VALUE
            MVC    MACTIVE, = CL6' '            BLANK 'ACTIVE' FLD
[9]         TM     FSTFLAGS,FSTFILEA            TEST 'ACTIVE' BITS
            BZ     SHOWIT                       IF ZERO, DONE
            MVC    MACTIVE, = C'ACTIVE'         SHOW FILE IN USE

*           ISSUE LINEWRT TO WRITE TO MY VIRTUAL CONSOLE
SHOWIT      EQU    *
            LINEWRT DATA = (MSGFILE,80),HILITE = HIGH,ERROR = *
            LINEWRT DATA = (MSGFILE2,80),HILITE = HIGH,ERROR = *
            B      GETFILE                      READ NAME AGAIN

ENDEXEC     EQU    *
            LH     R0,RETCODE                   GET RETURN CODE
            CVD    R0,DOUBLEWD                  CONV TO DECIMAL
            OI     DOUBLEWD + 7,X'0F'           TURN ON SIGN BITS
            UNPK   MSG803RC,DOUBLEWD            UNPACK
*           ISSUE LINEWRT TO WRITE TO MY VIRTUAL CONSOLE
            LINEWRT   DATA = (MSG803I,80),                     X
                      HILITE = HIGH,ERROR = *,ALARM = YES,     X
                      LINE = 21
*           RETURN TO CALLING PROGRAM

RETURN      EQU    *
            LH     R15,RETCODE                  GET RETURN CODE
            L      R13,4(R13)                   SAVE AREA ADDR
[10]        CMSRET  RC = (15)                   RETURN TO VM
*           NO FILE NAME ENTERED - WRITE ERR MSG AND RETRY
NODATA      EQU    *
            APPLMSG  APPLID = CMS,                             X
                     TEXT = 'YOU MUST ENTER A FILE NAME OR ''END'
                     ' TO STOP',DISP = TYPE
            B      GETFILE                      READ NAME AGAIN
```

Figure A4.1 (Continued)

```
*              ERROR IN SOME MACRO - DISPLAY AND END EXECUTION
MACROERR      EQU                        *
              CVD    R15,DOUBLEWD      -     CONV TO DECIMAL
              OI     DOUBLEWD+7,X'0F'        SET SIGN BITS
              UNPK   R15ERR,DOUBLEWD         UNPACK
              LINEWRT DATA=(MACMSG,40),HILITE=HIGH,ERROR=*
              B      ENDEXEC                 GIVE UP

*              ABEND REQUEST FOR DEBUGGING
ABENDUS  EQU  *
[11]          DMSABN  FFF


*              DATA AREAS
DOUBLEWD  DC    D'0'
SAVEAREA DC    18F'+0'
SAVEROR1 DS    2F
RETCODE  DC    H'0'
[12]
FILEFSCB FSCB  FORM=E

FILEIN    DC    CL20' '                   FILE NAME HERE
MSGFILE  DC    C'FILE:'
MNAME    DC    CL8' ',C' '
MTYPE    DC    CL8' ',C' '
MMODE    DC    CL2' ',C' LAST WRITTEN:'
MMMDD    DC    CL6' '
MYEAR    DC    CL3' ',C' AT '
MHHMM    DC    CL6' '
         DC    CL(MSGFILE+80-*)' '        FILLER
MSGFILE2 DC    C'      FORMAT:'
MRECFM   DC    C' ',C' RECORD LENGTH:'
MLRECL   DC    CL6' ',C' NUMBER OF RECORDS:'
MRECCT   DC    CL6' ',C' '
MACTIVE  DC    CL6' '
         DC    CL(MSGFILE2+80-*)' '       FILLER
FSSTERR  DC    C'ERROR - FSSTATE RETURN CODE:'
FSSTCODE DC    CL8' ',CL4'****' '

MACMSG   DC    AL1(40)                    LENGTH
ERRMACRO       DC                         CL8' '
         DC    CL32' MACRO HAD ERROR - R15:'
R15ERR   DC    CL8' ',CL4' '
```

Figure A4.1 (Continued)

```
WILDCARD DC       CL8'*'
MSG803I   DC      CL21'MSG803I END OF JOB - '
MSG803RC DC       CL2' '
          DC      CL57' WAS HIGHEST RETURN CODE'

*                 REGISTER EQUATES
                  REGEQU

                  LTORG

                  CNOP 0,4                    FULLWORD ALIGN
FMTFILE   DS      CL200                       PARM LISTS   HERE

[13]      FSTD            FILE STATUS TABLE DSECT

          END     SHOWFILE
```

Notes:
1. We are using APPLMSG to write out a message — in this case, it is similar to LINEDIT. The APPLID=CMS is required unless you have an alternative message dictionary defined.
2. We use LINERD to read in a file name from the virtual console. Note that the text in the PROMPT parameter is displayed on the CMS terminal.
3. We are testing here for the keywords END or ABEND. Note that since the literal is the first operand, the assembler will use the length of the literal for the comparison automatically and we don't have to code it.
4. We are using the SCAN macro here to parse the file name into a tokenized parameter list. We are not going to actually use the output as a tokenized parameter list.
5. Here we are searching for the end of the input file name as provided by the caller. The SCAN macro generated X'FF' at the end of the list for us earlier.
6. The FSSTATE macro will look for the file name formatted by the SCAN macro.
7. Here we use the LINEWRT macro to display an error message on the CMS terminal. Note the ALARM and HILITE operands, which will sound a 3270 alarm and display the text in higher intensity on a 3270 terminal.
8. Here we format the various FST fields. See the comments for the individual field names and descriptions.
9. The ACTIVE flag will be set on if the CMS file is open (e.g., by means of FSOPEN). This indicates if it is in use.

10. Here we use CMSRET to pass control back to CMS.

11. The DMSABN macro will force an ABEND for debugging.

12. Note that there is no file name on this FSCB. It is provided by the FSSTATE macro coded earlier.

13. This generates the File Status Table (FST) DSECT.

A4.5   CMS DATA-AREA DSECTs

In addition to the data-area macros we've listed above (e.g., FSTD), there are two additional DSECT macros that have generally used information. The first is the NUCON DSECT macro. This maps the CMS nucleus. The second is the CMSCVT macro. This maps the CMS OS compatibility version of the MVS Communications Vector Table (CVT). You may wish to review the DSECT output of these macro instructions.

A4.6   ACCESSING CP SERVICES

VM Control Program (CP) services are fundamentally different from those provided by CMS. While the difference between CP and CMS commands may not appear significant to you, CP services are provided at very basic levels.

We must use a different method of invoking CP services. CMS allows us to use the SVC instruction and uses SVC 202 and 203 to call CMS services such as CMSSTOR.

CP does not respond to SVC requests, however, since these must be performed within the virtual machine (e.g., by CMS) rather than by CP. To communicate with CP, we must use a different method. This is by using an instruction that is not normally used by either application programs or an operating system.

The instruction selected for this is the Diagnose instruction. Diagnose is used in hardware diagnostic programs and hardware error recovery routines. It does not typically appear in normal operation.

Diagnose is intended for very special operations and has no assembler opcode. We must generate it ourselves to invoke CP. This is usually done with the DC directive.

The hexadecimal machine operation code for Diagnose is X'83'. This is the first part of the code we must generate. Diagnose is a 4-byte instruction. The remainder of the generated code comprises three values.

The first two values are register numbers (in hexadecimal), which are referred to as Rx and Ry, respectively. These contain addresses and/or codes used by the function invoked by CP Diagnose. The Ry register will usually contain a return code.

The last value is a 2-byte hexadecimal function code that tells VM what service we are requesting. The service codes, along with other CP programming information, are listed in the System Facilities for Programming Manual. Figure A4.2 shows the format of the Diagnose instruction.

Figure A4.2 Format of Diagnose instruction.

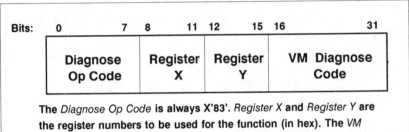

The wide variety of services provided through Diagnose is too large to document here. You should refer to the System Facilities for Programming Manual for more details on how to use Diagnose. However, we will provide an example that shows how to use a basic service through CP Diagnose — the "store extended identification code" service. This tells us information about the VM release and user ID we are running under.

In addition, we will show use of the STIDP (Store Processor ID) instruction. This can be used to determine the CPU type and serial number you are running on.

Figure A4.3 shows the pertinent code from a program called DIAG-NOSE. It issues Diagnose with a function code of X'0000'and then issues an STIDP to determine the CPU information. The output is displayed in hexadecimal and in formatted form. Note that the program initialization and other standard code is not shown, only what you would include in a program to do this function. (The numbers in brackets refer to the notes that follow the program.) Sample virtual console output from running the program is shown in Fig. A4.4.

The method by which this works is that both the Diagnose and STIDP instructions generate program interruptions. These would normally result in 0C2 ABENDs (Privileged operation exceptions) in MVS. However, CP recognizes these as valid requests for service, and processes them as needed — returning information in the case of our Diagnose example and for the STIDP instruction.

Figure A4.3 Example of Diagnose instruction.

```
*              ISSUE DIAGNOSE TO GET USER ID AND VM RELEASE INFO
*              TO DO THIS, WE MUST GENERATE A 4-BYTE CONSTANT
*              IN THE DIAGNOSE FORMAT.

*              THE FOLLOWING DIAGNOSE INSTRUCTION REQUESTS
*              THAT VM PROVIDE THE USER ID AND SOME VM
*              RELEASE AND CPU INFORMATION TO US.

[1]            LA      R2,DIAGAREA              DIAGNOSE O/P AREA
               LA      R3,L'DIAGAREA            LEN OF O/P AREA
[2]            DC      X'83230000'              DIAGNOSE

*              DISPLAY WHAT WE GOT BACK.
               MVI     DIAGOUT,105    SET UP 1-BYTE LINE LENGTH
[3]            LINEDIT TEXTA = DIAGOUT,DISP = TYPE,DOT = NO,        X
                       COMP = NO,SUB = (HEX4A,(2)),RENT = NO

*              NOW ISSUE A STORE CPU IDENTIFICATION (STIDP)
*              INSTRUCTION TO GET THE CPU TYPE AND SERIAL NUM.
[4]            STIDP CPUAREA                     STORE CPU INFO

*              DISPLAY STIDP RESULT.
               MVI     DIAGOUT,33                1-BYTE LINE LEN
               MVC     DIAGOUT + 1(8), = C' STIDP '  CHANGE TO 'STIDP'
               LINEDIT  TEXTA = DIAGOUT,DISP = TYPE,DOT = NO,        X
                       COMP = NO,SUB = (HEX4A,CPUAREA),             X
                       RENT = NO

*              NOW DISPLAY THE INFORMATION WE GOT BACK
*              FROM BOTH IN DISPLAYABLE FORMAT.
[5]            MVC     USERID,DIAGAREA + 16      MOVE USER ID
               MVC     OPSYS,DIAGAREA            MOVE VM ID
               MVC     RELNO, = X'4020204B2020'  MOVE EDIT MASK
               ED      RELNO,DIAGAREA + 36       EDIT RELEASE + VER
               MVC     CPUMODEL, = X'4020202020'  MOVE EDIT MASK
               ED      CPUMODEL,CPUAREA + 4      EDIT CPU TYPE
               MVC     SERIALNO, = X'4020202020202020'     EDIT MASK
               ED      SERIALNO,CPUAREA + 1      CPU SERIAL NUM
               WRTERM  IDLINE,80                 WRITE MSG TO TERMINAL
               . . . . . . . .
DIAGOUT        DC      AL1(99)
[6]            DC  C'DIAGNOSE OUTPUT:.....................................X
               .................................................................X
               ................',
```

Figure A4.3 (Continued)

```
*               THE 'DIAGAREA' MUST BE DOUBLEWORD ALIGNED
                CNOP  0,8
DIAGAREA DC     XL40'00'

CPUAREA DC      D'0'
IDLINE    DS    0CL80
          DC    C'USER ID:'
USERID  DC      CL8' ',C' '
OPSYS   DC      CL8' ',C' RELEASE'
RELNO   DC      CL6' ',C' CPU TYPE:'
CPUMODEL DC     CL5' ',C' SERIAL NUMBER:'
SERIALNO DC     CL7' '
          DC    CL(IDLINE+80-*)' '                    FILLER
*               VM NUCLEUS DSECT
[7]             NUCON
```

Notes:

1. The Rx and Ry registers for this request will be 2 and 3. These LA instructions set up their values.
2. This is the Diagnose instruction itself generated with a DC directive. '83' specifies the Diagnose machine opcode. '23' is the Rx and Ry field, specifying registers 2 and 3. '0000' is the CP Diagnose function code for getting the VM release and user ID.
3. This shows the results from the CP Diagnose.
4. The second part of our display will be the CPU ID and type. We use the STIDP instruction to do this, which returns an 8-byte value. We will also display this in hexadecimal.
5. Now display the information from the Diagnose and the STIDP in a more usable format. This code creates the output lines.
6. This begins the data areas used by this code.
7. This generates the CMS nucleus DSECT NUCON, which is not needed for this example but worth reviewing.

This code was assembled in a program called DIAGNOSE. Figure A4.4 shows the VM virtual terminal output generated when running it on an IBM 9370 model 60 from the OPERATOR user ID.

Figure A4.4 Output from Diagnose instruction.

```
load  diagnose
Ready; T = 0.02/0.06 18:40:07
start  *
Execution begins...
DIAGNOSE OUTPUT:    E5D461E2 D7404040 00000050 00000000 D6D7C5D9

                   C1E3D6D9 FE0000E0 00000000 FFFFC7C0 06000258

       STIDP  OUTPUT:FF010029 93750000

USER ID:OPERATOR VM/SP    RELEASE  6.00 CPU TYPE: 9375
                                    SERIAL NUMBER:  10029
```

The CMS commands used to run this program are shown in bold type. The layout of the print lines was changed slightly to fit the output into the dimensions of this book.

An Annotated Assembly Listing

This appendix presents the actual assembler listing from the assembler program shown in Fig. 1.2. Each page on the assembler listing is separated by a ruled line — one appears on the next page. Comments on the listing explaining its contents are enclosed in brackets ("[", "]"). Where there is not enough space to explain something, a note in brackets (e.g.,"[1]") is placed at the point of interest. The note is then explained below.

Where an explanation covers a topic which may be less frequently used, the note is preceded by "Esoterica" within the brackets.

[The first page of your assembly listing is usually the external symbol dictionary. This defines the names inside your program and the names of any other programs you refer to. Chapter 14 explains these concepts.]

```
                                      EXTERNAL SYMBOL DICTIONARY                      PAGE   1
                                                                        ASM H V 02 12.05 11/27/89
                                                                                [4]

SYMBOL   TYPE ID  ADDR   LENGTH  LD ID FLAGS
PROGNAME SD 0001 000000  0003D8
  [1]         [2]   [3]                                                    [5]      [6]   [7]
```

[Notes:
1. The SYMBOL column shows the control section (CSECT) names and any ENTRY names inside your program. It also shows any references to other program names (e.g., via EXTRNs).
2. The ADDR column shows where the name under the SYMBOL column is located within your program. In this case, PROGNAME is the first CSECT in the program, and begins at location zero within the program.
3. This column shows the length associated with the name in the SYMBOL column. In this case, the program called PROGNAME is hexadecimal X'3D8' long (984 bytes in decimal).
4. The assembler prints a page number on each page.
5. This is the assembler type (assembler H) and its version number (version 2).
6. This is the time the assembly started (12:05 P.M.).
7. This is the date the assembly started (November 27, 1989).]

[This begins the actual program listing. The columns below have the following meanings:

1. LOC is the location within the program. It is shown in hexadecimal. It begins at zero and increases by the data or instruction length of each statement.

2. OBJECT CODE is what the assembler generates from the instructions, macros, or directives you code. It is either one, two, or three columns for instructions, depending on how long the instruction is. It is one column for data, showing up to eight bytes of data generated as a result of a DC directive.

3. ADDR1 is the address of the first operand. This is usually the address of a label within your program. For example, follow the LOC column down until you find 000056. The source statement for this (column 6) is " MVC   DATA,INAREA ". You will note that the ADDR1 column contains 0018D. Now follow the LOC column down until you find an entry with with 00018D. If you look at the source statement, you should find "DATA" as the label field.

4. ADDR2 is the address of the second operand. Go back to the LOC column entry with 000056 in it. The ADDR2 column contains 0012C. Now follow the LOC column until you find a line with a location of 00012C. The label on the source statement field (column 6 again) should be INAREA.

5. STMT is the statement number assigned to the source line by the assembler. This does not have any relationship to a source line number assigned by TSO, ISPF, CMS, or any other program editor.

6. The SOURCE STATEMENT is the actual line of your program which the assembler is converting to code. (This may also come from a macro you have coded.)]

ASM H V 02 12.05 11/27/89

PAGE   2

[1]	[2]	[3]	[4]	[5]	[6]			
LOC	OBJECT CODE	ADDR1	ADDR2	STMT	SOURCE	STATEMENT		
000000				1	PROGNAME	CSECT		
000000	90EC D00C		0000C	2		STM	R14,R12,12(R13)	SAVE REGISTERS
000004	18CF			3		LR	R12,R15	GET PROGRAM ADDRESS
000000				4		USING	PROGNAME,R12	ESTABLISH ADDRESSABILITY
				6	*	CHAIN	SAVE AREAS	
000006	50D0 C0E8		000E8	7		ST	R13,SAVEAREA+4	SET OLD SAVE AREA ADDRESS
00000A	4120 C0E4		000E4	8		LA	R2,SAVEAREA	GET TO NEW SAVE AREA ADDR
00000E	502D 0008		00008	9		ST	R2,8(R13)	SET NEW SAVE AREA ADDRESS
000012	18D2			10		LR	R13,R2	UPDATE REGISTER 13

```
12 *        OPEN FILES
13          OPEN  (INFILE,INPUT,PRINTER,OUTPUT)
```

[Note that statement 13 uses the OPEN macro instruction. The next seven lines (statements 14 through 20) have a "+" (plus sign) after the statement number to indicate that they came from a macro rather than being coded in your program.]

[Esoterica: Also note that positions 73-80 of these generated statements have "01-OPEN" placed there by the assembler. The "01" signifies the macro nesting level — it is possible to use a macro instruction inside another macro. This number indicates which macro the assembler is processing at a given time. The "OPEN" part is he name of the macro being processed.]

```
000014                 14+  CNOP  0,4                   ALIGN LIST TO FULLWORD  01-OPEN
000014 4510 C020       15+  BAL   1,*+12                LOAD REG1 W/LIST ADDR.  01-OPEN
000018 00              16+  DC    AL1(0)                OPTION BYTE             01-OPEN
000019 000378          17+  DC    AL3(INFILE)           DCB ADDRESS             01-OPEN
00001C 8F              18+  DC    AL1(143)              OPTION BYTE             01-OPEN
00001D 000318          19+  DC    AL3(PRINTER)          DCB ADDRESS             01-OPEN
000020 0A13            20+  SVC   19                    ISSUE OPEN SVC          01-OPEN
000022 4110 C378       21+  LA    R1,INFILE             GET ADDRESS OF INPUT DCB
                       22+  USING IHADCB,R1             ESTABLISH ADDRESSABILITY TO DCB
000026 9110 1030       23+  TM    DCBOFLGS,X'10'        TEST FOR SUCCESSFUL OPEN
00002A 4780 C0D0       24+  BZ    OPENERR               NOT ZERO - OPEN FAILED
00002E 4110 C318       25+  LA    R1,PRINTER            NOW POINT TO PRINT OUTPUT DCB
000032 9110 1030       26+  TM    DCBOFLGS,X'10'        TEST FOR SUCCESSFUL OPEN
000036 4780 C0D0       27+  BZ    OPENERR               NOT ZERO - OPEN FAILED
```

[Esoterica: Here is another example of a macro invocation. Note that the first two generated statements (numbers 30 and 31) have "02-IHBIN" in positions 73 through 80. The 02 indicates that these lines are from the second-level macro nested in this call. PUT (what we coded as shown on statement 29) was the first level. PUT uses an inner macro called IHBINNRA to process parameters — this is where the IHBIN arose.]

```
                       29   PUT   PRINTER,HEADLINE      WRITE PAGE HEADING
00003A 4110 C318       30+  LA    1,PRINTER             LOAD PARAMETER REG 1    02-IHBIN
00003E 4100 C201       31+  LA    0,HEADLINE            LOAD PARAMETER REG 0    02-IHBIN
000042 58F0 1030       32+  L     15,48(0,1)            LOAD PUT ROUTINE ADDR   01-PUT
000046 05EF            33+  BALR  14,15                 LINK TO PUT ROUTINE     01-PUT
```

[Note that statement 36 has an EQU — equate — directive. The assembler prints the value of the EQU in the ADDR2 column. In this case, "*" represents the current program location, which is hexadecimal 00048.]

```
                                      00048     36 MAINLINE EQU  *
                                                37          GET  INFILE,INAREA        READ A RECORD
000048 4110 C378                00378  38+          LA   1,INFILE            LOAD PARAMETER REG 1   02-IHBIN
00004C 4100 C12C                0012C  39+          LA   0,INAREA            LOAD PARAMETER REG 0   02-IHBIN
000050 58F0 1030                00030  40+          L    15,48(0,1)     LOAD GET ROUTINE ADDR      01-GET
000054 05EF                            41+          BALR 14,15          LINK TO GET ROUTINE        01-GET
000056 D24F C18D C12C    0018D 0012C   42          MVC  DATA,INAREA         MOVE TO PRINT AREA
00005C FA30 C30D C312    0030D 00312   43          AP   RECNUM,ONE          ADD TO RECORD COUNT
000062 960F C310               00310   44          OI   RECNUM+3,X'0F'      SET SIGN BITS
000066 F363 C185 C30D    00185 0030D   45          UNPK NUMBER,RECNUM       MOVE TO PRINT LINE
                                       46          PUT  PRINTER,LINE        WRITE PRINT LINE
00006C 4110 C318               00318   47+          LA   1,PRINTER           LOAD PARAMETER REG 1  02-IHBIN
000070 4100 C17C               0017C   48+          LA   0,LINE              LOAD PARAMETER REG 0  02-IHBIN
000074 58F0 1030               00030   49+          L    15,48(0,1)     LOAD PUT ROUTINE ADDR     01-PUT
000078 05EF                            50+          BALR 14,15          LINK TO PUT ROUTINE        01-PUT
00007A FA10 C30B C312    0030B 00312   51          AP   LINECT,ONE          ADD TO LINE COUNT
000080 F911 C30B C313    0030B 00313   52          CP   LINECT,P50          ARE WE AT PAGE END?
000086 4740 C048               00048   53          BL   MAINLINE            NO - CONTINUE
00008A F810 C30B C311    0030B 00311   54          ZAP  LINECT,ZERO         RESET LINE COUNT
                                       55          PUT  PRINTER,HEADLINE    WRITE PAGE HEADING
```

LOC	OBJECT CODE	ADDR1	ADDR2	STMT	SOURCE STATEMENT		
000090	4110 C318		00318	56+	LA	1,PRINTER	LOAD PARAMETER REG 1	02-IHBIN
000094	4100 C201		00201	57+	LA	0,HEADLINE	LOAD PARAMETER REG 0	02-IHBIN
000098	58F0 1030		00030	58+	L	15,48(0,1)	LOAD PUT ROUTINE ADDR	01-PUT
00009C	05EF			59+	BALR	14,15	LINK TO PUT ROUTINE	01-PUT
00009E	47F0 C048		00048	60	B	MAINLINE	PROCESS NEXT RECORD	
				62 *	END-OF-FILE ROUTINE.		
000A2			000A2	63 ENDDATA	EQU	*		
				64	PUT	PRINTER,ENDLINE	WRITE ENDING LINE	
0000A2	4110 C318		00318	65+	LA	1,PRINTER	LOAD PARAMETER REG 1	02-IHBIN
0000A6	4100 C286		00286	66+	LA	0,ENDLINE	LOAD PARAMETER REG 0	02-IHBIN
0000AA	58F0 1030		00030	67+	L	15,48(0,1)	LOAD PUT ROUTINE ADDR	01-PUT
0000AE	05EF			68+	BALR	14,15	LINK TO PUT ROUTINE	01-PUT
				69	CLOSE	(INFILE,,PRINTER)	CLOSE FILES	
0000B0				70+	CNOP	0,4	ALIGN LIST TO FULLWORD	01-CLOSE
0000B0	4510 C0BC		000BC	71+	BAL	1,*+12	LOAD REG1 W/LIST ADDR	01-CLOSE
0000B4	00			72+	DC	AL1(0)	OPTION BYTE	01-CLOSE
0000B5	000378			73+	DC	AL3(INFILE)	DCB ADDRESS	01-CLOSE
0000B8	80			74+	DC	AL1(128)	OPTION BYTE	01-CLOSE
0000B9	000318			75+	DC	AL3(PRINTER)	DCB ADDRESS	01-CLOSE
0000BC	0A14			76+	SVC	20	ISSUE CLOSE SVC	01-CLOSE
0000BE	58DD 0004		00004	77	L	R13,4(R13)	GET OLD SAVE AREA	
				78	RETURN	(14,12),T,RC=0	RETURN TO OPERATING SYSTEM	
0000C2	98EC D00C	0000C		79+	LM	14,12,12(13)	RESTORE THE REGISTERS	01-RETUR
0000C6	92FF D00C		0000C	80+	MVI	12(13),X'FF'	SET RETURN INDICATION	01-RETUR
0000CA	41F0 0000		00000	81+	LA	15,0(0,0)	LOAD RETURN CODE	01-RETUR
0000CE	07FE			82+	BR	14	RETURN	01-RETUR
				84 *	ERROR WHEN OPENING A FILE. END WITH RETURN CODE = 16.		
0000D0			000D0	85 OPENERR	EQU	*		
0000D0	58DD 0004		00004	86	L	R13,4(R13)	GET OLD SAVE AREA	
				87	RETURN	(14,12),T,RC=16	RETURN TO OPERATING SYSTEM	
0000D4	98EC D00C	0000C		88+	LM	14,12,12(13)	RESTORE THE REGISTERS	01-RETUR
0000D8	92FF D00C		0000C	89+	MVI	12(13),X'FF'	SET RETURN INDICATION	01-RETUR
0000DC	41F0 0010		00010	90+	LA	15,16(0,0)	LOAD RETURN CODE	01-RETUR
0000E0	07FE			91+	BR	14	RETURN	01-RETUR

[We now begin to generate the data part of this program. Note that the assembler inserts slack bytes for alignment just as the COBOL compiler does. The next line, at address 0000E2, shows an example of this.]

```
0000E2 0000          93 *          DATA AREAS
```

[When the assembler generates data, it places the value of the data it creates in hexadecimal. Normally, only the first eight bytes's worth are shown.]

```
0000E4 0000000000000000   94 SAVEAREA DC    18F'0'                    PROGRAM SAVE AREA
```

[Conversely, when a DS — Define Storage — directive is coded, the assembler has no initial value to display, and the area is left blank, as it is below.]

```
00012C                     95 INAREA   DS   CL80                      INPUT DATA AREA
00017C 40                  96 LINE     DC   C' '                      CARRIAGE CONTROL
00017D 40D9C5C3D6D9C440    97          DC   C' RECORD '
000185                     98 NUMBER   DS   CL7                       RECORD NUMBER
00018C 7A                  99          DC   C':'
00018D                    100 DATA     DS   CL80                      DATA RECORD
0001DD 4040404040404040   101          DC   CL36' '                   FILLER
000201 F1405C405C405C40   102 HEADLINE DC   CL133'1 * * * RECORD LISTING * * *'
000286 F0405C405C405C40   103 ENDLINE  DC   CL133'0 * * * END OF REPORT * * *'
00030B 000C               104 LINECT   DC   PL2'0'                    LINE COUNT
00030D 0000000C           105 RECNUM   DC   PL4'0'                    RECORD NUMBER
000311 0C                 106 ZERO     DC   P'0'                      CONSTANT 0
000312 1C                 107 ONE      DC   P'1'                      CONSTANT 1
```

473

LOC	OBJECT CODE	ADDR1	ADDR2	STMT	SOURCE STATEMENT		
000313	050C			108	P50	DC	P'50' CONSTANT 50
				110	*	DATA CONTROL BLOCKS	
				111	PRINTER	DCB	DDNAME=PRINTER,DEVD=DA,MACRF=(PM),DSORG=PS, X
							RECFM=FBA,LRECL=133,BLKSIZE=0
							DATA CONTROL BLOCK
000315	000000	[Slack Bytes]					
000318				113+	*		
				114+	*		
000318				115+	PRINTER	DC	0F'0' ORIGIN ON WORD BOUNDARY 01-DCB
				117+	*	DIRECT ACCESS DEVICE INTERFACE	
000318	0000000000000000			119+		DC	BL16'0' FDAD,DVTBL 01-DCB
000328	00000000			120+		DC	A(0) KEYLE,DEVT,TRBAL 01-DCB
				122+	*	COMMON ACCESS METHOD INTERFACE	
00032C	00			124+		DC	AL1(0) BUFNO 01-DCB
00032D	000001			125+		DC	AL3(1) BUFCB 01-DCB
000330	0000			126+		DC	AL2(0) BUFL 01-DCB
000332	4000			127+		DC	BL2'0100000000000000' DSORG 01-DCB
000334	00000001			128+		DC	A(1) ICQE/IOBAD 01-DCB
				130+	*	FOUNDATION EXTENSION BFTEK,BFLN,HIARCHY	
000338	00			132+		DC	BL1'00000000' 01-DCB
000339	000001			133+		DC	AL3(1) EODAD 01-DCB
00033C	94			134+		DC	BL1'10010100' RECFM 01-DCB
00033D	000000			135+		DC	AL3(0) EXLST 01-DCB
				137+	*	FOUNDATION BLOCK	
000340	D7D9C9D5E3C5D940			139+		DC	CL8'PRINTER' DDNAME 01-DCB
000348	02			140+		DC	BL1'00000010' OFLGS 01-DCB
000349	00			141+		DC	BL1'00000000' IFLG 01-DCB
00034A	0050			142+		DC	BL2'0000000001010000' MACR 01-DCB
				144+	*	BSAM-BPAM-QSAM INTERFACE	
00034C	00			146+		DC	BL1'00000000' RER1 01-DCB
00034D	000001			147+		DC	AL3(1) CHECK, GERR, PERR 01-DCB
000350	00000001			148+		DC	A(1) SYNAD 01-DCB
000354	0000			149+		DC	H'0' CIND1, CIND2 01-DCB
000356	0000			150+		DC	AL2(0) BLKSIZE 01-DCB
000358	00000000			151+		DC	F'0' WCPO, WCPL, OFFSR, OFFSW 01-DCB

```
00035C 00000001                152+        DC    A(1)                         IOBA                        01-DCB
000360 00                      153+        DC    AL1(0)                       NCP                         01-DCB
000361 000001                  154+        DC    AL3(1)                       EOBR, EOBAD                 01-DCB
                               156+**                           QSAM INTERFACE—
```

```
000364 00000001                158+        DC    A(1)                         RECAD                       01-DCB
000368 0000                    159+        DC    H'0'                         QSWS                        01-DCB
00036A 0085                    160+        DC    AL2(133)   LRECL                                         01-DCB
00036C 00                      161+        DC    BL1'00000000'                EROPT                       01-DCB
00036D 000001                  162+        DC    AL3(1)                       CNTRL                       01-DCB
000370 00000000                163+        DC    F'0'                         PRECL                       01-DCB
000374 00000001                164+        DC    A(1)                         EOB                         01-DCB
                               165 INFILE   DCB  DDNAME=INFILE,DEVD=DA,MACRF=(GM),DSORG=PS,            X
                                                 RECFM=FB,LRECL=80,BLKSIZE=0,                          X
                                                 EODAD=ENDDATA
                               167+**                       DATA CONTROL BLOCK
                               168+**
000378                         169+INFILE   DC   0F'0'              ORIGIN ON WORD BOUNDARY              01-DCB
                               171+**              DIRECT ACCESS DEVICE INTERFACE
000378 0000000000000000        173+        DC    BL16'0'                      FDAD,DVTBL                  01-DCB
000388 00000000                174+        DC    A(0)                         KEYLE,DEVT,TRBAL            01-DCB
                               176+**              COMMON ACCESS METHOD INTERFACE
00038C 00                      178+        DC    AL1(0)                       BUFNO                       01-DCB
00038D 000001                  179+        DC    AL3(1)                       BUFCB                       01-DCB
000390 0000                    180+        DC    AL2(0)     BUFL                                          01-DCB
000392 4000                    181+        DC    BL2'0100000000000000'        DSORG                       01-DCB
000394 00000001                182+        DC    A(1)                         ICQE/IOBAD                  01-DCB
                               184+**                     FOUNDATION EXTENSION
000398 00                      186+        DC    BL1'00000000'                BFTEK,BFLN,HIARCHY          01-DCB
000399 0000A2                  187+        DC    AL3(ENDDATA)                 EODAD                       01-DCB
00039C 90                      188+        DC    BL1'10010000'                RECFM                       01-DCB
00039D 000000                  189+        DC    AL3(0)                       EXLST                       01-DCB
```

475

```
                                          FOUNDATION BLOCK
0003A0 C9D5C6C9D3C54040      191+*                                                        01-DCB
0003A8 02                    193+    DC   CL8'INFILE'             DDNAME                   01-DCB
0003A9 00                    194+    DC   BL1'00000010'           OFLGS                    01-DCB
0003AA 5000                  195+    DC   BL1'00000000'                   IFLG             01-DCB
                             196+    DC   BL2'0101000000000000'   MACR                     01-DCB
                             198+*                    BSAM-BPAM-QSAM INTERFACE
0003AC 00                    200+    DC   BL1'00000000'                          RER1      01-DCB
0003AD 000001                201+    DC   AL3(1)                  CHECK, GERR, PERR        01-DCB
0003B0 0000                  202+    DC   A(1)                    SYNAD                    01-DCB
0003B4 0000                  203+    DC   H'0'                    CIND1, CIND2             01-DCB
0003B6 0000                  204+    DC   AL2(0)                  BLKSIZE                  01-DCB
0003B8 00000000              205+    DC   F'0'                    WCPO, WCPL, OFFSR, OFFSW 01-DCB
0003BC 00000001              206+    DC   A(1)                    IOBA                     01-DCB
0003C0 00                    207+    DC   AL1(0)                  NCP                      01-DCB
0003C1 000001                208+    DC   AL3(1)                  EOBR, EOBAD              01-DCB
```

```
LOC    OBJECT CODE      ADDR1  ADDR2   STMT   SOURCE STATEMENT
                                       210+*                    QSAM INTERFACE
0003C4 00000001                        212+    DC   A(1)                    RECAD         01-DCB
0003C8 0000                            213+    DC   H'0'                    QSWS          01-DCB
0003CA 0050                            214+    DC   AL2(80)                 LRECL         01-DCB
0003CC 00                              215+    DC   BL1'00000000'           EROPT         01-DCB
0003CD 000001                          216+    DC   AL3(1)                  CNTRL         01-DCB
0003D0 00000000                        217+    DC   F'0'                    PRECL         01-DCB
0003D4 00000001                        218+    DC   A(1)                    EOB           01-DCB
                                       220 *   DATA CONTROL BLOCK DUMMY SECTION (IHADCB)

                                       221             PRINT ON,NOGEN
```

[The PRINT directive controls what is printed by the assembler. The NOGEN option tells the assembler not to print the output of macro instructions.]

[The DCBD macro generates a DSECT which describes the contents of a data control block (DCB). It generates a lot of output — about 20 pages. We will not print it here. Chapter 7 discusses the concept of a DSECT.]

```
          222    DCBD    DEVD=DA,DSORG=PS

          800  *        REGISTER EQUATES
```

[Here we define the symbols R0 through R15. These are used wherever we use a register in an instruction. The advantage to using equated labels for the registers is that they will appear in the cross-reference listing, which follows later.]

```
00000     801  R0      EQU   0
00001     802  R1      EQU   1
00002     803  R2      EQU   2
00003     804  R3      EQU   3
00004     805  R4      EQU   4
00005     806  R5      EQU   5
00006     807  R6      EQU   6
00007     808  R7      EQU   7
00008     809  R8      EQU   8
00009     810  R9      EQU   9
0000A     811  R10     EQU   10
0000B     812  R11     EQU   11
0000C     813  R12     EQU   12
0000D     814  R13     EQU   13
0000E     815  R14     EQU   14
0000F     816  R15     EQU   15
          817  PROGNAME END       END OF PROGRAM

000000
```

477

[The RELOCATION DICTIONARY is a list of all the address constants (ADCONS) within our program. The operating system program loader will convert these fields to hold the actual address where something is located. We normally don't reference this information.]

[The ADDRESS column shows where an address constant is located within the program. If you go to location 000019 in the program, you will see an address constant coded as " DC   AL3(INFILE) " .

POS.ID	REL.ID	FLAGS	ADDRESS
0001	0001	08	000019
0001	0001	08	00001D
0001	0001	08	0000B5
0001	0001	08	0000B9
0001	0001	08	000399

[The CROSS REFERENCE shows more than the COBOL cross reference. The column headings are:
1. SYMBOL shows the names of the fields being cross-referenced.
2. LEN is the assembler's computed length for the field in decimal.
3. VALUE usually contains the address of the symbol (the value of the LOC column). For EQU symbols, it shows the value assigned by the assembler.
4. DEFN is the statement number where the field or label is defined. Note that this is the statement number (STMT column), not the location (LOC column).
5. REFERENCES shows where the named field is used.]

   [1]   [2]   [3]   [4]   [5]

                                       CROSS REFERENCE

SYMBOL   LEN   VALUE   DEFN   REFERENCES
DATA   00080 00018D 0100   0042

[For the above line, the symbol DATA was defined at statement number 100. It is at location 00018D in the program. It has a length of 80. It is only used (referred to) at statement number 42.]

DCBBIT0 00001 00000080 0254 0340 0348 0361 0385 0418 0420 0421 0423 0446 0449 0469 0473 0488 0525 0580 0612 0650 0654
                            0667 0767 0769 0779

[A number of fields are defined by the DCBD macro instruction, but were not printed. These appear within the cross-reference, but we don't use any of them except DCBOFLGS. You can normally ignore them.]

DCBBIT1 00001 00000040 0255 0341 0349 0363 0386 0387 0396 0402 0418 0420 0422 0423 0451 0469 0471 0473 0491 0492 0493
                            0528 0529 0580 0614 0656 0658 0670 0714 0767 0771 0780
DCBBIT2 00001 00000020 0256 0342 0350 0364 0365 0366 0386 0387 0391 0397 0402 0418 0419 0424 0453 0474 0475 0496 0497
                            0498 0532 0533 0581 0619 0659 0675 0717 0720 0767 0781
DCBBIT3 00001 00000010 0257 0343 0364 0366 0367 0386 0399 0425 0456 0474 0477 0500 0501 0502 0536 0537 0581 0621 0623
                            0625 0661 0676 0717 0721 0767
DCBBIT4 00001 00000008 0258 0351 0400 0401 0402 0426 0457 0479 0484 0485 0505 0506 0540 0541 0543 0544 0582 0628 0677
                            0717 0722
DCBBIT5 00001 00000004 0259 0352 0407 0429 0430 0459 0479 0481 0482 0485 0485 0509 0511 0512 0513 0547 0548 0549 0550 0582

Symbol	Length	Value	Defn	References
DCBBIT6	00001	00000002	0260	0516 0517 0518 0519 0553 0554 0555 0556 0583 0630 0633 0636 0663 0679 0681 0712 0723
DCBBIT7	00001	00000001	0261	0345 0408 0410 0412 0429 0431 0460 0521 0522 0559 0560 0562 0563 0639 0665 0682 0725
DCBFDAD	00008	00005	0281	0284
DCBOFLGS	00001	000030	0445	0023 0026
ENDDATA	00001	000000A2	0063	0187
ENDLINE	00133	000286	0103	066
HEADLINE	00133	000201	0102	0031 0057
IHADCB	00001	00000000	0227	0022 0322 0371 0442 0571 0587 0594 0607 0702 0708 0735 0758
INAREA	00080	00012C	0095	0039 0042
INFILE	00004	000378	0169	0017 0021 0038 0073
LINE	00001	00017C	0096	0048
LINECT	00002	00030B	0104	0051 0052 0054
MAINLINE	00001	00000048	0036	0053 0060
NUMBER	00007	000185	0098	0045
ONE	00001	000312	0107	0043 0051
OPENERR	00001	000000D0	0085	0024 0027
PRINTER	00004	000318	0115	0019 0025 0030 0047 0056 0065 0075
PROGNAME	00001	00000000	0001	0004 0817
P50	00002	000313	0108	0052
RECNUM	00004	00030D	0105	0043 0044 0045
R1	00001	00000001	0802	0021 0022 0025
R12	00001	0000000C	0813	0002 0003 0004
R13	00001	0000000D	0814	0002 0007 0009 0010 0077 0077 0086 0086
R14	00001	0000000E	0815	0002
R15	00001	0000000F	0816	0003
R2	00001	00000002	0803	0008 0009 0010
SAVEAREA	00004	0000E4	0094	0007 0008
ZERO	00001	000311	0106	0054

[Newer versions of Assembler H will underline the reference numbers when an item is altered by an instruction. If the item is only referenced, the statement number is printed as shown here.]

[The assembler prints its statistics and diagnostic information as the last page of the assembly.]

DIAGNOSTIC CROSS REFERENCE AND ASSEMBLER SUMMARY

[**Success !**] NO STATEMENTS FLAGGED IN THIS ASSEMBLY

[If you specify any parameters for the assembler, they are printed here. You specify these through the JCL PARM.ASM parameter in MVS, or as the "(options" for the VM HASM or ASSEMBLE commands.]

OVERRIDING PARAMETERS- XREF(SHORT)

[This section lists the assembler's default parameters. Refer to the assembler programmer's guide for an explanation of each option.]

OPTIONS FOR THIS ASSEMBLY
DECK, NOOBJECT, LIST, XREF(SHORT), NORENT, NOTEST, NOBATCH, ALIGN, ESD, RLD, NOTERM, LINECOUNT(55),
   FLAG(0), SYSPARM()
NO OVERRIDING DD NAMES

[At this point, the assembler shows the number of input, output, and library statements it processed. This says that there were 96 input statements in the program we just assembled. The macro instructions we used had a total of 4564 statements. (These came from a library, DDNAME SYSLIB for MVS or GLOBAL MACLIB for VM.) The assembler printed 293 lines of output. Finally, 21 records of object text file were produced.]

```
  96 CARDS FROM SYSIN
4564 CARDS FROM SYSLIB
 293 LINES OUTPUT
  21 CARDS OUTPUT
```

Index